RSPB

RSPB
WHERE TO DISCOVER
NATURE
IN BRITAIN AND NORTHERN IRELAND

MARIANNE TAYLOR

**a million
voices for
nature**

The RSPB works for a healthy environment rich in birds and wildlife. It depends on the support and generosity of others to make a difference. It works with bird and habitat conservation organisations in a global partnership called BirdLife International.

If you would like to know more about The RSPB, visit the website at www.rspb.org or write to: The RSPB, The Lodge, Sandy, Bedfordshire, SG19 2DL; 01767 680551.

NATURA 2000

Natura 2000 is a European Union-wide network of protected sites.
Find out more at www.natura.org

First published 2009 by A & C Black Publishers Ltd, 36 Soho Square, London W1D 3QY
www.acblack.com

Copyright © 2009 text by Marianne Taylor
Copyright in the photographs remains with the individual photographers (listed on pp338–341)

The right of Marianne Taylor to be identified as the author of this work has been asserted by her in accordance with the Copyright, Design and Patents Act 1988.

ISBN 978 1 4081 0864 2

A CIP catalogue record for this book is available from the British Library.

This book is produced using paper that is made from wood grown in managed, sustainable forests. It is natural, renewable and recyclable. The logging and manufacturing processes conform to the environmental regulations of the country of origin.

Commissioning Editor: Nigel Redman
Project Editor: Julie Bailey
Design by Julie Dando, Fluke Art, Cornwall
Reserve maps by Brian Southern

Printed and bound in Milan by Rotolito

10 9 8 7 6 5 4 3 2 1

CONTENTS

NORTH SCOTLAND

WALES

DATES WITH NATURE

Goldeneye

INTRODUCTION

The UK can feel like a small and busy land at times, with the few remaining scraps of wilderness pressured on all sides by our need for more roads, more buildings, more blocks of commercial conifers or sheets of monoculture arable fields. When we think of wildlife on the grand scale, our thoughts tend to fly far from our own shores to the Kenyan savanna, the Brazilian rainforest or the Russian wildwoods.

Back in 1889, when the RSPB was founded, the UK was a wilder land and attitudes towards wildlife a good deal more cavalier than they are today. The original RSPB membership was a group of well-to-do women, united in protest at the slaughter of wild birds for their feathers – used to decorate hats and other garments. This organisation, then called the Fur and Feather Group, quickly grew to encompass other wildlife-related issues and received its Royal Charter in 1904.

Throughout the last century, the shrinking of the UK's green spaces caused growing concern for the RSPB – what's the point of lobbying for the protection of wild birds if their habitats are being destroyed around them? The Society bought its first dedicated nature reserve in 1930, and through the second half of the 20th century more and more sites were bought, with more than 200 nature reserves now under RSPB care today. The RSPB's efforts have brought 130,000 hectares of superb wildlife habitat under permanent protection, helping to safeguard the futures of some of the UK's special wildlife communities.

RSPB reserves today

It goes without saying that at RSPB reserves you can enjoy some of the best wildlife-watching that the UK has to offer. Golden Eagles gliding along towering mountain ridges, the riot of noise and action on a cliffside seabird colony, Red Deer stags roaring and antler-clashing at dawn or hundreds of thousands of Starlings swirling over a reedbed at dusk... wildlife wonders are all around us in profusion and diversity. Each reserve is unique – some offer many facilities and attract hundreds of visitors a day, while others are quiet and remote. Every kind of wild habitat in the UK is represented within RSPB reserves, from rolling violet heathland to mature woodland, riverside and reedbed to estuary and breathtaking sea-cliff. Some 80 per cent of the UK's rarest birds can be found on RSPB reserves, along with hosts of other wildlife from the familiar to the fascinatingly obscure.

This book is your guide to the wonderful wildlife reserves founded and managed by the RSPB throughout the UK. Here you'll find all you need to know about getting to each reserve and getting the most from your visit. Chances are there are several reserves within striking distance of your home, and if you love wildlife and nature and enjoy travel about the UK you can base numerous holiday itineraries around visiting reserves. As a member of the RSPB, you can visit all of these wonderful places absolutely free, and your support of the society will help fund the purchase of even more wildlife habitat.

It's easy to be gloomy about the future of our wildlife, but thanks to the efforts of the RSPB we are holding on to some of our most precious wild places. And there is more – the RSPB has recently established several exciting habitat restoration projects. Reserves like Saltholme and Lakenheath Fen represent the future of conservation – creating brand new prime wildlife habitat from what was previously uninteresting arable or waste land.

The RSPB's work is ongoing, and new reserves are being established all the time. A couple of the very newest could not be included in this book, including the seabird spectacular at Dunnet Head in northern Scotland. This reserve and other new acquisitions will be incorporated into subsequent editions. In the meantime, you can find out about them on the RSPB's website – visit www.rspb.org.uk/reserves.

Sea air, incredible views, the racket of thousands of nesting seabirds – Marwick Head is one of many RSPB reserves to offer all of this.

USING THIS BOOK

Dormice

USING THIS BOOK

This book is designed to help you discover the RSPB reserves around the UK and how to get the most from any visit to a reserve. The book is set out geographically by country and by region within the countries for England and Scotland. Within each region, the reserves are arranged alphabetically.

The RSPB designates its reserves as either 'active engagement' or 'quiet enjoyment' reserves. The former are the RSPB's flagship reserves, which have more developed visitor facilities including shops, visitor centres and often a busy programme of events. Quiet enjoyment reserves have fewer facilities and offer a different but equally enjoyable experience. In this book most active engagement reserves are covered over four pages, the quiet enjoyment reserves over two.

Each account is structured in the same way – the sections are described below:

Introduction gives you a quick overview of where the reserve is situated and what it has to offer. Any official conservation designations awarded to the reserve, such as SSSI (Site of Special Scientific Interest) are given here (for more on conservation designations see p13, and for a list of what the abbreviations stand for see p338).

Access, facilities, contact details and accessibility lays out the practicalities of planning a visit – opening times and entry fees, facilities available (represented by symbols, see next page), what sort of walking terrain you can expect, information for dog owners and for disabled visitors, and how to contact the reserve by phone or email.

P Parking

Refreshments

Picnic area

Toilets

Access for disabled people

Accessible toilets for disabled people

Baby changing facilities

The map illustrates the main trails around the reserve and the locations of other facilities, such as hides and viewpoints. It also shows the road access point or points to help you plan your journey. Colour shadings indicate the different habitat types on each reserve – each map has its own key for ease of reference.

The main text takes you on a tour around the reserve, describing in detail the wildlife you're likely to see at various different times as well as providing interesting background information about the place and the way the RSPB is managing the land to benefit its special wildlife.

At the end of the book, you'll find a 12-page section on the RSPB's Date With Nature events. These events take place at a variety of locations across the UK – urban and rural – and their purpose is to bring visitors face to face with some of our most exciting wild birds and other animals. Here you'll find details of where to watch nesting Peregrine Falcons in our city centres, how to book a cruise to sail among Puffins and Gannets, places to explore nature on wildlife-friendly working farms, and where to see hunting Ospreys, rutting Red Deer and other wonderful and iconic animals.

Wildlife by Season summarises the main wildlife highlights you can expect to see during the four seasons.

When to Visit highlights any details about how best to time your visit, taking into account wildlife activity through the day, tide times, light conditions and so on.

How to Get Here provides the postal district and OS grid reference for the reserve, followed by basic directions to reach the site by road and by public transport.

Most of us will recognise this as a Kingfisher but how many of us have seen one? On many RSPB reserves you can have great views of them.

Public Hide
East Hide

Scrape hides

Swallow

HINTS FOR ENJOYING YOUR VISIT

The RSPB's nature reserves are, primarily, places for wildlife to thrive and flourish. However, they are also places for you to come and see this wildlife, and the nature trails, hides and viewpoints are designed and placed to help you to see as much as possible.

There are no hard-and-fast rules for watching wildlife – you can see the most astonishing sights with no special preparation at all – but there are definitely many things you can do to give yourself the best chance of seeing plenty of wildlife.

When you're walking around the reserve, move quietly and speak softly. Wearing dull-coloured clothing can help, as can choosing clothing that doesn't rustle. Look all around you as you go, and take opportunities to sit down and just quietly observe what's around you.

In general, visiting early in the day or towards evening is more productive than a midday visit – especially in woodlands. Insects, however, are most active in the warmest hours. Weather is important – obviously it's more pleasant for you if it's not raining while you're out walking,

but also be aware that on very windy days birds tend to lay low and can be hard to see. Birds of prey are most active on sunny days, while cold weather can be good for seeing wildfowl in wintertime.

Bringing binoculars will add immeasurably to your enjoyment of the visit, as with them you'll have close views of birds without needing to get so close to them that you'll disturb them. Many reserves have binoculars available for hire if you don't have your own, and at many Date With Nature events the RSPB volunteers on site will have telescopes and binoculars available for you to use. If you're new to binocular use, remember to fold or push the eyecups down if you wear glasses, and try to keep your eyes relaxed and don't squint as you use them.

Finally, remember to always treat the country-side with respect. That means 'take nothing but photographs and leave nothing but footprints' as the saying goes – don't litter, don't pick flowers, and leave gates closed and hide doors shut – essentially, leave the reserve as you found it.

HIDES

Most hides resemble large wooden sheds, equipped with benches inside and slots in the walls to look through, but on some reserves you'll find some very fancy and comfortable hides. In any case, the purpose of the hide is to give you a place to watch birds and other wildlife at close quarters without them knowing you are there. The approach to the hide is usually screened off. Most hides overlook a lake, lagoon, river shore or other area of water.

Hides often bring you much closer to the birds than you'd otherwise be able to get, but even though you

are concealed inside you can still startle them if you're not careful so make sure that you don't talk loudly or shout, or wave your arms through the viewing slots. It might also be wise to switch off your mobile phone before you enter a hide.

Some hides can get busy, especially at popular reserves on weekends. Be considerate of others and let someone take your place when you have finished viewing if there is a backlog of people waiting to sit down. If you spot something exciting, the others in the hide will appreciate it if you point it out for them – and if you see something you can't identify, don't be afraid to ask for help from someone else.

RSPB reserves protect not only the best wildlife habitats in Britain, but also some of the most beautiful and diverse countryside you'll find anywhere – you don't have to be a nature buff to enjoy a walk in the lovely pine woods around Loch Garten.

WHAT TO EXPECT

Barn Owl

WHAT TO EXPECT ON YOUR VISIT

The advice on facilities and the more detailed information in the reserve accounts will give you an idea of what to expect when you arrive and how to prepare for your visit. For the larger reserves, there will be toilets, easy car parking and a shop or café selling refreshments, while for others there will be a place to park on the roadside, a trail to follow and nothing else. Some general advice applies whichever reserve you are visiting.

Wear sturdy footwear Virtually every reserve has at least some sections of path that are a little uneven or could potentially become muddy, so it's wise to wear walking boots, especially if you plan on a long walk.

Carry a bottle of water Even on cool days walking can be thirsty work, and although a nature trail may not constitute a long walk by its distance alone, you'll often be so absorbed by what you see on the way that you end up being out longer than you anticipated.

Take sunscreen Or apply a long-lasting sunscreen before you go out even if it doesn't look that bright – don't rely on the British weather to stay the same!

Take a mobile phone Just in case you get lost or get into other difficulties.

Lock valuables in the car boot Sadly, thieves are aware that birdwatchers often have expensive optical equipment with them, so it's especially important to lock everything away out of sight at known birdwatching places.

If you're visiting a more remote reserve without facilities, you might also want to consider bringing an OS map of the area and perhaps some food. Wellington boots are a good idea at some wetland sites in winter, while you should wear a hat if you visit a skua or tern colony as these birds may divebomb visitors.

Larger reserves will have information posters on display in the hides to help you identify the birds you see. You can also ask staff at the visitor centre for help on identification conundrums. Carrying a field guide is a good idea, though if you are interested in all kinds of animals and plants it's difficult to find a really comprehensive book that's also portable. You may also want to take a notebook and pencil, so you can make sketches and take notes about any unfamiliar plants or animals, to be checked against the books later.

CONSERVATION DESIGNATIONS

Alongside the reserve names in this book you'll notice sets of capital letters – SSSI, SPA and so on. These letters stand for various different official conservation designations that reflect the site's importance for wildlife. A list of all the designations used in this book, and what the abbreviations stand for, is found on page 338.

Protecting the best places for wildlife from damage or destruction has been a cornerstone of nature conservation for decades. Setting up nature reserves is a sure and certain way of ensuring that the best habitat is protected and managed especially for wildlife. But nature reserves are only part of the story. Our countryside contains a patchwork of protected areas, places where their wildlife riches are protected by law and based on careful, scientific evaluation.

Most of the places featured in this book are designated for their wildlife. Some of them are among the most important places for wildlife in Europe: part of a network of sites called Natura 2000. Part of this vital network is made up of sites that are important for birds. These are known as Special Protection Areas (SPAs) and are one of the measures the European Birds Directive sets out to protect and restore bird populations across the European Union. The European Birds Directive is one of the most effective pieces of environmental legislation in

the world and is a key reason that very few of our best sites have been damaged in recent years. The Natura 2000 network also contains Special Areas of Conservation (SACs) designated under the Habitats Directive, a more recent piece of legislation that complements the Birds Directive.

All Special Protection Areas and many more sites besides are designated as Sites of Special Scientific Interest (SSSIs) or Areas of Special Scientific Interest (ASSIs) in Northern Ireland. These are the UK's best sites for wildlife and their role is to conserve specific biological or geological features of interest. National Nature Reserves (NNRs) contain some of the best examples of particular habitats – they are managed especially for wildlife. Ramsar sites are wetlands of international importance, as designated under the Ramsar Convention of 1971.

In some cases, the designation covers part of the reserve but not its entirety. Additionally, sometimes nature reserves make up a part of a larger protected area, in a sort of Russian doll set of designations. For example, the RSPB's nature reserve at Dungeness is part of the Dungeness National Nature Reserve that, in turn, is part of the Dungeness to Pett Level Special Protection Area. Dungeness is also a Special Area of Conservation, reflecting the area's huge importance for plants and animals. In short, it means these places are great for wildlife, it's official!

RSPB Mersehead, on the Solway Firth in south-west Scotland, is a designated Ramsar site. This designation is given in recognition of its importance for marine wildlife.

SOUTH-WEST

ARNE   SSSI, SPA, SAC, RAMSAR, AONB, NATURA 2000

Imagine a gently rolling landscape of sweet-scented purple heather and yellow gorse flowers under a warm blue summer sky. This is Arne, a beautiful, peaceful haven just across the harbour from the bustling town of Poole on the Dorset coast. The heathland is home to some of Britain's most localised and fascinating wildlife, including all six of our native reptiles, and wonderful birds like Dartford Warblers and Nightjars. The trails wind through stretches of deciduous woodland, out across the open heathland and eventually take you down to the harbour shore, where you can watch yachts and water birds going about their business side-by-side.

● Access, facilities, contact details and accessibility

Arne has two hides, the one on the Shipstal trail is a two-floor hide giving panoramic views across the area. There is no visitor centre but there is a reception building. Guided walks are available.

- **Telephone** 01929 553360; **email** arne@rspb.org.uk; **web** www.rspb.org.uk/arne
- **Opening hours** Dawn till dusk
- **Entry fees** Car park charges per car: 1 April to 30 September – £2 for up to two hours, £4 all day; 1 October to 31 March – £2 all day. Free entry for RSPB members – display your membership card on car dashboard.
- **Accessibility** The trails around the reserve are on rough ground – they are navigable with pushchairs but more difficult for wheelchairs. Contact the reserve office for more information.
- **Dogs** Allowed but must be kept under close control

WILDLIFE BY SEASON

SPRING

Birdsong at its best. Summer visitors start to return to the woods and heath, while the last winter water birds are leaving the harbour. On warm days Adders and other reptiles emerge from their hibernating places to bask in the sun.

SUMMER

Best time for reptiles and insects. Later in summer the flowering heather is at its best. Early migrating waders start to arrive in the harbour.

AUTUMN

Ospreys visit the harbour to fish, wader numbers peak and wildfowl numbers start to build up. Sika Deer begin their rut in October. Migrating songbirds may visit the heath and woodland en route to their winter quarters.

WINTER

Water birds reach their highest numbers (30,000) in the harbour. Birds of prey like Hen Harrier and Peregrine Falcon visit the area to take advantage of the concentrations of other birds. Dartford Warblers and Stonechats are still present on the heath.

What to look for

The whole of the Isle of Purbeck is great for wildlife, but on the Arne reserve the RSPB protects and manages some of the finest wildlife habitat you'll find anywhere – Arne is the largest area of lowland heath in England outside the New Forest. The scenery is beautiful – fans of the writer Thomas Hardy's work will enjoy wandering in the landscapes that inspired him, while local archaeological interest includes nine bowl

you'll probably need to choose just one walk, but you can easily do both in a day or less.

The heathland at Arne is actively managed to maximise its attractiveness to a whole range of wildlife. The RSPB uses selective grazing alongside a regime of controlling bracken and eradicating rhododendrons and self-seeded pines to maintain a mixed-age balance of heather and gorse – the different micro-habitats this produces help increase the wildlife

Large flocks of Avocets spend their winters in Poole Harbour.

barrows. The spectacular Corfe Castle is also nearby.

There are two main areas to explore, both of which you can reach from the RSPB car park at Arne village. You can head east along the Shipstal trail, which skirts around Arne farm and then to the heaths and woodland of Big Wood, or go south-east to explore the more open Coombe Heath. Other parts of the reserve, including the farm, are not open to the public. If you only have a couple of hours

diversity on the reserve. As you walk along the trails in summer, tread quietly and keep your eyes open for reptiles basking in sunny spots. Britain's rarest snake (the Smooth Snake) and rarest lizard (the Sand Lizard) live here alongside their more widespread relatives. The boggy areas are breeding grounds for numerous insects, food for the reptiles. Some of the insects are hunters themselves, such as the dragonflies that cruise menacingly over the heather,

The predatory Green Tiger Beetle can often been seen bustling along the trails in summer.

and the striking Green Tiger Beetle which chases other insects over the bare ground.

The heaths are also home to the lively little Dartford Warbler, a dark charcoal-and-maroon bird with a scratchy song and long, flicky tail. Dartford Warblers live in Britain year-round, unlike most warblers, so can suffer huge population losses in severe winters – the warm climate in this corner of Dorset means that this is one of their strongholds. Other inhabitants of the heath include Woodlarks, Stonechats, and the enchanting Nightjars, which sing their strange churring song and hawk for moths after dusk. The attractive Silver-studded Blue butterfly is one of many butterfly species that fly over the reserve in summer.

As autumn progresses, migrating birds may fly over, and some could stop off for a few days. Species like Redstart and various warblers may stop off in the woodlands to feed up before heading south. Out in the harbour, migrating waders call in to feed on the muddy banks and saltmarsh, migrating Ospreys may stop off for several weeks to fill up on fish before the next leg of their journeys to Africa, and ducks start to arrive for their winter stay.

There are two hides at the harbour's edge, one for each main trail, each overlooking areas of saltmarsh, reedbed and open water. Trails also pass close to the shore, giving good views. Winter is the best time for water birds, but year-round you'll see interesting species here. This is one of the UK's strongholds for the Little Egret, a dainty white heron which is a recent addition to our countryside following a population expansion of the species in Europe. Another striking water bird shows up in winter – the dapper black-and-white Avocet. There may be grebes and divers as well as the flocks of diving and dabbling ducks in the harbour, and rarities like Spoonbill show up regularly.

The heath and woodland is quieter in winter, as some of the birds here (like Hobby, Nightjar and various warblers – not including Dartford Warbler though) are summer visitors. However,

WHEN TO VISIT

Small birds are most easily seen and heard in the early mornings. If you're visiting in summer, your best chance of seeing reptiles and insects is to visit a little later in the day, when the air and ground have really warmed up. For Nightjars, visit late on summer evenings.

you may be lucky enough to see a Hen Harrier or even a Great Grey Shrike on the heath, while woodland birds visit the car park to scavenge scraps – look out for Nuthatches and Marsh Tits. The RSPB is managing Arne Farm for wildlife, providing rough pasture for Barn Owls, and winter crops for seed-eating birds, and the farm attracts flocks of finches in winter – other farmland species like Yellowhammer should hopefully be attracted too.

The Sika Deer, an introduced species from Japan, lives at Arne in quite large numbers and you may see them at any time, on the heath, in the woods or even down in the saltmarsh – they are most obvious in late autumn when the rut takes place – the males are especially noisy as they establish their temporary rutting territories and try to gather a harem of females. A much more elusive mammal here is the Otter – your best chance of seeing one is to visit early or late, on a falling tide, and keep quiet.

Unlike most other warblers, the Dartford Warbler stays in the UK all year round, though very hard winters can hit its populations hard.

How to get here

Grid ref./postcode SY971876/BH20 4
By road From Wareham town centre, head south over the causeway to Stoborough. Arne is signposted from here – the car park is located at the beginning of the village.

By public transport The nearest railway station is Wareham (4 miles from the reserve).

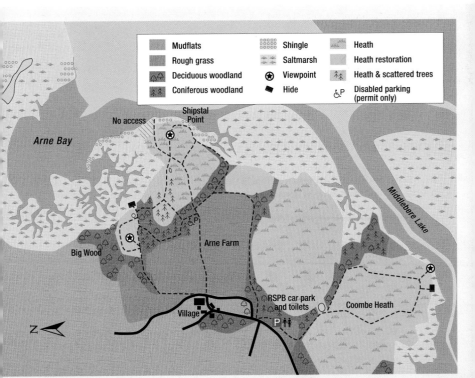

AYLESBEARE COMMON

SSSI, SPA, SAC, AONB, NATURA 2000

Aylesbeare Common is a reserve of glorious heathland and scattered woodland with streams and ponds, and it holds an array of special breeding birds, butterflies, dragonflies and other wildlife. The terrain is quite hilly, which means there are wonderful views across the east Devon countryside from the high points.

● Access, facilities, contact details and accessibility

A quiet reserve with minimal facilities, Aylesbeare Common is ideal for self-sufficient walkers and those who want to enjoy heathland wildlife in a particularly tranquil setting. **P**

- **Telephone** 01395 233 655; **email** aylesbeare.common@rspb.org.uk; **web** www.rspb.org.uk/aylesbearecommon
- **Opening hours** Open at all times, all year round
- **Entry fees** None, though donations are appreciated
- **Accessibility** Although the paths are unimproved, the main trail across the heath is usually firm underfoot and suitable for pushchairs, possibly also wheelchairs with care. Some stretches can become muddy, especially in winter.
- **Dogs** Only allowed on public footpaths and bridleways

What to look for

From the car park, two trails (one 3 miles long, the other three-quarters of a mile) lead you out across the heathland. This reserve is part of the unique east Devon pebble-bed heath – the pebbles on the trails underfoot look most out of

place this far from the sea, and were in fact left behind by fast-flowing rivers in the Triassic era.

In spring and summer, you'll hear many birds singing and this is a great place to learn the songs of some of the less common

WILDLIFE BY SEASON

SPRING
Look out for singing Dartford Warblers, Yellow-hammers, Tree Pipits, Stonechats and other heathland birds. Reptiles and insects start to appear.

SUMMER
Nightjars sing at dusk, while in the heat of the day butterflies and dragon-flies are abundant, and you may find snakes and lizards basking in the sun.

AUTUMN
Warm days remain good for reptiles and insects, while migratory birds are on the move.

WINTER
Snipes arrive to feed on the boggy areas, Redwings and Fieldfares visit the scrubby areas for berries.

species. The Yellowhammer gives a characteristic rapid rattling phrase, ending with a shrill drawn-out note – often transcribed as 'a-little-bit-of-bread-and-no-cheeeeeeeese'. Tree Pipits perform an eye-catching 'parachuting' song flight. Stonechats give a jumbled but melodious song from prom-inent perches, although their *tack-tack* call, like two stones being knocked together is more commonly heard. The star of the heath, the dainty long-tailed Dartford Warbler, has a rattling warble that may pass unnoticed among other, stronger songs. Unlike most other warblers, 'Darties' are here all year round, although you're most likely to hear them singing in the spring.

Each year's new crop of dragonflies emerge from the pools and streams to hawk over the heath in summer, and they in turn are prey for Hobbies. Butterflies feed from the heather flowers by day, while by dusk Nightjars are out hunting for moths and defending their terri-tories. It is well worth staying on into the evening to listen to their hypnotic churring song and to watch their light, agile and silent flights between pine trees.

Winter is a quieter time for wildlife, but you may see flocks of finches or even a Hen Harrier or Great Grey Shrike.

WHEN TO VISIT
Like all heathlands, Aylesbeare Common is best in spring and summer, when birds are singing and reptiles and insects are active. Visit at dusk to see and hear Nightjars. The heath is much quieter in winter.

How to get here
Grid ref./postcode SY 057898/ EX10 0
By road The reserve is 8 miles east of Exeter and 6 miles east from the M5 on the A3052. Travel half a mile past the Halfway Inn, turn right towards Hawkerland and the car park is immediately on the left.
By public transport Exeter St Davids/Central is the nearest railway station but is 8 miles away. From Exeter, buses 52A and 52B stop by request at nearby Joneys Cross.

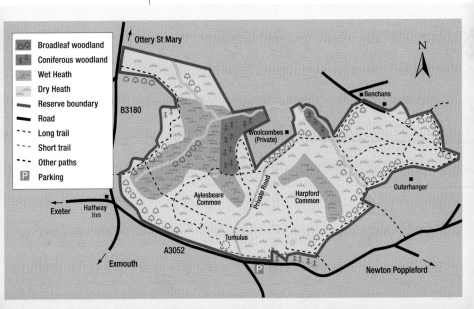

EXE ESTUARY SSSI, SPA, RAMSAR, NATURA 2000

The Exe Estuary nature reserve comprises two areas of grazing marsh on opposite sides of the River Exe; Exminster and Powderham Marshes on the west, Bowling Green Marsh on the east. Between them they hold some 40,000 birds in winter. You can also take an RSPB cruise from Exmouth, Starcross or Topsham across the estuary to look for Avocets in winter (see page 335).

● Access, facilities, contact details and accessibility

Bowling Green Marsh has a hide and viewing platform, while Powderham Marshes has a nature trail about three-quarters of a mile long, and also a viewing platform. You can book group visits or guided walks.

- **Telephone** 01392 824614; **web** www.rspb.org.uk/exeestuary
- **Opening hours** The footpaths and the hide and viewing platform at Bowling Green Marsh are open at all times. The RSPB Shop at Darts Farm is open Monday to Saturday 9am–5.30pm, Sundays 10.30am–4.30 pm (closed Christmas Day, Boxing Day and Easter Sunday).
- **Entry fees** None, but donations are welcomed
- **Accessibility** The hide at Bowling Green Marsh is wheelchair-accessible but the trails may be difficult
- **Dogs** Dogs are only allowed on footpaths on Exminster Marshes and Bowling Green Marsh. Only registered assistance dogs are allowed on Powderham Marshes.

What to look for

The UK's estuaries, especially on the south coast of England, are largely overdeveloped and have lost much of their wildlife interest. This makes the more unspoilt estuaries like that of the River Exe especially precious, as their marshland and

saltmarsh are so important for wetland birds.

The Exminster Marshes/Powderham Marshes reserve is the larger of the two sites, and you can explore it at length from several public footpaths, or take the RSPB trail down to the Powderham

WILDLIFE BY SEASON

SPRING

Look out for displaying waders and Shelducks, warblers singing in the reeds, and Swifts, Swallows and House and Sand Martins feeding over the water.

SUMMER

Lapwing and Redshank chicks have hatched and feed by the pools. Dragonflies and damselflies hunt over the water.

AUTUMN

Migrating waders gather at Bowling Green Marsh. You may see an Osprey fishing in the estuary. Avocets start to arrive.

WINTER

The estuary is full of waders and wildfowl, and hunting Peregrines dash overhead regularly.

viewpoint, in a part of the reserve known as Powderham Marshes. Lapwings and Redshanks breed here. Both are very visible and vocal in the spring.

Through spring and summer dragonflies and damselflies abound. Sedge, Reed, Grasshopper and Cetti's Warblers sing, Hobbies hunt overhead and migrating Whimbrels visit the meadows.

In autumn, migrating waders will arrive in large numbers. The other site here, Bowling Green Marshes on the eastern side of the estuary, is an even better place than Exminster for observing them, and dedicated birdwatchers here have found a number of very rare species among the commoner birds. As the season goes on, wildfowl numbers also build up, including a large wintering flock of Dark-bellied Brent Geese.

The RSPB manages water levels on the marshes to maintain their attractiveness for waders and wildfowl throughout the year.

How to get here

Grid ref./postcode SX 954872/ EX6 8

WHEN TO VISIT

Visit at high tide to see the highest numbers of birds on the reserves. Perhaps the best birdwatching is in spring and autumn for migrating waders, but winter is best for wildfowl.

By road The RSPB shop is located at Darts Farm off the A376 Exmouth road, 5 minutes from Junction 30 (Exeter Services) of the M5. Exminster Marshes and Powderham Marshes are east of Exminster Village, and are accessible off the A379 Dawlish road – reach the car park via a tight turn off Station Road. Bowling Green Marsh is on the outskirts of Topsham, and is signposted from the Holman Way car park. Both are 5 miles south of Exeter on either side of the Exe Estuary.

By public transport Stagecoach bus 57 (Exeter–Exmouth) stops at Darts Farm. This service also stops near Bowling Green Marsh – service 2 goes to Exminster. Topsham railway station is three-quarters of a mile away from Darts Farm.

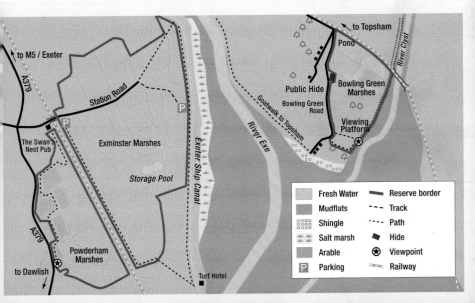

to Topsham
Pond
River Clyst
to M5 / Exeter
A379
Station Road
Public Hide
Bowling Green Marshes
Bowling Green Road
Goatwalk to Topsham
The Swan's Nest Pub
Exminster Marshes
Exeter Ship Canal
River Exe
Viewing Platform
Storage Pool
A379
Powderham Marshes
to Dawlish
Turf Hotel

Fresh Water		Reserve border	
Mudflats		Track	---
Shingle		Path	-·-·-
Salt marsh		Hide	
Arable		Viewpoint	
Parking	P	Railway	

GARSTON WOOD SSSI, AONB

This beautiful ancient woodland, a fragment of a once much more extensive forest, teems with wildlife throughout the year, although it is especially delightful in springtime. The terrain is easy to walk and with care you'll be able to take a pushchair around as well, making this a perfect spot for a family walk.

● Access, facilities, contact details and accessibility

- **Telephone** 01929 553 360; **email** garston.wood@rspb.org.uk; **web** www.rspb.org.uk/garstonwood
- **Opening hours** Open at all times
- **Entry fees** Free, but donations to help continue the work here are welcome
- **Accessibility** The trails here are unimproved – it is possible but challenging to get around in a wheelchair. Contact the reserve for more advice.
- **Dogs** Only allowed on public footpaths and bridleways, and must be kept on a lead

What to look for

There are various footpaths at Garston Wood – the reserve leaflet (available at the reserve) recommends several routes. If you visit in spring, you'll be treated to carpets of Bluebells, Wood Anemones and Primroses. Birdsong adds to the peaceful atmosphere – early in spring you'll hear resident species like tits, finches, Nuthatches, Treecreepers and thrushes, and through April and May they will be joined by summer visitors – Willow Warblers, Blackcaps, Garden Warblers and hopefully Turtle Doves. Nightingales have occurred in recent years, so listen out for them too as they could return.

Woodland birds of prey found here occasionally include the rare and impressive Goshawk. This big bird of prey stages aerial

WILDLIFE BY SEASON

SPRING
Woodland flowers bloom and birds sing, including Turtle Dove.

SUMMER
Woodland butterflies on the wing from late June through to August include the stunning Silver-washed Fritillary and White Admiral.

AUTUMN
The wood is colourful with autumn leaves and a great variety of mushrooms and toadstools. Look for Fallow Deer.

WINTER
Traditional forest mainten-ance, such as coppicing, is taking place. Resident and wintering birds form roving flocks, and you may see a Woodcock feeding on muddy ground.

courtship displays in late winter, but you may also see one gliding high overhead on any fine day. Buzzards and Sparrowhawks also occur here.

South-west England is probably the best part of the UK for butterflies, and a flowery woodland perhaps the best environment to see a good variety of them – 29 species have been seen in Garston Wood. Traditional coppicing helps maintain the open woodland structure that they require. In high summer you could see Silver-washed Fritillaries with their golden, black-spotted wings, and elegant White Admirals, dapper in smoky black with a bold white stripe.

Woodland mammals are not easy to see, but autumn is one of the better times to look. Deer (Fallow and Roe occur here) are rutting from late summer so are more active and vocal. Dormice are most active in late summer, especially early in the day, though they tend to remain high up in the treetops.

Winter is quiet, but the woods remain picturesque

WHEN TO VISIT
Visit in spring for the dazzling display of woodland flowers and the wonderful chorus of birdsong. Still, sunny summer days will be best for watching butterflies, similar days in late winter for displaying Goshawks.

and peaceful, with small birds such as tits, Goldcrests and Treecreepers forming lively travelling feeding flocks.

How to get here
Grid ref./postcode SU 003194/ SP5 5
By road From Sixpenny Handley, take the Bowerchalk road (Dean Lane). Keeping right proceed for approximately 1.5 miles and you'll find Garston Wood car park on the left-hand side of the road, indicated by a finger post on the opposite side of the road.
By public transport The nearest station is in Salisbury – from Salisbury bus station, take Wilts & Dorset bus 184 to Sixpenny Handley (Roebuck Inn).

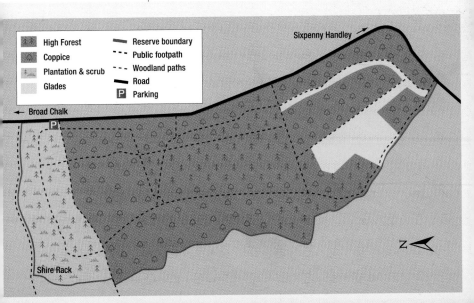

High Forest
Coppice
Plantation & scrub
Glades

Reserve boundary
Public footpath
Woodland paths
Road
P Parking

Sixpenny Handley

Broad Chalk

Shire Rack

N

SOUTH-WEST

GREYLAKE

This new reserve was an area of arable farmland in the year 2000. The RSPB is working to restore it to its previous incarnation – as an area of wet grassland with numerous ditches and pools. This regime is designed to attract wildfowl in winter and grassland waders and other wetland-nesting species in summer, and so far the results have been impressive.

● Access, facilities, contact details and accessibility

There is a car park and a picnic area. There is a viewing platform in the car park, and a hide 300m from the car park.
- **Telephone** 01458 252805 or 07774 620879 (to book walks); **email** west.sedgemoor@rspb.org.uk; **web** www.rspb.org.uk/greylake
- **Opening hours** Open at all times
- **Entry fees** Free, though donations are welcomed
- **Accessibility** The boardwalk trail is 700m and is accessible by wheelchair
- **Dogs** No dogs allowed, except registered assistance dogs

What to look for

You don't need much time to cover the available ground at this reserve – the boardwalk to the hide is just 700m long – but there is a great deal to see, especially in winter, and views from the hide are often excellent.

In summer, look out for the breeding birds of the wet grassland, such as the attractive Yellow Wagtail, which often follows the reserve's cattle as they graze – the birds hoping to snap up insects disturbed by the cows. Sedge Warblers and Reed Buntings are noisy and noticeable breeding birds of the reserve, and Skylarks and Meadow Pipits breed here too – both springing out of the long grass to deliver their songs in an aerial display.

WILDLIFE BY SEASON

SPRING
Breeding birds like warblers, Reed Buntings and Yellow Wagtails are singing and displaying.

SUMMER
The best time to see Roe Deer, Brown Hares and other mammals, as well as insects. Breeding birds are feeding their chicks.

AUTUMN
Migrating Wigeons and other wildfowl start to arrive along with waders and attendant birds of prey such as Merlins.

WINTER
Little Egrets, Lapwings and Golden Plovers are on the floods, and this is the best time for birds of prey like Peregrines.

The grasslands visible from the hide already attract breeding Snipes and Lapwings. Summer is also a good time to look for mammals. Water Voles have colonised the ditches, while Otters have also been seen. Roe Deer and Brown Hares both feed in the fields – these two shy animals are best seen early or late in the day. Look out too for Stoats and Grass Snakes. Dragonflies such as the Four-spotted Chaser hunt their prey around the pools throughout summer and into autumn.

The RSPB manages the water levels to make sure that there are plenty of pools and flooded feeding areas in spring and more extensive water cover in winter – necessitating the boardwalk but also making the area very attractive to wintering wildfowl. Flocks of Wigeons arrive in late autumn, along with Teal and sometimes other ducks. On the fields, large flocks of Lapwings gather to feed. You might also find Golden Plovers, Ruffs and perhaps other waders among them. Inevitably they attract predators, such as Peregrine Falcons and Merlins.

WHEN TO VISIT
An early or late visit gives you the best chance of seeing mammals, especially in summer. Smaller birds may be more active early in the day, but the water birds can usually be observed easily throughout the day.

How to get here
Grid ref./postcode ST399346/ TA7 1

By road The reserve is on the A361 (Taunton to Glastonbury) midway between the villages of Othery and Greinton. Leave Bridgwater on the A372 heading east towards Langport. After passing the old airfield take a left turn past the recycling centre to join the A361 at Greylake. Turn left and follow the road for about one and a half miles to the reserve car park.

By public transport Take the 29 bus from Taunton or Glastonbury. The nearest bus stop is in Othery at the London Inn or in Greinton at the phone box. A request to stop at the reserve can be made.

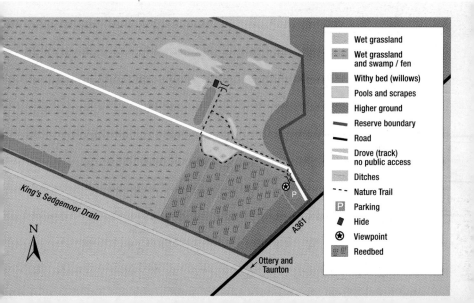

King's Sedgemoor Drain

N

A361

← Ottery and Taunton

Wet grassland

Wet grassland and swamp / fen

Withy bed (willows)

Pools and scrapes

Higher ground

Reserve boundary

Road

Drove (track) no public access

Ditches

Nature Trail

P Parking

Hide

Viewpoint

Reedbed

SOUTH-WEST

HAM WALL   NNR

Conservation isn't just about preservation, it's also about creation. At Ham Wall in the Avalon Marshes, the RSPB has created a new wetland – the project began in 1994, and today the extensive reedbed and open waters hold an impressive and ever-increasing variety of wildlife, all viewable from a network of trails and viewpoints. The reserve famously holds a huge Starling roost.

● Access, facilities, contact details and accessibility

This reserve offers easy wildlife-watching for the mobility-impaired, and has educational resources.
- **Telephone** 01458 860 494; **email** ham.wall@rspb.org.uk; **web** www.rspb.org.uk/hamwall. For information on the roosting Starlings please phone the Avalon Marshes Starling Hotline on 07866 554142.
- **Opening hours** Open at all times (note the car park has a 2-metre restriction barrier)
- **Entry fees** None, but donations are welcome
- **Accessibility** The railway line trail and walkways are accessible to wheelchairs, as are the viewscreens
- **Dogs** Only allowed on the public footpath and disused railway line

What to look for

The Avalon Marshes previously held rich peat deposits, which have been extensively dug out. Following peat extraction, the land naturally becomes wet once again. Here, the RSPB has landscaped the terrain, seeded a reedbed and managed the emergent vegetation to create a varied wetland habitat, suitable for rare water

birds and many other animals and plants. As the landscape at Ham Wall matures, its biodiversity will continue to grow, but the site already holds an impressive range of species.

The main track follows the old Glastonbury to Highbridge railway line, and will take you to several viewing screens, some roofed and some

WILDLIFE BY SEASON

SPRING

Bitterns boom from early spring. Newly arrived migrants may include dozens of Hobbies.

SUMMER

Insects like dragonflies are on the wing. Barn Owls are active from early evening. Ducks and grebes have chicks.

AUTUMN

The best time to see Bearded Tits and Kingfishers. Hedgerow berries attract thrushes, finches and warblers.

WINTER

The Starling flock is at its most impressive. Winter wildfowl numbers build, with Gadwalls, Shovelers and Teals most numerous. Look out for birds of prey.

open, which overlook interesting points of the reserve. Beyond this short track, there are other, rougher trails to explore.

The reeds hold a very special breeding bird: the Bittern. One of the RSPB's aims here was to attract this rare heron to breed, and in 2008 two nests were discovered here, the first in Somerset for 40 years. Other reedbed birds include Cetti's, Reed and Sedge Warblers, and the tiny, long-tailed Bearded Tit, the male sporting an impressive black 'moustache'. Overhead you should see Swifts, Swallows, House and Sand Martins and Hobbies.

The pools attract breeding wildfowl, while you may also be lucky enough to see a Water Vole or even an Otter swimming across the open water. By autumn, the bushes lining the main track are packed with berries and seeds, and busy with hungry thrushes, finches and other birds. As winter draws near, more wildfowl arrive on the marsh to spend their winter here, while the roosting Starling flock grows to epic proportions, attracting Sparrowhawks and Peregrine Falcons to its after-

noon show. Bitterns and Water Rails may become easier to see in winter – look out too for Barn Owls hunting the fields at dusk.

How to get here

Grid ref./postcode ST 449397/ BA6 9

By road From Glastonbury, take the B3151 to Wedmore. At the village of Meare go past the garage on your left, then take the next left into Ashcott Road. The reserve entrance is 1 mile on the left after the Railway Inn. The access roads are narrow and bumpy – park only in designated car parks.

By public transport The nearest bus stop is in the village of Meare, a mile or so from the reserve. Bus 668 from Shipham calls at Meare; services from Bristol serve Shipham.

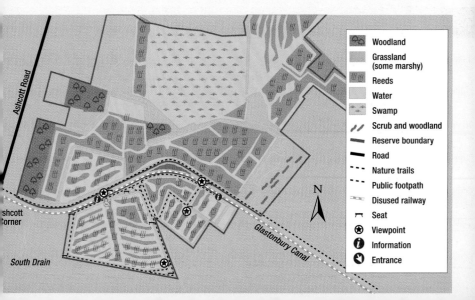

	Woodland
	Grassland (some marshy)
	Reeds
	Water
	Swamp
	Scrub and woodland
	Reserve boundary
	Road
	Nature trails
	Public footpath
	Disused railway
	Seat
	Viewpoint
	Information
	Entrance

Ashcott Road

Ashcott Corner

South Drain

Glastonbury Canal

N

SOUTH-WEST

HAYLE ESTUARY SSSI

This small estuary is the most south-westerly in the UK, and so is very attractive to water birds, especially when cold weather freezes other wetland sites further north. In winter, huge numbers of ducks and waders pack onto the muddy banks, while autumn is a great time to see a variety of migrating waders and perhaps find yourself a real rarity among them.

● Access, facilities, contact details and accessibility

There is one hide overlooking the lagoon at Ryan's Field, and a short circular walk from here. This reserve's convenient urban location makes it popular with local birdwatchers, who can easily make short, regular visits.

P

- **Telephone** 01736 711 682; **email** hayle.estuary@rspb.org.uk; **web** www.rspb.org.uk/hayleestuary
- **Opening hours** Open at all times
- **Entry fees** None, though donations to help continue the work here are welcome
- **Accessibility** Although the paths are unimproved, most are flat and navigable with a pushchair
- **Dogs** Only allowed on public footpaths and bridleways – they must be kept under control

What to look for

There is a hide overlooking a lagoon at Ryan's Field, which birds use at high tide. Cross the main road (carefully) here to view the estuary.

In spring, waders you might see here include Oystercatchers, Ringed Plovers, Sanderlings, Dunlins, Black-tailed and Bar-tailed Godwits, Whimbrels, Curlews, Greenshanks and

Redshanks. A few ducks will linger into spring, and the gull roost may contain Black-headed, Lesser Black-backed, Herring and Great Black-backed Gulls until mid-spring, with the more unusual Mediterranean Gulls often joining them.

The short summer season is quiet, although Oystercatchers have stayed on to breed at

WILDLIFE BY SEASON

SPRING
Winter wildfowl are moving on, while migrating waders stop off on their journeys north.

SUMMER
High summer is quiet, but the return migration of wading birds is already in full swing by late July and August.

AUTUMN
The best time to see waders, including scarcities. The gull roost may contain rarities as well.

WINTER
Winter wildfowl numbers reach their peak, with Teals and Wigeons most abundant. Look out for predators, like Peregrine and Merlin.

the lagoon. Waders on return migration are soon coming through, and autumn sees even greater variety and numbers than in spring. In addition to the species mentioned above, you may also see Golden and Grey Plovers, Lapwings, Knots, Little Stints, Curlew Sandpipers, Ruffs, Snipes and Turnstones. Hayle is also a good place to look for rarities – North American birds blown off course on migration turn up most autumns.

Good numbers of autumn waders will linger on through the winter, joining hundreds of Teals and Wigeons that feed on the mudflats. At high tide, when the mud is covered, many of the birds decamp to the lagoon at Ryan's Field, giving great views from the hide there. The RSPB manages the lagoon to maintain its appeal for these birds, and also works with local authorities to minimise disturbance to birds both here and on the estuary itself. In cold conditions, disturbance is particularly dangerous for birds as they need to conserve their energy and not waste precious feeding time.

WHEN TO VISIT
The birds on the estuary peak during winter, although spring and autumn can both be exciting times as migrants are passing through.

How to get here
Grid ref./postcode SW 551364/ TR27 6

By road To get from Foundry Square in Hayle to Ryan's Field, head west along the B3301 (Carnsew Road) road under the railway viaduct and bear left along the raised cycleway parallel to Carnsew Road until it terminates at the St Erth road opposite the entrance to Ryan's Field.

By public transport From St Erth railway station, take the Western Greyhound bus 501 to Foundry Square in Hayle (summer only). From here, go back under the railway viaduct and bear right across the waste ground and through the gate by the Jewsons yard. Carry on along the track and after about 30m, cross the lock gates and the pool is in front of you.

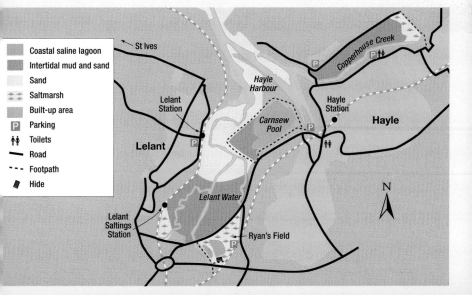

Legend:
- Coastal saline lagoon
- Intertidal mud and sand
- Sand
- Saltmarsh
- Built-up area
- P Parking
- Toilets
- Road
- Footpath
- Hide

St Ives · Lelant Station · Lelant · Lelant Saltings Station · Hayle Harbour · Carnsew Pool · Hayle Station · Hayle · Copperhouse Creek · Lelant Water · Ryan's Field

N

SOUTH-WEST

Nightingale

HIGHNAM WOODS

This area of ancient deciduous woodland, lying not far from Gloucester in the Severn Vale, is a haven for a wide range of birds, mammals, flowers and insects. The RSPB purchased the site in 1987 to protect its population of Nightingales, and they use traditional coppicing to maintain the dense understorey that suits the nesting requirements of these fabulous songsters.

● Access, facilities, contact details and accessibility

This quiet reserve is ideal for self-sufficient walkers, although guided walks can be arranged. There is one hide, overlooking the feeding station and a pond.

P

- **Telephone** 01594 562 852: **email** highnam.woods@rspb.org.uk; **web** www.rspb.org.uk/highnamwoods
- **Opening hours** Open at all times
- **Entry fees** None, although donations are welcome
- **Accessibility** The trail, although not very hilly, is often muddy so not suitable for wheelchairs or pushchairs
- **Dogs** Only allowed on public footpaths and bridleways

What to look for

From the car park, a nature trail leads you on a 1.25-mile walk around the wood. Listen for Nightingales if you're visiting in May or June – the rich, liquid notes are very beautiful and once heard, never forgotten. Catching sight of one is more of a challenge, as they often sing from deep in thick cover. Coppicing the trees (cutting them back close to the ground) encourages a cluster of new shoots to grow, forming the impenetrable low-level thickets that Nightingales need.

The RSPB's work here also focuses on encouraging a diverse population of insects and other invertebrates – this is achieved by measures such as removing non-native tree

WILDLIFE BY SEASON

SPRING

Nightingales and many other woodland birds are singing. Treetop birds are easier to see before the trees come into leaf.

SUMMER

Butterflies including White-letter Hairstreaks and White Admirals feed on the flowers that line the woodland rides

AUTUMN

This is the season to see a great variety of fungi in the wood. Activity at the feeding station increases.

WINTER

Look for Marsh Tits, Nuthatches and Great Spotted Woodpeckers at the feeding station.

species and leaving dead wood to rot. Plenty of insects means plenty of woodland birds – in early spring look (and listen) for Lesser Spotted Woodpeckers, which have become rare over much of England. They 'sing' by drumming rapidly on suitably resonant branches. More conventional songsters to listen for include warblers and (from mid-May) Spotted Flycatchers.

The flowers that grow in the interior of the woodland must flower before the trees' leaves come out and steal their light. However, in the sunny, open rides other flowers bloom into spring and summer. Look for the nationally rare Tintern Spurge among them – an unassuming green-flowered plant of open areas. If you visit late in the day in summer you're likely to see bats, and possibly Woodcocks patrolling their territories overhead.

Once the flush of autumn colour has passed, winter can be a quieter time in the woods. The feeding station becomes a focal point of bird activity now, and this is a great time to watch Marsh Tits.

WHEN TO VISIT

Highnam's star bird, the Nightingale, can be heard from mid-April into June. They sing through the day as well as at night – early morning is a great time to hear them as the song carries well in the clear air.

How to get here

Grid ref./postcode SO 778190/ GL2 9

By road The reserve is situated 3.75 miles west of Gloucester. Take the A40 west from Gloucester signposted to Ross. Proceed along A40 for 1.25 miles and go straight on at the roundabout and continue towards Ross for 0.6 mile and the reserve is on the right and clearly signposted.

By public transport Several bus services from Gloucester call nearby – bus 33 to Ross calls every 45 minutes past the hour Monday to Saturday; bus 24 to Joys Green every 15 minutes past the hour Monday to Saturday; and bus 325 to Ruardean, every two hours from 8.05am on Sundays only.

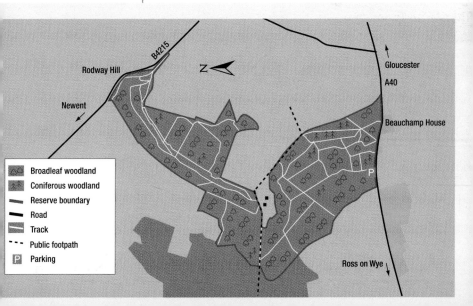

- Broadleaf woodland
- Coniferous woodland
- Reserve boundary
- Road
- Track
- Public footpath
- P Parking

SOUTH-WEST

LODMOOR sssi

Weymouth is a great town to live or stay in if you like wildlife, as you'll have not one but two RSPB reserves on your doorstep. Like its neighbour Radipole Lake, Lodmoor is a reserve of open water, saltmarsh, wet grassland and reedbed, with rare breeding birds and many water birds visiting in autumn and winter, and it also has the potential to attract rarities.

● Access, facilities, contact details and accessibility

This quiet reserve has a nature trail and a viewing shelter.
- **Telephone** 01305 773 519; **web** www.rspb.org.uk/lodmoor
- **Opening hours** Open at all times
- **Entry fees** Free, although donations to help continue the work here are welcome
- **Accessibility** The level trails are narrow in places. The nature trail is wheelchair-friendly.
- **Dogs** Only allowed on public footpaths and bridleways

What to look for

You can approach Lodmoor from the east or west. The trails give you views across open water and over saltmarsh and wet grassland as well as leading you through corridors of tall reeds. This dense reedbed offers a hiding place for a variety of birds, most of them superbly camouflaged and rather difficult to see. Bitterns, Sedge Warblers, Water Rails and Bearded Tits, although very

different in shape and size, all have boldly streaky plumage that enables them to disappear into the dark-and-light pattern of the reed stems, and you'll need patience and perhaps some luck to see them. In spring, the warblers at least will be singing noisily, and you may also hear the metallic 'ping' calls of Bearded Tits or the agonised squealing cry of the Water Rail. Bitterns

WILDLIFE BY SEASON

SPRING

Watch ducks and grebes courting. Warblers sing in the reeds and Swallows and House and Sand Martins hawk overhead.

SUMMER

Butterflies, dragonflies and other insects abound, especially on sunny days, and Hobbies patrol the skies for dragonflies.

AUTUMN

Young Kingfishers and family groups of Bearded Tits are around. Migrating waders visit the lake shores.

WINTER

With luck you may see a wintering Bittern, while Little Egrets are harder to miss. Cetti's Warblers may be easier to see in leafless winter bushes.

are only here in winter, when they are silent, but if you're here at this time keep checking overhead in case you're lucky and get a flypast of this large reedbed bird which can look surprisingly owl-like in flight.

From many points around the reserve you'll have a view across Lodmoor's open water. In summer the islands hold a large colony of raucous Common Terns, which commute to the sea to fish for their chicks. You'll also see Shelducks with their ducklings. Hobbies come to Lodmoor to hunt dragonflies, which they deftly dismember in flight, removing the wings and letting them flutter to earth.

In autumn, waders call in at the reserve, and you can best see them from the hide. Black-tailed Godwits wade belly-deep, while Green and Wood Sandpipers are more likely to stick to the shoreline. A sudden commotion among the birds on the lake may be a warning sign that a bird of prey is overhead – at this time of year it could be an Osprey, on its southbound migration.

Wintering wildfowl start to

WHEN TO VISIT

There is much of interest to see at Lodmoor throughout the year, and time of day is not critical for a visit. If you're not local to the area, it is well worth allowing enough time to visit the nearby Radipole Lake reserve (see page 38) as well.

arrive in late autumn, and by winter they are numerous and varied – look for Shovelers, Gadwalls,, Shelducks, Pochards, and Tufted Ducks.

How to get here

Grid ref./postcode SY 688809/ DT3 6
By road North-east of Weymouth, Lodmoor is 1 mile from Weymouth town centre. Take the A353 to Wareham.
By public transport The reserve is about a mile's walk along the seafront from Weymouth rail station, or you can take a bus (services are frequent) from Weymouth to Overcombe Corner and Lodmoor Country Park.

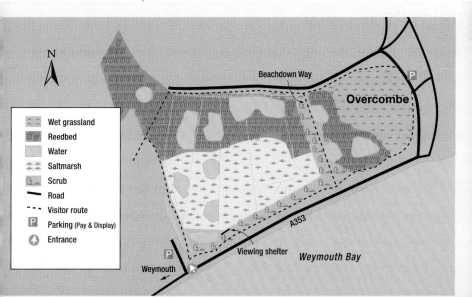

N

Beachdown Way

Overcombe

P

	Wet grassland
	Reedbed
	Water
	Saltmarsh
	Scrub
	Road
	Visitor route
P	Parking (Pay & Display)
	Entrance

A353

Viewing shelter · **Weymouth Bay**

Weymouth

P

SOUTH-WEST

MARAZION MARSH

SSSI, SPA, NATURA 2000

In a county of mainly rocky coastlines, Marazion Marsh is a rare coastal wetland, boasting Cornwall's largest reedbed. It is important for many breeding and visiting birds – including the Aquatic Warbler, one of Europe's most threatened species. Many families will enjoy a walk here as part of a visit to the area's many other attractions, such as the stunning St Michael's Mount.

●Access, facilities, contact details and accessibility

Regular guided walks are held here to help visitors see all the reserve has to offer.

- **Telephone** 01736 711682; **email** marazion.marsh@rspb.org.uk; **web** www.rspb.org.uk/marazionmarsh
- **Opening hours** At all times
- **Entry fees** None, but donations are welcome
- **Accessibility** The terrain here is flat, but the trails are unimproved, so access may be difficult for the mobility-impaired
- **Dogs** Must be kept under control and not allowed to enter the open water areas

What to look for

The western parts of this reserve can be viewed from the seaside road. The footpath from the car park runs north through the eastern end of the reserve, across the railway to Ludgvan village.

Grey Herons start to nest early in the year, so by late winter you'll see breeding activity – unusually, Marazion's population nests in the reedbeds rather than in trees. Little Egrets are usually noticeable too – Bitterns are more skulking but cold weather may force them into the open.

By mid-spring, the Bitterns and other winter birds have moved on, replaced by summer migrants. The resident Cetti's Warblers and

WILDLIFE BY SEASON

SPRING
Winter birds depart in early spring, and summer migrants like Reed and Sedge Warblers and Sand Martins start to arrive.

SUMMER
The Yellow Flag Irises and other marshland plants are flowering, and dragonflies hawk over the water, perhaps attracting a Hobby or two.

AUTUMN
Migrant waders may stop at the reserve, and migrant songbirds could include the secretive Aquatic Warbler.

WINTER
There may be a large roost of Starlings in the reedbeds. Look out for Bitterns and Water Rails feeding at the reed edges.

Reed Buntings are joined by noisy Sedge and Reed Warblers. Their songs are similar, but the Sedge's is more varied, with twittering, grinding and rattling notes. The marshland flowers are at their best in early summer, and insect numbers soon peak, with dragonflies, bumblebees and many others on the wing.

In autumn, many migrating Reed and Sedge Warblers visit along with a few Aquatic Warblers – Marazion is a vital staging post for this endangered eastern European species.

Autumn also brings other migrants – waders stop at the reserve to feed in the shallow water, and countless Swallows and martins fuel up on insects here before tackling their first sea crossing. The rare Spotted Crake may also put in an appearance.

Marazion's reedbeds hold a large roosting flock of Starlings in some winters – the birds perform sweeping aerial manouvres against the dusk sky before dropping down into the reeds. Winter also brings ducks such as Teals to the reserve, and you could see a Bittern.

WHEN TO VISIT
The reserve is interesting year-round. To see the Starlings coming in to roost visit before dusk in winter (check with the reserve first, as the flock uses other sites in some years).

How to get here
Grid ref./postcode SW 510312/ TR17 0

By road From Penzance follow the A30 east. At the heliport roundabout take the third exit to Longrock, go straight across the Morrison's roundabout and through Longrock. At the mini roundabout beyond the pedestrian crossing, take the second exit to Marazion. Follow signs from here - park by the reserve entrance or on the seafront.

By public transport First Group buses 2, 7 and 8 and Sunset 'Bay2Bay' service 340 go from Penzance bus terminus to Marazion. Get off at Green Lane. From here, cross the road and head north up Green Lane for about 30m. Take the first left, cross the bridge and the reserve entrance gate is on your right.

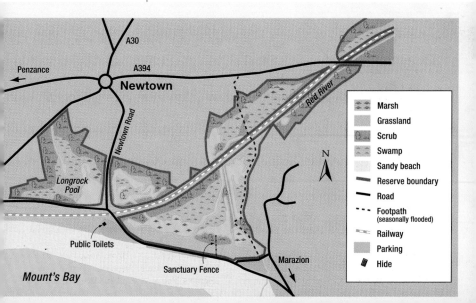

SOUTH-WEST

NAGSHEAD   SSSI

This exceptionally rich oak woodland, part of the Forest of Dean, is one of the best places to see woodland birds in the UK, with a long list of breeding species that includes some of the most coveted songbirds, such as Hawfinch and Wood Warbler, and the impressive and rare Goshawk. It is a lovely place for a ramble, with each season offering something special.

●Access, facilities, contact details and accessibility

The woodland has two hides overlooking ponds. There are two nature trails; one a mile long, the other 2.25 miles. You can book guided walks and group visits.

- **Telephone** 01594 562 852; **web** www.rspb.org.uk/nagshead
- **Opening hours** The reserve is open at all times, year-round. The reception/information centre (with toilet facilities) is open 10am–4pm at weekends only between Easter and August bank holidays inclusive.
- **Entry fees** None, though donations are welcome
- **Accessibility** Wheelchair access to part of the woodland is possible, although the nature trails are not suitable for wheelchairs, due to muddy surfaces, kissing gates and steep inclines.
- **Dogs** Only allowed on footpaths under the strictest control and on leads during the bird breeding season

What to look for

Nagshead is a lovely setting to enjoy springtime woodland birds. Visit before the leaves are out to see them more easily, especially species like Lesser Spotted Woodpecker that tend to spend most of their time in the canopy. Hawfinches nest here – they are very shy and hard to see but it will help if you learn to identify the characteristic loud ticking call. The hides overlooking the ponds are good places to see this ever-thirsty finch.

Summer migrants soon arrive, with Wood Warblers, Redstarts, Chiffchaffs and Pied

WILDLIFE BY SEASON

SPRING

Woodland birds sing in earnest from March, with migrants arriving into early May. Lesser Spotted Woodpeckers are easiest to see before the leaves come out.

SUMMER

Butterflies like White Admirals visit flowers in sunny patches. Nightjars churr at dusk.

AUTUMN

The seasonal colours are wonderful. Fallow Deer rut in October, and winter birds start to arrive.

WINTER

Look out for Bramblings, Redpolls and Redwings among the resident birds. Goshawks begin displaying on fine days in February.

Flycatchers in the wood and Nightjars on the open edges. Bluebells flourish in mid-May.

By summer the woodland birds are quieter, discreetly feeding their chicks and taking advantage of the leaf cover. The ancient oaks look impressive in full leaf, and in sunny clearings look out for Silver-washed Fritillaries, White Admirals and other woodland butterflies.

Beeches, oaks, Rowan, Aspen, willows and Wild Cherry provide fine autumn colours. Large beechmast crops attract many Chaffinches and sometimes Bramblings. In October, you may hear Fallow Deer bucks calling during the brief rutting season.

In winter proper, the non-migratory woodland birds travel extensively, often in flocks, from tree to tree in a constant search for food. Look out for Siskins, Redpolls and winter thrushes.

The breeding season kicks off early in the Forest of Dean, with the local Goshawks beginning to display from February. Most visitors will be eager to obtain views of this powerful and charismatic raptor, and RSPB

WHEN TO VISIT

To see Goshawks displaying at New Fancy View, visit on a still, sunny day in February or March. The later spring months are best for birdsong. Still summer evenings are the time to listen for Nightjars.

staff are on hand at New Fancy View, just east of Nagshead, to help you see one – you should also see Buzzards and perhaps other birds of prey here.

How to get here

Grid ref./postcode SO 606085/ GL15 4

By road From Parkend, take the B4431 in a westerly direction towards Coleford and Nagshead is signposted on the right on leaving Parkend village. Parkend is situated 3.75 miles north of Lydney on the B4234.

By public transport Lydney station is 3.75 miles away. Buses run from Lydney Bus Station (circular), to the stop along the B4431 signposted to Coleford. The reserve entrance is on the right on leaving the village.

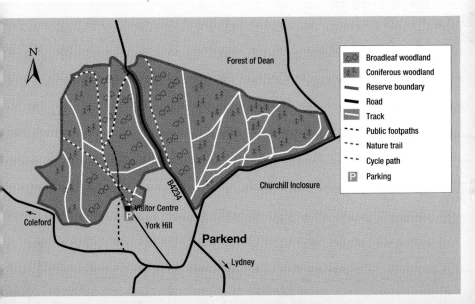

N

Forest of Dean

Coleford

Visitor Centre
York Hill
B4234

Churchill Inclosure

Parkend

Lydney

Broadleaf woodland
Coniferous woodland
Reserve boundary
Road
Track
Public footpaths
Nature trail
Cycle path
P Parking

SOUTH-WEST

RADIPOLE LAKE SSSI

Radipole Lake is on the River Wey, lying close to Weymouth town centre and flowing into Weymouth Harbour. It is surrounded by extensive reedbeds, which support rare breeding birds – the lake itself attracts large numbers of water birds throughout the year, reaching a peak in wintertime. In the migration season, a variety of waders stop off at the lake, and great flocks of Swallows and martins hunt tiny flying insects overhead. Summer sees butterflies feeding on the flowers that line the trails through the reserve, and dragonflies hawking overhead. Despite its town-centre location, Radipole offers rich and exciting wildlife-watching throughout the year.

● Access, facilities, contact details and accessibility

The seaside town of Weymouth is the perfect setting for this exciting and highly accessible reserve, which offers plenty of facilities for all the family including binocular hire, a picnic area, and regular wildlife-related events. A wide range of wildlife-related merchandise is available from the shop.

- **Telephone** 01305 773 519; **email** radipole.lake@rspb.org.uk; **web** www.rspb.org.uk/radipolelake
- **Opening hours** The visitor centre is open daily from 9am–5pm (4 pm in winter). The hide is open from 8.30am–4.30pm. Both are closed Christmas and Boxing Day. There are toilets (including disabled toilets) in the council-owned Swannery car park.
- **Entry fees** Entry is free for all visitors, though donations are welcome
- **Accessibility** The main trails are all level and wheelchair-accessible, though a little rough in places. There are several benches along the way. The visitor centre, hide and viewpoints are all accessible too.
- **Dogs** Only allowed on public footpaths

WILDLIFE BY SEASON

SPRING

As the new season's insects appear, so do the insect-eating birds – Swallows and martins hawk over the water, while in the reeds Sedge and Reed Warblers are singing and preparing to breed. Occasionally 'overshooting' migrant birds from continental Europe show up.

SUMMER

Hobbies chase the numerous dragonflies overhead, while butterflies may include migrant Painted Ladies or Clouded Yellows. Breeding wildfowl will be escorting their broods on the lake.

AUTUMN

Water levels in the lake are lowered at this time of year, exposing muddy shorelines that attract migrating waders. Family groups of Bearded Tits are feeding on the reed heads, or foraging along the muddy lake shore. Ospreys visit most years.

WINTER

The skulking Cetti's Warbler becomes (slightly) easier to see – listen too for its short, fruity song, given throughout the year. You may be lucky enough to spot a Water Rail or even a Bittern picking through the reeds, while on the lake gull and duck numbers reach their peak.

What to look for

From the Swannery car park, head for the visitor centre. You'll probably notice an assortment of wildfowl and gulls hanging around the car park or swimming in the small creek adjacent to the reserve, hoping for handouts. Look out for Little Grebes in the creek, perhaps ferrying fish to their stripy chicks in summer, and take a close look at the gulls – scarcer species show up here now and then, especially in winter.

The visitor centre looks out over the lake and there are

Osprey. Ospreys tend not to hang around when returning to their breeding grounds in spring, but birds heading south in autumn may linger for days around good fishing grounds. An Osprey overhead will cause panic among the gulls and waders on the lake. Another migrant predator, the Hobby, may be seen chasing dragonflies throughout summer, while you could see Sparrowhawks, Kestrels, Peregrines and Buzzards at any time of year.

The dense reedbeds that

The lovely Mediterranean Gull stands out among commoner Black-headed Gulls with its white wingtips and sturdy red bill.

telescopes permanently set up for anyone to use. In spring and autumn, look for waders such as Black-tailed Godwits feeding on the shore or in shallow water – also check the muddy banks for foraging Bearded Tits. These tiny birds, with their sharp metallic calls, can be hard to spot among the reeds, but here you will often see them feeding on the exposed lake shore.

Migrating birds of prey are also a feature of Radipole, the star among them being the

surround the lake are a valuable wildlife habitat – many birds breed in the dense mesh of reed stems and other marshy vegetation. They can be hard to spot – none more so than Cetti's Warbler, a shy, chestnut-brown bird with an arrestingly loud and emphatic song. They are present all year round and you may hear a dozen or more of them as you walk around the trail, but you'll need a lot of patience to see one. Reed and Sedge Warblers are also shy songsters, giving

One of the most distinctive reedbed birds, the Bearded Tit is not closely related to our other tit species, but shares their agility and engaging character. Only the males have the distinctive black face markings – more of a moustache than a beard.

their dry, pulsing, interminable songs in concert around you in the spring and summer, but the Sedge Warbler does sometimes give itself away with a short song-flight.

In winter, two of the reedbed birds become slightly easier to see as shorter days and scarcer food supplies mean they have to move around more than usual. You may see a Bittern flopping in heavy flight out of the reeds, like a brown, heavy-set Grey Heron. Water Rails, twitchy-tailed Moorhen-like birds with long red bills,

WHEN TO VISIT

You can walk the main trail at any time – small birds tend to be more active around dawn and dusk, but many of Radipole's specialities can be seen and heard just as well at more civilised hours. Summer is best for insects and the birds (Swallows, House and Sand Martins and Hobbies) that hunt them, while in winter all attention turns to the lake itself, with its gatherings of gulls and wildfowl. The transitional seasons of spring and autumn are characterised by visiting waders, birds of prey and other migratory birds.

are reluctant fliers but you may spot one picking its way along the water's edge or even dashing across the trail in front of you – or listen out for its shrill 'scream', rather like a piglet.

This site is specially managed to maintain a balance of open water with reed and scrub – without this management much of the open water would disappear, and willow and other trees would replace the reedbeds. At the furthest point of the main trail, a viewing shelter looks out across open water. Here, you may see wildfowl like Shovelers, Wigeons, Gadwalls, Pochards and Teals in winter. There is less variety in spring and summer but look out for handsome Great Crested Grebes, performing their elaborate courtship dance in early spring and giving piggyback lifts to their humbug-striped chicks in summer. This is a good place to watch for birds of prey overhead.

Another trail, recently opened up to all visitors, leads to the comfortable and roomy North Hide, which overlooks a shallow, marsh-fringed pool in the middle of the reserve. A large pre-roost gathering of Little Egrets can be seen here – you can watch these small white herons fly in as dusk approaches. This is also the likeliest spot to see a Bittern hunting at the edge of the

ACCIDENTALS HAPPEN

Most RSPB reserves have been established to protect and encourage the UK's regularly breeding, wintering or migrating birds, but some RSPB reserves enjoy, by virtue of their location, a higher than average number of non-British birds appearing as vagrants each year. These extreme rarities or 'accidentals' originate from as far away as Siberia or North America, but a few individuals completely lose their way on migration and (if they survive the sea crossing) will stop at the first land they find. The Dorset headland of Portland Bill is the first landfall for many a lost bird, and for water birds Radipole Lake may be the first suitable habitat they find. Radipole Lake is therefore popular with serious 'twitchers' looking for mega-rarities, especially during the migration seasons. In 2008 sightings included a Little Bittern from continental Europe and a Hooded Merganser from North America.

A rare clear view of a Cetti's Warbler – a rapidly disappearing tail is the usual sighting of this very shy and furtive little bird.

How to get here

Grid ref./postcode SY671804/DT3 5
By road The reserve entrance is in the Swannery car park in Weymouth town centre, off the A353.
By public transport The reserve is close to the town centre, and less than half a mile from Weymouth train station. The town centre is well served by buses.

water, as well as the more familiar Grey Heron. Other long-legged wading birds seem drawn to this lake as well – rarities like Spoonbill and Cattle Egret have been seen in recent years.

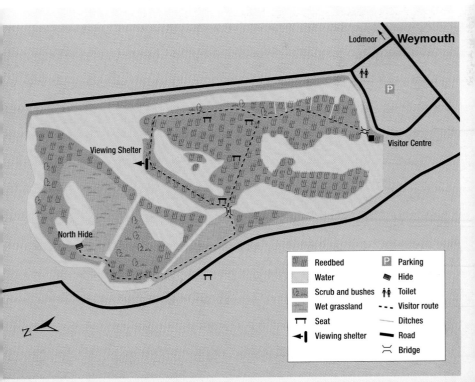

Reedbed		Parking	
Water		Hide	
Scrub and bushes		Toilet	
Wet grassland		Visitor route	
Seat		Ditches	
Viewing shelter		Road	
		Bridge	

SOUTH-WEST

WEST SEDGEMOOR

SSSI, SPA, RAMSAR, NATURA 2000

Once, the Somerset Levels were a great expanse of reed and water in winter and wet grassland in summer. Gradually agriculture drained this precious habitat, but now, thanks to the RSPB, West Sedgemoor is once again returning to its former glory and wildfowl gather in huge numbers in winter and waders breed here in spring – filling the air with their evocative calls.

● Access, facilities, contact details and accessibility

A guided walk is one of the best ways to see wildfowl on the reserve in winter and breeding waders in the spring. This is a great place for a short family walk if you have a pushchair, and a longer exploration if you don't.

- **Telephone** 01458 252805 or 07774 620879 (to book walks); **email** west.sedgemoor@rspb.org.uk; **web** www.rspb.org.uk/westsedgemoor
- **Opening hours** Open at all times
- **Entry fees** Free, but donations to help us continue our work here are welcome
- **Accessibility** The Heronry Hide and part of the Woodland trail are wheelchair-accessible
- **Dogs** Not allowed, except registered assistance dogs

What to look for

From the car park, the Woodland walk leads you on a loop around Swell Wood. If you are visiting in late winter or spring, you'll definitely want to head for the Heronry Hide, a short distance from the car park, to view the busy nesting colony of Grey Herons in the treetops here.

From February the adults are renovating their nests and soon have chicks. A few pairs of Little Egrets nest here too.

Bluebells, orchids and other woodland flowers flourish at this time of year, and migrants like Nightingale, Blackcap, Garden Warbler and

WILDLIFE BY SEASON

SPRING

Herons are breeding. Waders display over the pastures, and the woodlands are full of birdsong and spring flowers.

SUMMER

Insect season – the flowery meadows are alive with butterflies, hoverflies and bees. Listen for Quails calling from the long grass.

AUTUMN

A good time to see Roe Deer grazing on the woodland edges. Winter visitors such as Redwings and Fieldfares start to arrive.

WINTER

The feeders at Swell Wood attract woodland birds. Flooded fields attract large flocks of ducks, Lapwings and Golden Plovers.

Chiffchaff add their voices to the chorus of resident songbirds.

From the viewpoints out over the meadows, you might see Curlews delivering their beautiful bubbling song as they fly over the fields. If you feel inclined, you can continue your walk by taking the more rugged Scarp trail through the eastern end of Swell Wood, with views over the wet fields below. At the bottom of the hill, a public footpath runs east–west skirting the edge of the moor.

A wide variety of butterflies can be seen in the fields and hedgerows in summer. The last to emerge is the Brown Hairstreak, on the wing from mid-August into September. This attractive and scarce species lays its eggs on Blackthorn twigs – to prevent destruction of the eggs the RSPB cuts its Blackthorn hedges in early August, rather than doing the more traditional winter cutting.

In winter, rain may cause the wet meadows to flood – if they do, you'll see large flocks gathering. The numbers of these birds can be staggering, with up to 20,000 Wigeons, 10,000

WHEN TO VISIT

West Sedgemoor teems with wildlife throughout the year. Early-morning visits in spring are best for birdsong in the woodland, and butterflies are most active toward midday.

Teals and even 500 Pintails. Add to these the 30,000 Lapwings and 18,000 Golden Plovers, and you can have no doubt that the return to traditional management of the Levels is a tremendous boost to these wetland-loving species.

How to get here

Grid ref./postcode ST 361238/ TA3 6
By road The reserve is signed off the A378 between the villages of Curry Rivel and Fivehead. Take the first turning on your left after leaving Fivehead or first turning on your right after leaving Curry Rivel.
By public transport Taunton station is 11 miles away. Southern National Taunton to Yeovil bus service stops in Fivehead on the A378, 1 mile away.

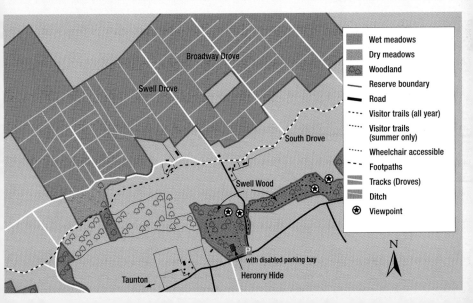

Broadway Drove

Swell Drove

South Drove

Swell Wood

Taunton

P with disabled parking bay

Heronry Hide

	Wet meadows
	Dry meadows
	Woodland
—	Reserve boundary
—	Road
----	Visitor trails (all year)
·····	Visitor trails (summer only)
·-·-·	Wheelchair accessible
- - -	Footpaths
	Tracks (Droves)
	Ditch
✪	Viewpoint

N

Heath Fritillary

BLEAN WOODS SSSI, NNR, SAC

The Canterbury woodlands have a very special community of wildlife. Blean Woods is an area of woodland that is managed by the RSPB in partnership with Natural England, Woodland Trust and three local authorities to ensure the plants and animals here prosper. The network of mainly level trails take you through the richest habitats. A dawn or dusk visit is especially magical.

● Access, facilities, contact details and accessibility

There are five colour-marked trails, the longest 8 miles. Guided walks can be booked.

- **Telephone** 01227 455 972; **email** blean.woods@rspb.org.uk; **web** www.rspb.org.uk/bleanwoods
- **Opening hours** The car park is open from 8am–9pm; you can visit on foot at all times.
- **Entry fees** Free, but donations are welcome
- **Accessibility** The green trail is suitable for wheelchair users, with reasonably firm surfaces and gentle gradients. Some sections could be muddy after heavy rain.
- **Dogs** Allowed on the white trail and on public footpaths

What to look for

As soon as you enter the reserve from the car park, the smells and sounds of the woodland take over. If you're visiting in mid-spring, you will probably soon hear your first Nightingale, pumping out its beautiful song from some well-concealed hiding place in the foliage. The RSPB coppices the woodland here to maintain the thick understorey that Nightingales require. Nearly as sweet is the warbling song of the Blackcap from high in the treetops.

Part of this reserve is open heathland, and the RSPB has increased the size of the heathy area to encourage birds like Nightjars. The open areas also benefit butterflies. It is well worth visiting

WILDLIFE BY SEASON

SPRING

Woodland and heathland birdsong is at its best with Nightingales, warblers, thrushes, finches and many others.

SUMMER

Listen for Nightjars and Woodcocks at dusk. Heath Fritillaries and other butterflies are on the wing.

AUTUMN

Fungi sprout from dead wood and on the woodland floor. Migratory birds are feeding up on seeds and berries.

WINTER

Foraging flocks of tits sometimes attract Goldcrests and Treecreepers. Woodcocks feed in muddy areas in the woodland.

in June to see one of the real stars of this reserve, the Heath Fritillary butterfly. This beautiful little orange-and-black insect is one of Britain's rarest species.

A summer visit here would not be complete without spending some time at sunset listening to and watching Nightjars as they churr and glide over the heath. You will probably also see and hear a male Woodcock or two at dusk, a portly, long-billed bird flying overhead in neat straight lines. Tawny Owls are most vocal either in late summer or late winter but you may see one at any time, silently flapping across a clearing.

Winter is generally quieter, but is the best time to see Lesser Spotted Woodpeckers as they are no longer hidden by tree foliage. They may join noisy foraging flocks of tits and other woodland birds. These small woodpeckers have become very scarce in the UK in recent years.

How to get here

Grid ref./postcode TR 126592/ CT2 9
By road From the A2 heading

WHEN TO VISIT

To hear Nightingales and other woodland birds at their best, visit from mid-April to mid-May. For Nightjars, visit on still summer evenings from late May. Heath Fritillaries are on the wing from late May into early July.

east into Canterbury, take the A2050 and turn left at signs for Rough Common and Blean. Drive up the steep hill into Rough Common village. After 900m, look out for the brown RSPB sign and take the access track to the car park.
By public transport Canterbury East and West stations are nearest. From Canterbury bus station bus 27 (Bay A4 at bus station) runs at 7 minutes past the hour to Rough Common Monday–Saturday, stopping by the reserve access track (ask for Lovell Road). Buses 4 and 4A (Bay B1 or B2 at bus station) run to Rough Common about every 15 minutes Monday to Saturday and every 30 minutes on Sunday.

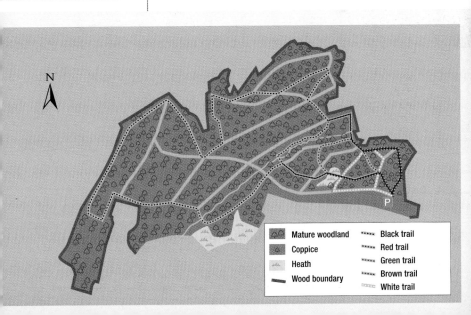

Mature woodland	·····	Black trail
Coppice	·····	Red trail
Heath	·····	Green trail
Wood boundary	·····	Brown trail
	·····	White trail

N

BRADING MARSHES

SSSI, SPA, NATURA 2000

This is the RSPB's first reserve on the Isle of Wight. From the many public footpaths, you can explore this area of marshland, woodland, fields and hedges along the lower River Yar from the town of Sandown to the quiet harbour at Bembridge. In winter, flocks of wildfowl gather on the fields, and in spring and summer the flowery fields and woodland host masses of butterflies.

● Access, facilities, contact details and accessibility

You can explore the reserve via a network of footpaths from Brading Station, Bembridge Harbour and Culver Down NT. Brading station on the island's railway line makes a perfect starting point.

- **Telephone** 01273 775 333; **web** www.rspb.org.uk/bradingmarshes
- **Opening hours** Open at all times, but the station (run by Brading Town Council) has limited opening times
- **Entry fees** None, but donations to help continue the work here are appreciated
- **Accessibility** None of the public footpaths are suitable for wheelchairs. Many can be wet or muddy in winter.
- **Dogs** Are allowed on public footpaths and bridleways, but are not permitted on guided walks

What to look for

This scenic river valley is a great place to enjoy a quiet walk, whether you are already on the Isle of Wight or making a special trip from the mainland. Public footpaths allow good open views over much of the area, and it's possible to plan a variety of interesting long or short routes.

In spring, look out for Lapwings calling and displaying out over the marshes. Their numbers are increasing as the RSPB restores the wetlands. Yellow Wagtails and Skylarks also favour the open fields, while in bushes around the edges you are almost certain to hear the explosive song of the Cetti's Warbler – this relative newcomer to the British Isles is doing well here.

WILDLIFE BY SEASON

SPRING

Lapwings are giving their extraordinary yodelling cries above the marshes, and Buzzards and other birds of prey glide overhead on sunny days.

SUMMER

Birds are breeding – you may see families of fledglings – and butterflies and other insects are on the wing in the grasslands.

AUTUMN

Little Egret numbers peak. Darter dragonflies make the most of the last warm days, often resting on the ground.

WINTER

Winter wildfowl gather on the marshes. Look out for the colourful berries of Spindle and Stinking Iris.

Alongside the wetlands and bordering the abandoned railway line, there are patches of scrub and woodland with a variety of commoner woodland birds. Centurion's Copse is a delightful woodland to visit with beds of Wild Daffodils in early spring and the chance to spot entrancing Red Squirrels. The Isle of Wight fortunately still has a healthy population of these attractive animals.

Summer butterflies to look out for in the fields include Common Blues, Marbled Whites and Meadow Browns, and other downland species should flourish as the RSPB restores some of the meadows on the valley sides.

In winter, water birds congregate on the reserve. Large flocks of Brent Geese and Wigeons arrive to graze on the open grasslands, and Teals are also present in large numbers. Little Egrets are commoner in autumn, but in winter another scarce heron, the shy Bittern, may visit areas of reedbed. One or two Hen Harriers sometimes spend winter here – look out for them gliding low over the fields,

WHEN TO VISIT

There is interesting wildlife to see at Brading Marshes throughout the year, and time of day is not critical.

in search of an unsuspecting bird or rodent.

How to get here

Grid ref./postcode SZ 609868/ PO36 0

By road The best access is by the island train to Brading station, which also makes an easy and fun day-trip from the mainland by directly-connecting train and ferry (Portsmouth to Ryde). Cars can park at the National Trust's Bembridge Duver and Culver Down nearby.

By public transport From Brading station, walk up the road away from the station and turn right at a brown pedestrian sign into a housing estate. After 50m, turn right at another brown sign between two houses. The path leads through a gate, across the railway then across the meadow to the old sea wall. Turn right to enter the reserve.

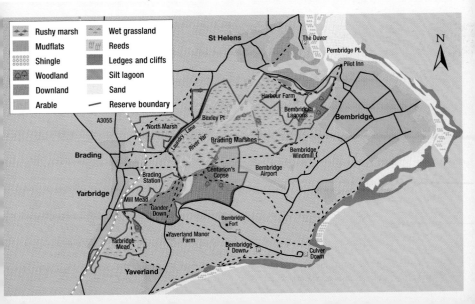

Rushy marsh
Mudflats
Shingle
Woodland
Downland
Arable
Wet grassland
Reeds
Ledges and cliffs
Silt lagoon
Sand
Reserve boundary

St Helens
The Duver
Pembridge Pt.
Pilot Inn
Harbour Farm
Bembridge Lagoons
Bembridge
A3055
North Marsh
Bexley Pt
Laundry Lane
River Yar
Brading Marshes
Bembridge Windmill
Brading
Centurion's Copse
Bembridge Airport
Yarbridge
Brading Station
Mill Mead
Gander Down
Bembridge Fort
Yaverland Manor Farm
Bembridge Down
Culver Down
Yarbridge Mead
Yaverland

N

SOUTH-EAST

Nightjar

BROADWATER WARREN AONB

Broadwater Warren is a new and exciting reserve within the High Weald Area of Outstanding Natural Beauty. It is currently largely conifer plantation, but the RSPB plans to restore the glorious historic mix of ancient deciduous woodland and heathland that was once common across this High Weald Forest Ridge.

●Access, facilities, contact details and accessibility

There is a small car park, open 7am–7pm or dusk if earlier, plus a long nature trail for you to explore. There are no plans for major visitor facilities here.

- **Telephone** 01273 775 333; **web** www.rspb.org.uk/broadwaterwarren
- **Opening hours** Open at all times
- **Entry fees** Free
- **Accessibility** The paths are mainly flat but there are a few steep slopes. They can be also uneven and sometimes muddy. An all-abilities track to the Nightjar viewpoint is planned.
- **Dogs** Welcome but must be kept under control

What to look for

This is 'one to watch', a reserve that is just opening its doors up to visitors and is going to get better and better for the wildlife too. The RSPB plans many changes, but it is already a wonderfully restful place to visit and, in time, rare heathland birds like Woodlark and Dartford Warbler should flourish here. Already there are

heathy areas, ponds, an area of Sweet Chestnut coppice and a patch of boggy mire, and it hosts a correspondingly varied flora and fauna.

Common woodland and open-country birds are most obvious in spring, when males are singing to proclaim their territories. Listen for the fluty warbles of Blackcaps, the sweet

WILDLIFE BY SEASON

SPRING

The last winter finches move on through March, and the first Chiffchaffs and Willow Warblers are singing.

SUMMER

Nightjars churr at dusk, with Woodcocks roding overhead. You could see Glow-worms by the track. Dragonflies are on the wing by day. Wood Ant nests are busy.

AUTUMN

Woodland birds start to form flocks, and wintering visitors begin to arrive. The best time for fungi.

WINTER

Parties of thrushes and finches roam the woods. Flocks of Siskins and Redpolls visit.

descending notes of Willow Warblers and the steady two-note song of Chiffchaffs. Yellowhammers sing on the few open, heathy areas. A few Nightjar pairs cling on, and you can hear their strange churring song through summer. A late-evening summer vigil will almost certainly also produce a Woodcock or two, the males flying in neat straight lines above the trees, giving periodic squeaks or grunts in their own form of song and display – known as 'roding'. There's a chance you'll bump into a Badger as well, and look out for the green lights of female Glow-worms (actually a kind of beetle) along the trail edges.

Things quieten down in autumn, but winter finches and thrushes provide interest, with flocks of Redpolls and Siskins visiting the birches, and Redwings and Fieldfares passing overhead.

What you will also see is a landscape reawakening. Over a period of 10 years, the RSPB will remove some of the conifer plantations, allowing the heathland and woodland seeds

WHEN TO VISIT

To hear Nightjars, visit on still summer evenings, aiming to arrive soon before dusk. Otherwise, spring and summer is generally best, and time of day is not important.

buried in the soil to germinate. It won't look pretty at first, that's unavoidable – but soon the heather will start to flower again and long lost wildlife will return.

How to get here

Grid ref./postcode TQ 561370/ TN3 9

By road From the A26 from Tunbridge Wells heading towards Crowborough road, take the minor road on the right, Broadwater Forest Lane.

By public transport The nearest railway station is Tunbridge Wells – the town is well served by buses too. From the railway station, turn left and then right onto Vale Road, and at the end of Vale Road turn left onto London Road – this is the A26, follow directions as above.

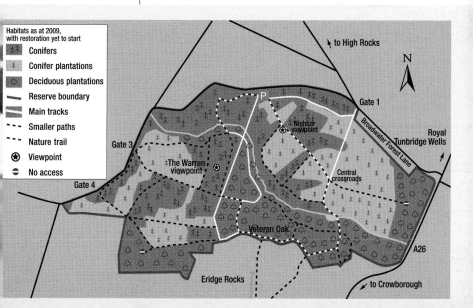

Habitats as at 2009, with restoration yet to start

- 🌲 Conifers
- 🌲 Conifer plantations
- 🌳 Deciduous plantations
- — Reserve boundary
- ══ Main tracks
- - - Smaller paths
- - - Nature trail
- ✦ Viewpoint
- ⊖ No access

SOUTH-EAST

CLIFFE POOLS

SSSI, SPA, RAMSAR, NATURA 2000

Cliffe Pools is a spectacular reserve of open water, big skies and huge wheeling flocks of wetland birds. This wonderful space was recently earmarked for a new London airport, but RSPB campaigning has saved it from destruction, and it is now a flourishing wildlife haven.

● Access, facilities, contact details and accessibility

A car park and way-marked nature trails with interpretation boards are new additions to the site. Further visitor infrastructure is still being developed. Existing paths are pushchair-friendly.

- **Telephone** 01634 222 480; **email** northkentmarshes@rspb.org.uk; **web** www.rspb.org.uk/cliffepools
- **Opening hours** At all times; car park gates open 8am–5pm (or sunset if earlier)
- **Entry fees** Free, though donations to help continue the work here are welcome
- **Accessibility** The trails are mostly flat but may be rough in places
- **Dogs** Only allowed on public footpaths and bridleways

What to look for

The reserve consists of a number of large, shallow, saline lagoons that are highly attractive to birds. Waders in particular rely on habitats like this, to use as roosting and feeding places when the tide is high and the mudflats of the Thames Estuary are covered by water. The lagoons were formerly clay pits – as work was abandoned,

the pits flooded and a wet grassland habitat developed around them.

There are currently four nature trails, ranging from half a mile to 4.5 miles. Purpose-built viewing mounds provide good vantage points across the lagoons and the Thames Estuary. Further visitor facilities are planned – the RSPB

WILLDLIFE BY SEASON

SPRING

Marshland and wetland bird are breeding. Nightingales sing along the Saxon Shore Way. Migrating waders pass through.

SUMMER

Up to 30 species of waders on return migration stop off from midsummer. Insects visit marshland flowers.

AUTUMN

Large flocks of Avocets and Black-tailed Godwits visit the reserve. Seabirds are moving on the Thames.

WINTER

Large flocks of ducks and waders overwinter. The best time to see harriers, Short-eared Owls and other birds of prey.

is also carrying out landscaping and water management work to further enhance the reserve's attractiveness to wildlife.

In spring, the star bird here is the Avocet, once extinct in the UK but now thriving here and at other RSPB reserves on the south and east coasts of England. Avocets are great fun to watch as they bicker over nest sites and, later in the year, escort their enchanting fluffy grey chicks on feeding forays. Common Terns nest on lagoon islands, while the scratchy songs of Whitethroats are all around.

From mid-summer, the reserve plays host to many species of waders – birds which bred in more northerly climes and are now migrating south, stopping at Cliffe en route to feed. The adults come through first, then a few weeks later the young birds of the year, looking smarter than their parents in brand new juvenile plumage.

These 'passage migrants' move on by mid to late autumn, and the winter birds arrive. Large flocks of ducks spend the cold months here. You may also see grebes or divers on the

WHEN TO VISIT

With an exciting variety of breeding and wintering birds, along with good numbers of migrants visiting in spring and autumn, Cliffe is an exciting place to visit at any time of year. Visit at high tide to see waders on the lagoons.

deeper lagoons, and elsewhere wintering waders including up to 5,000 Dunlins.

How to get here

Grid ref./postcode TQ722757/ ME3 7

By road Take the A289 off the A2 near Strood. From the A289 follow the B2000. Salt Lane will be the main reserve entrance, but parking opportunities there are limited at present. Turn second left after the 'Cliffe' village sign, turn right at the next T-junction, and Salt Lane is the next left.

By public transport Higham, 3 miles away, and Strood, 5 miles away, are the nearest stations. Bus 113 from Chatham via Rochester and Strood stops at the Six Bells pub in Cliffe.

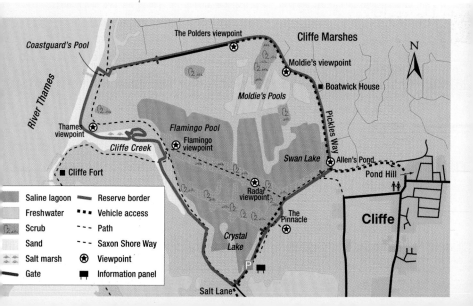

SOUTH-EAST

DUNGENESS SSSI, NNR, SPA, SAC, NATURA 2000

Dungeness is a huge triangular projection into the English Channel, with no towns and only a couple of roads. This unique wilderness of shingle is dotted with lakes but little vegetation; it has a tiny village and a hulking power station guarding the tip of the promontory. The headland's position makes it a springboard for departing migratory birds, and the first landfall for them on their return. The lakes attract large numbers of water birds, especially when inland and more northerly waters freeze up, and the power station's outflow warms the sea which attracts fish and therefore seabirds. It's also an incredibly atmospheric place to visit.

● Access, facilities, contact details and accessibility

This flagship reserve is well-equipped for visitors. There is ample parking close to the visitor centre, which doubles as a shop selling books, optical gear, garden bird feeders, and so on. You can also buy hot drinks and snacks, and get the latest wildlife information from the staff at the reception desk. The events programme includes guided walks, optics demos and workshops. Around the main trail, which is flat and easy walking, you'll find six hides, with another plus a viewing screen at the Hanson ARC site (which has its own car park).

● **Telephone** 01797 320588; **email** dungeness@rspb.org.uk; **web** www.rspb.org.uk/dungeness
● **Opening hours** Open daily (except 25 and 26 December) from 9am–9 pm (or sunset if earlier). The visitor centre is open from 10am–5pm (closing 4pm November–February).
● **Entry fees** Free to all RSPB members. Non-members £3, children £1, concessions £2, family ticket £6.
● **Accessibility** The main trail is 2 miles long, the Hanson ARC trails are both 380m long (one leading to the hide, the other to the viewing screen). The trails are flat and accessible to wheelchairs and pushchairs, although some areas have looser shingle and will be a little trickier to navigate.
● **Dogs** No dogs allowed, except registered assistance dogs

WILDLIFE BY SEASON

SPRING
Bird migration is under-way, and there's a good chance of a rarity turning up. Breeding birds will be singing, displaying and nest-building. Skuas, terns and other seabirds pass along the coast in May.

SUMMER
Hobbies hunt dragonflies over the pits, and Marsh Frogs are in full voice in the creeks and ditches. Oystercatchers and other breeding birds will be attending to their chicks. The shingle flowers are out, and this is the best time for insects.

AUTUMN
Numbers of Swallows and martins build up over the pits. Again there is a good chance of a rarity. Waders are passing through on their return migration. As autumn progresses, winter visitors begin to arrive.

WINTER
Numbers of wildfowl reach their peak, and more unusual water birds are likely to show up. Bitterns may be wintering in the reeds. There may be rare wintering songbirds about, with Penduline Tits and Firecrests occasionally visiting. The best time for birds of prey, with Merlins, Peregrines, Short-eared Owls and sometimes Hen Harriers all visiting the area.

What to look for

The RSPB established their very first reserve here in 1931, to protect the rare breeding birds that lived on the unique shingle ridges. The area's status as a National Nature Reserve is because of this remarkable habitat – the largest of its kind in Europe. Over the years, the RSPB has worked to protect and develop new areas of wildlife habitat here, in particular the flooded gravel pits, their islands and vegetation, and the reedbeds that have grown around them.

Pit. There are telescopes set up here so you can do some birdwatching in warmth and comfort. This is particularly welcome when cold winter winds are sweeping across the peninsula – although chilly conditions often mean exciting birdlife is around.

From the visitor centre, the main trail leads you alongside the shore of Burrowe's Pit. You can view the water birds without disturbing them from the four hides that overlook

The smartest and most sought after Dungeness duck, the Smew is a real charmer. Cold winter weather usually brings several to the reserve.

The road to the RSPB visitor centre weaves through 'fields' of shingle, with a few scattered bushes and small ponds. In summer you'll see a colourful display of shingle-loving flowers here, like the Yellow-horned Poppy and the blue-flowered Viper's Bugloss. In winter, look for wildfowl on the ponds and birds of prey overhead. The visitor centre has a board detailing recent wildlife sightings and looks out through large windows onto the biggest of the reserve's gravel pits, Burrowe's

the pit on the way round. In winter, there will be many common ducks like Shovelers, Wigeons, Teals, Tufted Ducks and Pochards. Among them, look out for grebes, divers and more unusual ducks like Pintail, Smew, Long-tailed Duck and Goldeneye. You may see birds of prey like Merlins or Peregrine Falcons harrying the water birds. In summer, there will be breeding gulls, Oystercatchers and Ringed Plovers on the pit's many islands. Hobbies may hawk overhead, and ducks, geese

The male Great Crested Newt becomes a flamboyant little dragon in spring, with his fine crest and spotty pattern.

and Mute Swans lead their fluffy broods across the water. If you visit in spring or autumn, you'll see migrant waders on the shore and in shallow water, and perhaps warblers and other small songbirds in the patches of scrub around the trail.

The trail carries on away from the coast – you'll notice that the shingle is becoming more vegetated. You'll soon reach the Denge Marsh hide, overlooking a reedy lake. Here, the thick reedbeds are alive with the songs of Reed and Sedge Warblers in summer, while Reed Buntings, Cetti's Warblers and Bearded Tits are here all year round. You may hear the pig-like squeal of the Water Rail and, if you're very lucky, see one picking its way around the edges of the reeds. Marsh Harriers have recently begun to breed

WHEN TO VISIT

The reserve has a lot to offer at any time of year. If you are interested in birds you will probably get most out of a winter visit, but be aware that this exposed area can become bitterly cold. Midday at weekends will be busiest, although the main areas of interest are well-screened from the trails so disturbance isn't usually a problem.

at Dungeness – look for a big, long-tailed bird of prey, its wings held in a shallow 'V', cruising low over the reedbeds and fields. In winter, you could also see its smaller relative, the Hen Harrier.

The reedbeds here are the result of extensive landscaping work by the RSPB, the aim being to connect them up with reedbeds at the nearby Hooker's Pit. One of the aims of management here is to attract Bitterns to breed – these shy brown herons already overwinter, and the first 'booming' spring male was heard in 2009.

As the trail takes you back towards the visitor centre, you'll pass rough grassy fields, over which Lapwings give their weird, whooping calls in spring. Throughout summer the ditches will resound with the chorus of gurgling croaks from the reserve's many Marsh Frogs, newts including the rare Great Crested breed there too, and butterflies feed on the flowers – they may include newly arrived Painted Ladies and Clouded Yellows from the near continent.

Although they're less obvious than the birds, many other creatures live at Dungeness, including national rarities like the Medicinal Leech, Dotted Bee-fly, Sussex Emerald moth and an impressive 11 species of bumblebee.

The RSPB has recently opened new visitor

trails at the nearby Hanson ARC pit, which lead
to a hide and viewing screen by the lake.

The whole Dungeness peninsula is famous for
attracting rare birds. Serious birdwatchers will
want to visit the bird observatory, particularly
in spring and summer. If you have time, it's
worth visiting the beach, to watch the masses of
gulls and terns that gather to feed on abundant
fish at the 'Patch' – an area of water warmed by
the power station's outflow – while the power
station itself is home to breeding Black Redstarts.
Seabird enthusiasts pass many happy hours
here in spring and autumn, watching for passing
seabirds like the striking Pomarine Skua. Of
more general interest, Derek Jarman's famous
shingle garden is in the village, and from spring
to autumn you can also enjoy a ride on the
narrow-gauge Romney, Hythe and Dymchurch
railway, which terminates at Dungeness point.

How to get here

Grid ref./postcode TR062197/TN29 9
By road One mile out of the village of Lydd on
the Dungeness Road, turn right for the reserve
entrance. The visitor centre and car park are 1
mile along the track. The entrance to the Hanson
ARC site and car park is opposite the main

Brent Geese migrate past Dungeness at sea in their thousands
each autumn, and sometimes head inland to visit the reserve.

reserve entrance on the left of the Dungeness
Road.

By public transport Trains go to Rye (10 miles
from the reserve) from Hastings and Ashford.
From Rye take bus 711 to Lydd and bus 12
from Lydd to the reserve. From Folkestone
station (20 miles from the reserve), take bus 12
to the reserve. From Ashford station (16 miles
from the reserve) take bus 11 to reserve. The
buses stop about a mile's walk from the reserve.

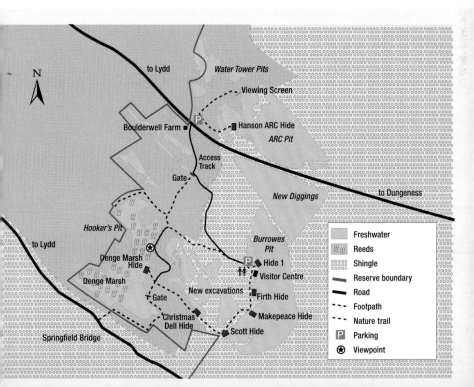

SOUTH-EAST

Wigeon

ELMLEY MARSHES

SSSI, SPA, RAMSAR, NNR, NATURA 2000

The spectacle of masses of wild birds over a great vista of wetland and pasture is a magical sight anywhere, but perhaps especially wonderful in the most built-up corner of Britain. Here, at the mouth of the Thames Estuary, is a real paradise for wildlife and wildlife enthusiasts alike, with a sense of endless space and wilderness.

● Access, facilities, contact details and accessibility

Elmley has five birdwatching hides, and two trails (6 miles and 2 miles).

- **Telephone** 01795 665 969; **email** northkentmarshes@rspb.org.uk; **web** www.rspb.org.uk/elmleymarshes
- **Opening hours** Daily (closed Tuesdays) 9am–9pm or sunset when earlier
- **Entry fees** No fixed entrance fees. However, suggested donations for non-members of £2.50 adults, 50p child, £1.50 concession, and £4.50 for a family, are gratefully received to help maintain the reserve.
- **Accessibility** The trails are mostly flat. Disabled visitors may drive up to the first hide by arrangement.
- **Dogs** Not allowed, except registered assistance dogs

What to look for

Check the fields around the rough track leading to the entrance for feeding waders and partridges. Park by the reserve buildings and head out on foot to the reserve proper. There is a feeding station by the track just beyond the car park.

The trail leads you down beside the sea wall. The open fields are interspersed with small, reedy pools and ditches. In winter you'll constantly see parties of Wigeons, various other ducks and waders overhead. You might also see White-fronted Geese, and perhaps Whooper or Bewick's Swans. Small birds around in the

WILDLIFE BY SEASON

SPRING
Breeding waders (one of the highest densities in lowland Britain), ducks and Marsh Harriers are preparing to nest.

SUMMER
Many young waders and ducklings are out. Look for Yellow Wagtails in the fields, and dragonflies and damselflies around the pools and ditches.

AUTUMN
Migrating waders visit the lagoons – visit at high tide to see the largest numbers. Little Egret and Marsh Harrier numbers increase.

WINTER
Flocks of ducks, geese and waders descend on the pools. A variety of brids of prey can be seen.

winter include Stonechats and Meadow Pipits.

In winter Elmley is wonderful for birds of prey – look out for Short-eared Owls, Peregrine Falcons, Merlins, Marsh and Hen Harriers and Common Buzzards. Elmley is probably the best place in Britain to see the Rough-legged Buzzard, a scarce winter visitor.

There are three hides overlooking the Flood, a sizeable lagoon with breeding waders in summer and large numbers of ducks and waders in winter. Another hide overlooks the Swale itself, giving wonderful views of waders on a rising tide. In autumn, you may see seabirds moving along the channel.

In spring and especially autumn, migrant waders, Black Terns and Little Gulls visit the Flood. Early to mid-summer can be quieter but you'll see butterflies and dragonflies, and wader chicks from the Flood hides. Yellow Wagtails breed in good numbers at Elmley and will be feeding their fledged chicks in the summer. Mammals here include Brown Hares and Water Voles.

WHEN TO VISIT
Elmley is perhaps at its best in winter, with the most wildfowl and birds of prey. High tide will push more birds onto the reserve. The Swale hide will be most exciting on a rising tide, as the climbing water level pushes birds closer to the hide.

How to get here
Grid ref./postcode TQ 937678/ ME12 3
By road From Junction 5 on the M2, follow the A249 to Sheerness. Take the road signposted Iwade and Ridham Dock. At the roundabout take the second exit onto the old road bridge. On the Isle of Sheppey, after 1.25 miles, turn right following RSPB sign.
By public transport Swale station, on the Sittingbourne to Sheerness line, is 3 miles from the reserve car park. From the station, walk alongside the A249 onto the Isle of Sheppey, turn right after 1 mile where the reserve is signposted. Follow the rough track for 2 miles to the car park at Kingshill Farm.

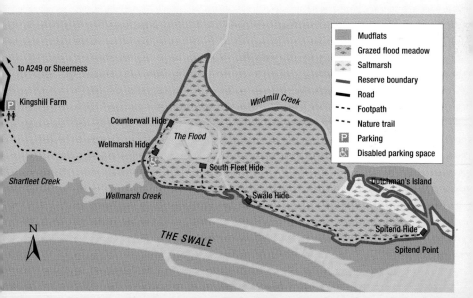

SOUTH-EAST

FARNHAM HEATH AONB

A new reserve and still very much a work in progress, Farnham Heath has nevertheless already attracted Nightjars, Tree Pipits and Woodlarks to its heathy slopes, which until 2002 were covered with conifer plantations. There are three nature trails and several public footpaths, so you can spend hours walking here and enjoying the sight of a heathland coming back to life.

● Access, facilities, contact details and accessibility

This new reserve shares the facilities of the Rural Life Centre, with car parking, toilets and a tearoom.

● **Telephone** 01252 795 632; **email** farnham.heath@rspb.org.uk; **web** www.rspb.org.uk/farnhamheath

● **Opening hours** Open at all times. The car park opens at 9.30am (10.30am on weekends) and closes at 5.30pm, but you can park nearby outside those hours.

● **Entry fees** Free, but donations to help continue the work here are welcome

● **Accessibility** The orange and purple routes are generally accessible to the mobility-impaired – call for more information – the green trail is more difficult.

● **Dogs** Allowed on the trails but must be kept under close control, especially during the nesting season

What to look for

There are areas of heathland to explore on either side of the Reeds Road, although the larger section where the RSPB trails are lies on the north side and is accessible from the Rural Life Centre. The orange and purple trails stick mainly to the open heath, while the longer green trail

skirts areas of Sweet Chestnut coppice as well.

Two of the characteristic heathland birds are well known for their songs, which you'll hear in spring. The Tree Pipit gives its sweet, trilling song while performing an eyecatching song-flight that begins from a tree and culminates in

WILDLIFE BY SEASON

SPRING
There is a brilliant woodland show of Blue-bells. Woodlarks and Tree Pipits sing on the heath.

SUMMER
Nightjars sing and display at dusk on the heath, while Woodcocks 'rode' into the night. Serotine and Pipistrelle Bats are on the wing. Heather blooms in August.

AUTUMN
More than 150 species of fungi are on show. Late-flying dragonflies like Common Darter and Migrant Hawker are still about.

WINTER
The feeding station attracts a range of woodland birds. Parties of finches roam the wooded edges.

the bird 'parachuting' slowly down to the ground on fanned-out wings. The Woodlark, another unassuming brown bird, has a deliciously melodious song – look out for it in the areas most recently cleared of trees.

At dusk in summer Nightjars deliver their otherworldly churring songs and staccato wing-clapping and flit between stands of pine trees. At this time also listen for the squeaks and grunts of roding male Woodcocks, flying straight-line patrols high over their territories.

Summer days see Grayling and Silver-washed Fritillary butterflies out in sunny patches of heath and woodland respectively, while the heather is at its glorious best in August. Into autumn, many of the heathland birds move south, but winter visitors include Crossbills, heavy-duty finches which prise open pinecones with their crossed bill-tips, and Siskins and Redpolls, colourful and vocal smaller finches with a liking for Alder seeds. Parties of tits and finches roam the wood and visit the feeding station through the winter.

WHEN TO VISIT
To see and hear Nightjars and Woodcocks, visit an hour before dusk on a still summer's day and be prepared to be out till it's virtually dark. For spring birdsong, early morning visits are best. The heath is quiet in the winter.

How to get here
Grid ref./postcode SU 859433/ GU10 2
By road Take the B3001 south from Farnham. Take the right-hand fork, signposted Tilford, immediately past the level crossing. Just outside Tilford village follow signs to the Rural Life Centre. The entrance is on the right after half a mile.
By public transport The nearest station is Farnham. Bus 19 runs from Farnham to Hindhead and calls at Millbridge village, outside the entrance to Pierrepont House. The reserve is 1 mile away from here, along Reeds Road (follow signs to the Rural Life Centre).

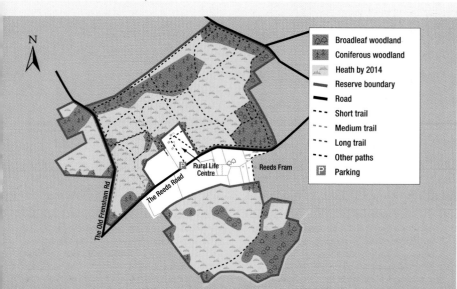

Nuthatch

FORE WOOD SSSI, AONB

Fore Wood is a small but very picturesque woodland reserve, lying on sandstone soil and cut through with ghylls (deep, steep-sided mini ravines) that are full of exotic-looking ferns and other vegetation. It is home to many woodland birds, insects and mammals, and is carpeted with flowers in the early spring. It is wonderful for a woodland walk at any time of year.

● Access, facilities, contact details and accessibility

There are two nature trails, three-quarters and 1.5 miles long (note that there is also a half mile walk across fields to reach the reserve). This is a good place for a peaceful walk.

- **Telephone** 01273 775 333; **web** www.rspb.org.uk/forewood
- **Opening hours** Open at all times
- **Entry fees** None, but donations to help continue the work here are welcomed
- **Accessibility** Not suitable for pushchairs or the mobility-impaired, parts of the trails are steep and may be muddy
- **Dogs** Allowed on the reserve but must be kept strictly under control

What to look for

A walk across peaceful fields brings you to the reserve entrance, where the nature trails begin. Woodland birdwatching can be difficult when the trees are in leaf, but if you come earlier in spring while the twigs are still bare, it's easier to see the Great Spotted Woodpeckers, Nuthatches, Marsh Tits, Chiffchaffs and other woodland birds that live here. In some places the woodland floor is covered by Bluebells – you'll also see many delicate white Wood Anemones, and a few early Purple Orchids. Botanists will also notice unusual mosses and ferns like the Hay-scented Buckler Fern growing in the ghylls.

Coppicing the oak and Hornbeam trees helps to maintain a mixed woodland that supports lots of wildlife. The dazzling White Admiral butterfly

WILDLIFE BY SEASON

SPRING
Birdsong is at its best, and woodland flowers and birds are best seen before the trees come into leaf.

SUMMER
White Admirals and other butterflies are on the wing from spring through summer. Look for Beautiful Demoiselle damselflies.

AUTUMN
Wintering thrushes and finches start to arrive. The trees are a blaze of colour, and a wide variety of fungi grows on dead wood and the woodland floor.

WINTER
Woodland birds forage in flocks, while you may see large gatherings of Rooks, finches and thrushes in the fields.

lays its eggs on Honeysuckle, a plant that thrives in coppice woodlands. The butterflies themselves, marvellously elegant flyers, are on the wing in July, often patrolling a small territory and basking on favourite leaves. The Silver-washed Fritillary is another striking high-summer butterfly. The Beautiful Demoiselle, a stunning dark-winged damselfly, can be seen flitting around the trees in summer.

There is a small pond in the reserve, where Common Frogs and Palmate Newts breed.

Birds come down to the water to drink, especially finches, which get very thirsty on their diet of mainly seeds. In autumn and winter there can be large flocks of Chaffinches feasting on fallen tree seeds – their northern cousin the Brambling is a possibility too.

Once the trees have shed their leaves and the autumn fungi have disappeared, the wood is at its quietest, but can suddenly come to life when a feeding party of tits goes by, perhaps joined by the odd Goldcrest or Treecreeper.

WHEN TO VISIT
Visit early on a spring day to enjoy the dawn chorus. Spring and summer are best for flowers and butterflies respectively, while the wood as a whole looks spectacular in its autumn colours.

How to get here
Grid ref./postcode TQ 752127/ TN33 9

By road The reserve is on the edge of Crowhurst village. From Telham on the A2100, take the lane heading south-west through Crowhurst. Park at the village hall, turn right and follow the main road uphill for 200 yards. Look for the finger post pointing to Fore Wood, on the left at the first bend. Follow the path half a mile across the fields to the reserve.

By public transport Crowhurst, on the London to Hastings line, is the nearest station. Follow the lane from the station until it joins the main Forewood Lane. Turn right and pass the village hall. Follow directions from village hall (see above).

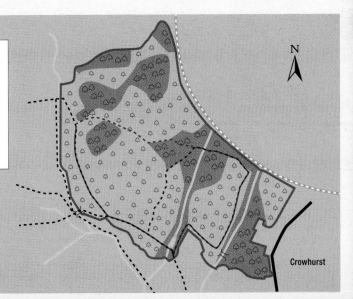

Coppice
High Forest
Reserve boundary
Road
Public footpath
Short trail
Long trail
Bridge

N

Crowhurst

SOUTH-EAST

Grey Heron

NORTHWARD HILL

SSSI, SPA, NATURA 2000

A high, wooded ridge overlooking the flood-meadows of this quiet part of the Thames marshes, Northward Hill is famous for its large heronry. Since 2000 the wood has also been home to a growing colony of Little Egrets. The reserve includes parts of the marshland as well as the woodland.

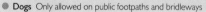

●Access, facilities, contact details and accessibility

There are 4 trails (0.5–4 miles) and guided walks can be arranged. Exciting events are held year-round.

- **Telephone** 01634 222480; **email** northkentmarshes@rspb.org.uk; **web** www.rspb.org.uk/northwardhill
- **Opening hours** At all times
- **Entry fees** Free, but donations to help continue the work here are welcome
- **Accessibility** The unimproved trails may not be suitable for mobility-impaired visitors. Please contact the reserve for more information.
- **Dogs** Only allowed on public footpaths and bridleways

What to look for

The trails through the woodland take you through to the Heronry Viewpoint, where you can watch activity in the large colony of breeding Grey Herons and Little Egrets if you visit in spring or early summer. The wood looks and sounds magnificent in spring, with a lavish carpet of Bluebells and a chorus of birdsong led by a healthy population of Nightingales.

The wet grassland below the wood also has special breeding birds. Redshanks and Lapwings have both declined in the UK in the 20th century, so the RSPB takes particular care to maintain the dampness and grass height here to suit both species and encourage them to breed. Both of

WILDLIFE BY SEASON

SPRING
Grey Herons and Little Egrets are nesting in the woods, Avocets on the islands. Nightingales can be heard from mid-April.

SUMMER
Hobbies hunt dragonflies over the marsh. Summer butterflies include the rare White-letter Hairstreak.

AUTUMN
Migrating waders may visit the reservoirs. Swallows gather in pre-migration flocks, and Jays are very obvious as they collect acorns in the wood.

WINTER
Wildfowl flock on the marsh, finches, buntings and thrushes are busy feeding on seeds and late berries in the scrub.

these waders can be very noisy in the breeding season.

In winter, the meadows often flood and attract flocks of ducks. You can see large numbers of Wigeons and Teals here.

Another speciality of the reserve is its owls – the mixture of woodland and open habitat suits them very well. They are not as easy to see as the herons and waders, but in winter, if you are extremely lucky, you could see all five British species of owls in one day at this remarkable reserve.

How to get here
Grid ref./postcode TQ 781757/ ME3 8
By road Leave the M2 at Junction 1 and join the A228, signposted Grain. Turn left off A228 for High Halstow. In the village both reserve car parks are signed at the T-junction. The 'Woodland' car park is in the village, the 'Main' car park is located at Bromhey Farm, signposted left from the road from High Halstow to Cooling.
By public transport Strood is the nearest station (trains are hourly

WHEN TO VISIT
Activity at the heronry begins in late winter and continues through the summer. Come in spring for Nightingales, and in winter to see flocks of wildfowl on the marsh.

from London). Buses from Strood depart about every 30 minutes to High Halstow village. The reserve trail connects with the long-distance Saxon Shore Way path.

EGRETS, WE'VE HAD A FEW...
The Little Egret was a rare bird in Britain through most of the 20th century. Its nearest breeding places were in southern France, and only a few odd birds showed up in the UK. However, in the 1980s there were more and more arrivals, and eventually some of the birds started to breed. Northward Hill had two pairs of breeding egrets in the year 2000, and by 2008 there were 110 pairs – nearly as many as there are Grey Herons here.

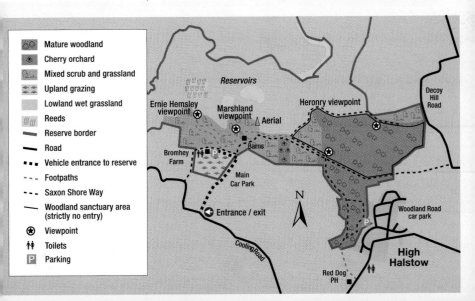

Legend:
- Mature woodland
- Cherry orchard
- Mixed scrub and grassland
- Upland grazing
- Lowland wet grassland
- Reeds
- Reserve border
- Road
- Vehicle entrance to reserve
- Footpaths
- Saxon Shore Way
- Woodland sanctuary area (strictly no entry)
- Viewpoint
- Toilets
- P Parking

Reservoirs

Ernie Hemsley viewpoint

Marshland viewpoint

Aerial

Heronry viewpoint

Decoy Hill Road

Bromhey Farm

Barns

Main Car Park

Entrance / exit

N

Woodland Road car park

Cooling Road

High Halstow

Red Dog PH

SOUTH-EAST

PULBOROUGH BROOKS

SSSI, RAMSAR

The beautiful Arun Valley in West Sussex includes low-lying grazing marsh inland from the South Downs. The fields are interspersed with small pools (becoming bigger in winter) and cut through by numerous ditches and channels. Pulborough Brooks is a flagship RSPB reserve in the heart of this gentle landscape, with trails, hides and expert help on hand to help you find and enjoy the wildlife. The RSPB's work here is helping to restore and expand the existing wetland habitats, and to restore former areas of heathland to encourage an even greater variety of wildlife.

● Access, facilities, contact details and accessibility

Pulborough's facilities include a well-stocked shop, a tearoom serving hot meals and light refreshments, and a well-appointed visitor centre full of information about the reserve and its wildlife. The trails offer easy, pushchair-friendly walking, and there are numerous benches if you fancy a breather. A telescope is useful here, as the hides and viewpoints overlook quite broad vistas rather than intimate corners of the brooks. There is a busy events programme, including themed and general guided walks, talks, children's activities, optics demonstrations and workshops. There is a play area by the visitor centre.

- **Telephone** 01798 875851; **email** pulborough.brooks@rspb.org.uk;
  web www.rspb.org.uk/pulboroughbrooks
- **Opening hours** Visitor centre open 9.30am–5pm daily; nature trail open sunrise to sunset. The reserve is closed on Christmas Day, visitor centre is also closed on Boxing Day.
- **Entry fees** RSPB members free. Non-members £3.50, children £1, concessions £2.50, families £7.
- **Accessibility** The trail is accessible to wheelchair-users with strong helpers. There are disabled-adapted toilets, and three of the four hides are accessible. A buggy is available for use on the trail.
- **Dogs** Dogs are only allowed on public footpaths and bridleways. They must kept under close control.

WILDLIFE BY SEASON

SPRING

Breeding birds are singing and starting to set up their territories. Nightingales and warblers including Blackcap, Garden Warbler and Whitethroat add their voices to the chorus. There may be a few wintering ducks and swans on the brooks.

SUMMER

The best time to see mammals and insects. Broods of ducklings on the brooks. Later in summer, migrating waders will start to appear. Brown Hairstreak butterflies emerge in early August.

AUTUMN

Migrating waders are visiting in larger numbers, and the wintering birds (ducks, swans and more waders) start to arrive. Flocks of Redwings and Fieldfares arrive to feed on hedgerow berries, as the warblers about to migrate south do the same.

WINTER

The brooks are now teeming with wildfowl, especially Wigeon and Teal but you could also see Bewick's Swans, Pintails and Shovelers. Look for waders too – Snipes will be feeding in the marshy spots while Ruffs wade in the shallows. Best time for a variety of birds of prey.

What to look for

The character of Pulborough Brooks changes dramatically through the seasons. In winter, wildfowl and waders come in their thousands to the wet meadows and marshland to feed. In summer, the hedgerows are alive with flowering plants, insects and songbirds. Spring and autumn are exciting transitional times, with many birds stopping off here on migration.

The reserve is a relatively recent acquisition for the RSPB, bought in 1989 thanks to a generous bequest from a single RSPB member who lived in the area. Winifred Smith Wright wanted the brooks to be restored to the wildlife-rich flooding maintains the water balance to suit the needs of Pulborough's wetland birds. The brooks themselves are a collection of wide but shallow pools which are busy with flocks of wildlfowl and waders from late summer through to early spring.

Before you set out on the nature trail, take some time to look at the feeding station by the Visitor Centre. It is especially busy in winter, with finches, tits, Nuthatches and Great Spotted Woodpeckers all coming in for free food. The latter's little cousin, the Lesser Spotted Woodpecker, isn't so keen on the feeders but you may spot

To see Barn Owls hunting, you will usually need to get to the reserve an hour or two before dark, though they do occasionally hunt in broad daylight.

landscape she remembered from her childhood – her bequest and the hard work of the RSPB has made her dream a reality. The meadowland was formerly drained for farming. The RSPB has restored the wet grazing marsh by raising water levels – achieved by disabling the deep, narrow drains that take moisture out of the fields and instead digging 'grips' – shallow, meandering watercourses that provide feeding grounds for wetland birds. Controlled one in the trees around the car park – this is a particularly good spot for this hard-to-see little bird. Another fairly scarce bird you may find at the feeders or elsewhere in the reserve is the Marsh Tit.

The circular trail here is a manageable 2 miles (3.5 km), and takes you downhill through flowery fields to four hides and three viewpoints that look out across the low-lying flood-meadows with their ditches and pools. From here you should

The pretty Brown Hairstreak butterfly is a highlight in late summer and early autumn.

see plenty of wildfowl and waders in autumn and winter, including Wigeon and Teal. In spring and summer there are breeding Lapwings and Redshanks on the grazing marsh – the former are particularly entertaining with their tumbling display flights and bizarre whooping calls. As summer wears on, wading birds start to arrive on the brooks, including some, like Wood Sandpiper, that only make brief stop-offs on their migratory journeys and will move on before winter. Blackcaps and Garden Warblers will be feeding avidly on berries in the hedgerows before they migrate, and whatever they don't finish off will be gobbled up by the first Redwings and Fieldfares that arrive in autumn and will stay over the winter.

The trail winds through pleasant and varied scenery, with broad hedgerows flanked by flowery banks, and many open, sunny patches which are full of wild flowers and thrumming with insect life in summer. An arable field near the visitor centre usually attracts Skylarks and Yellowhammers. A plan of controlled grazing by cattle along with carefully timed hay-cutting maintains a good diversity of habitats in the fields and rides. You'll notice many small birds in the woody copses and hedgerows, which in spring and summer include both whitethroats, Garden Warblers and Nightingales. Another summer visitor you might spot over the open patches is the Hobby, an elegant falcon that makes its living chasing down dragonflies and other flying insects. In winter, the Hobbies will have migrated, but new birds of prey will arrive to take advantage of the mass arrivals of ducks and waders. They include Hen Harriers and Short-eared Owls – the latter our only owl species that is mostly active in the daylight hours. Later in the day, look out for hunting Barn Owls. These ghostly white owls tend to work their way slowly and methodically across the fields so may give you prolonged close views if you're standing in the right place and willing to be patient. A pair of Barn Owls have in the past made use of a nestbox on the Visitor Centre – even when they are not using the nest box you can still enjoy encounters at any time of year.

WHEN TO VISIT

This reserve has a lot to offer throughout the year. Perhaps winter is best of all from a wildlife-watching point of view. If you want to see Barn Owls, you'll need to be at the reserve an hour or two before dark, but otherwise you will not lose much by visiting at other times. The hides and trails will be busy on sunny weekends.

Pulborough is home to plenty of other wildlife besides the birds. It is as good a place as any to bump into a Stoat or Weasel – these lithe little hunters take advantage of the reserve's numerous mice, voles and (in the case of the Stoats) Rabbits. A highlight of late summer and early autumn is the Brown Hairstreak butterfly, a scarce and pretty insect with its subtle fawn-and-white pattern. Look out for Brown Hairstreaks around blackthorn bushes in sunny spots. If you visit at a quiet time and make your way around with minimum noise, you could easily surprise a Fallow Deer in the woods, or find an Adder or a Grass Snake basking in the sun.

How to get here

Grid ref./postcode TQ 058164/RH20 2
By road The reserve is located approximately 2 miles (3.2 km) from Pulborough village. Follow the A283 towards Storrington. The reserve is located on the right-hand side.
By public transport The nearest railway station is Pulborough (2 miles/4 km); you can take a taxi from here or the 100 bus. The reserve is a request stop so ask the driver to drop you outside Pulborough Brooks reserve when you board. Alternatively you can walk from the station – it is a pleasant countryside walk along public footpaths.

The trees around the car park at Pulborough Brooks are a good place to look for the small and shy Lesser Spotted Woodpecker.

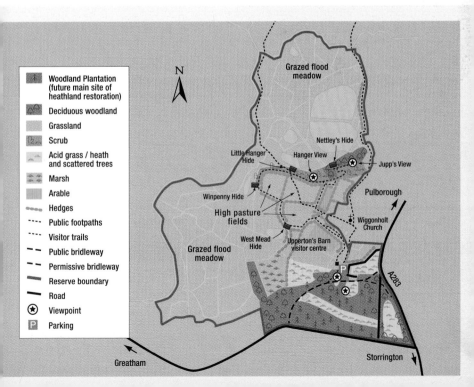

SOUTH-EAST

RAINHAM MARSHES SSSI

The Thames is the UK's largest river, and the marshlands around its lower stretches have always been important for wildlife, even though many areas have been extensively developed over the years as London sprawled eastwards. One area that escaped the attention of the town planners is Rainham Marshes – instead this complex of marshland had been closed to the public and was used as a military firing range for nearly 100 years. Since buying the site in 2000, the RSPB has worked hard to restore this landscape of wet grassland, pools and ditches into a haven for wetland wildlife, and also a place that people of all ages can enjoy visiting.

● Access, facilities, contact details and accessibility

Although Rainham Marshes is a new reserve, the RSPB has already established a good visitor infrastructure and further improvements are planned. There is a network of nature trails currently in place, and approximately 2.5 miles of nature boardwalks, all designed for wheelchair and pushchair access. The reserve has one hide and several viewpoints. The visitor centre provides refreshments as well as general birdwatching merchandise, and there is a lively events programme with all ages catered for. The visitor centre provides great views across the reserve, and there is a new wildlife garden and children's adventure play area too.

● **Telephone** 01708 899 840; **email** rainham.marshes@rspb.org.uk; **web** www.rspb.org.uk/rainhammarshes

● **Opening hours** 1 November–31 March, 9.30am–4.30pm; 1 April–31 October, 9.30am–5pm.

● **Entry fees** Car park: voluntary £1 donation. Reserve: free to RSPB members and residents of Havering and Thurrock; non-members £2.50 adult, £1 child, £7 family (two adults and up to four children). Some events may incur additional charges, please check on booking.

● **Accessibility** The paths and trails are suitable for wheelchairs, pushchairs and people with limited mobility

● **Dogs** Only registered assistance dogs allowed, but dog-walkers can use the adjacent riverside path

WILDLIFE BY SEASON

SPRING

Migrating songbirds like Wheatears, Whinchats and Sand Martins pass through, while breeding birds are singing and displaying. Migrating birds of prey pass overhead. Frogs are breeding in the ponds and ditches – you may see Grass Snakes hunting them.

SUMMER

From mid-summer a great variety of migrating waders stops off at the reserve – look out for godwits, Ruffs, Whimbrels and Greenshanks. Marsh Frogs are breeding in the ponds and ditches, and Water Voles are quite easy to see.

AUTUMN

Migrating waders continue to pass through – gull and duck numbers start to noticeably increase. Young birds and mammals disperse to look for new homes – this is a good time to see Marsh Harriers, Barn Owls, Bearded Tits, Stoats and Weasels.

WINTER

Ducks and waders flock on the reserve, and birds of prey come to hunt them. You could see Short-eared Owls, Peregrine Falcons and even Merlins. Look out for wintering Water Pipits and rare visitors like Penduline Tits.

What to look for

Rainham Marshes, so recently a neglected wasteland, now fully deserves inclusion among the very best birdwatching sites in the south-east – all the more remarkable given how close it lies to London. The superb, environmentally friendly new visitor centre gives you views across the whole area, so you can appreciate just how much work has gone into restoring the floodplain habitats, as well as how committed the RSPB is to this new reserve. The site opened to the public in 2006, and already it has been placed firmly on the birdwatching map

semi-permanent pools. This will also encourage more wildfowl to spend winter here.

As you walk around the reserve, look at the small details as well as the big picture. For example, the ditch systems at Rainham Marshes are home to one of the UK's most threatened mammals, the Water Vole. Look out for these portly, short-tailed and small-eared rodents chewing vegetation at the water's edge or swimming across, blunt nose held just clear of the surface. The ditches also attract noisy Marsh Frogs in the breeding season, and you may

Why swim when you can ride? Little Grebe chicks often hop up a parent's back, for safety and perhaps a better view.

having attracted several national rarities as well as a good variety of commoner birds.

With a telescope, you can see far across the wet meadows from the visitor centre. In spring, you may spot Lapwings flying in extravagant tumbling display flights above their territories. Redshanks also breed in the grassland – the RSPB plans to enhance the habitat for these birds by creating a mosaic of wet tussocky grassland, flooded short grassland and

see a Grass Snake swimming along in search of a frog for supper.

If you visit early in spring, you could see various newly arrived migrant birds. Wheatears are perky and striking, with attractive peachy-buff, grey and black plumage and a broad white rump patch that catches the eye as they fly away. Over the water you may see Sand Martins, agile fly-chasers that are soon joined by their more familiar relatives – House

You could see Grey Plovers on the Thames foreshore, distinctive with their stocky build and stop-start running in search of prey.

Martins and Swallows. Spring water birds may include little Ringed Plovers and Garganeys.

By summer, waders of the far north are already on their return migration after their short breeding season. This is the time to look for species such as Greenshanks, Whimbrels, Black-tailed Godwits and Common Sandpipers. Summer is also a great time for children to explore the mini-beasts of the reserve, perhaps getting involved in the pond-dipping and bug hunting events. Among the flying insects you might see in summer is the beautiful Scarce Emerald Damselfly.

As summer merges into autumn, other migrants call in, like Arctic Terns and Avocets. Species that breed locally may also be easier to see at this time, as the young birds of the year become independent. This is a particularly good time to see migrant Marsh Harriers – the youngsters dark chocolate-brown with pale foreheads and shoulders like their mothers.

The lagoons here, while very attractive to birds, are still being commercially used for dredging silt from the Thames. One of the RSPB's challenges is to balance this with the needs of the wildlife – so some lagoons will be 'retired' while others will be managed rotationally so there is always undisturbed habitat for the birds.

In winter, wrap up warm as the flat landscape offers little protection from easterly winds, and head out in search of water birds, birds of prey and, perhaps, some of the other special winter species that have helped make Rainham Marshes such a popular destination with birdwatchers. Golden Plovers and Lapwings gather in large flocks, dramatic to see when they all take to the wing, perhaps disturbed by a passing Peregrine Falcon. On the wet grassland, look for Water Pipits – a little larger than the more familiar Meadow Pipits, with greyer plumage and darker legs. In the reeds, you may see Reed Buntings demolishing old bulrush heads. Another bird fond of bulrushes is the Penduline Tit, a tiny and very pretty bird that is a real rarity and something of a Rainham Marshes speciality – one or more have been seen here most winters since work began on the site here. Ask at the visitor centre – the staff will be able to tell you what's about and the best places to look.

WHEN TO VISIT

This reserve is well worth a visit at any time of the day and throughout the year. Probably the largest numbers of birds will be seen in the winter, but there are weekly guided walks to help you discover the best of Rainham's Marshes wildlife through the changing seasons.

How to get here

Grid ref./postcode TQ 552792/RM19 1
By road From London, join A13 eastbound. After Dagenham the A13 goes onto an elevated section. Stay on the A13 to the A1306 turn-off

(signposted Wennington, Aveley and Purfleet.)
At the slip road roundabout turn right, following
signs for Purfleet on the A1306 heading east.
Continue along the A1306 for half a mile.
At the traffic lights, take a right-hand turn,
signposted Purfleet and RSPB onto New Tank
Hill Road flyover. The entrance to the reserve is
signposted approximately 300m along this road,
just after the bottom of the flyover on the right
hand side. From the M25 exit the motorway at
Junction 31. At the roundabout take the A1306
west, signposted to RSPB Rainham Marshes.
Continue along the A1306 for 1.5 miles. At
the traffic lights turn left, signposted Purfleet
and RSPB onto New Tank Hill Road flyover.
The entrance to the reserve is signposted
approximately 300m along this road.
By public transport The nearest station is
Purfleet. Alternatively, bus 44 runs daily between
Grays and Lakeside via Purfleet. From Purfleet
station, turn right, follow the road until The
Royal pub, on the left-hand side. At the pub,
head down to the Thames and join the Riverside
Path (a joint foot and cycle path). Follow the
riverside path, which eventually crosses the
Mardyke River at a small bridge. After the
bridge, turn left and follow the pavement around
to the RSPB Environment & Education Centre.

In pastel blue and shimmering green, the Scarce Emerald
Damselfly is a real beauty and a Rainham Marshes speciality.

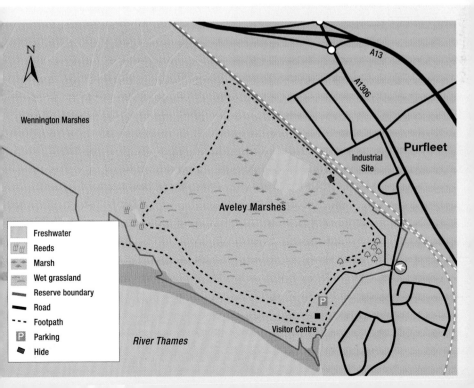

N

Wennington Marshes

A13

A1306

Purfleet

Industrial
Site

Aveley Marshes

Freshwater
Reeds
Marsh
Wet grassland
Reserve boundary
Road
Footpath
P Parking
Hide

Visitor Centre

River Thames

SOUTH-EAST

RYE MEADS   SSSI, SPA, RAMSAR, NATURA 2000

The River Lee, which runs north-south into north London, boasts a number of good wildlife-watching sites along its valley. The star among them is Rye Meads RSPB reserve, a wonderful place to enjoy close encounters with a variety of wetland and hedgerow birds and other animals. This is a family-friendly destination, with a busy programme of events for all and many superb hides offering a look in on nesting Common Terns, close views from the visitor centre of garden birds visiting busy feeding stations, flocks of winter wildfowl and much more. Easily accessible from London, this reserve offers splendid wildlife-watching and excellent facilities for all.

● Access, facilities, contact details and accessibility

Rye Meads is geared towards offering full facilities for all visitors, whatever their interests and levels of experience. There are numerous hides, live cameras relaying images from the reserve to the visitor centre, binocular hire is available, and you can purchase hot drinks at the visitor centre. A varied events programme offers walks and talks for all ages, and a range of activities for younger visitors. Group bookings and school visits can be arranged. A Saturday Wildlife Explorer Club and holiday activities are available for children.

- **Telephone** 01992 708383; **email** rye.meads2@rspb.org.uk; **web** www.rspb.org.uk/ryemeads
- **Opening hours** Open daily 10am–5pm (or dusk if earlier). Gates are locked when the reserve closes. Please note that the reserve is closed on Christmas Day and Boxing Day.
- **Entry fees** None
- **Accessibility** The visitor centre and most hides and paths are wheelchair-accessible. A wheelchair can be hired free from the visitor centre.
- **Dogs** Not allowed, except registered assistance dogs

WILDLIFE BY SEASON

SPRING
The time for birdsong, flowers and early butterflies. The feeding station by the visitor centre is busy well into spring. Overwintering and newly emerged butterflies are about from the first warm spring days. Hobbies hunt dragonflies over the meadow.

SUMMER
The noisy Common Tern colony on the lagoon rafts is in full swing, and Gadwalls and Tufted Ducks have chicks too. Kingfishers may be nesting close to the Kingfisher hide, giving stunning views.

AUTUMN
Out on the scrapes, look for Snipes, Green Sandpipers and other waders. Redwings and Fieldfares join the resident thrushes, and Starlings and buntings begin to form winter roosting flocks.

WINTER
The cold weather brings flocks of ducks from further north to winter on the lagoons. The Shovelers, Gadwalls, Pochards and Tufted Ducks may be joined by the occasional Smew or Goldeneye. The feeding station is at its busiest, and this is also the time to spot a Bittern in the reedbed.

What to look for

Rye Meads is a great place for a family day out, with an exciting mix of wildlife within easy reach of London. There are three nature trails at this reserve, ranging from 0.3 miles to 1 mile long. All of them allow you to visit several of the hides, so you can see birds on the lagoons as well as on the trails themselves. Kingfishers may nest within metres of the Kingfisher Hide, giving stunning views.

Rye Meads reserve has several lagoons and also a

The Gadwalls and Tufted Ducks that nest here don't have to fetch food for their ducklings but instead escort them across the water in safety while the babies find their own food.

From the reedbeds you will hear Reed and Sedge Warblers singing in spring. Where there are Reed Warblers there are often Cuckoos, looking out for an unattended warbler nest into which to lay an egg. More often heard than seen, Cuckoos look like long-tailed hawks when they

It's no ordinary cow – European Buffaloes graze the wet meadow on the Herts and Middlesex Wildlife Trust part of the reserve to maintain the habitat for breeding waders.

stream, along which the first section of the trail runs. In spring and summer, the Gadwall hide lets you observe family life in the colony of Common Terns – they nest here on rafts provided for just that purpose by the RSPB. This is the only species of tern breeding in the UK that regularly nests inland – once the chicks have hatched, the adults hunt for fish over the river and nearby lakes and lagoons, and bring their catch home to their fluffy offspring.

swoop by in territorial chases. Another agile flyer, the Hobby, is attracted by Rye Meads' large dragonfly population. You can often watch Hobbies chasing and deftly seizing dragonflies over the lagoons through summer into autumn.

If you venture to the furthest part of the reserve, to the adjoining Hertfordshire and Middlesex Wildlife Trust reserve, you may be surprised to see some particularly hefty black cattle grazing the meadow

Perhaps our most dazzling bird, the spectacular Kingfisher often obliges visitors to Rye Meads with close views from the hides.

– actually they are European Buffaloes. Grazing is an environmentally friendly way to manage the fields, and the animals' droppings attract insects that in turn provide food for birds. Rye Meads is a good place to see a much smaller grazing animal, especially the Muntjac Deer, which is no taller than a medium-sized dog. Unlike the buffaloes, the Muntjacs are wild, albeit not native but introduced from China over 100 years ago. Keep quiet as you walk around, and you could see one or perhaps a Fox, Harvest Mouse or Water Shrew – all of them live on the reserve.

As the breeding season winds down, some of the reserve's birds prepare to depart for their southerly winter homes. So it's time to

say goodbye to the terns and warblers, but this is also the time when winter visitors start to arrive. Just as our resident Blackbirds and thrushes thought they had the berry crop all to themselves, Redwings and Fieldfares from Scandinavia arrive to clear the hedgerows of their autumn bounty. Starlings gather to feed on the berries too, and to roost in large flocks in the reeds. Migrating waders, such as Green Sandpipers, may visit the lagoons at this time as well. The male ducks lose their distinctive colours in late summer and moult into their confusing autumn 'eclipse' plumage – camouflage for the weeks when they are growing new wing feathers and are, therefore, flightless. Later in autumn, many more ducks arrive from northern Europe to spend winter at the reserve.

Wildfowl are a big feature of the winter scene here, but many visitors will be particularly hoping to catch sight of a Bittern. There are very few Bitterns breeding in the UK, but the population rises a little in winter, when some of the birds from the Netherlands and elsewhere on the continent move over to the UK, especially if things get too chilly for them on the European mainland. These big brown herons are perfectly camouflaged to slink through the reedbeds unseen, but if you are very patient you may see one as it comes out to the edge of the reeds, or perhaps witness its heavy, ponderous flight as it travels over the top of the reeds to new hunting grounds.

Much easier to see are the birds coming to the feeding station by the visitor centre. Winter is the time when natural food sources may run out, and birds need to keep their energy up to survive the cold nights. Blue and Great Tits, Dunnocks, Chaffinches, Greenfinches, Goldfinches, Great Spotted Woodpeckers, Collared Doves, Song Thrushes, Pheasants and Reed Buntings all come for a free meal. The small birds run the risk of becoming a meal themselves when one of the local Sparrowhawks launches a surprise attack – every bit as dramatic a spectacle as anything you'll see on a wildlife programme from the Masai Mara.

How to get here

Grid ref./postcode TL 389103/EN11 0
By road From the A10: (note that this route is only accessible for vehicles with axle weights less than 5T) take the Hoddesdon turning and head towards Hoddesdon, down the Dinant Link road

(a dual carriageway). Go straight over the large roundabout (you will have the Sun pub on your left) onto another section of dual carriageway. At the next roundabout, turn left into Pindar Road. Turn left into a one-way system (before the railway crossing) and follow the road round. The one-way system leads back to Pindar Road. Turn left onto a bridge on Normandy Way. Turn left into Fisherman's Way (a housing estate), follow this road until a T-junction. Turn right over the bridge. Follow this road (passing the Rye House Pub and the Lee Valley Gate House) until you see a large blue and yellow building – the Rye Meads Visitor Centre. The car park is through the big green gates by the electricity pylon.
By public transport Rye House station, on the Hertford East branch of the Cambridge–Liverpool Street line, is very close. Climb the steps out of the station and turn right towards Rye Meads, with the Historic Rye House Gatehouse on your left and Rye House Public House to your right. Follow a footpath on the left side of the minor road for 300m until you reach the visitor centre entrance. The nearest bus stop is in the Old Highway, which is off Rye Road. Walk down towards Rye House Station and over two bridges, then follow directions as above.

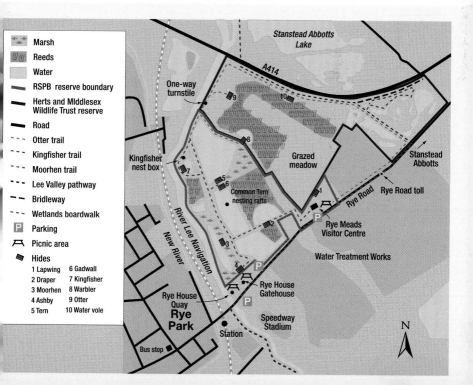

TUDELEY WOODS

Tudeley Woods lies in a quiet corner of the High Weald of west Kent, a few miles from the busy town of Tunbridge Wells. It is a rich area of wood and heathland, alive with wildlife all year round. The reserve is managed in partnership with the Hadlow Estate.

● Access, facilities, contact details and accessibility

There is a car park, leaflet-dispensers and an information board here, and the trails are clearly marked out. It is possible to book group visits or guided walks.

- **Telephone** 01273 775333; **web** www.rspb.org.uk/tudeleywoods
- **Opening hours** Open at all times, but note that the car park has a 6' 6" height barrier, also a locked vehicle barrier when the car park is closed at night.
- **Entry fees** Free for everyone, but please make a donation to the RSPB if you can
- **Accessibility** The trails are steep in places and may become muddy, but most are negotiable with a pushchair in dry weather.
- **Dogs** You can walk dogs on the public footpaths and bridleways only

What to look for

Deciduous woodland and patchy heathland once cloaked much of Kent's High Weald, but now the woodland is fragmented by tracts of farmland and plantations of fast-growing conifers. At Tudeley Woods, one such fragment, the RSPB is building the diversity of habitats to encourage woodland and heathland wildlife to prosper.

From the car park, a short trail leads you into the woods and a crossroads where you can choose between three nature trails. The shorter two take you through various types of woodland, while the longest traverses the area of newly restored heathland. In spring, Bluebells bring the forest floor to life, and birdsong is everywhere.

WILDLIFE BY SEASON

SPRING

Early butterflies are on the wing. Best time to see Lesser Spotted Woodpecker.

SUMMER

Mammals are active early and late in the day. Woodland butterflies are out, dragonflies patrol the heath. Nightjars 'churr' in early summer.

AUTUMN

Mushrooms and toadstools abound in the woodlands. Winter finches and thrushes arrive.

WINTER

Finches, tits and other woodland birds are roaming the woodland, dodging Sparrowhawk attacks. Crossbills visit heathside conifers.

Look – and listen – for Marsh Tits, Blackcaps and other songsters.

Where taller trees grow, you may see woodpeckers – all three British species breed here. The rare Lesser Spotted Woodpecker is easiest to see in early spring, before there are leaves on the trees. Woodland mammals include the delightful Dormouse.

On the longer trail, you'll cross the extensive area of heathland that the RSPB has established by removing the conifer plantation that was here before. This project, the first of its kind undertaken by the RSPB, has been a great success, and now the heath is home to several scarce summer visitors like the Tree Pipit and Nightjar. Summer is also the time to see butterflies like the stunning White Admiral.

Autumn in the woods sees an impressive display of mushrooms and toadstools – more than 1,000 species occur. Winter can be quiet but on an invigorating walk you may encounter flocks of tits and finches roaming the woods.

WHEN TO VISIT

Tudeley Woods is perhaps at its best in spring. Most birds are more active in early mornings and evenings. Summer is good for mammals and insects, and (at dusk) Nightjars.

How to get here

Grid ref./postcode TQ617433/ TN11 0

By road Just over half-a-mile south of Tonbridge along the A21, take the left turn into Half Moon Lane, immediately before the petrol station on the left. The car park is 300m along the lane, on the left.

By public transport The nearest railway station is High Brooms, 2.5 miles away, on the outskirts of Tunbridge Wells.

A FAIR COPPICE

In the woodlands, coppicing (cutting back young trees to encourage bushier growth) has for decades produced a wildlife-friendly mixture of plants by creating open spaces. The RSPB today makes charcoal from Tudeley Woods's coppiced trees.

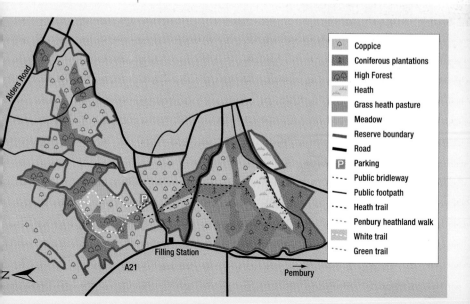

Key
- Coppice
- Coniferous plantations
- High Forest
- Heath
- Grass heath pasture
- Meadow
- Reserve boundary
- Road
- P Parking
- Public bridleway
- Public footpath
- Heath trail
- Penbury heathland walk
- White trail
- Green trail

Alders Road

P

Filling Station

A21

Pembury

N

MIDLANDS

Blackcap

CHURCH WOOD

Not far from the M40, this lovely woodland reserve with a flourishing wild flower meadow. It is a beautiful place for a quiet walk, with the opportunity to see a good variety of woodland birds, butterflies and flowers, with Red Kites overhead. Visit on a spring morning to see the reserve at its very best.

● Access, facilities, contact details and accessibility

There is a 1.25-mile nature trail exploring the woods and meadow.
- **Telephone** 01865 351 163; **web** www.rspb.org.uk/churchwood
- **Opening hours** Open daily, dawn to dusk
- **Entry fees** Free, though donations are welcome
- **Accessibility** The trail passes through a kissing gate and is often wet and muddy, so problematic for wheelchair users but possible with a pushchair.
- **Dogs** Should preferably be kept on a lead, but especially during the breeding season (April to June) to reduce disturbance to nesting birds.

What to look for

If you visit early on a spring morning, you'll enjoy a fine show of Bluebells and an enthusiastic chorus of song from the woodland's resident birds, including tits, finches and thrushes. On warm days, early butterflies will be on the wing from mid-morning, including dazzling yellow male Brimstones and creamy-white females, Orange-tips and Green-veined Whites. Nettle patches attract Small Tortoiseshells and Peacocks.

Migrants soon join the resident songbirds, and the fluty warblings of Blackcaps and metronomic two-note refrains of Chiffchaffs are added to the confusion of birdsong. The drumming

WILDLIFE BY SEASON

SPRING
The woods are full of birdsong, with Chiffchaffs and Blackcaps joining the resident species, and Bluebells and other spring flowers are blooming.

SUMMER
The rides and meadow attract many butterflies, including White Admirals and Marbled Whites.

AUTUMN
Dying leaves and sprouting fungi liven up the woods. Birds become easier to see.

WINTER
You may see Roe or Muntjac Deer moving quietly between the leafless trees. Buzzards and Red Kites circle overhead.

of Great and Lesser Spotted Woodpeckers and yaffling of Green Woodpeckers ring through the woods. The wild flower meadow is a good place to see the latter species, hopping on the ground like a thrush and feeding on ants.

Summertime is quiet for birds, as they concentrate on nesting and stay out of sight. New butterfly species appear in the warmer months, with elegant White Admirals flitting through the coppiced woodland and Marbled Whites along the southern hedge. Browns and skippers exploit the nectar bounty in the wild flower meadow.

A wide variety of fungi appears in autumn, including Parasol Mushrooms, Fly Agarics and various bracket fungi on the dead wood. Redwings and Fieldfares arrive in search of berry-bearing bushes. As winter nears, the falling leaves reveal the woodland birds again, now tending to join together in feeding flocks. New arrivals for winter include flocks of Redpolls. Overhead, Buzzards and Red Kites soar, the latter

WHEN TO VISIT
Early mornings in spring are the most rewarding times, with birdsong and flowers everywhere, but other times and seasons can be good too.

originating from the RSPB's hugely successful reintroduction project in the Chilterns. You may also glimpse Roe or Muntjac Deer.

How to get here

Grid ref./postcode SU 971872/ SL2 3
By road Take the A355 at Junction 2 on the M40, and follow signs to Hedgerley village (about 3 miles), where you should park. Walk down the private track right of the village pond. Follow the footpath for 200m; the reserve entrance is on your left through a kissing gate.
By public transport The nearest station is Gerrards Cross, 3 miles away. Bus 40 from Slough goes to Hedgerley, and bus 74 from Slough calls at Hedgerley en route to Farnham Common.

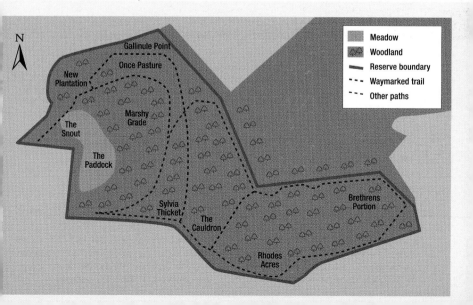

MIDLANDS

COOMBES & CHURNET _{SSSI}

Coombes Valley is a lovely woodland on the edge of the Peak District. Its slopes rise around the Coombes brook, which flows rapidly along its rocky course. As well as oak and birch woodland, there are meadows, glades and clearings, filled with flowers and butterflies in summer. This is a beautiful scenic place to enjoy walking and wildlife-watching all year.

● Access, facilities, contact details and accessibility

This reserve has simple facilities, making it ideal for a quiet family walk with children old enough to negotiate the steeper paths. Contact the reserve to book group walks and school activities.

- **Telephone** 01538 384017; **email** coombes.valley@rspb.org.uk; **web** www.rspb.org.uk/coombeschurnet
- **Opening hours** The reserve is open daily (except Christmas Day) from dawn until dusk. There is a small visitor centre with information on wildlife currently present.
- **Entry fees** Free, but donations to help continue the work here are welcome
- **Accessibility** The unimproved paths are steep in places – use of pushchairs and wheelchairs is not recommended
- **Dogs** Only registered assistance dogs allowed, except on public footpaths (please keep them on leads)

What to look for

From the car park, the trail leads you first through pastures and meadows. Lightly grazed by cattle or mown for hay, these fields encourage a wealth of flowers and insects to flourish. Visit in late spring or early summer to see them at their best.

The RSPB's management includes gradually opening glades and clearings so that there are trees of different ages and more sunlight to encourage flowers, insects and birds. The spring woodland flowers make the most of the sunlight before the leaves on the trees emerge, with Lesser Celandines, Wood Anemones, Primroses

WILDLIFE BY SEASON

SPRING
Birdsong and woodland flowers are at their best. Redstarts and Pied Flycatchers arrive, orchids flower in the meadows.

SUMMER
Pied Flycatchers and Redstarts easily visible to early July. Butterflies and flowers including orchids in the meadows, dragonflies at the pond.

AUTUMN
Fungi flourish in the forest. Birds flock for the winter.

WINTER
Tits and finches patrol the woodland in flocks. On fine days in late winter (into spring) Sparrowhawks and Buzzards display overhead.

and then carpets of Bluebells (which are best in May).

In spring and summer look out for Pied Flycatchers, which hawk insects from favourite branches. They nest in tree holes, and to give them more potential homes the RSPB provides nestboxes, which Great Tits, Blue Tits and Nuthatches also use. The Redstart is another summer visitor typical of this woodland; one often sings near the old cottage in the middle of the reserve. Great Spotted Woodpeckers sometimes nest in trees close to the paths. Rotting wood teems with beetle grubs, all providing food for the birds.

The long loop passes a pond where you can see dragonflies in the summer. A Kingfisher visits occasionally.

In autumn the leaves fall in a blaze of glory and the forest floor becomes a show ground for a great variety of fungi, in all their outlandish shapes and colours. Late summer also sees the departure of the flycatchers, Redstarts and warblers, followed by the arrival of Redwings and Fieldfares, intent on clearing the berry bushes of their crops. Jays

WHEN TO VISIT
Early spring mornings are best for birdsong, summer midday for butterflies. If you're hoping to see woodland mammals visit early or late and move around slowly and quietly.

fly overhead, carrying acorns to store for the winter.

How to get here
Grid ref./postcode SK 009534/ ST13 7

By road The reserve lies 3 miles east of Leek. Leave Leek on the Ashbourne road (A523). After passing Bradnop, turn up the minor road (and across a disused railway line) to Apesford (signposted to RSPB Coombes Valley) – after a mile the reserve is on the left.

By public transport The nearest station is Macclesfield, 17 miles away. Bus 108 from Leek to Ashbourne stops 1.2 miles from the reserve entrance twice a day. Walk in Ashbourne direction and take the first right over the disabled railway line, to the reserve entrance on the left.

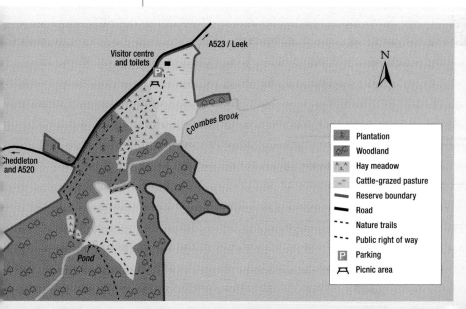

Legend	
Plantation	
Woodland	
Hay meadow	
Cattle-grazed pasture	
Reserve boundary	
Road	
Nature trails	
Public right of way	
P	Parking
Picnic area	

MIDLANDS

MIDDLETON LAKES

The RSPB purchased this former gravel quarry in the Tame Valley in 2007. With this came a vision to create a wonderful haven for wildlife and a place to inspire people. We expect the reserve to open for general visitors in 2010 and for access and habitat improvements to continue in stages over the next several years.

●Access, facilities, contact details and accessibility

The reserve is very new and facilities are limited at present to paths around the site, but more facilities will be added in due course.

- **Telephone** 01827 259 454; **email** middletonlakes@rspb.org.uk; **web** www.rspb.org.uk/middletonlakes
- **Opening hours** Please contact the reserve for details
- **Entry fees** Free
- **Accessibility** Limited – please contact the reserve for details
- **Dogs** Allowed on some parts of the reserve, under close control. Contact the reserve for more information.

What to look for

The reserve encompasses a mosaic of different habitats from semi-ancient woodland to lakes and rough grassland. The dominant feature is the River Tame which meanders through the reserve feeding the pools, ponds and ditches that characterise the wetlands. Kingfishers, grebes and Little Egrets hunt fish in the pools and are joined by terns in the summer. The quieter areas are used by Grass Snakes, Water Rails and Otters, though these are rarely seen.

Perhaps the greatest spectacles you'll see are in the woodlands to the west of the reserve where carpets of Bluebells give off a heady scent in April. High in the trees above a group of over

WILDLIFE BY SEASON

SPRING

The heronry becomes fully active and Bluebells rush to put on a show before the woodland canopy closes over them.

SUMMER

Terns fish the river and lakes and Hobbies, Swallows and Swifts hunt the insects high in the sky.

AUTUMN

Starlings form large flocks. Migrants may stop over. Jays store acorns for the winter.

WINTER

Waders and waterfowl gather in large flocks whilst Short-eared and Long-eared Owls join the resident Barn Owls on the grassland.

20 pairs of Grey Herons raise large noisy young, providing great views and regular flybys of these charismatic birds. The drumming of Great and Lesser Spotted Woodpeckers add to the wildlife soundtrack.

The calls of warblers, Turtle Doves and Cuckoos emanate from the scrub in the summer while resident finches, thrushes and tits find food and cover here throughout the year. The open grassland provides opportunities for ground-nesting birds such as Lapwings and Skylarks whilst Harvest Mice and other small mammals hide from hunting Barn Owls and Kestrels.

Ponds and ditches ensure that a myriad of dragonflies are present across the reserve in the summer and early autumn, these in turn providing a meal for Hobbies. Open water attracts large flocks of ducks, geese and gulls in the winter and Oystercatchers, Dunlins, Redshanks and other waders are present all year round on the spits and scrapes in the shallower lakes.

WHEN TO VISIT

There is something to see all year round and the habitats and wildlife change constantly so visit at any time of day and year.

How to get here

Grid ref./postcode SP 195982/ B78 2
By road The reserve is accessed from minor roads off the A4091.
By public transport The nearest railway stations are Wilnecote and Tamworth.

A Grey Heron takes a break from fish-watching to spruce up its plumage. These birds combine patience and power to lethal effect when stalking their aquatic prey.

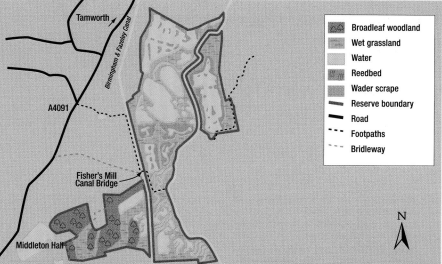

Tamworth

Birmingham & Fazeley Canal

A4091

Fisher's Mill Canal Bridge

Middleton Hall

Kingsbury Water Park

Broadleaf woodland
Wet grassland
Water
Reedbed
Wader scrape
Reserve boundary
Road
Footpaths
Bridleway

N

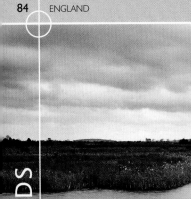

MIDLANDS

OTMOOR

At Otmoor, the RSPB has saved a fragment of what was once a great wetland, in the floodplain of the River Ray, and is now working to return the arable land to its former glory. Today, this lovely, tranquil reserve is home to increasing numbers of breeding and wintering water birds and other wildlife.

● Access, facilities, contact details and accessibility

Otmoor has many footpaths intersecting the 1.5-mile main visitor trail, which in dry weather is navigable with pushchairs and medium-sized wheelchairs.

- **Telephone** 01865 351163; **web** www.rspb.org.uk/otmoor
- **Opening hours** Daily, dawn til dusk
- **Entry fees** None, but donations to help continue work here are appreciated
- **Accessibility** There are ramps to the viewing screens, but only adventurous wheelchair users should attempt the trails. In winter paths often become muddy, making wheelchair access potentially much more difficult.
- **Dogs** Only allowed on public footpaths and bridleways

What to look for

There is a 1.5-mile visitor trail here from the car park, which intersects with other existing public footpaths if you want a longer walk and more thorough exploration of the reserve. You'll begin your walk alongside wet grassland, cut through with numerous ditches and channels. These provide plenty of muddy edges, ideal for

wader chicks to feed on worms, tiny snails and other invertebrates. Breeding pairs of Lapwings and Redshanks have increased five-fold since the RSPB began managing the reserve.

The trail leads to viewing screens overlooking the fields and also a 22-hectare reedbed, which was created from scratch by the RSPB in the

WILDLIFE BY SEASON

SPRING
Breeding waders display over the fields, while warblers sing from the reedbeds. Migrating waders may stop off.

SUMMER
Dragonflies are active, including Hairy Dragonfly and Ruddy Darter. The very rare Black Hairstreak butterfly is on the wing from late June through July. Hobbies hunt overhead.

AUTUMN
Brown Hairstreak butterflies are out from early August through September.

WINTER
Wildfowl arrives en masse, large flocks of Lapwings and Golden Plovers assemble, and birds of prey hunt overhead.

hope that Bitterns and other reedbed birds will return.

The RSPB uses cattle to graze the fields, creating a mixture of vegetation heights and a variety of habitat types to appeal to a diversity of wildlife. The cattle themselves attract Yellow Wagtails, which hang around and snap up insects disturbed by the browsing mammals. In winter, the wet fields, ponds and ditches attract feeding Golden Plovers and Lapwings, and also wildfowl – especially Teals and Wigeons, but also Pintails, Gadwalls and Shovelers. The ducks in turn attract birds of prey – look out for Hen Harriers, Short-eared Owls or Peregrine Falcons cruising low over the fields in search of lunch.

How to get here

Grid ref./postcode SP 570126/ OX3 9
By road From A34 take B4027 to Islip. Through Islip, continue along B4027 towards Wheatley. After 4 miles turn left to Horton-cum-Studley. Turn left to Beckley, then right before Abingdon Arms. Turn sharp

WHEN TO VISIT
Small birds are more active at dawn and dusk. For dragonflies and other insects, visit on sunny days from mid-morning. Reedbed birds tend to keep out of sight in windy weather.

left into Otmoor Lane. Follow this to the end for the reserve entrance.
By public transport The nearest rail station is Islip, around 6 miles by road from the reserve, so you will need a bicycle or to take a taxi.

REEDING MATERIAL
The RSPB designed the brand-new reedbed at Otmoor to be large enough to support a breeding pair of Bitterns. The 150,000 reeds were sown in a pattern that left plenty of channels and open areas for these rare herons to hunt for fish. As the reedbed matures, hopefully a passing Bittern will decide to move in. The reeds also help regulate water levels by holding excess rainwater in winter.

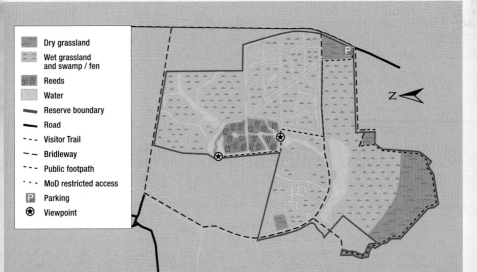

- ▨ Dry grassland
- ⌃⌃ Wet grassland and swamp / fen
- ▥ Reeds
- ▦ Water
- ▬ Reserve boundary
- ━ Road
- - - - Visitor Trail
- ∼∼ Bridleway
- - - - Public footpath
- ⋯ MoD restricted access
- 🅿 Parking
- ✷ Viewpoint

MIDLANDS

SANDWELL VALLEY LNR

The Sandwell Valley lies on the River Tame, and Forge Mill Lake, produced to control flooding of the river and now the centrepiece of the RSPB reserve, sits in a meander of the river. Here, the RSPB has developed a diverse and attractive reserve with a good mix of habitat types, and equipped it with everything you could want to enjoy an interesting and relaxing day out. The reserve's location, close to Birmingham, places it within easy reach for many, and it offers a welcome opportunity for seeing a variety of wildlife within this generally very built-up area.

● Access, facilities, contact details and accessibility

Sandwell Valley, an urban oasis of a reserve, is well equipped with family-friendly facilities to enable visitors of all ages to enjoy a fine day out. The information centre gives details of latest wildlife sightings, and from here you can hire binoculars and buy refreshments. There are interactive educational displays for children, and a remote camera showing live footage from the reserve. Events are held throughout the year, and group bookings and guided walks can be arranged.

- **Telephone** 0121 357 7395; **email** sandwellvalley@rspb.org.uk; **web** www.rspb.org.uk/sandwellvalley
- **Opening hours** The visitor centre, car parks and wheelchair access are open from 9am–5pm from Tuesday to Friday and 10am–5pm on Saturday and Sunday (closes at dusk in winter). The reserve is open at all times; hide – usually open 10.30am–3.30pm every day except Mondays (please phone to confirm before making a special journey).
- **Entry fees** Free
- **Accessibility** All trails, viewscreens and the hide are wheelchair-accessible with assistance but may become muddy in wet weather. The trails are mostly level, with several benches. There are disabled toilets.
- **Dogs** Allowed anywhere, but they must be kept on a lead

WILDLIFE BY SEASON

SPRING

It's all change at the reserve as the winter wildfowl depart and the summer visitors – warblers (nine species occur here) martins and Swallows – arrive. Summer insects like butterflies and dragonflies become more numerous as the weather warms up.

SUMMER

The breeding waders and wildfowl have fluffy chicks in tow, while the songbirds are also feeding their young – you may see family groups of Willow Tits, Reed Warblers or other small birds later in summer.

AUTUMN

Migrating waders visit the lake to feed. Look out for a Jack Snipe among the more numerous Common Snipes. Departing warblers and newly arrived winter thrushes are busy feeding up on the rich crop of hedgerow berries, and wintering ducks are starting to arrive.

WINTER

The feeding station gets busier as the weather gets colder – look out for handsome Bullfinches among the commoner birds. On the lake, Wigeons, Teals, Pochards, Shovelers and Goosanders may be joined by scarcer ducks like Goldeneyes.

What to look for

The visitor trail does a complete circuit of the lake, although you can walk a shorter loop if you prefer and still see much of what the reserve has to offer – the hide, two viewing screens, wildlife garden and reedbed all lie close to the visitor centre. At the visitor centre, take a moment to appreciate the stunning carpet with its specially commissioned wildlife art theme.

If you visit in summer, you'll find the wildlife garden

tits and finches may be joined by something scarcer, such as a Brambling. A few pairs of Willow Tits breed on the reserve – look out at the feeding station for this smart little bird with its distinctive 'sneering' nasal call. The visitor centre also has telescopes set up to overlook a small nearby pool and the lake beyond.

Following the trail clockwise through a reedy, scrubby area, you'll reach a viewing screen overlooking the small pool,

That hook-tipped, saw-edged bill looks oddly predatory for a duck, and Goosanders are indeed skilled hunters of fish.

at its best, with native flowers in bloom and a wealth of butterflies taking advantage of the abundance of nectar on offer. Look out for Small Coppers and Common Blues alongside the more familiar Small Tortoiseshells, whites and Peacocks.

There is a feeding station near the visitor centre which is viewable from inside the centre itself – if you visit in winter this will be especially worthy of your attention as the usual

which is surrounded by reeds, wet grassland and marshland, and a viewing platform at the far end of the reedbed, overlooking the main lake. If you head anticlockwise, you'll reach the other viewing screen which overlooks grassland, with the hide just ahead. Through spring and summer Reed and Sedge Warblers give their tireless songs from deep within the reeds; the former has a squeakier tone to its song while the latter's is more varied, with dry rattling sounds.

Smaller and noticeably shorter-billed than the commoner Snipe, the Jack Snipe is a shy bird with an engaging clockwork-toy way of bobbing along.

Less shy is the Reed Bunting; males have a neat black head and white collar and sing their simple song from more exposed perches.

In autumn the RSPB cuts back the reedbed to encourage regrowth. This management encourages Water Rails and Water Voles, both of which you may see if you're lucky. In winter the marsh attracts several Snipes – look at each of them closely in case there is also a Jack Snipe present – smaller, shorter-billed and a little stripier than its cousin, the Jack Snipe has an endearingly jerky, 'clockwork toy' way of moving around.

The large island in the south-eastern corner of Forge Mill Lake is managed specifically to attract

WHEN TO VISIT

Weekends and term-time days can be quite busy – early-morning trips are quieter. The birdfeeders will be liveliest during the winter and this is also the best time to see wildfowl, so this is a perfect place to bring the family for an interesting winter walk. However, the reserve has much to offer throughout the year.

breeding waders – the vegetation is kept low so that the waders and their chicks can forage for prey more easily. These include a few Lapwings and sometimes Little Ringed Plovers, Redshanks and Oystercatchers. If you're visiting in winter, you'll see much larger numbers of Lapwings feeding and resting on the island. Also look for wildfowl on the water, like Goldeneyes, Gadwalls, Goosanders, Pochards and Shovelers. The lake also attracts hundreds of Black-headed Gulls, and a few other gull species. The hide, which is placed directly in front of the large island, is staffed by volunteers at most times, who will be able to help you with any identification problems you might have.

The trail goes outside the RSPB reserve boundary and into the adjacent Sandwell Valley Country Park to circle the lake – from here things can get very muddy indeed so those with pushchairs or wheelchairs should take particular care. After turning south and following the River Tame for some time (look out for Kingfishers on the river) it rejoins the RSPB reserve on the south-eastern corner of the lake. If you took this route, you can now explore the remainder of the reserve, depending which way round you walked the trail. Besides the birds already mentioned, you could see many other species, depending on the time of year. In spring and summer, warblers such as Whitethroats, Blackcaps and Garden Warblers sing from the hedges and scrubby areas, while Common Terns may fish in the lake. In winter, Redwings, Fieldfares, Siskins and Redpolls may visit in flocks, searching for berries or seeds. Birds of prey you might see at any time include Buzzards, Sparrowhawks and Kestrels. Seeing mammals is never easy, but you might be lucky enough to see a Fox or a Weasel.

How to get here

Grid ref./postcode SP 035928/B43 5
By road From Birmingham city centre, take the Walsall Road (A34) to Scott Arms and turn left into Newton Road (A4041). Take Hamstead Road (B4167), which is fifth on the left near the bottom of the hill by the church (look for the brown sign marked RSPB nature centre). Take Tanhouse Avenue on the right. The reserve entrance is through a gateway on the left (there is another brown sign marked RSPB).
By public transport Hamstead is the nearest rail station. Turn right onto the main road –

An odd combination of brilliant colour and a shy and retiring nature, the Bullfinch is sometimes seen at or around the feeding station.

the Hamstead Hill/Old Walsall Road. Follow directions from Hamstead Road as above. Alternatively take the 16 bus from Birmingham centre, and ask for Tanhouse Avenue.

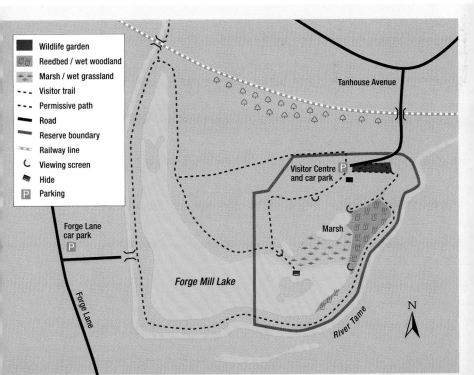

	Wildlife garden
	Reedbed / wet woodland
	Marsh / wet grassland
- - -	Visitor trail
- - -	Permissive path
	Road
	Reserve boundary
	Railway line
C	Viewing screen
	Hide
P	Parking

Tanhouse Avenue

Visitor Centre and car park

Marsh

Forge Lane car park

Forge Mill Lake

Forge Lane

River Tame

N

BERNEY MARSHES

SSSI, SPA, pSAC, NP, NATURA 2000

Berney Marshes is probably the most remote RSPB reserve in England – you can only reach it by train, boat or on foot. It lies on the River Yare, and incorporates part of Breydon Water, the large tidal estuary that where the Rivers Yare, Bure and Waveney meet. Waders breed in summer, and wildfowl and waders flock here in winter.

●Access, facilities, contact details and accessibility

The RSPB has no public access arrangements to this reserve, but you can view it easily from various public footpaths and enjoy a long walk in the area.

- **Telephone** 01493 700 645; **email** berney.marshes@rspb.org.uk; **web** www.rspb.org.uk/berneybreydon
- **Opening hours** The reserve can be viewed at all times
- **Entry fees** Free, though donations are welcome
- **Accessibility** The paths are level but can become very muddy and slippery in winter so may currently not be suitable for all
- **Dogs** Only allowed on public footpaths and bridleways

What to look for

The wild open spaces of Norfolk attract birds and birdwatchers equally – this is probably the most popular county in England for birdwatching and this reserve is a perfect illustration of why that is. When you disembark from the train at Berney Arms station, you are surrounded by miles of pasture and marshland with not a road in sight – paradise for wildlife and people who enjoy unspoilt wild places. One of a handful of buildings here is the Berney

WILDLIFE BY SEASON

SPRING
The calls of Lapwings and Redstarts ring across the marshes. Look for migrants like Garganeys and Yellow Wagtails.

SUMMER
Meadow flowers bloom. A good time to visit the windmill. Barn Owls hunt from early evening.

AUTUMN
Wildfowl and waders start to return to the marshes and estuary, including Wigeons, Pink-footed Geese and godwits.

WINTER
Some 100,000 waders and wildfowl overwinter, including tens of thousands of Wigeons, Pink-footed Geese, Lapwings and Golden Plovers.

Arms windmill, recently restored and the tallest of its kind. South-east of the station is the tip of Breydon Water, a huge tidal expanse with muddy shores that attract masses of wading birds, especially in winter.

The area is intersected by several public footpaths, including the Wherryman's Way, a long-distance path for walkers and cyclists. It is easily possible to walk for a whole day here, and as the Wherryman's Way runs alongside the rail line you can, with a bit of forward planning, walk a long section of it and then return to your starting point by train if you wish.

The marshes are home to breeding waders in spring and summer – Redshanks pipe loudly to let you know they've seen you, while Lapwings whoop and yodel overhead. Yellow Wagtails, glowing in the sunshine, snap up small insects close to the ground, while Garganeys may hide in the ditches.

Some 100,000 birds congregate here in winter – this is the time to see great flocks of

WHEN TO VISIT
The most exciting time to visit is probably winter, when marshland and estuary birds are present in large numbers.

Pink-footed Geese, Wigeons, Lapwings and Golden Plovers, while Short-eared Owls and Hen Harriers hunt over the marshes.

How to get here
Grid ref./postcode TG 464048/ NR30 1

By road There is strictly no access by road, you will need to travel to one of the other railway stations on the Norwich–Great Yarmouth via Reedham line and take the train from there to Berney Arms (see below).

By public transport Get off at the Berney Arms station for Berney Marshes. Follow the footpath signs south-east and you will get to the office. For Breydon Water, get off at Great Yarmouth and follow the Wherryman's Way path on the northern side of the estuary.

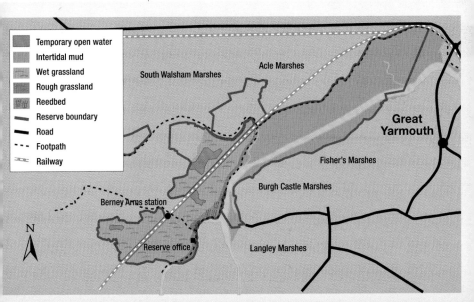

Legend	
▨	Temporary open water
▦	Intertidal mud
▤	Wet grassland
▩	Rough grassland
▦	Reedbed
—	Reserve boundary
━	Road
- - -	Footpath
⌗⌗⌗	Railway

South Walsham Marshes

Acle Marshes

Great Yarmouth

Fisher's Marshes

Burgh Castle Marshes

Berney Arms station

Reserve office

Langley Marshes

N

EAST ENGLAND

BOYTON MARSHES

SSSI, SPA, SAC, RAMSAR, AONB, NATURA 2000

Situated between the Butley river and Ore estuary, Boyton Marshes is a reserve of wet grassland and shallow open water, which attracts ducks, waders and birds of prey in winter, and has breeding waders and various songbirds in summer. It is also a great place to watch butterflies and dragonflies in summertime.

● Access, facilities, contact details and accessibility

This peaceful reserve is a great place for a birdwatching visit, or to include in a long walk on the Suffolk coast.

- **Telephone** 01394 450732; **email** havergate.island@rspb.org.uk; **web** www.rspb.org.uk/boytonmarshes
- **Opening hours** Open at all times
- **Entry fees** Free, but donations are appreciated
- **Accessibility** Some of the paths may be difficult for the mobility-impaired
- **Dogs** Allowed on public footpaths and bridleways

What to look for

This peaceful marshland reserve has areas of wet grassland to attract breeding waders in summer and flocks of wildfowl in winter – it also has a scrape that draws in passing waders to feed, especially when the tide is high and the riverside mud is covered over.

Throughout the year, you'll see Little Egrets and Grey Herons waiting to grab some prey by the ditches or out in the fields. Little Egrets are especially numerous in autumn. Do check carefully any distant pale bird in flight, as this is a good spot for Barn Owls and they do

WILDLIFE BY SEASON

SPRING

The breeding birds are on the marsh – look out for Lapwings, Redshanks, whitethroats, Shovelers and Gadwalls.

SUMMER

The meadows are full of flowers and butterflies such as Meadow Browns, Ringlets and various skippers. Barn Owls hunt in the evenings.

AUTUMN

Birds on migration visit the marsh and winter wildfowl start to arrive.

WINTER

Pintails are among the ducks that gather in winter, with Curlews, Dunlins and other waders on the marsh. Thrushes scour the fields for invertebrate prey.

sometimes hunt in daylight. A good view will reveal the owl's beautifully patterned grey and golden upperparts, and the long, melancholy, dark-eyed face.

The RSPB manages Boyton's wet meadows to provide suitable nesting places for Redshanks and Lapwings, and foraging grounds for their chicks. Gadwalls and Shovelers nest here too.

The grassland has a diverse and flourishing insect population – this is a great place to watch butterfly species that aren't in the habit of visiting gardens and so may be less familiar. Meadow Browns and Ringlets are slow, fluttery fliers, frequently stopping to feed on grassland flowers. Skippers are much smaller, with bright red-gold wings. Large, Small and Essex Skippers are all likely to be present. The Large Skippers emerge at the end of May, the other two species a few weeks later.

As with many marshland sites, Boyton sees a large influx of waders and wildfowl in autumn and winter. You'll

WHEN TO VISIT

This reserve is well worth a visit at any time of year, and time of day is not crucial.

see many Wigeons, the drakes handsome with their silvery bodies and orange heads with neat cream crown-stripes.

How to get here

Grid ref./postcode TM 387475/ IP12 3

By road The reserve is about seven miles east of Woodbridge. Follow the B1084 to the village of Butley. Turn right and follow the road through to Capel St Andrew. Turn left and follow the road towards Boyton village. Approximately 400m before the village, go left down a concrete track on a sharp right-hand turn.

By public transport Woodbridge is the nearest railway station. Bus route 160 (Ipswich–Bealings–Woodbridge–Orford) stops at Boyton village – the reserve is half a mile north-east of the village.

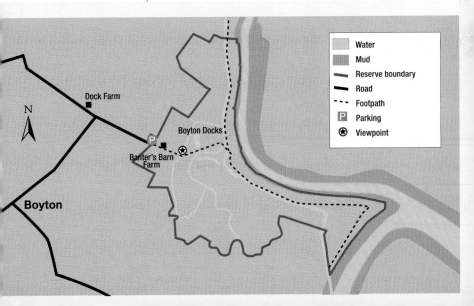

Dock Farm

Boyton Docks

Banter's Barn Farm

N

Boyton

	Water
	Mud
—	Reserve boundary
—	Road
- - -	Footpath
P	Parking
✹	Viewpoint

EAST ENGLAND

BUCKENHAM MARSHES <small>SSSI</small>

This traditionally managed grazing marsh attracts many ducks, geese and waders in autumn and winter. In spring and summer it is home to breeding waders. The reserve, along with the adjacent Cantley Marshes, is particularly well known for being the wintering ground for England's only regular flock of Taiga Bean Geese.

● Access, facilities, contact details and accessibility

The nature trail here is 1 mile long each way. Strumpshaw Fen and other RSPB reserves are nearby.

- **Telephone** 01603 715 191; **email** buckenham.cantley@rspb.org.uk; **web** www.rspb.org.uk/buckenham
- **Opening hours** Open at all times. The Meadow Trail is open only between late May and the end of August.
- **Entry fees** None, but donations are appreciated
- **Accessibility** The trail is not suitable for wheelchairs or pushchairs
- **Dogs** Only allowed on public footpaths and bridleways

What to look for

As with the RSPB's other wet grazing marsh reserves here in East Anglia, Buckenham Marshes is a vital breeding ground for a select group of uncommon birds, and if you visit in spring you'll probably see at least some of them. Redshanks and Lapwings have both declined as inland breeding species so sites like this are very important for them. They are both noisy in early spring, and if you hear them making a particularly loud fuss that may mean a bird of prey is around, so scan the skies for a Marsh Harrier. Avocets are here throughout spring and summer, and Reed and Sedge Warblers sing along the trails.

WILDLIFE BY SEASON

SPRING

Avocets, Lapwings, Snipes, Redshanks and Oystercatchers busily establish their nest sites. Yellow Wagtails arrive and prepare to breed.

SUMMER

Watch the waders with their chicks, and look out for hunting Barn Owls in the evening. Little Egret numbers increase.

AUTUMN

Peregrines arrive for winter. Winter wildfowl and waders start to arrive.

WINTER

Teals, Wigeons, Lapwings and Golden Plovers gather in large flocks. White-fronted and Taiga Bean Geese arrive.

Management of water levels is key to keeping habitats like this attractive to wildlife. Ditch management helps keep things dry enough for delicate wader chicks to survive, without allowing the fields to dry out and deprive the birds of their water-edge feeding grounds. The RSPB also uses cattle to keep the grass length down – cows graze selectively on longer, coarser grasses, allowing a mosaic of grassland plants to thrive. Of course, it is necessary to keep cattle and nesting waders apart at the crucial time!

Autumn and winter brings flocks of Wigeons, Teals and Shovelers to the grazing marshes – at this time water levels are allowed to increase, to suit these ducks. November onwards is the time to see the local speciality – the Taiga Bean Goose. This is the larger and rarer of the two subspecies of Bean Goose that visit the UK in winter – only one other regular flock of Taiga Beans occurs in Britain, many miles away in the Avon Valley in Scotland.

WHEN TO VISIT

To see the Taiga Bean Geese, visit between November and January. The reserve is interesting year-round.

How to get here

Grid ref./postcode TG 351056/ NR13 4

By road Taking the A47 from Norwich, head for Brundall village at the roundabout, Drive through the village and continue on the same road out towards Strumpshaw. Soon after you pass the Strumpshaw sign, turn right into Stone Road, then take the second right (also Stone Road). Take the first turn on the right onto Station Road, which leads to Buckenham train station and Buckenham Marshes.

By public transport A number of trains on the Norwich to Great Yarmouth and Lowestoft (Wherry Lines) services call at Buckenham station by request at the weekend. The entrance to the reserve is by the station. On other days, the closest station is Brundall (2.5 miles from reserve) on the same line.

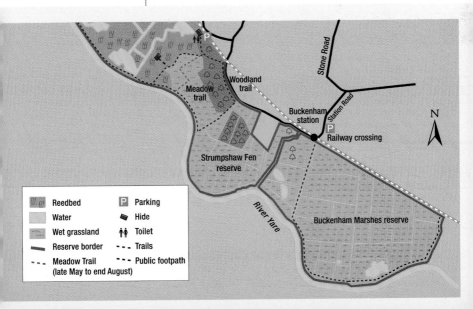

🏚	Reedbed	P	Parking
	Water	◣	Hide
	Wet grassland	♀♂	Toilet
▬	Reserve border	- - -	Trails
- - -	Meadow Trail (late May to end August)	- - -	Public footpath

EAST ENGLAND

Reed Warbler

FOWLMERE SSSI

A natural oasis surrounded on all sides by large tracts of agricultural land, Fowlmere is a small wetland nature reserve south-west of Cambridge, where watercress was grown until the early 1960s. It has easy, pushchair-friendly walking in an interesting mix of habitat types, with a wide range of wildlife to see in tranquil surroundings.

●Access, facilities, contact details and accessibility

A pleasantly paced walk around Fowlmere will take no more than a couple of hours.

- **Telephone** 01763 208978; **email**: fowlmere@rspb.org.uk; **web** www.rspb.org.uk/fowlmere
- **Opening hours** Open at all times
- **Entry fees** Free for everyone, but please make a donation to the RSPB if you can
- **Accessibility** The main nature trail and Drewer hide are comfortably wheelchair-accessible. The two other hides are more tricky, and other paths are rougher.
- **Dogs** Not allowed on the reserve

What to look for

Fowlmere is a remnant of Cambridgeshire fenland, fed by pure water from chalk springs. An extensive reedbed formed where the watercress beds used to be, attracting a variety of wildlife. The RSPB purchased the site in 1977, with funds raised by the then children's division of the society, the Young Ornithologists'

Club (YOC). Appropriately, Fowlmere is today a great place for families to visit and enjoy.

A 1.9 mile circular nature trail takes you around the best parts of the reserve. Little Grebes, Sedge and Reed Warblers, Water Rails and Reed Buntings nest in and around the

WILDLIFE BY SEASON

SPRING

Warblers (nine species occur) and Turtle Doves sing. Little Grebes and other water birds breed on the meres.

SUMMER

The best time for insects, especially dragonflies and damselflies. Dawn and dusk are good for mammal-watching.

AUTUMN

Migrating birds pass through, including large numbers of thrushes, and occasional waders.

WINTER

The meres may attract visiting ducks and geese. Starlings, winter thrushes, finches and buntings gather in pre-roost flocks.

reedbeds, with Grasshopper Warblers and Turtle Doves in the drier areas. You may well see a Kingfisher flashing down the stream. Listen out for the 'jangling-keys' song of the declining Corn Bunting on adjacent farmland. Hobbies hunt dragonflies overhead in summer and early autumn, chasing down their quarry with effortlessly agile flight. Migrating waders like Green Sandpipers may stop off in autumn, and Long-eared Owls sometimes roost in the scrub in winter. Roosting Starlings, thrushes and buntings may attract birds of prey like Sparrowhawks and Merlins. Badgers and Muntjac Deer live in the woods – visit early or late and keep quiet for your best chance of seeing them – and in the wetland areas Otters and Water Shrews may be seen.

As well as maintaining the reedbeds by periodically clearing areas of reed to prevent drying out, the RSPB is also working to restore the site's chalk grassland, to encourage wild flowers such as Cowslips and Southern Marsh Orchids. This habitat is also attractive to butterflies,

WHEN TO VISIT

To enjoy the reserve's dawn chorus at its best, visit early on a still spring day. Mornings or evenings are also best for seeing mammals. Dragonflies and butterflies will be most active on warm, still summer days. Water Rails may be easier to see in cold winter weather.

beetles and grasshoppers – in high summer the chalk grassland is alive with insects.

How to get here

Grid ref./postcode TL 406461/ SG8 6
By road From the A10 (Cambridge to Royston) turn towards Fowlmere at the Fowlmere–Shepreth crossroads; after 1 mile, turn right by the cemetery (RSPB sign); after about half a mile, turn left into the reserve.
Public transport The nearest railway station is 2 miles away at Shepreth, while buses call at Dunsbridge Turnpike, which is 1 mile away.

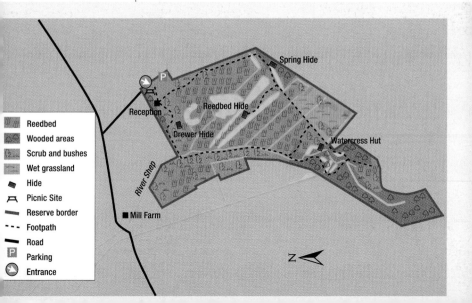

Reedbed	
Wooded areas	
Scrub and bushes	
Wet grassland	
Hide	
Picnic Site	
Reserve border	
Footpath	
Road	
Parking	
Entrance	

Spring Hide
Reedbed Hide
Reception
Drewer Hide
Watercress Hut
River Shep
Mill Farm
N

EAST ENGLAND

FRAMPTON MARSH

SPA, SAC, NATURA 2000

For birdwatchers, there is little to rival the excitement of a walk along a remote east-coast saltmarsh in autumn. At Frampton Marsh the rising tide covers the saltmarsh and forces birds over the sea wall and onto the fields. The reserve is also an important refuge for many breeding and wintering birds. Brand new visitor facilities help bring you really close to the wildlife.

● Access, facilities, contact details and accessibility

There is a new visitor centre overlooking the reedbed reservoir, and several hides overlooking freshwater scrapes.
- **Telephone** 01205 724 678; **email** lincolnshirewashreserves@rspb.org.uk; **web** www.rspb.org.uk/framptonmarsh
- **Opening hours** Open at all times
- **Entry fees** None, but donations to help continue the work here are appreciated
- **Accessibility** The paths and trails may be difficult to access for wheelchairs
- **Dogs** Allowed on public footpaths, bridleways and the saltmarsh, provided they are kept under control

What to look for

From the visitor centre, there are fantastic views across a reedbed reservoir with nesting wildfowl and waders, and from here the trails take you out across a marvellous wild landscape. In springtime, you will almost certainly hear many territorial Redshanks giving their shrill piping calls. These striking waders are easily identified

by the broad white stripe on the trailing edge of the wing, and the white rump. You may also see some late winter waders, such as Knots, before they head north to breed. Over the fields, Skylarks rise in their towering song flights, while in scrubbier areas you may hear the simple song of a male Reed Bunting, resplendent with glossy

WILDLIFE BY SEASON

SPRING

Brent Geese are passing through until May, while Whimbrels flock on the saltmarsh in April. Redshanks are breeding.

SUMMER

A quieter time, although good for Marsh Harriers and marshland flowers.

AUTUMN

High tides push flocks of Curlews, Golden Plovers and Redshanks onto the fields. Kingfishers fish the saltmarsh creeks. Brent Geese start to arrive.

WINTER

Masses of Brent Geese graze on the marshes. You may see flocks of Twites, Snow Buntings and the odd Lapland Bunting. Also look out for raptors.

black head and neat white collar.

By late summer, there is a steady trickle of migrants returning, in the form of waders like Greenshanks and Whimbrels. Autumn, however, is the best time to visit this reserve, as this is when you are almost guaranteed amazing close-up views of waders sheltering on the highest parts of the marsh, just over the sea wall, at high tide. You must make sure that you pick the right day and time to observe this spectacle. You'll need to consult a local tide table, and visit when high tide will be during daylight hours. Also note that the biggest tides happen when the moon is new or full.

From the hides, you'll get fantastic close views of nesting birds on the scrapes, including Avocets and Little Ringed Plovers.

Winter at Frampton means Brent Geese, grazing on the saltmarsh in their thousands and often giving excellent views. Twites, small finches of the northern highlands, move to the coast in winter and you may encounter a flock of them

WHEN TO VISIT

There is interesting wildlife to be seen year-round, but to witness the particularly exciting spectacle of waders forced off the marsh by high tides, visit on a rising tide in autumn.

feeding on plant seeds – look out for the males' pink rumps in flight. Two buntings that breed in northern climes may also visit in winter – Snow and Lapland Buntings. Both can be extremely approachable.

How to get here

Grid ref./postcode TF 356392/ PE20 1

By road The reserve is reached from Frampton village, south of Boston. Turn off the A16 at Kirton, signposted to Frampton, pass through Frampton village and follow the signposts from there to RSPB Frampton Marsh nature reserve.

By public transport The nearest station is Boston, 5 miles away. Buses 5, 13, 51 and 58 from Boston all go through Kirton, 3 miles away.

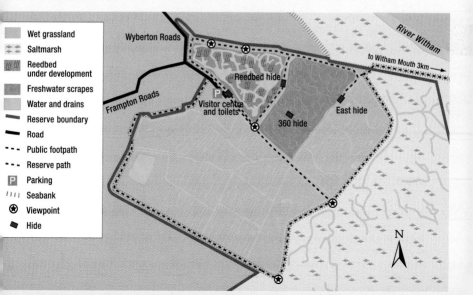

	Wet grassland
	Saltmarsh
	Reedbed under development
	Freshwater scrapes
	Water and drains
—	Reserve boundary
▬	Road
- - -	Public footpath
- - -	Reserve path
P	Parking
'''''	Seabank
✪	Viewpoint
◣	Hide

Wyberton Roads
River Witham
to Witham Mouth 3km →
Reedbed hide
Frampton Roads
Visitor centre and toilets
East hide
360 hide
N

EAST ENGLAND

FREISTON SHORE

SSSI, SPA, SAC, RAMSAR, NATURA 2000

For centuries the Wash has been surrounded by man-made banks, and the land behind them drained for agriculture. Now, as sea levels rise and saltmarshes in front of these sea walls start to disappear, important wildlife habitat is being lost. On purchasing several hectares of coastal farmland here, the RSPB, in conjunction with the Environment Agency, allowed the sea to broach the sea wall and inundate the farmland. As a result, the land is now reverting to saltmarsh, helping to preserve this important habitat for shore birds and other wildlife of intertidal areas. Additionally, a newly constructed saline lagoon here has provided a breeding place for Avocets, and a safe high-tide roost for many more species of waders.

● Access, facilities, contact details and accessibility

There are two nature trails (one of them newly opened) and one birdwatching hide here. You can arrange guided walks, and group bookings are accepted too.

- **Telephone** 01205 724 678; **email** lincolnshirewashreserves@rspb.org.uk; **web** www.rspb.org.uk/freistonshore
- **Opening hours** Open at all times
- **Entry fees** None
- **Accessibility** The bird hide and part of the wetland trail are accessible to disabled visitors. Excellent views of parts of the reserve can be had from the car park.
- **Dogs** Allowed on all footpaths

P
♿

WILDLIFE BY SEASON

SPRING

Avocets and Ringed Plovers are nesting on the lagoon, and Skylarks can be heard singing high over the fields.
Tree Sparrows are holding territory around the nest boxes. Increasing numbers of Lapwings and Redshanks are nesting on the wetlands.

SUMMER

Autumn waders start to arrive midway through summer, while the breeding species are still attending their growing chicks.

AUTUMN

Wader numbers peak, and at high tide masses of Knots and Dunlins assemble on the lagoon. Winter wildfowl start to arrive. Hen Harriers and other birds of prey start to be seen more frequently.

WINTER

Brent Geese gather in large numbers on the reserve, while Teals and Wigeons come to the lagoon. Flocks of Lapwings and Golden Plovers feed on the marsh too. This is the best time to see birds of prey, with Hen Harriers, Merlins, Peregrine Falcons and Short-eared Owls all seen regularly.

What to look for

The main parking area here is adjacent to the lagoon, so you don't need to walk far at all to see many of the reserve's special birds. In fact, you may see Tree Sparrows around the car park – these smart birds are distinguished from House Sparrows by their black cheek spots. Tree Sparrows have undergone catastrophic declines in the second half of the 20th century, but providing nestboxes and suitable habitat has helped them to increase in number ones confidently swimming beside them. Young Avocets look so different from their parents that you could be forgiven for thinking them another species entirely when they are small – over the summer their short, stubby bills grow long and upswept, and the familiar black-and-white plumage replaces their grey fluff.

The wetland trail explores an area of newly created wet grassland, south of the car park. Here you could see breeding

Shelducks are large and handsome ducks with a strong tie to the sea. You could see them on the lagoon here or flying overhead at any time.

on this and some other RSPB reserves.

A footpath leads from the car park to the lagoon hide. This is screened off by high hedgerows to avoid disturbing the birds. If you visit in spring you should see breeding Avocets and Ringed Plovers from the lagoon hide; the Avocets in particular are extremely active and vocal at this time of year. By summer they and their chicks will be out feeding together, the adults wading belly-deep with the little Redshanks – look out too for Brown Hares, lying low in their shallow scrapes or 'forms', or bounding away on their immensely long legs. You'll know you're looking at a hare and not a Rabbit when you see the black tips to its ears, or its staring amber eyes.

In autumn, the lagoon really comes into its own as a roosting place for waders. These birds, many of them just visiting while on their southbound migration, feed out on the mudflats and use

Speed demon: the Brown Hare is a sprinter par excellence, using those long legs to escape danger and to race each other in wild spring courtship chases.

the time when high tide covers the mud to rest, bathe and sleep. It is well worth timing your visit so you will be on the reserve at high tide to see the Knots, Dunlins, Oystercatchers and other waders at close quarters. Winter brings more new arrivals to the lagoon in the form of ducks – mostly Teals and Wigeons.

The expanding saltmarsh at Freiston attracts many waders and also Brent Geese in winter. Flocks of Golden Plovers and Lapwings feed on the marsh, taking off en masse when a Peregrine Falcon flies over – you might even witness one of these powerful predators stooping headfirst into a panicking flock and knocking an unlucky victim to the ground. Other birds of prey visit in

winter too – you may see Hen Harriers gliding elegantly, the females brown with prominent white rumps, the males ghostly grey with neat black wingtips. A small and very dashing falcon that visits in winter is the Merlin, here to hunt Meadow Pipits, Twites and other small birds which, like the Merlins themselves, abandon their moorland breeding grounds for wild coastlines like this in winter. Barn Owls could be seen at any time of year, but Short-eared Owls are usually a winter treat, twisting and turning on long, boldly patterned wings as they search for rodents in the grassland.

Freiston Shore lies very close to Frampton Marsh, so you may want to visit both reserves while in the general area. The county of Lincolnshire has tremendous potential as a place for keen visitors to find more unusual birds, especially in the migration seasons, as its best coastal sites are not as intensively 'watched' as neighbouring Norfolk. So be on the lookout for the unexpected as you explore this beautiful area.

WHEN TO VISIT

Like neighbouring Frampton Marsh, this reserve offers particularly exciting birdwatching in autumn at high tide, but it is well worth a look at any time.

SALT OF THE EARTH

Balancing the needs of people and wildlife is problematic when it comes to the sea. Coastal animals are adapted to cope with the constant change brought about by the tides, from day to day and year to year. People, however, generally prefer their homes and land to stay in the same place for as long as possible. Sea defences, by their very nature, destroy the special transient habitats like saltmarshes that so many animals depend on, so the RSPB were eager to take the opportunity to create new areas of saltmarsh at Freiston, as well as to protect the saltmarsh that was already there. The saltmarsh also creates a buffer zone for encroaching sea water that is actually an effective flood defence in its own right for fields further inland.

Once extinct as a British breeding bird, the Avocet is now back with a vengeance, nesting at sites all up the east coast including Freiston Shore.

How to get here

Grid ref./postcode TF 398425/PE22 0
By road From Boston, take the A52 road towards Skegness. Upon reaching Haltoft End after two miles, turn right and follow the brown tourist signs from here directing you to RSPB Freiston Shore reserve.
By public transport Boston, 4 miles away, is the nearest station. Local buses serve the nearby Butterwick and Freiston villages.

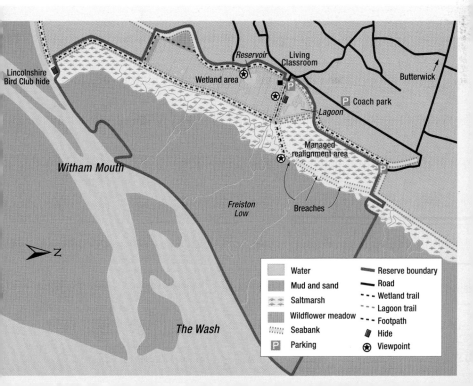

Common Tern

HAVERGATE ISLAND SSSI, NNR,
SPA, pSAC, RAMSAR, STATUTORY BIRD SANCTUARY, AONB, NATURA 2000

A narrow and low-lying sliver of land between Orford beach and the Suffolk mainland, Havergate Island is a very special place for the history of conservation in Britain. Erosion means it will eventually be lost to the sea, probably sometime this century, so visit while you can!

● Access, facilities, contact details and accessibility

Access is by boat. There are five hides and one viewing screen, and a 1.5-mile nature trail.

- **Telephone** 01394 450 732; **email** havergate.island@rspb.org.uk; **web** www.rspb.org.uk/havergate
- **Opening hours** You can visit on certain days all year, check the website for details. Visits last five hours. Book via the RSPB Minsmere reserve visitor centre – tel: 01728 648281.
- **Entry fees** Adults: members £5; non-members £7. Children (under 16): members £2; non-members £3
- **Accessibility** The nature trail is unsuitable for wheelchairs or pushchairs
- **Dogs** Not allowed, except registered assistance dogs

What to look for

When you disembark from the boat, you'll find a nature trail taking you the whole length of the island, with hides giving you close views of the birds that visit the lagoons. In spring, the lagoon islands are home to Avocets, Lesser Black-backed and other gulls, and Common Terns. The terns are loud-voiced and lively, squabbling among themselves in their busy colonies. The RSPB keeps the islands tern-friendly by clearing them of excess vegetation in winter, when the birds themselves are away on their African wintering grounds.

The island has a healthy population of Brown Hares, which you might see indulging

WILDLIFE BY SEASON

SPRING
Avocets and ducks are displaying to their partners and preparing to breed. You may see boxing Brown Hares. Terns start to return from Africa.

SUMMER
Terns are busy fetching fish for their chicks. Sunny days see plenty of butterfly activity.

AUTUMN
Migrating waders such as Spotted Redshanks start to arrive. The Sea Aster on the saltmarsh comes into colourful flower.

WINTER
Birds of prey, such as Hen Harrier, are more numerous, and ducks including Wigeons, Teals and Pintails gather on the lagoons.

in spectacular courtship chases across the grassy areas in spring. By summer, the grassland is full of butterflies – one of the earlier species is the handsome Wall Brown with its fiery orange and black patterned wings.

Havergate's vegetated shingle habitat has a special community of plants and insects, which the RSPB carefully monitor and manage. More than 20 Spoonbills have gathered on the reserve in recent summers, making this reserve one of the best places in the UK to see this rare and spectacular bird with its incredible ladle-shaped bill.

By winter, the lagoons are home to a range of ducks, such as Wigeons, Teals and Pintails, and birds of prey are often seen.

How to get here
Grid ref./postcode TM 425495/ IP12 2
By road Access by boat from Orford Quay. The village of Orford is located 11 miles to the north-east of Woodbridge; the village is signposted off the A12. There is a large pay-and-display car park adjacent to the quay.

WHEN TO VISIT
Visiting opportunities are more numerous in summer, for visitors keen to see the breeding terns and Avocets. However, the island is still busy with birdlife in autumn and winter.

By public transport Wickham Market Station. From the station, follow the B1078 east through Tunstall to the B1084. Turn left and follow through to the village of Orford.

MAKING HISTORY
The Avocet, famous icon of the RSPB, became extinct as a breeding bird in Britain early in the 19th century, so the arrival of a few pairs on Havergate Island in 1947 was cause for celebration. The birds were attracted by lagoons created when a stray bomb damaged the sea wall, but this helped conservationists develop ways of creating more suitable habitat at other locations. The RSPB acquired Havergate Island in 1948, and adopted the Avocet as its logo.

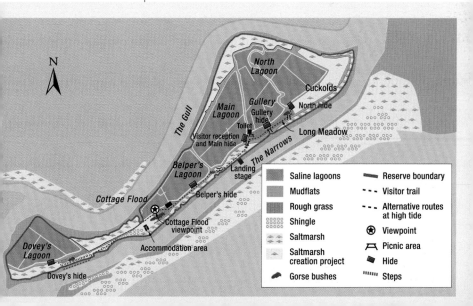

EAST ENGLAND

LAKENHEATH FEN SSSI

At Lakenheath Fen, the RSPB has converted an area of arable farmland, bought in 1995 and 1997, into a large wetland of reedbeds and grazing marshes. The new reedbeds have attracted many wetland birds, and Otters and Water Voles have now arrived. The reserve also includes three areas of Poplar plantations that in summer are home to the rare and stunning Golden Oriole, and in 2007 two pairs of Cranes nested in reedbeds here. Bitterns seem poised to colonise too. The reserve is not just for keen birdwatchers – it is family-friendly with good (and still improving) visitor facilities and plenty of events for all.

● Access, facilities, contact details and accessibility

The visitor centre has family explorer backpacks for hire. There are two nature trails – a 3.4-mile out-and-back route and a 3.5-mile circular trail – and from the trails there are four viewpoints. Please note: from time to time sections of these trails are closed, and diversions opened. Facilities for mobility-impaired visitors are still being actively developed and improved. Events are held throughout the year, and guided walks can be booked.

- **Telephone** 01842 863400; **email** lakenheath@rspb.org.uk;
  web www.rspb.org.uk/lakenheathfen
- **Opening hours** Dawn till dusk
- **Entry fees** Free, but donations to help continue the work here are appreciated
- **Accessibility** The wheelchair/pushchair path (150m) from the car park to the riverbank viewpoint is possible with assistance. The wheelchair/pushchair path from car park to visitor centre is fully accessible. The wheelchair/pushchair circular-route footpath (1,000 metres) is fully accessible from the car-park.
- **Dogs** Only allowed on public footpaths and bridleways

WILDLIFE BY SEASON

SPRING
The star breeding bird of Lakenheath, the Golden Oriole, returns to the plantations mid-spring. Other nesting birds are much in evidence, with Blackcaps in the plantation and Sedge and Reed Warblers singing from the reedbeds, and there's a chance you may hear a Bittern 'booming'.

SUMMER
Hobbies hunt for dragonflies overhead, and breeding Marsh Harriers can be seen carrying prey to their nests. There are many insects on the wing at the reserve, especially dragonflies over the wetter parts, scarce reedbed moths, and butterflies in the wooded areas.

AUTUMN
Bearded Tits are easiest to see in autumn as they travel in vocal family groups. Warblers feed up prior to migration, and later in autumn the winter wildfowl start to arrive.

WINTER
The best time to see Cranes, Barn Owls and Kingfishers. Winter wildfowl may include Teals, Gadwalls, Tufted Ducks, Wigeons, Shovelers and sometimes Whooper Swans.

What to look for

There are two long trails to enjoy at Lakenheath Fen, so make a day of it and explore them both. The staff at the visitor centre will be able to tell you what's about, and the centre itself is full of information on the history of the reserve and the wildlife that lives here.

It is hard to imagine, looking at Lakenheath Fen today, that in 1996 it was an area of unremarkable carrot fields. Five years of heavy earth-moving

specialists of this kind of habitat. The RSPB aimed to build a reedbed that could support at least 800 pairs of Reed Warblers – now there are 850 pairs here, along with 130 pairs of Reed Buntings and seven of Marsh Harriers. Bearded Tits have moved in too, while Bitterns are now here throughout the year – hopefully they too will soon breed.

A highlight of a spring visit to Lakenheath is the beautiful

The stateliest of our birds, the Crane is an extremely rare breeding species in the UK and Lakenheath's staff are rightly proud to have attracted them here.

work constructed a network of pools and ditches, with the displaced earth being used to build up embankments between the dug-out areas. Next, reed seedlings were planted. Given that the land was, historically, fenland that had been drained to make it suitable for agriculture, it did not take long for it to become flooded again, and the reedbed has flourished. Now, if you visit in spring, you'll hear the churring, squeaky singing of numerous Reed Warblers,

and exotic fluty song of the male Golden Oriole. Just hearing one of these birds won't be enough for most visitors, even though seeing them can be quite a challenge – it's amazing how difficult it can be to spot a biggish bright yellow and black bird in the tops of the Poplar trees – the dull green females are even more difficult to find. Be patient and keep checking – the birds can range quite widely in the Poplar plantation and are present until late summer.

A stunning flower of the wetlands, Purple Loosestrife is much appreciated by butterflies, like this Brimstone, as well as by humans.

The reserve has areas of grazing marsh as well, and here in 2007 two pairs of displaying Cranes were discovered. The spectacular birds stayed on to breed – yet another remarkable record for this fledgling nature reserve. A viewpoint has been built so you can watch them without causing disturbance. If you see one flying overhead (which could happen at any time of year), you'll recognise one by the way its neck is extended, rather than tucked in like a heron.

Wildfowl come to Lakenheath in winter, and you may see flocks of Wigeons, Teals, Shovelers and Gadwalls, with a chance of Whooper Swans. The chances of seeing a bird of prey go up in winter, with the resident Marsh Harriers being joined by Hen Harriers and the occasional Peregrine Falcon or Merlin. Water Pipits join Meadow Pipits in the fields, while yet another special reedbed bird was found for the first time here in January 2009 – a Penduline Tit, a species found on the near continent that has long been tipped as a potential colonist to Britain.

It isn't all about birds here, though. Roe Deer are seen regularly and, excitingly, Otter sightings are on the increase. One Otter obligingly fished in the pool nearest the visitor centre on several mornings between 9 and 11am in winter 2008/2009.

This beautiful reserve is a wonderful living testament to the power of imagination and the dividends paid by serious hard work. Progress is ongoing, with more reeds to be planted and visitor facilities to be improved to allow even more people to enjoy the scenery and wildlife here. The project was primarily conceived by Norman Sills, an RSPB veteran of 36 years, and after planning and overseeing the first phases of the work, he has now taken on the role of site manager here. Come to one of the guided walks to gain the benefit of his and his colleagues' expertise, and to see and learn about all aspects of life and work at Lakenheath Fen.

WHEN TO VISIT

To see the Golden Orioles and the Cranes (if present), you'll need to visit in spring or early summer. Otherwise, there is interesting wildlife to see here throughout the year, and time of day is not important.

How to get here

Grid ref./postcode TL 722864/IP27 9

By road From Lakenheath village, travel north on B1112 for about 2 miles. Go over the level crossing and after 200m, turn left into the reserve entrance. From Hockwold village, travel south on B1112 for nearly 1 mile, go over the river bridge and after 200m, turn right into the reserve entrance.

By public transport At weekends a number of trains on the Norwich-Ely-Cambridge service call at Lakenheath (request stop). On Sundays and public holidays, there are three trains a day, and on Saturdays there is one train in each direction (allowing a day trip from Norwich). A new footpath links the visitor centre with Station Road north of the railway station. On other days, the closest station is Brandon, with an hourly service. The reserve is 4.7 miles away along the Hereward Way if you fancy a walk or bring your bike with you. Alternatively, you can use the on-demand Brecks Bus, available Monday–Friday, to reach the reserve from Brandon and Thetford. To book, phone Brecks Bus on 01842 816 170 by noon the weekday before travel.

The Lakenheath reedbed was designed to be big enough for Bitterns to nest in, and so far three different males have 'boomed' in the reedbeds in spring.

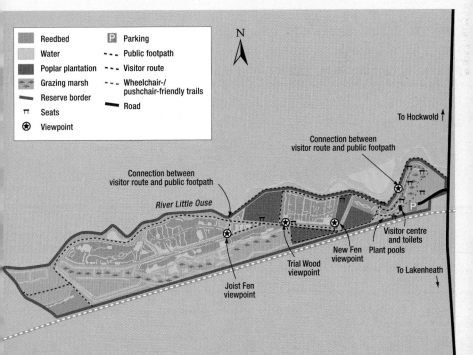

EAST ENGLAND

MINSMERE

SSSI, SPA, cSAC, RAMSAR, AONB, NATURA 2000

Tucked away at the end of an impossibly quiet, wooded lane is the gateway to a spectacular wetland paradise. At Minsmere the RSPB have recreated a fragment of the once extensive marshes and reedbeds of Suffolk, but you'll experience a real sense of space and wilderness as you look across the acres of swaying reeds and lagoons sparkling under a big East Anglian sky. Minsmere teems with wildlife all year round, and is home to some of the UK's most iconic animals, many of which are easy to see here. As a flagship RSPB reserve, Minsmere is also replete with top-notch visitor facilities, making it the perfect destination for a day out.

● Access, facilities, contact details and accessibility

Minsmere is a very popular reserve, especially on sunny weekends. The flipside of this is the array of facilities and activities on offer. The reserve has ample parking, toilets, a teashop that sells light refreshments and meals, and a fully equipped gift shop. The large visitor centre has many displays and, usually, an art exhibition. In addition, a busy programme of events includes regular guided walks, children's events, including Easter egg hunts and pond-dipping days, art workshops and moth-trapping nights.

- **Telephone** 01728 648281; **email** minsmere@rspb.org.uk; **web** www.rspb.org.uk/minsmere
- **Opening hours** 9am until dusk (or 9pm if earlier) year-round, except for Christmas Day and Boxing Day
- **Entry fees** Free to all RSPB members. Non-members £5, children £1.50, concessions £3, family ticket £10.
- **Accessibility** Most trails and hides are wheelchair-accessible. For more information see www.rspb.org.uk/reserves/guide/m/minsmere/accessibility.asp.
- **Dogs** No dogs are allowed on the nature trails or in hides, except assistance dogs

WILDLIFE BY SEASON

SPRING

Avocets and other breeding birds on the Scrape. Nightingales and other summer visitors will be singing. Bitterns 'boom' and Marsh Harriers display over the reedbeds, and Sand Martins are breeding in the purpose-built bank near the visitor centre.

SUMMER

Lots of dragonflies and other insects on the wing over much of the reserve. Migrating waders start to arrive. Best time to see reptiles on Dunwich heath, and summer mornings and evenings are often the best times to see mammals like Stoats, Weasels and deer.

AUTUMN

A good time to see family groups of Bearded Tits in the reedbeds. Red Deer stags rut in the woods and heaths. Migrating songbirds and waders are on the move – this is the best time of year to find a rare bird.

WINTER

Good numbers of wintering ducks and geese visit the Scrape, grazing marsh and meres. Snow Buntings may be found on the beach. Marsh Harriers gather to roost at dusk and Otters may be seen with luck.

What to look for

From the car park, the main nature trail first leads you into a small area of woodland. In spring you'll hear a riot of birdsong here – listen especially for the full-throated, fluty notes of Nightingales. The woodland soon opens up to marshland, and the path takes you alongside an expanse of reedbeds. Many of Minsmere's special birds live in this habitat. At any time of year you might see Marsh Harriers gliding low over the reeds – these big birds of prey the reedbeds for fish which, in turn, are food for Bitterns. Also look out for Reed Buntings, Bearded Tits and (in summer) Reed and Sedge Warblers. The reedbeds support a wealth of other wildlife including a healthy population of Water Voles and very rare wainscot moths, including the White-mantled Wainscot, a species whose entire UK population lives in reedbeds on the Suffolk coast.

Close to the coast lies Minsmere's famous Scrape, a

The heaths around Minsmere are home to sizeable – and readily observed – herds of Red Deer.

were once driven to extinction in Britain, and in 1971 Minsmere had the UK's only breeding pair. Conservationists here and elsewhere have worked hard to protect the harriers and their habitat and now about 360 pairs live in Britain, 5 per cent of them at Minsmere and nearby marshlands. Another rare bird of the reedbeds is the Bittern, a brown-streaked, shy heron – Minsmere is one of its strongholds and here the RSPB has specially managed collection of shallow, brackish lagoons with numerous small islands. The Scrape was first dug in the 1960s by Bert Axel, Minsmere's second – and perhaps most visionary – warden. The Scrape soon became home to another once-extinct British bird, the dazzling Avocet. About 100 noisy pairs now breed here – you'll recognise them by their black-and-white plumage, gangly legs and upturned bills. The Scrape also has breeding

Marsh Harriers can be seen year-round, but visit in spring to catch their stunning breeding display.

Mediterranean Gulls – smarter than the average gull with their white wings, jet-black heads and bright red bills. The Scrape is busy with visiting waders like Greenshanks and Spotted Redshanks in late summer and autumn, and attracts flocks of wildfowl in winter. Hides overlook the Scrape from all angles.

The main path continues around the Scrape, providing good views of the beach and dunes, reedbeds and marshy fields. The fields may be dotted with snowy-white Little Egrets and, in winter, you may see flocks of Wigeons and Teals and sometimes Bewick's Swans, with a chance of a hunting Short-eared Owl.

There is a handy bench by the beach, where you can sit and look out to sea. If you have a telescope it will be useful here to scan the sea for interesting birds such as divers or scoters, especially in winter. You may also find a seal bobbing in the shallows – both Common and Grey Seals live nearby. The beach itself sometimes attracts Snow Buntings in winter, while a few pairs of Little Terns breed in the summer (these rare birds' nest sites will be fenced off to prevent accidental damage).

The path returns to woodland, where you have the opportunity to return to the visitor centre or to continue towards the Bittern Hide, overlooking several small lagoons and reedbeds, and eventually you'll reach Island Mere, a deep lake with its own hide. The deeper water here means that you may see some different birds than on the shallow lagoons, including diving ducks like Goldeneye and Pochard in winter. Island Mere is the likeliest spot to see one of Minsmere's most exciting animals – the Otter. If you continue along the path you'll rejoin the minor road leading to the main entrance of the reserve, through a more extensive patch of woodland. Here you'll find the Canopy Hide, positioned 10 metres high in the treetops and accessed by several solid flights of stairs. Up here you could enjoy eye-level views of woodland birds.

WHEN TO VISIT

You will get a lot out of a visit to Minsmere at any time of year and any time of day. In terms of variety there is probably most to see in late spring and early summer, but the great flocks of wintering wildfowl and waders – and the birds of prey they attract – make a winter visit a memorable experience. Many birdwatchers like the early autumn when rare migrants from Europe and elsewhere may arrive unexpectedly – at Minsmere you never know what may turn up! Much of the reserve is quite exposed, and the reedbed birds tend to lay low on windy or rainy days, though you can still take to the hides and watch water birds on the Scrape. If you want maximum peace and tranquility try visiting on a weekday, early in the morning, before most of the visitors arrive!

If you turn left instead of right at the beach, you can walk on to the National Trust's reserve at Dunwich Heath, which adjoins Minsmere. Alternatively, drive on to the RSPB's reserve at Westleton Heath (grid ref TM 465701), which has similar habitat. The heathland is home to herds of Red Deer – the stags do noisy battle for their mating rights in autumn, with much clashing of mighty antlers. You'll see masses of heathland insects in spring and summer, including a host of dragonflies, moths and the lovely Silver-studded Blue butterflies, while heathland birds like Dartford Warblers sing and flit across the heather. Summer evenings up here are magical, with churring Nightjars vying with Nightingales for your attention.

How to get here

Grid ref./postcode TM 473672/IP17 3
By road Follow brown tourist signs from A12 at Yoxford (if coming from south) or Blythburgh (from north) to Westleton. From Westleton, take the Dunwich road, then take the first right, following brown tourist signs. Turn left at the crossroads, then follow the reserve entrance track, with speed bumps (20 mph limit). Turn left at Scotts Hall and the car park is a further half a mile away.

Prettiest of all our pigeon and dove species, the Turtle Dove is also the rarest. Look out for it resting on bare trees or telegraph poles in the area.

By public transport The nearest rail station is Darsham (five miles away) and the nearest calling point for scheduled buses is Leiston (four miles away). The new on-demand bus service Coastlink visits both villages – call 01728 833526 to book or visit www.suffolkcoastandheaths.org and search for Coastlink.

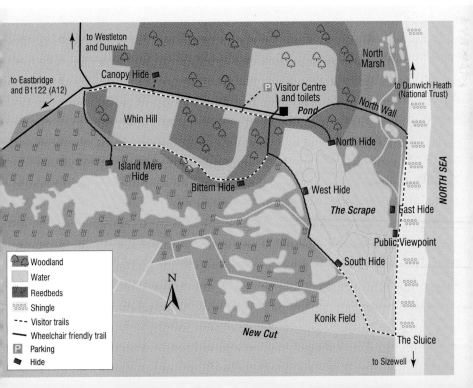

EAST ENGLAND

NORTH WARREN

SSSI, SPA, LNR, AONB, NATURA 2000

Close to the RSPB's flagship Minsmere reserve is this more low-key but no less exciting reserve of marshes, heathland, woodland and seashore. Bitterns, Marsh Harriers and Nightingales breed here, while winter brings important numbers of White-fronted Geese to the grazing marshes.

● Access, facilities, contact details and accessibility

North Warren is easily accessible on an extensive network of public footpaths – this is a reserve for quiet long walks in unspoilt surroundings.

- **Telephone** 01728 648281; **email** minsmere@rspb.org.uk; **web** www.rspb.org.uk/northwarren
- **Opening hours** At all times
- **Entry fees** Free, but donations to help continue the work here are welcome. The main car parks in Aldeburgh and Thorpeness are pay-and-display in summer
- **Accessibility** Most of the reserve is difficult for wheelchair users. An all-terrain wheelchair can be hired from Aldeburgh Tourist Information Centre.
- **Dogs** Only allowed on public footpaths and bridleways

What to look for

There is such a diversity of habitats here that it is worth planning to spend several hours exploring the trails and visiting the beach. You can also arrange to be taken on guided walks here by contacting the Minsmere visitor centre (see page 110).

The grazing marshes attract noisy breeding Lapwings and Redshanks in spring – the nesting Shovelers and Gadwalls are more discreet. By mid-spring the reedbed is alive with Reed and Sedge Warblers. The RSPB manages the reedbed

WILDLIFE BY SEASON

SPRING
Breeding birds include Bitterns, Marsh Harriers, warblers, Nightingales and waders.

SUMMER
Yellow-horned Poppies and Sea Peas flower on the shingle, heather blooms on the heath. Grayling and other butterflies are on the wing.

AUTUMN
Migrating waders and songbirds visit, including occasional rarities. Seabirds are on the move offshore.

WINTER
Many ducks and White-fronted Geese winter on the marsh. Many Red-throated Divers winter on the sea here.

to benefit Bitterns, so it is kept flooded from April to July to ensure that there are enough fish and other aquatic animals to sustain two pairs of Bitterns and their chicks. Look out for male Marsh Harriers passing food to their mates in mid-air.

A spring visit wouldn't be complete without a visit to the wooded and scrubby patches, where you can hear Nightingales delivering their matchless song from mid-April through into June. Another impressive songster, the Woodlark, can be heard on the heaths from as early as late January, while summer on the heaths means blooming heather and heathland insects on the wing.

Autumn is an exciting season, with northern waders and other migrants calling in, a few rarities among them most years. At sea, shearwaters and skuas may fly past, close inshore, when the wind is blowing the right way.

In winter, attention shifts to the grazing marsh, as flocks of wildfowl arrive. Among them are White-fronted Geese from the far north and, some years, you may also see a few Tundra

WHEN TO VISIT
To hear Nightingales and other songbirds, visit early in the day from mid-spring to mid-summer. The reserve is full of wildlife throughout the year.

Bean Geese. Internationally important numbers of Red-throated Divers spend winter at sea just off the Suffolk coast, and with them you may also see Scoters, auks and other seabirds.

How to get here
Grid ref./postcode TM 467576/IP16 4
By road Leave the A12 on the A1094 for Aldeburgh. Follow this to Aldeburgh town centre. After passing the church, go straight on at the crossroads, then left onto Thorpe Road. Soon after leaving the town, there is a large pay-and-display car park on the right.
By public transport Saxmundham is the nearest station. Buses (First Buses service 64) run regularly between Saxmundham and Aldeburgh.

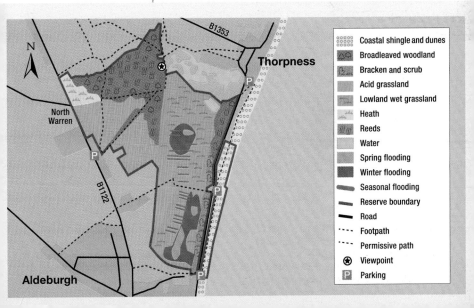

OUSE WASHES

SSSI, SPA, pSAC, RAMSAR, NATURA 2000

These days fenland is all flat fields of dark soil and endless moody skyscapes. In a few special and unspoilt places, like this reserve, it's about grazing pasture that in winter is transformed into gleaming expanses of floodland, alive with flocks of ducks, waders and wild swans.

● Access, facilities, contact details and accessibility

There are 10 hides along the reserve boundary. You can arrange group visits and guided walks.

- **Telephone** 01354 680 212; **email** ouse.washes@rspb.org.uk; **web** www.rspb.org.uk/ousewashes
- **Opening hours** The hides are open at all times. The visitor centre is open from 9am to 5pm (not Christmas Day and Boxing Day).
- **Entry fees** Free, but donations are welcome
- **Accessibility** The visitor centre and Welches Dam hide are accessible, though the path to the latter is steep in places
- **Dogs** Only allowed on public footpaths and bridleways

What to look for

From the car park there is one short nature trail, which ends at the first hide approximately 300m away. From here there are a further nine hides set out at intervals in a line along the reserve boundary – the furthest is 1.8 miles away. Look out for Tree Sparrows at the visitor

centre feeding station while you're here.

Breeding birds are numerous, and with the visitor centre and 10 hides from which to view their breeding grounds you should see some, if not all, of the special species that nest here, including Lapwings, Redshanks, Garganeys,

WILDLIFE BY SEASON

SPRING

Waders and wildfowl nest on the reserve, and passage migrant waders visit, including hundreds of Icelandic Black-tailed Godwits.

SUMMER

You'll see ducklings and cygnets in the ditches, numerous dragonflies, and butterflies over the fields.

AUTUMN

Wintering wildfowl start to arrive by mid-autumn, with flocks of Bewick's and Whooper Swans growing daily.

WINTER

Some 100,000 waders, ducks and swans may be on the reserve. Short-eared Owls and Hen Harriers patrol the fields.

Snipes, Shelducks, Gadwalls and Shovelers. Icelandic Black-tailed Godwits visit on migration.

As the year progresses, growing grass provides cover for the small chicks, hiding breeding birds in summer. You could still easily see Yellow Wagtails, Kingfishers, Grey Herons stalking frogs or fish, and hunting Marsh Harriers in the day and Barn Owls in the evenings.

By mid-autumn, the first of the wintering swans will be back on the washes. Their numbers build steadily and they are joined by many species of dabbling ducks, as well as Lapwings, Golden Plovers and other waders.

How to get here

Grid ref./postcode TL 471860/ PE15 8

By road From the south and east head to Ely, take the A142 to Chatteris and follow signs to Manea. Entering the village, turn right at the RSPB sign towards Welches Dam, continuing to the signposted car park.

WHEN TO VISIT

This reserve is at its best in winter into early spring.

By public transport Manea station is 3 miles from the reserve and is served by two trains a day on the Peterborough–Stansted Airport line. Buses from local towns including Chatteris, St Ives and March also serve the village.

A TALE OF TWO SWANS

The Ouse Washes is one of the best places in the UK to see all three of our swan species. We all know Mute Swans from our local park lake, but the other two, Bewick's and Whooper, are much less familiar and can be difficult to tell apart. Both have black-and-yellow bills, but the Whooper has more yellow than black, the opposite with Bewick's. Also, the Whooper is a bigger bird, as long-necked as a Mute Swan, while Bewick's is smaller and shorter-necked.

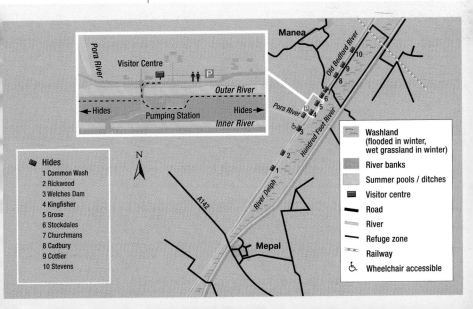

Hides
1 Common Wash
2 Rickwood
3 Welches Dam
4 Kingfisher
5 Grose
6 Stockdales
7 Churchmans
8 Cadbury
9 Cottier
10 Stevens

Washland (flooded in winter, wet grassland in winter)
River banks
Summer pools / ditches
Visitor centre
Road
River
Refuge zone
Railway
Wheelchair accessible

SNETTISHAM

SSSI, SPA, SAC, RAMSAR, AONB, NATURA 2000

This RSPB reserve is tucked in the corner of north-west Norfolk on the edge of the Wash. Whether it's wild geese streaming across a technicolour sunrise, or waders swirling over the mudflats as the tide rolls in, Snettisham is all about spectacular moments and breathtaking grandeur.

●Access, facilities, contact details and accessibility

The nature trail is 3.5 miles long, and passes four hides. There are three sets of steps to negotiate but otherwise the trail is pushchair-friendly. You can book guided walks and group visits.

- **Telephone** 01485 542 689 (call 01485 210779 to book guided walks); **email** snettisham@rspb.org.uk; **web** www.rspb.org.uk/snettisham
- **Opening hours** Open at all times – note the car park has a height restriction of 2.2 metres
- **Entry fees** Free, though donations are welcome
- **Accessibility** Disabled visitors may drive to the first hide by arrangement. Two hides are accessible.
- **Dogs** Only allowed on public footpaths and bridleways

What to look for

It is difficult to overstate the importance of the Wash for wildlife. The vast mudflats exposed when the tide retreats are teeming with invertebrate life, which in turn attracts masses of wading birds to feed, especially in autumn. At Snettisham, the lagoons provide a retreat for many of these birds when high tide covers the mud, and from the hides you can watch them at very close quarters. The famous Pink-footed Geese of the Wash roost here, rather than feed, but Snettisham is the perfect spot to watch them as they set off at dawn for the sugar beet fields inland. Around full moons their habits are more erratic.

The reserve is lively in spring and summer,

WILDLIFE BY SEASON

SPRING
Breeding water birds are establishing nest sites on the lagoons and beach. Migrant waders and songbirds call in.

SUMMER
Yellow-horned Poppy and Viper's Bugloss are in full colourful bloom. Migrant Knots flock on the Wash.

AUTUMN
Large flocks of waders feed out on the Wash and take refuge on the lagoons at big high tides. Thrushes and finches migrate overhead.

WINTER
The lagoons attracts many ducks, while vast flocks of Pink-footed Geese roost on the Wash overnight and flocks of Snow Buntings feed on the beach.

especially in the Common Tern and Black-headed Gull colonies on the lagoons. Mediterranean Gulls and Avocets also nest here, with Ringed Plovers and Oystercatchers nesting on the shingle beach.

Late summer and autumn brings the waders back to the Wash. You'll see thousands of Knots and many others, including Bar-tailed Godwits, Grey Plovers and Dunlins, out on the mudflats. As the tide comes in, the birds move in waves, closer and closer to view. If the tide is big enough, the birds must abandon the mud and many wait it out on the lagoon shores.

Wildfowl numbers build in winter – the reserve attracts important numbers of Brent and Pink-footed Geese, Gadwalls, Shelducks and many others.

How to get here

Grid ref./postcode TF 650328/ PE31 7
By road The reserve is clearly signposted down Beach Road from the A149 Snettisham and Dersingham bypass.
By public transport The nearest

WHEN TO VISIT
Visit at high tide in autumn to see waders roosting in front of the hides. To see the Pink-footed Geese leaving their roost, you'll need to visit at dawn on a winter day.

railway station is Kings Lynn. Buses from Kings Lynn stop 2 miles away. Contact Traveline East Anglia for all public transport enquiries, tel: 0871 200 2233.

THE GOLDEN GEESE
A winter dawn, and from out on the darkened Wash comes the hubbub of thousands of voices. As the sky becomes streaked with fiery orange, the voices suddenly rise in pitch and pace as the first birds take to the wing. They come overhead in strings and 'V's, a few at first but soon in huge skeins, all constantly giving their wild, musical calls as they swarm over against the glowing dawn sky. Snettisham's Pink-footed Geese truly put on a show to rival anything on earth.

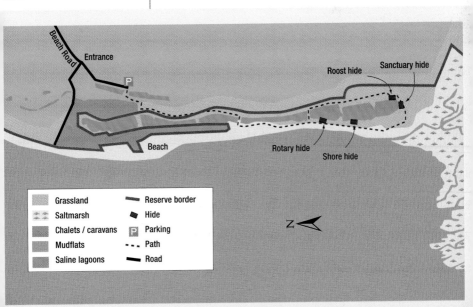

Grassland
Saltmarsh
Chalets / caravans
Mudflats
Saline lagoons

Reserve border
Hide
Parking
Path
Road

Beach Road
Entrance
Beach
Roost hide
Sanctuary hide
Rotary hide
Shore hide

EAST ENGLAND

SOUTH ESSEX MARSHES

The South Essex Marshes are on the north coast of the Thames Estuary and lie within its flood-plain. Here the RSPB are creating and protecting a large area of connected wetland habitat. Work to improve habitats and create visitor facilities at West Canvey Marsh is just beginning while Vange Marsh has well-established wildlife populations and good visitor facilities.

● Access, facilities, contact details and accessibility

Vange Marshes has a mile-long nature trail, with three viewing mounds overlooking the fresh marsh and a viewing screen which overlooks the newly created saline lagoon. There is an RSPB Visitor Centre in the nearby council owned Wat Tyler Country Park.

- **Telephone** 01268 559158; **web** www.rspb.org.uk/vangemarshes, www.rspb.org.uk/westcanveymarshes
- **Opening hours** The reserve is open at all times, the visitor centre 10am–5pm from April to September, 10am–4pm from October to March.
- **Entry fees** Free
- **Accessibility** The Vange Marsh trail is not wheelchair-accessible. Wat Tyler Country Park has good disabled access.
- **Dogs** Only allowed on public footpaths and bridleways

What to look for

Coastal grassland and saltmarsh is a scarce and valuable wildlife habitat, full of life at all times of year. In spring, waders dominate the scene here. Northbound migrants often stop off at the lagoons on Vange Marsh, including handsome red breeding-plumaged Black-tailed Godwits, while Avocets and Little Ringed Plovers are preparing to breed here. The damp grassland and saltmarsh has breeding Redshanks and Lapwings. Skylarks nest on the drier grassland,

WILDLIFE BY SEASON

SPRING

Breeding waders display over the grassland. Water Voles are breeding. Black-tailed Godwits and other northern waders stop off on migration.

SUMMER

Hobbies hawk overhead. Marbled White butterflies and Scarce Emerald damselflies are among the many insects around.

AUTUMN

Migrating waders visit the lagoons. A good time to see Bearded Tits.

WINTER

Teals, Wigeons and other wildfowl overwinter on the reserve. A good time for farmland birds with Yellowhammers and Corn Buntings feeding together.

with Whitethroats in the scrub. Common Terns join the lagoon waders in mid-spring.

In summertime, there are many insects on the wing including Marbled White and Essex Skipper butterflies. Swallows and House Martins hawk for insects over the marsh while in pursuit of the larger dragonflies are Hobbies, deftly swiping and dismembering their prey on the wing. The Scarce Emerald damselfly is one of the most attractive members of its group and is easily seen here. Adders bask in sunny spots on the drier grassland, while Water Voles are present around the reeds and ditches.

At West Canvey Marsh, the tidal creeks attract Knots, Dunlins, Oystercatchers and Black-tailed Godwits in autumn, and Little Egrets – present all year round – are most numerous at this time of year. As the autumn waders move on, winter wildfowl arrive. Large flocks of Wigeons and Teals lead the way, feeding on the lagoons and damp meadows. Look out for Barn and Short-eared Owls, and Peregrines and Merlins.

WHEN TO VISIT

With breeding and migrating waders, Hobbies and insects in summer and wildfowl over winter, there is something to see all year, and time of day isn't important.

How to get here

Grid ref./postcode TQ 731871/ SS16 4UH

By road Turn off the A13 at the Pitsea Junction and follow signs for Wat Tyler Country Park. Park your car in the car park there and walk back along Pitsea Hall Lane to the railway crossing. Just beyond this take the gravel footpath on the left, over the railway line into Vange Marsh. Alternatively, for quicker access, you could park at Pitsea railway station.

By public transport Pitsea is the nearest station. From here walk straight down the entrance road with the car park on your left. Cross the road at the T-junction, continuing straight ahead, and take the public footpath. Follow the path over the railway line to Vange Marsh.

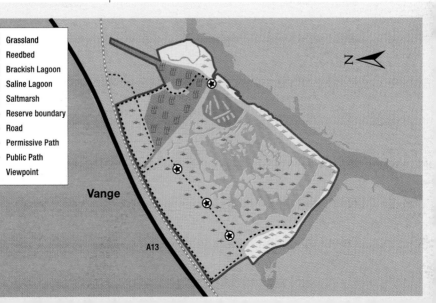

Grassland
Reedbed
Brackish Lagoon
Saline Lagoon
Saltmarsh
Reserve boundary
Road
Permissive Path
Public Path
Viewpoint

Vange

A13

EAST ENGLAND

STOUR ESTUARY

SSSI, SPA, RAMSAR, NATURA 2000

A woodland walk leads to a wide expanse of prime estuarine habitat at this attractive reserve on the south side of the River Stour. Nightingales sing and flowers bloom in the woods in spring, while winter brings masses of waders and wildfowl to the estuary.

● Access, facilities, contact details and accessibility

Guided walks can be arranged in this interesting reserve, and there is a picnic area.
- **Telephone** 01473 328006; **email** stourestuary@rspb.org.uk; **web** www.rspb.org.uk/stourestuary
- **Opening hours** Trails are always open but the car park is locked from 7pm (or dusk) until 6am
- **Entry fees** Free, but non-members are invited to make a voluntary donation
- **Accessibility** The two picnic tables are not built to disabled standard, but are still suitable for wheelchair access. The woodland trail is accessible during dry periods.
- **Dogs** Not allowed in Copperas Wood, or onto foreshore. Dogs are allowed in Stour Wood, and along public rights of way elsewhere.

What to look for

From the car park, you can walk a short circular trail through the woods, or choose a longer walk to view the estuary and visit one or all three of the hides that overlook it.

Springtime is magical in Stour Wood and Copperas Wood, with the former full of Wood

Anemones and primroses, and the latter sprouting a luxuriant carpet of Bluebells. The resident woodland birds, including Bullfinches and Great Spotted Woodpeckers, are joined by summer migrants in spring, with Chiffchaffs and Blackcaps singing from late March and the star of the

WILDLIFE BY SEASON

SPRING

The woods are full of spring flowers from late March. Nightingales arrive mid-April.

SUMMER

White Admiral butterflies fly from July into August, while all summer is great for dragonflies and damselflies.

AUTUMN

The woods are stunning in their autumn colours. Estuary waders start to arrive.

WINTER

Parties of tits and finches roam the woods. On the estuary there are important numbers of Knots, Dunlins, Redshanks, Brent Geese, Pintails and Ringed and Grey Plovers.

show, the Nightingale, arriving mid-April. The resident Stock Doves are occasionally joined by a few Turtle Doves by May. If you visit early in the day, you may be lucky and see a sleepy Badger returning to its sett.

The woodland is good for butterflies, including White Admiral and Brown Argus, and many moths, attracted by sunny clearings produced by coppicing. Dragonflies and damselflies breed in the reserve ponds.

The estuary can be quiet through summer, but as autumn advances so flocks of wading birds start to build, including more than 5,000 each of Knots and Dunlins, hundreds of god-wits, Grey and Golden Plovers, Curlews and Redshanks, and a few other species, like Green-shanks. Some of these stay for winter, when they are joined by large numbers of Brent Geese, Wigeons, Teals and Pintails.

How to get here

Grid ref./postcode TM 190310/ CO12 5
By road From Manningtree

WHEN TO VISIT

Pick an early morning in spring to hear Nightingales and other woodland birds. The estuary birdlife is best in autumn and winter – high tide gives the best views.

follow B1352 through Mistley into Bradfield. At the Strangers Home public house, turn left onto Harwich Road (signposted Pamsey, Harwich). Continue on B1352, turn left to the reserve car park at the brown tourist board sign. Tall vehicles can park by the roadside west of the car park.
By public transport The nearest station is Wrabness – take the main road through the village until the next right-hand bend, then take the public footpath (which is a surfaced track) into the wood. After about 100m, turn right at the next T-junction. Continue on this main circular trail until you arrive at the car park/information point. Buses running between Harwich and Colchester via Manningtree will stop at the entrance to the woods if it is safe.

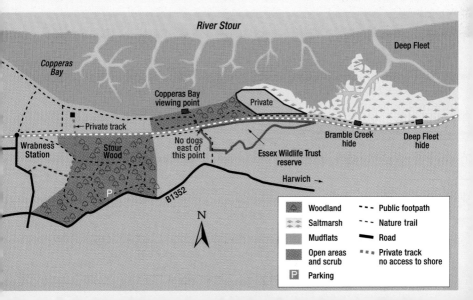

EAST ENGLAND

STRUMPSHAW FEN

SSSI, NNR, SPA, SAC, RAMSAR

In the floodplains of the River Yare, in the heart of Broadland, this beautiful reserve is a haven for all kinds of wetland wildlife, and is the flagship reserve among a string of RSPB sites in the area. All Broadland habitats are here, with acres of reedbed and open water, wet meadowland with numerous small pools, ditches and boggy patches, and wet woodland. See Bitterns, Marsh Harriers, Cetti's Warblers, the wonderful Swallowtail butterfly and much more as you enjoy a walk through a highly distinctive corner of Britain. Spring and summer are especially exciting but the sweeping Broadland skies and scenery are always unforgettable.

● Access, facilities, contact details and accessibility

The visitor centre incorporates a hide with a viewing platform. There are two other hides (including a tower hide giving far-reaching views across the fen). Events here include guided walks and fun activities for children, but this is also a reserve where you can enjoy a quiet walk along the two nature trails (the two trails combined provide a 3-mile circuit). The Meadow Trail is open in summer only.

- **Telephone** 01603 715191; **email** strumpshaw@rspb.org.uk; **web** www.rspb.org.uk/strumpshawfen
- **Opening hours** Open from dawn until dusk every day (except Christmas Day)
- **Entry fees** Non-members: £2.50 adults; 50p children; £1.50 concessions and £5 families. RSPB members: free.
- **Accessibility** There are wheelchair accessible picnic tables, a disabled toilet and a wheelchair-accessible viewing platform at the reception hide. Accessibility of trails varies with weather – wheelchair users are advised to contact the reserve to check trail conditions before visiting.
- **Dogs** Not allowed, except registered assistance dogs

WILDLIFE BY SEASON

SPRING

You'll hear Cuckoos and warblers singing in the fen, perhaps also Bitterns 'booming', and you may see Marsh Harriers performing their stunning aerial courtship displays. Listen for drumming Great and Lesser Spotted Woodpeckers in the wood.

SUMMER

From mid-May look out for Swallowtail butterflies visiting fenland flowers, and Norfolk Hawkers among the many dragon-flies. The meadow has several species of orchids and many other flowers.

AUTUMN

The best time of year to see Bearded Tits. Marsh Harriers start to form their communal winter roosts. Migrating waders may stop off at the pools, there's also a good chance of seeing an Osprey on migration.

WINTER

Bittern numbers increase as a few continental immigrants arrive. Hen Harriers may join the roosting Marsh Harriers. Many wildfowl gather on the reedbed pools. Look out for Otters from the hides from autumn into winter.

What to look for

Strumpshaw Fen is divided into two nearly equal halves – to the west is the reedbed and open water, eastwards the wet pasture with patches of woodland. The visitor centre sits neatly between the two sides, and from here you can take the fen trail or the shorter woodland trail.

Spring is a great time to visit the reserve, as much of its birdlife will be making itself seen and heard in the run-up to the breeding season. Bitterns breed here, and the males also pass food to females mid-air, a skilled manouvre requiring great skill and timing from the bird underneath. By testing males' ability to find a suitable food item as well as their aerial agility, the females are perhaps assessing their potential partners' ability to provide for a nest of chicks. The tower hide is a great place from which to watch them.

In bushes around the fen, listen for the loud, exuberant song of the Cetti's Warbler – a

Marsh Harriers are particularly handsome and colourful birds of prey, decked out in cream, black, silver-blue and rich red-brown.

will be giving their bizarre 'booms' from March. It closely resembles the sound produced by blowing across the top of a half-filled bottle – airy but deeply resonant. It carries over a couple of miles – male Bitterns often pair with multiple females so they need to make themselves heard over a wide area.

Marsh Harriers court one another with dance rather than song. Not only do males indulge in an aerial sky dance, with the male rising and falling, but they species that only colonised Britain in the 1970s but which has thrived in many suitable sites, including Strumpshaw. You'll need patience to spot one as it creeps through tangled undergrowth, almost like a mouse. Summer is also probably the best time to see Kingfishers, especially when they are busy feeding young.

One of the most celebrated Strumpshaw species is a large and beautiful butterfly – the Swallowtail. This species is

Not all introduced animals bring unbridled disaster. The Chinese Water Deer seems content to keep a fairly low profile and is rarely seen anywhere outside the Norfolk Broads.

confined to Broadland in the UK, laying its eggs only upon milk parsley plants. On sunny days in late May and June you could see dozens of Swallowtails – wait by some suitably enticing-looking flowers (Ragged Robin is a favourite) if you want to see one rest and feed. Summer also means dragonflies – among the 20 or so species found here is the Norfolk Hawker, one of the UK's largest and scarcest species. More butterflies and diurnal moths patrol the meadows, visiting the many flowers that grow here. The flowery display includes six species of orchid – the Southern Marsh Orchids are particularly bright and eye-catching.

Migrating birds of prey are a feature of autumn, with Ospreys calling in most years. Hobbies are regularly seen through the summer, but depart for warmer climes in autumn. Two pairs of Barn Owls nest on the reserve and are easiest to see over the meadows on summer evenings. Migrating waders may visit the reedbed pools, and look out for Bearded Tits picking their way along the bases of the reed stems. Little Egrets are commonest in late summer and autumn.

In winter, there are usually more Bitterns on the reserve, especially if cold weather on the near continent has frozen significant areas of wetland. If you are keen to see one, wait in one of the hides – the Fen Hide is a good place to pick out flying birds, while at ground level you may get good views of one feeding at the reeds' edge. Autumn and winter are the likeliest times to see an Otter from one of the hides.

The open water and the wet meadows both attract wildfowl in winter. You'll see Shovelers, Teals and Gadwalls on the pools, with Pochards and Tufted Ducks diving in deep water.

As the light fades on winter afternoons, you could see Marsh Harriers flying in to their communal roosts – ten or more birds may gather in the same area of reeds. Sometimes they are joined by a few Hen Harriers.

WHEN TO VISIT

This is a reserve with much to offer throughout the year, and time of day is not generally important, though you'll need to visit near dusk in winter to see the roosting harriers and Starlings (if present).

How to get here

Grid ref./postcode TG 341065/NR13 4

By road The reserve is best aproached from the village of Brundall which lies east of Norwich just off the A47. From the A47 roundabout, drive through Brundall and continue on the same road out towards Strumpshaw. Soon after you pass the Strumpshaw sign, turn right into Stone Road, and immediately right again into Low Road. The reserve car park is 500m down Low Road on the right. The route is signed with brown signs from Brundall.

By public transport A number of trains on the Norwich to Great Yarmouth and Lowestoft (Wherry Lines) services call at Buckenham station by request at the weekend. Four trains each way call on Sundays and public holidays, one on Saturdays. Strumpshaw Fen is about a mile away, via quiet lanes. On other days, the closest station is Brundall (1.4 miles from the reserve) on the same line. From the station walk up the hill (Station Road) towards Brundall village. At the main road turn right and walk through Brundall. Continue under the bridge towards Strumpshaw. Soon after you pass the Strumpshaw sign, turn right into Stone Road, and immediately right again into Low Road. The reserve is 500m down Low Road on the right.

The Southern Marsh Orchid is an eye-catching glamorous species with its overblown and bright pink flower spikes.

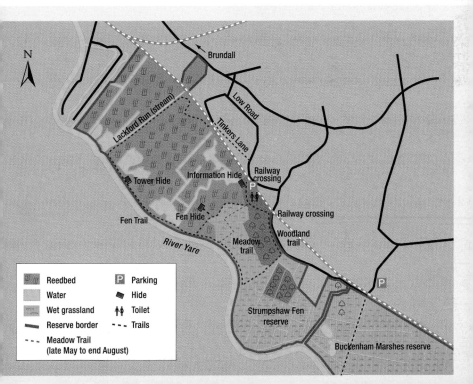

Legend:

- Reedbed
- Water
- Wet grassland
- Reserve border
- Meadow Trail (late May to end August)
- P Parking
- Hide
- Toilet
- Trails

Swallowtail

SURLINGHAM CHURCH MARSH
NNR

Surlingham Church Marsh lies on the River Yare, upstream of the larger reserve of Strumpshaw Fen, and has much in common with its neighbour. The reserve consists mainly of reedbed and open pools, and you can explore it from the circular nature trail in a couple of hours – this is therefore a good place to visit if you're in the area but only have a short time spare.

● Access, facilities, contact details and accessibility

This small reserve gives you the opportunity to enjoy a delightful circular walk and see some fenland flora and fauna within a compact area – the trail is a mile long.

- **Telephone** 01603 715191; **web:** www.rspb.org.uk/surlingham
- **Opening hours** Open at all times
- **Entry fees** Free, but donations are welcome
- **Accessibility** The trail is not suitable for wheelchairs or pushchairs
- **Dogs** Only allowed on public footpaths and bridleways

What to look for

The marsh lies on the south of the river, and the trail loops around alongside the river and then back between the reedbeds and adjacent farmland. Come in spring to hear a chorus of warbler song from the reedbeds. That harbinger of spring, the Cuckoo, is likely to be close at hand – the males calling to attract females, and the females lurking and waiting for a chance to lay an egg in an unattended Reed Warbler nest.

You could spot a Marsh Harrier cruising over the reeds. The males are distinctive with ginger-brown, cream and blue-grey plumage, but the

EAST ENGLAND

WILDLIFE BY SEASON

SPRING

Warblers sing and Marsh Harriers 'skydance' over the reeds. Cuckoos call and chase each other over the reserve.

SUMMER

Fenland flowers are in bloom, attracting butterflies. Hobbies hawk after dragonflies overhead.

AUTUMN

Migrating waders visit the pools, and as water levels rise the winter wildfowl start to arrive.

WINTER

Duck numbers increase. Harriers may form winter roosts in the reedbeds, and this is the best time to look for Bitterns.

females are mostly dark and you could mistake one for a crow at first glance. Kingfishers are often seen here at all times of year, and Otters visit regularly.

The fenland flowers make a colourful display in summer, with Yellow Flag Iris, Bogbean and Purple Loosestrife among the more striking species. Butterflies including a few Swallowtails visit the flowers, while a variety of cryptically patterned moths live in the reeds and sedges. By mid spring, the first dragonflies and damselflies are on the wing – in summer look out for the brown-bodied and green-eyed Norfolk Hawker.

The River Yare, while offering more good wildlife habitat, is a potential source of pollution to the reserve pools. The solution the RSPB has employed is to isolate the reserve from the river and to control water levels using sluice gates. In winter, water levels are allowed to rise, and the resultant flooding means more wildfowl are attracted to the reserve. Shovelers and Gadwalls work their way across the ponds, while the shyer Teals tend to

WHEN TO VISIT

There is wildlife interest here throughout the year, and time of day is not critical.

stick to the edges. With luck, you could see a Bittern in winter, perhaps stepping out from a curtain of reeds to stalk a fish, or flying ponderously overhead. Water Rails are present year-round, and they too are easier to see in winter, or listen for their shrill, piglet-like call.

How to get here

Grid ref./postcode TG 304066/ NR14 7

By road From Surlingham village centre, head west via Walnut Hill for about half a mile, then turn right into Church Lane. A footpath leads directly down to the reserve from the church.

By public transport From Norwich, bus service 001 goes to Surlingham village, Monday to Saturday. It is operated by Anglian Coaches, from All Saints Green, John Lewis layby.

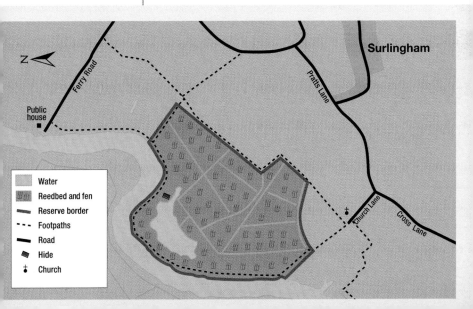

EAST ENGLAND

THE LODGE SSSI

It is most fitting that the RSPB headquarters should nestle within a beautiful nature reserve. The building itself, a grand Victorian house, is where many RSPB staff carry out their work, while the nearby 'Swiss Cottage' has been converted into a visitor centre. The house sits within spectacular landscaped wildlife-friendly gardens that are open to visitors. The surrounding land is mainly broadleaved woodland and some conifers with ancient fragments of heath, but since 2005 a heathland restoration project has been underway, the aim being to return one square kilometre of the area to new heathland to improve the reserve's biodiversity.

● Access, facilities, contact details and accessibility

At the shop and information point you can buy hot drinks and a variety of merchandise. You can borrow binoculars, or explorer rucksacks and other items to help children enjoy their visit. There is a full programme of events and guided walks for all ages.

- **Telephone** 01767 680541; **email** thelodgereserve@rspb.org.uk; **web** www.rspb.org.uk/thelodge
- **Opening hours** The reserve is open from 9am–9pm (or sunset when earlier). The shop is open from 9am–5pm on weekdays and 10am–5pm at weekends and Bank Holidays.
- **Entry fees** Non-members £4 per motor vehicle, members and those only visiting the shop park may enter the reserve free. Please obtain a ticket in the shop or welcome hut, and display it in your vehicle.
- **Accessibility** The garden hide and shop are accessible by wheelchair. The trails on the reserve may be problematic as they are steep in places – contact the reserve for more information.
- **Dogs** Only allowed on the bridleway, not on other paths due to the sensitive nature of wildlife and presence of sheep

WILDLIFE BY SEASON

SPRING
Woodland birds are singing (and woodpeckers drumming), and Bluebells bloom on the woodland floor. Buzzards circle above and Cuckoos call from mid-April. From mid-May the gardens are filled with flowering azaleas and rhododendrons.

SUMMER
Grass Snakes and Common Lizards are active on the heath. Many insects are on the wing – Hobbies cruise around deftly catching dragonflies over the heath. July is the best month for butterflies, and in late summer the heather comes into bloom. The Lodge gardens are in full flower.

AUTUMN
Jays fly overhead carrying acorns to bury. Migrating birds of prey and flocks of winter thrushes fly overhead. The wood is colourful with changing leaves and emerging fungi.

WINTER
The feeders are busy with tits and finches. Winter thrushes flock to clear the bushes of berries. Snowdrops flower as spring approaches.

What to look for

From the visitor car park, you have a choice of trails leading you through the woods, around the heath, or to the gardens. If you follow signs to the Meadow hide, an easy path will take you to a hide overlooking some bird feeders, and small pools that attract drinking and bathing birds.

Springtime is delightful here, with woodland flowers blooming and birdsong everywhere. Listen out for the drumming of Great Spotted Woodpeckers – the

woodland include Coal Tits and Goldcrests. In some years the Scots Pines attract Crossbills. You may hear the plopping of discarded cones before seeing the birds themselves.

Green Woodpeckers favour more open ground, although they still require good-sized trees to nest in. These handsome birds are voracious ant-eaters, lapping up the insects directly from the anthills with their long, sticky tongues. They have quickly colonised the new

Hobbies spend long spells on the wing on sunny days, chasing insects and devouring them in flight. With patience you may see one land in a tree for a breather.

rapid staccato beats can be hard to differentiate and the resulting sound may remind you of a creaky branch. As well as drumming, the woodpeckers also indulge in noisy territorial chases.

The deciduous woodlands hold many other birds, with summer visitors like Blackcaps, Garden Warblers and Chiffchaffs joining them in summer. The conifers are less bird-friendly, but species that do live in this kind of

heathland, and you're likely to spot their striking yellow rear ends as they fly by in deeply undulating flight. Whitethroats also prefer the more open spaces.

The newly planted heathland should in due course attract birds such as Woodlarks, Dartford Warblers and Nightjars to breed here when it becomes mature. All three have been seen on the reserve since the heathland restoration began, so hopefully they will be breeding

The Natterjack Toad is smaller, a bit more colourful and considerably noisier than the Common Toad, and prefers drier terrain.

here before too long. Already thoroughly exploiting the opportunity to bask in the heath's open sunny patches are Grass Snakes and Common Lizards. Both are shy animals, and very sensitive to the human footfall, so scan the path ahead and step lightly to give yourself the best chance of seeing them. The reserve also has a small colony of reintroduced Natterjack Toads, the UK's most threatened amphibian.

From the hide, you could see any of the local woodland birds having a drink or a bath. Sparrowhawks enjoy prolonged and vigorous bathes, although their presence will of course scare off other birds. Seed-eating birds tend to be thirstier than insectivores, so the birds you're most likely to see here are members of the finch family although any species could come for a cool bath on a hot day.

WHEN TO VISIT

Spring and summer are the best seasons to visit this reserve, and to see the Lodge gardens at their best. Visit early on a spring day to enjoy the dawn chorus in the wood and on the heath. To see insects and reptiles, pick a sunny summer day and don't come too early.

The gardens around the RSPB headquarters are an inspirational blend of diverse ornamental plants and wildlife-friendly features. One of the latter is the pond in the formal gardens – once a swimming pool – which has actually attracted a Kingfisher! The flowers attract many butterflies in spring and summer, while the birdfeeders become increasingly important to birds as autumn progresses and natural food becomes harder to find.

Follow signs to Galley Hill to see the banks and ditches of an ancient hill fort. Buzzards fly overhead regularly, but in autumn there's a chance of seeing the much rarer Honey Buzzard, moving between summer and winter quarters. This is a good spot to observe migration of thrushes and finches too, with parties of Redwings dropping in to denude any berry bushes they spot. Finches like Siskins may be seen in good numbers in some winters.

The coldest months do tend to be quieter here. One bird that's hard to see is the Woodcock, a portly relative of the Snipe with beautifully patterned brown plumage that enables it to forage on the woodland floor unseen by all but the keenest eye. Of course, if you get too close the Woodcock's nerve will break and it will spring into flight. There are mammals here as well. Around you will be signs of Mole and Rabbit activity, and if you are lucky you may catch sight of a Muntjac Deer.

The RSPB moved its headquarters to the Lodge in 1961 – the society's sixth premises since their first office was established in 1907. The investment of time and effort put into the gardens and the reserve would seem to indicate that no further moves are likely for the foreseeable future, making the building and its surrounding reserve truly 'home' for the society. With the 50-year anniversary fast approaching, what better way to celebrate than to visit the reserve and see how the RSPB handles conservation on its own doorstep?

How to get here

Grid ref./postcode TL 191485/ SG19 2
By road From Sandy town centre, take the B1042 Potton road, passing the railway station and cemetery on your right. After 1.2 miles (1.75 km), at the top of the hill, turn right into the RSPB marked entrance. Toilets, picnic area and bicycle stand are just outside the 'Swiss Cottage' style gatehouse, which houses the shop.
By public transport The nearest railway station is in Sandy, on the King's Cross to Peterborough main line, less than a mile from the reserve

One of the species the RSPB hoped to attract to The Lodge's restored heathlands is the Woodlark, and in April 2009 one was heard singing on the reserve.

entrance. From the railway station, turn towards the main road (B1042 to Potton). Follow the path next to the road, past the cemetery, and continue to a gate at the bottom of the hill, where RSPB signs welcome you onto the reserve.

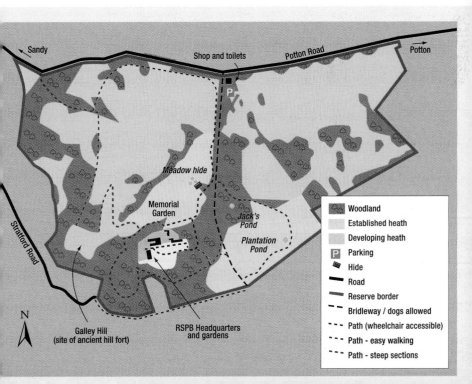

EAST ENGLAND

Avocets

TITCHWELL MARSH

SPA, SAC, NATURA 2000

One of the RSPB's best-known reserves and star of several television wildlife programmes, Titchwell Marsh offers the kind of wildlife-watching that could convert those once disinterested into enthusiastic naturalists for life. Every season offers something different, and the mix of habitats – from damp woodland, grazing marsh and reedbed to saline lagoon, foreshore and open sea – means that variety is always on the cards. The reserve offers a real taste of wilderness with its far-reaching views and dramatic Norfolk skies, but you're never too far from the comforts of the visitor centre with all its well-appointed facilities. Titchwell is a wonderful place for a family day out as well as for prolonged appreciation of the best of British wildlife.

● Access, facilities, contact details and accessibility

The reserve has three nature trails and three hides. From the shop you can buy hot and cold drinks and snacks, and browse an extensive stock of binoculars, books, garden bird supplies and gifts. You can hire binoculars here too if required. The reserve runs a busy programme of walks, talks and courses.

- **Telephone** 01485 210779; **email** titchwell@rspb.org.uk; **web** www.rspb.org.uk/titchwellmarsh
- **Opening hours** The reserve is always open. The centre is open from 9.30am–5pm (9.30am–4pm from mid-November to mid-February).
- **Entry fees** There is a facility charge of £4 per car for non-members
- **Accessibility** All three hides have disabled access and viewing facilities and all paths are hard surfaced. The disabled toilets are located in the car park along with eight specified parking bays.
- **Dogs** Only permitted on the west bank path, which is a public right of way. They must be kept on a lead and under close control.

WILLDIFE BY SEASON

SPRING

Newly arrived migrants such as Wheatears and Sand Martins are on the reserve, migrating Spotted Redshanks and other waders visit the lagoons. You may hear Bitterns booming or see Marsh Harriers 'skydancing'.

SUMMER

Summer Avocets are nesting on the lagoon, and male Marsh Harriers are out hunting for their families. Dragonflies and damselflies are abundant, with almost 20 species on the wing here every year.

AUTUMN

Waders are on their way back south again and, with the year's young birds on the wing, numbers and variety are even higher than in spring. Bearded Tits are often easy to see from the Island hide.

WINTER

Masses of Brent Geese gather in the fields and visit the lagoons, joined by many species of ducks including Pintail and Goldeneye. At sea, rafts of Common Scoters are sometimes seen, along with Eiders and Long-tailed Ducks. At dusk you may see Barn Owls hunting and Pink-footed Geese heading for their roosts.

What to look for

The habitats at Titchwell along the main beach trail grade smoothly from damp woodland around the visitor centre, through freshwater reedbed, tidal marsh and finally to the beach itself. There are three hides along the way, but you can enjoy great views from the path itself.

The visitor centre has a feeding station which attracts a good variety of common woodland birds throughout the year. Away from the feeders,

the reedbed. That other big reedbed specialist, the Marsh Harrier, is more easy to see as it patrols the reedbeds.

The freshwater lagoon is large with numerous islands of varied sizes. These islands provide suitable nest sites for Avocets, and you will see dozens of them in spring and summer, wading deep in the water and swishing their upcurved bills side to side to filter out tiny aquatic morsels. They are excitable birds, particularly in spring, and

Elegant and long-necked, Spotted Redshanks have no aversion to water and frequently wade in up to their bellies as they snap up flies and other morsels.

you could see Blackcaps, Garden Warblers and Lesser Whitethroats by mid-spring. As you move into the reedbed area, Sedge and Reed Warblers take over, their ceaseless songs the soundtrack of Titchwell in spring. In recent years they have been joined by Cetti's Warblers with their powerful bursts of song. Listen too for the deep breathy boom of a Bittern – since 2005 this species has bred here, vindicating much hard work managing and expanding

you could well witness noisy chases and minor skirmishes among them as they argue about territorial boundaries.

In spring both the fresh and saltwater lagoons attract migrating waders. Here is a great place to see Spotted Redshanks at close quarters and sort out their identification from the more familiar Common Redshank. 'Spot-shanks' have an unmistakeable smoky-black breeding plumage, but before this develops they are similar to

Migrating Painted Lady butterflies often make their first UK landfall at East-coast sites like Titchwell. May 2009 saw an astonishing arrival involving tens of thousands.

their relatives. The key features to look for are the Spotted Redshank's longer legs, taller and slimmer build, longer bill (which often seems to 'droop' slightly at the tip) and paler overall plumage. Spotted Redshanks feed with a great deal of energy, happily wading belly-deep in the water.

Summer is quieter for birds as the migrant waders have moved on, but the breeding species can often be seen very well, especially Marsh Harriers. The non-bird inhabitants of the reserve come into their own at this time as well – a new crop of dragonflies and damselflies emerges from the pools and ditches, and butterflies (including Painted Ladies freshly arrived from the continent) visit flowering plants. Summer

can be good for mammals – be alert for Water Voles jumping into the water with a loud 'plop', Weasels darting across the path ahead of you, and seals (both Grey and Common may be seen here) sometimes coming close to the beach.

Late summer and autumn means a return of the waders. The adults come first, many still wearing some or all of their breeding plumage (look out for Ruffs with their spectacular head-gear, and deep-red Black-tailed Godwits), and then the young birds of the year, looking pristine in their first set of feathers. The young Curlew Sandpipers are particularly beautiful with their peach-washed underparts, while young Little Stints are delightful with their pint-size proportions, bright back-braces and rich shades of cream and brown. Numbers and variety are greater in autumn than spring, and you could easily see 20 species in a day – perhaps including a rarity if you're lucky.

The reedbed hides and the paths are good for Bearded Tit-watching in autumn. These enchanting little birds feed on reed seeds and family groups often gather on the ground in front of Island hide to hoover up the fallen autumn crop.

WHEN TO VISIT

Titchwell offers exciting wildlife watching throughout the year, and time of day is not critical. The busiest times are weekends, especially in summer, so visit mid-week if you want a quieter walk.

SEA CHANGES

Titchwell Marsh is an ever-changing landscape and the natural processes that shape our coastlines are having a dramatic effect on the reserve and its future. Coastal erosion is placing the freshwater habitats under increased pressure and to protect these and the wildlife that relies on them the RSPB has embarked on a three-year Titchwell Marsh Coastal Change Project (2009–2011). This project will allow salt water into a small part of the reserve to protect the freshwater habitats, to ultimately improve the reserve for all visitors, both human and wildlife. For more information about the project contact the reserve or visit the website.

The sea offers exciting birdwatching into winter. If you have a telescope you'll be glad you brought it – there is a purpose-built platform at the top of the beach offering a good vantage point from which to scan the waves. Large rafts of Common Scoters, the males pitch black and the females dusky brown, may loiter offshore, the ducks periodically diving or taking off en masse to move to a different patch of sea. A flash of white-edged wings in the flock means you've found a Velvet Scoter, a rarer species that

occasionally joins the Common Scoters in small numbers. Eiders and Long-tailed Ducks, two seaducks that represent opposite extremes of heftiness versus daintiness, may also be seen in good numbers. Inland, the lagoons attract many other species of ducks, and large flocks of Brent Geese graze on the surrounding fields.

Back at the visitor centre, the feeders will be at their busiest in winter. The wood often attracts a large flock of redpolls, and offers keen birdwatchers the chance to hone their redpoll identification skills as among the Lesser Redpolls there are often a few Common (actually much rarer) Redpolls and, occasionally, an Arctic Redpoll with its telltale white rump and frosty appearance.

How to get here

Grid ref./postcode TF 750438/PE31 8
By road Take the first left after driving eastwards along the A149 through Thornham village. The reserve is signposted with a brown tourist sign.
By public transport The nearest railway station is King's Lynn – 22 miles away. From here you can take buses to the north coast villages and connect with the Coasthopper 36 bus, which runs between Hunstanton and Sheringham and stops outside the reserve.

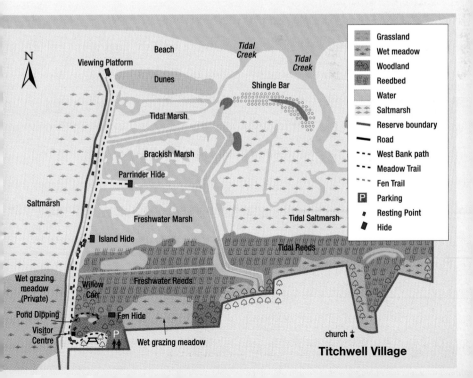

EAST ENGLAND

Long-tailed Tit

WOLVES WOOD

This reserve holds one of the few remaining fragments of ancient woodland in East Anglia, and by managing the trees with coppicing, a light and sunny woodland has been developed that is home to a good variety of birds and many other living things. Singing Nightingales are the stars of the show.

● Access, facilities, contact details and accessibility

There is a mile-long nature trail, good for a couple of hours of leisurely walking. Guided walks and group bookings can be arranged. The reserve is occasionally closed for management purposes beyond 9am.

- **Telephone** 01473 328006; **email** stourestuary@rspb.org.uk; **web** www.rspb.org.uk/wolveswood
- **Opening hours** The trails are open at all times, but the car park is locked from 6pm (or dusk if earlier), until 9am
- **Entry fees** Free, but donations are welcome
- **Accessibility** The nature trail is often wet and muddy, and so is not suitable for wheelchairs or pushchairs
- **Dogs** Not allowed, except registered assistance dogs

What to look for

A sunny spring day at Wolves Wood is a delight. When Nightingales return from Africa from mid-April onwards, their song can be heard throughout the day. The song is incredibly rich, liquid and varied, and each Nightingale somehow seems to conjure up its own magically atmospheric acoustics to give the song a transfixing quality – once heard, never forgotten. Seeing this shy songster presents a real challenge, but wait patiently and you may get a view.

The backing singers include Blackcaps and Garden Warblers, both very gifted songsters, as well as resident thrushes, Robins, Dunnocks and

WILDLIFE BY SEASON

SPRING

Nightingales lead the dawn chorus of birdsong. Look out for the striking Light Orange Underwing Moth, a local speciality.

SUMMER

Many species of butterflies patrol the sunny rides. Purple Hairstreak butterflies fly around the oak canopy in July.

AUTUMN

Woodcocks start to arrive for winter. The woodland colours are magnificent, and diverse fungi sprout everywhere.

WINTER

Vocal parties of tits, Redpolls and Siskins move through the otherwise quiet wood. Resident birds are singing from February.

finches. Another local speciality, the Marsh Tit, is also often located by sound, in this case its explosive '*pitchou*' call. Belying its name, the Marsh Tit actually prefers drier woodland.

The woodland here is managed to admit plenty of light to the woodland floor, which encourages flowering plants and also butterflies. July is the best month to see them, with skippers, Ringlets, Gatekeepers and Meadow Browns all moving from flower to flower. The Purple Hairstreak is an attractive small butterfly with a deep attachment to oak trees – it lays its eggs on them and spends most of its life fluttering high in the treetops, feeding not on flower nectar but on honeydew secreted onto the oak leaves by leaf-eating aphids. Scan the treetops to see it – or you may be lucky and see one making a rare groundwards sortie to visit a tempting bramble flower or drink from a puddle.

Once the showy colours of autumn have faded away, the wood becomes quiet through the winter. Woodcocks arrive

WHEN TO VISIT

Nightingales are singing from mid-April through to mid-June. Spring is generally the best time to visit but other seasons are interesting too.

but are skulking and shy – you may disturb one as you walk along the trail. You may also startle a Roe Deer – if you hear a sudden clatter in the woods look out for the deer's distinctive white bottom as it canters away.

How to get here

Grid ref./postcode TM 054437/ IP7 6

By road From Hadleigh town centre, head north up Angel Street. At the junction of the A1071, turn right towards Ipswich. The reserve is signposted after a mile on the left-hand side.

By public transport Ipswich, 8 miles away, is the nearest station. From Old Cattle Market bus station, board the 90, 91 or 94 bus and ask the driver if they can stop at Wolves Wood.

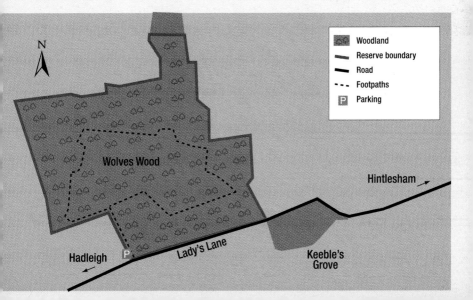

N

	Woodland
	Reserve boundary
	Road
	Footpaths
P	Parking

Wolves Wood

Hintlesham

Hadleigh

Lady's Lane

Keeble's Grove

BEMPTON CLIFFS SSSI, SPA, NATURA 2000

The three miles of sheer cliffs at Bempton hold one of the UK's best-known and most important seabird colonies. A summer visit is unforgettable, the sweeping seascape and the masses of noisy, ceaselessly active birds providing a high-octane assault on the senses. From several safe viewpoints you can look right into the heart of this avian metropolis, and get to know the city's inhabitants. Though the main spectacle is over by autumn, the reserve has much wildlife interest into winter with farmland birds and Short-eared Owls on show, and marvellous views across this wild coastline whatever the season.

● Access, facilities, contact details and accessibility

There are five safe cliff-top viewpoints, the furthest 900m from the visitor centre. You can buy refreshments, hire binoculars and arrange guided walks from the shop.

- **Telephone** 01262 851 179; **email** bempton.cliffs@rspb.org.uk; **web** www.rspb.org.uk/bemptoncliffs
- **Opening hours** The reserve is open at all times. From March to October, the visitor centre is open daily 10am–5pm; from November to February, 10am–4pm. For Christmas week opening times, please call 01262 851179.
- **Entry fees** Free of charge to members. Charge for non-members is £3.50 per car, mini-bus £6 and coach £8.
- **Accessibility** The visitor centre is accessible to wheelchair users. From the centre, there is a short 1:10 descent leading to a gently sloping, 0.9m-wide, rolled limestone path. The nearest viewpoint is 250m away and gives good views of the breeding seabirds.
- **Dogs** Welcome on the reserve, however they must be kept on leads at all times. This is to ensure that ground nesting birds are not disturbed, and also to ensure the safety of dogs on the cliff-top.

WILDLIFE BY SEASON

SPRING

The cliffs soon become packed with thousands of Guillemots, Razorbills, Kittiwakes, Puffins, Fulmars and Shags. Large numbers of Gannets breed here and from the viewpoints you can get up close to them. Look out for Harbour Porpoises on calm days. Northbound migrating songbirds may touch down here.

SUMMER

The colony is seething with activity as adult birds come and go, fetching food for their chicks. Butterflies and diurnal moths can be seen on sunny days, especially when it isn't too windy. Look out for orchids along the trails.

AUTUMN

The seabirds and their young leave the colony – the Gannets are last to go. There is plenty of seabird activity offshore through autumn, with skuas and shearwaters passing near the cliffs when onshore winds force them close to the shore.

WINTER

Several Short-eared Owls are usually present. The feeding station attracts many Tree Sparrows along with other small birds. Roe Deer and farmland birds can be seen.

What to look for

No wildlife education is complete without a visit to a seabird colony. Here in the UK we are blessed with many, but Bempton is one of the most southerly and also one of the most accessible. The family-friendly facilities make this a perfect place to bring children, who are guaranteed to enjoy the sights, sounds and even the smells of one of the UK's classic wildlife spectacles.

There isn't far to walk here (look out for Pyramidal, expression and big comedy bill. Less familiar are its two relatives, the Guillemot and Razorbill. Both look at first glance like miniature penguins – short-legged but standing tall, dark above and white below. Their stubby wings must beat very hard to keep them airborne, but underwater those same wings become powerful flippers, allowing the birds to swiftly pursue fish to depths of 50m or more.

Guillemots are not big on

Flying is one thing, landing is another. Gannets have to touch down carefully in their packed colony to avoid embarrassing collisions.

Common Spotted and Northern Marsh Orchids along the trail) but you could while away hours at any of the five viewpoints. The seabirds start to arrive from the end of February, and by the end of April some 200,000 individuals are here, courting, bickering over the top nesting spots and sallying forth to sea to hunt fish.

Three of Britain's four species of auk breed here. Everyone knows the Puffin, with its portly figure, mournful personal space and pairs will nest in very close proximity, occupying even the narrowest ledges. Guillemot eggs, laid straight onto the bare rock, are famously rather cone-shaped as an adaptation to this precipitous start in life – if nudged they spin on the spot and are less likely to roll off the edge. There are some 59,000 Guillemots here – it is the second most numerous bird on the cliff-face.

Look for Razorbills in the rock crevices. They are black

Bee Orchid flowers are shaped to resemble, and therefore attract, bees. This one has apparently malfunctioned though, and attracted an Elephant Hawk-moth.

above (the Guillemot is dark chocolate-brown) and have larger bills with a single white vertical stripe. Some 15,000 birds nest here.

The commonest cliff bird is the Kittiwake, and given that it also has a loud and distinctive voice, it also contributes the major part of seabird noise with its drawn-out '*kitt-i-waaark*' calls. It is a gull, but a particularly attractive one with a pleasant, dark-eyed expression and wings that shimmer silver as it flies. Two or three eggs are laid in a simple nest of seaweed plastered to the cliff ledge. Unlike other gulls, young Kittiwakes are not brown but quite boldly patterned in black and white – perhaps because their high-rise homes are safe from most predators so camouflage is not required.

Shags nest on flatter rocks, often close to the sea. They are all black (though show a greenish sheen when the light hits them), snaky-necked

WHEN TO VISIT

Come in spring or summer to see the 'seabird city' in full swing. By autumn the breeding season is over, but you could see large numbers of seabirds moving past offshore. Winter is quietest, but the feeding station is busiest at this time.

birds, and sport a curly topknot of feathers in summer.

Gannets, the biggest cliff birds, are superb fliers and divers and are quite mesmerising to watch as they hang, open-winged, above the sea, before tipping forward, drawing the wings back and together and diving in headfirst. Those long wings make them less competent swimmers underwater than the auks, so they compensate with these deep, high-speed dives.

The trailside flowers attract butterflies and moths, including migrants such as the beautiful Clouded Yellow butterfly and the remarkable Hummingbird Hawkmoth, the latter looking exactly like a tiny Hummingbird as it hovers before the flowers on a blur of wings, probing for nectar with its extended, beak-like proboscis. Out at sea, you could see Harbour Porpoises on still days – these small, blunt-nosed animals often sleep near the surface, lying langorously with a fin poking in the air.

The young seabirds leave the colony in late summer. The young Guillemots and Razorbills fledge before they can fly and so must jump into the sea, encouraged by a parent who then keeps them company on the open sea through the autumn as the chick grows and learns to fend for itself.

By autumn, all is quiet on the cliffs. The

reserve is still worth a visit – strong onshore winds may provide you with good views of migrating seabirds that breed further north, such as Manx Shearwaters and Arctic and Great Skuas. Now is also a time to appreciate the land birds and rare migrants from the east such as Supalpine, Arctic and Yellow-browed Warblers have all been seen in the cliff-top scrub and around the Dell.

Peregrine Falcons nest on the cliffs – they can be hard to pick out among the throngs of other birds in summer but in winter they are still around and are easier to see. Short-eared Owls come in winter – sometimes a dozen or more of them – and hunt over the fields, elegantly twisting and turning in flight as they home in on an unlucky vole.

How to get here

Grid ref./postcode TA 197738/YO15 3
By road The reserve is on the cliff road from the village of Bempton, which is on the B1229 road from Flamborough to Filey. In Bempton village, turn northwards at the White Horse public house and the reserve is at the end of the road after 1 mile (follow the brown tourist signs).
By public transport Bempton is the nearest

Flight doesn't come easily to Puffins – their undersize flying equipment functions much more effectively as flippers than wings.

railway station, 200m south of Bempton village. Exit the station and turn left, follow the road down to the church, walk up the lane adjacent to the church to a staggered cross-road junction. Walk across the road and take the road adjacent to the White Horse public house, northwards to the reserve. Total walking distance is about 1.6 miles. Cycle parking facilities are also available.

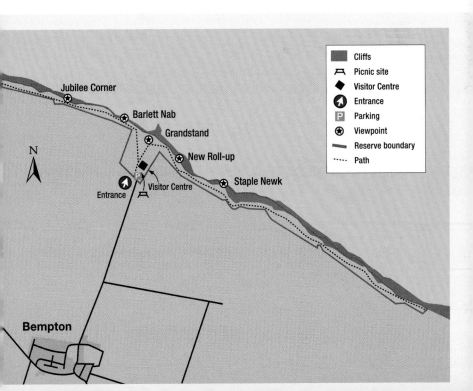

Jubilee Corner
Barlett Nab
Grandstand
New Roll-up
Staple Newk
Visitor Centre
Entrance
N
Bempton

Cliffs
Picnic site
Visitor Centre
Entrance
P Parking
Viewpoint
Reserve boundary
Path

NORTHERN ENGLAND

BLACKTOFT SANDS

SSSI, SPA, SAC, RAMSAR, NATURA 2000

On the south bank of the River Ouse, close to where it widens to meet the sea, sits this fabulous reserve of tidal reedbed and open water. Here is the second largest tidal reedbed in the UK, home to Bitterns, Marsh Harriers and Bearded Tits at one of their more northerly outposts. The lagoons in the reedbeds attract nesting and migrating waders, and the row of hides can give you wonderfully close views of these birds as they go about the business of feeding, resting and raising a family. Winter brings wildfowl and exciting birds of prey. This is a great place for visitors of all ages to get close to the special birds of this unusual and rare habitat.

● Access, facilities, contact details and accessibility

Blacktoft Sands is a well-appointed reserve, with six hides and a viewing screen strategically placed to give great views across the lagoons and reedbeds. You can hire binoculars if you need them, and guided walks and group visits can be arranged – there are also regular events. Children can borrow Wildlife Explorer backpacks from the visitor centre.

- **Telephone** 01405 704 665; **email** blacktoftsands@rspb.org.uk; **web** www.rspb.org.uk/blacktoftsands
- **Opening hours** Open daily (except Christmas Day) from 9am–9pm (or dusk if earlier)
- **Entry fees** Free for members. Non-members: adults £3, under 16s £1, concessions £2, family ticket £6.
- **Accessibility** All trails and hides are wheelchair-accessible, although the path to Ousefleet hide is grassed and can be difficult in wet weather
- **Dogs** Not allowed, except registered assistance dogs

WILDLIFE BY SEASON

SPRING

Bitterns boom and up to eight species of warblers sing as the breeding season begins. Avocets establish their nest sites on the islands, while from the Ousefleet hide you may see migrating waders. Look out for Marsh Harriers performing their courtship flights.

SUMMER

Marsh Harriers are busy hunting for food for their chicks, as are Barn Owls from late afternoon. Insects and flowers are much in evidence, and chicks of the Avocets and other breeding birds can be seen.

AUTUMN

Migrating Spotted Redshanks, Greenshanks, Black-tailed Godwits, Ruffs and Dunlins can be seen on the lagoons. This is also a good time to look for Water Rails and Bearded Tits.

WINTER

Hen Harriers and Merlins hunt on the reserve by day, and roost in the reedbeds at dusk. A large flock of Tree Sparrows assembles by the flood bank. Short-eared Owls join the resident Barn Owls, and wildfowl winter on the lagoons.

What to look for

From the car park, the nature trail runs east–west, with hides in both directions. These hides (seven in all, including the reception hide which doubles as a visitor centre) overlook a series of lagoons, with a viewing screen adjacent to the most westerly hide (Ousefleet). Although you will often enjoy very close views of birds here, this is also a good place to bring your telescope, as you won't have to carry it very far and it will enhance your enjoyment of the hides if you are

and pools, and keeping scrub in check.

The large reedbed at Black-toft makes it one of the best sites in the UK for Bearded Tits. Careful cutting of areas of reeds creates lots of nesting habitat for these attractive birds, which are easiest to see here in early summer. Marsh Harriers are doing very well here, and you'd be very unlucky not to have several sightings.

Marshland hide is probably the best one from which to

The spring soundtrack at Blacktoft features prominent contributions from the many Skylarks that sing from high above the fields beyond the reedbeds.

able to scan further horizons.

A visit in spring gives you a good chance of hearing Bitterns booming. This reserve is very important for Bitterns, holding one or two 'boomers' most years, and occasionally they overwinter here as well. Tidal reedbed is different in several ways to its freshwater equivalent, and management is necessarily different. The RSPB manage the habitat and keep it Bittern-friendly by cutting reed on rotation, creating new ditches

watch Avocets. Some 30-40 pairs nest on the purpose-built islands in the lagoons – the chicks are scampering about by June and are as appealing as the adults are elegant. Another nesting wader here is the Lapwing – this species has disappeared as a breeding bird from the countryside around, so it is especially important to encourage nesting birds on the reserve. They favour grassy islands – choosing islands for nest sites helps keep the birds

Scan along the edge of the reeds and you might just see a Water Vole, tucking into a healthy lunch while keeping a wary eye out for predators.

and their young safe from predatory mammals like Stoats and Foxes. Other mammals on the reserve include Water Voles and Water Shrews – with luck and patience you could see either species close to the water's edge, and summer is a good time to look.

As autumn advances, migrant waders call in at Blacktoft – the Ousefleet hide is often the best one from which to see them. Spotted Redshanks, Greenshanks, Black-tailed Godwits, Ruffs and Dunlins can all be seen, often in motley half-moulted breeding plumage. Male Ruffs may still be wearing all or part of their elaborate breeding head-dresses, while the Spotted Redshanks are often dappled in a combination of their blackish breeding attire and the silvery-grey and white plumage of winter. Dunlins may retain their black belly-patches, while the godwits are in various transitional states between brick-red

WHEN TO VISIT

The reserve offers exciting wildlife throughout the year, and is well worth a visit at any time. Be here at dusk on a winter's day to see birds of prey flying into their reedbed roosts.

and pale brownish-grey and white. The young birds of the year, in non-showy but sleekly brand-new feathers, stand out among their slightly threadbare-looking parents. If you are a little daunted by the details of wader identification, here is a great opportunity to sort out the basics.

Marsh Harriers are joined by Hen Harriers in winter. The latter are smaller and more agile birds, and quite different in plumage, but still hold their wings in the characteristic harrier shallow 'V' as they fly low and slow on a search for prey. A predator with none of the harriers' langour is the Merlin, a small and high-speed falcon that you may only glimpse for a moment as it tears past in pursuit of some unlucky Stonechat or other small bird. If you do get a good view of one, you'll notice its round-headed, rather 'cute' look (made all the more so by its slightly grumpy expression). The males are distinctively blue-grey above and cream below. The females are brown, superficially similar to female Kestrels but darker, duller and more compact-looking. Both Hen Harriers and Merlins roost in the reedbeds.

Barn Owls are a feature of Blacktoft all year round, with birds sometimes using purpose-built nestboxes within view of the hides. In winter there are also Short-eared Owls here – much more diurnal than their relatives so you have a good chance of seeing one in broad daylight.

Winter wouldn't be winter at a wetland reserve without ducks – in this case masses of Teals and Wigeons, calling loudly as they feed in front of the Ousefleet hide. The reserve's compact area of grazing marsh attracts many Lapwings and Golden Plovers in winter – the flocks occasionally taking to the air in a panic of tawny and black-and-white wings as a hunting Peregrine hoves into view.

How to get here

Grid ref./postcode SE 843232/DN14 8
By road From Goole, take the A161 road to Swinefleet, turn left at the mini-roundabout in Swinefleet, turn right at the next T-junction and follow the minor road for the next five miles through Reedness, Whitgift and Ousefleet. About a third of a mile out of Ousefleet heading towards Adlingfleet, turn left into the reserve car park (all turns described are marked with brown tourist signs).
By public transport From Goole railway station take the 357 bus Goole to Scunthorpe. The bus leaves from North Street in Goole and calls at

Autumn waders stopping off on the lagoons include Ruffs, which have a distinctive small-headed look and scaly-patterned plumage.

the reserve entrance, with several services a day (call Traveline on 0871 200 2230 or visit www. sweyne.co.uk for an up-to-date timetable).

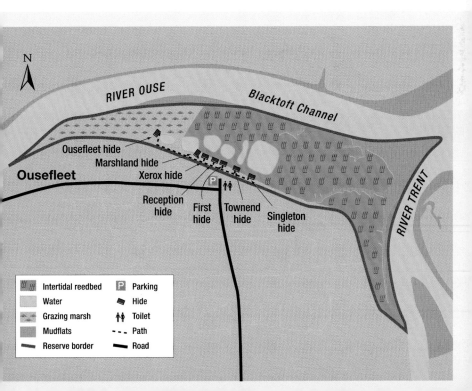

Intertidal reedbed   P Parking
Water   Hide
Grazing marsh   Toilet
Mudflats   - - - Path
Reserve border   Road

CAMPFIELD MARSH

SSSI, SPA, SAC, RAMSAR, AONB, NATURA 2000

A long strip of land in the mouth of the Solway Firth, this reserve is a mosaic of saltmarsh, peat bogs, farmland and wet grassland, attracting breeding waders in summer and flocks of geese, waders and other water birds in winter. You can enjoy a long walk here, with a chance of seeing Brown Hares, Roe Deer and many other species.

● Access, facilities, contact details and accessibility

This reserve offers good disabled access to a hide, and a network of trails and public footpaths on more challenging terrain for the able-bodied. There are also three viewing screens.

- **Telephone** 01697 351 330; **email** campfield.marsh@rspb.org.uk; **web** www.rspb.org.uk/campfieldmarsh
- **Opening hours** Open at all times
- **Entry fees** Free, though donations are welcome
- **Accessibility** Disabled visitors may drive along the lane to the hide. The hide has a wheelchair access ramp and viewing bay.
- **Dogs** Only allowed on public footpaths and bridleways

What to look for

An 800m trail leads from the car park at North Plain Farm to the hide, passing viewing screens on the way. The trail continues for 1.5 miles across fields and peat bog to Rogersceugh Farm, from where public rights of way allow you to make a round trip of 7 miles back to North Plain Farm via Bowness on Solway. What you'll see en route depends on the time of year – in spring

WILDLIFE BY SEASON

SPRING
Breeding waders are displaying over the fields. You may see Brown Hares and Roe Deer on the farmland. Skuas fly up the Solway on their way to their breeding grounds.

SUMMER
The peat bog swarms with dragonflies, and specialist plants flower. Migrant waders start to arrive.

AUTUMN
At high tide, thousands of roosting waders are visible from the roadside laybys. Winter wildfowl start to arrive.

WINTER
The farmland holds flock of Barnacle and Pink-footed Geese, other wildfowl and waders.

you're bound to notice the many breeding Lapwings performing aerobatics and whooping like toy trumpets overhead. Redshanks and Snipes breed here too; the former will call loudly when they see you coming, to let you know they know you're there – not for nothing are they called 'sentinels of the marshes'. Snipes tend to keep quiet and hope you won't see them – you're only likely to see one on your walk if you disturb it from a nearby ditch.

A feature of summer here is the migration of skuas up the Solway. All four species – Arctic, Great, Pomarine and Long-tailed – may be seen. The Great Skua is a big brown barrel of a bird with striking white wing-flashes. The other three are slighter, with the Long-tailed positively dainty. Your best chance of seeing them is to visit on a rising tide with a strong south-westerly wind blowing.

Big autumn tides push the waders off the mudflats, and you can see them at their high-tide roosts from the roadside laybys. From the hide, you should see Pintails, Teals, Shovelers and Wigeons from

WHEN TO VISIT
The reserve is interesting throughout the year. To see the wader roosts, visit as high tide approaches on an autumn day.

autumn through into winter – this is also a regular spot for Hen Harriers.

The farm fields attract Barnacle Geese in the depths of winter. These very attractive small geese are joined by Pink-footed Geese in late winter.

How to get here
Grid ref./postcode NY 197615/ CA7 5

By road The main entrance is at North Plain Farm, 1.5 miles west of Bowness on Solway on the unclassified coast road.

By public transport Carlisle, 13 miles away, is the nearest railway station. Bus 93 from Carlisle terminates at the eastern end of Campfield Marsh reserve at Bowness on Solway. Access to North Plain Farm and Bowness Common is 1.5 miles west along the road by the saltmarsh.

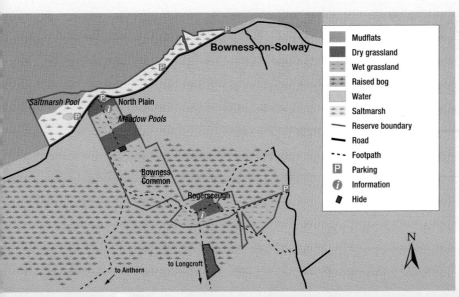

▨	Mudflats
▨	Dry grassland
▨	Wet grassland
▨	Raised bog
▨	Water
▨	Saltmarsh
—	Reserve boundary
▬	Road
- - -	Footpath
P	Parking
i	Information
◀	Hide

COQUET ISLAND SSSI, SPA, NATURA 2000

This Northumbrian island holds important numbers of breeding seabirds, including the very rare Roseate Tern. There is no public access to the island, but you can view CCTV images of them from the Northumberland Seabird Centre in the town of Amble on the mainland, and you can also take an RSPB-chartered boat around the island to see the birds in person.

● Access, facilities, contact details and accessibility

- **Telephone** 01665 710835; **web** www.rspb.org.uk/coquetisland or www.northumberlandseabirdcentre.co.uk
- **Opening hours** Northumberland Seabird Centre is normally open daily 10am–5pm (Sundays 10.30am–2.30pm) from April to the end of September. We recommended you call the Tourist Information Centre on 01665 712 313 to confirm times.

What to look for

This island is now uninhabited, apart from the RSPB wardens who live here year-round. A lighthouse and cottages were built on the remains of a monastery in the 19th century, but today the lighthouse is solar-powered and automatic, so the island belongs to the thousands of pairs of breeding birds and a handful of RSPB staff staying in the lighthouse. All the terns depart in autumn, not returning until the following spring.

Whether you view the birds on the CCTV screens in Northumberland Seabird Centre or take a boat trip around the island, there are several species to look for. The most numerous nesting species is the Puffin, with some 18,000 pairs. The island has plenty of accessible low ground, making it ideal for nesting Eider ducks. Many pairs make their famously downy nests on the grassy plateau. Kittiwakes and Fulmars represent cliff-nesting species on the island,

WILDLIFE BY SEASON

SPRING

Nesting activity gets underway, with courtship and territorial battles taking place before eggs are laid and things calm down.

SUMMER

The parent birds work throughout the day provisioning their chicks with fish, so there is much intense activity until the young ones are ready to fledge.

using the rockier parts on which to nest. There are no towering cliffs to suit the larger auks so these species are absent, but ample compensation is provided in the form of four species of nesting terns – Common, Arctic, Sandwich and Roseate.

The Roseate Tern is one of the UK's scarcest breeding species, and about 90 per cent of the population nests on Coquet Island. Nesting on the ground as they do, terns of all species are very vulnerable to disturbance from people and attacks on their nests from predatory mammals like Foxes. Many mainland colonies have disappeared due to beach disturbance and

WHEN TO VISIT

Birds are nesting on the island from April to September. Outside of these months there are no boat trips or CCTV footage.

development, and those that remain are especially vulnerable to predators – on Coquet and other islands, these problems are less significant. The wardens help to protect the birds further by supplying nestboxes, which give the chicks shelter from bad weather (another major killer) and airborne predators like gulls. For a gull, a fluffy tern chick is an easily captured little morsel, and individual gulls can become a real menace to tern colonies.

Roseates are similar to Common and Arctic Terns, but have longer, blacker bills, paler plumage and longer tails.

If you are in the Amble area for a short while, it's well worth visiting the visitor centre to watch some close-up footage of the Coquet birds going about their business in the busy colony. For a longer stay, a boat trip will provide thrilling close views of the birds as they forage at sea to feed their families.

How to get here

Grid ref./postcode
NU 293045/n/a
It's not possible to visit the island itself, though you can watch CCTV images at the Northumberland Seabird Centre in Amble during the breeding season. The nearest railway station is at Acklington. Buses run from Alnwick to Ashington, stopping at Amble (Monday–Saturday). A local boatman is licensed by the RSPB to run boat trips around the island – details are available at www. northumberlandseabirdcentre. co.uk

Roseate Terns are the most glamorous of tern species, longer-tailed and paler silvery-grey than the others, and some show a delicate rosy flush on the underparts.

DEARNE VALLEY – OLD MOOR

The Dearne Valley, with its associated wetlands, cuts through one of the most industrialised areas of northern England, skirting the edges of several big cities. Until quite recently, many of the good wildlife spots along the course of the River Dearne didn't have much in the way of protection, although they were well-known to local birdwatchers. The RSPB has now acquired some of the key sites, and the reserve at Old Moor is the centrepiece. Here, the existing habitat has been improved, providing lakes, wet meadows and copses that appeal to a whole range of wildlife. Additionally, the RSPB has added a suite of top-notch facilities for visitors.

● Access, facilities, contact details and accessibility

Old Moor is an ideal reserve for family visits. Children can enjoy the adventure playground and can play 'bird bingo' from the wildlife spotting den. The café serves delicious food and offers great views across the reserve. The trails are short and pushchair friendly. Guided walks are available and there is a busy programme of events.

- **Telephone** 01226 751593; **email** old.moor@rspb.org.uk; **web** www.rspb.org.uk/dearne-oldmoor
- **Opening hours** Between 1 November–31 January the visitor centre is open 9.30am–4pm; reserve gates open until 4.30pm. Between 1 February–31 October the visitor centre is open 9.30am–5pm; gates open until 5.15pm. The reserve is closed on Christmas Day and Boxing Day.
- **Entry fees** RSPB members free; adults £2.50; children £1.25; family ticket £5 (any number of children); concessions £2.
- **Accessibility** The trails and all hides are accessible to wheelchair users, as are the visitor centre facilities. Wheelchairs and an electric scooter are available for free hire.
- **Dogs** No dogs allowed, except registered assistance dogs

WILDLIFE BY SEASON

SPRING

The last winter visitors depart in early spring, migrating waders pass through, and summer visitors like warblers will start to arrive. Birdsong is at its best. Tree Sparrows will be staking claims to the nestboxes with loud territorial chirping.

SUMMER

Breeding birds will be attending their chicks, and the wet grasslands are full of insect life. This is also the likeliest time to encounter mammals such as Brown Hares, especially early or late in the day.

AUTUMN

The waders are back again on their return migration, other migrating birds may pass through and winter visitors start to arrive. Unusual visitors like Little Egrets or scarce waders may visit.

WINTER

Ducks and other water birds spend winter on the lakes. The impressive Golden Plover flock reaches its peak, and the feeding station is at its busiest. Ducks begin their courtship displays in late winter. Bitterns have recently begun to overwinter.

What to look for

From the car park, you'll proceed directly to the attractive new visitor centre, which has a shop selling an extensive range of books, optics and garden wildlife-attracting bits and bobs on the ground floor, and a delightful restaurant upstairs that gives views across the whole reserve.

Heading out from the visitor centre you will first pass through the new wildlife garden – complete with wildflower walks and insect hotels –

nestboxes around the reserve to encourage this species, and the Tree Sparrows have responded very well – this is one of the easiest places in Britain to see them and once you're used to their looks and distinctive call, you'll probably notice them all around the reserve, and especially standing guard over their nestboxes in spring. A Little Owl sometimes frequents the trees around the visitor centre – ask at reception about this and other sightings (a board

A colourful bunting, the Yellowhammer nests on scrubland and several regularly visit the Old Moor feeding station.

helping visitors understand the simple things they can do to bring nature to their doorstep. Children can spot birds and mammals from the wildlife spotting den, or make their way to the adventure playground with its dramatic bird-themed equipment. Next door, Tree Sparrow Farm is a real-life illustration of the relationship between food, farming and wildlife and a special chance to get close to Tree Sparrows. The RSPB has placed many

lists what's been seen recently).

There is a choice of two main nature trails onto the wider reserve, one of which leads to a further trail into the newly developing reedbed. The green lane trail takes in five bird-watching hides which overlook the scrapes and lakes from various angles. The second trail – 'ponds and picnics' – takes you around a network of pools and ditches that have become the perfect home for the shy Water Vole. Wooden sculptures

With its dark wing markings, gleaming blue body and rather show-offy personality, the male Banded Demoiselle is one of our most striking insects.

and carved picnic tables allow you to literally lunch with wildlife and enjoy an abundance of wild flowers and dragonflies and damselflies in summer. Leading off from the ponds and picnics trail is the reedbed trail which takes you to another more secluded part of the site. From a well-placed screen you should see Kingfishers in summer and perhaps the elusive Bittern in winter.

Thousands of Lapwings and Golden Plovers provide a stunning spectacle in winter. Winter is also the best time for ducks. Wigeons and Teals are numerous, and there will also be plenty of Shovelers, all in their best plumage at this time of year as the males are gearing up for a busy season of courting the females. Commoner diving ducks may be joined by scarcer visitors like the handsome Goosander.

In spring, waders stop by on their return journeys to their northern breeding grounds. Look out for Black-tailed Godwits wading belly-deep in the water, resplendent in their brick-red summer plumage, as well as less gaudy creatures

WHEN TO VISIT

This site is excellent throughout the year and at all times of the day, though sunny weekends will be busiest.

like Green and Wood Sandpipers. Some waders stay on to breed here. Around the shores of the lakes and their islands (especially from the first hide) look out for Little Ringed Plovers from early spring – smartly marked little clockwork toys of birds that nest on exposed inland beaches and rely on good luck and their own feistiness to keep their well-camouflaged eggs and chicks safe from predators. Redshanks, Snipe and Lapwings breed here too, favouring the meadowland areas, which are kept in an optimum state for them by the use of grazing cattle. Cows make excellent land managers, and the RSPB makes good use of them on reserves like this where damp grassland – a nationally rare but important habitat – still exists.

Summertime sees an explosion of insect life on the reserve, with dragonflies hawking up and down the trails, damselflies, mayflies and other small flying creatures emerging en masse from the ditches, and numerous moths, some of which get caught at the regular moth-trapping evening events. This wealth of insect life supports the small birds that breed on the reserve – warblers and Stonechats, but also seed-eaters like Reed Buntings and Tree Sparrows, which switch to an insect diet while rearing their chicks. Little Owls are larger insectivores – several live on the reserve; look out for them perched low in trees or resting on posts or buildings in the daytime. Breeding birds that exploit the reserve's substantial freshwater fish population include Kingfisher and Little Grebe. A vegetarian water creature is the endearing Water Vole. You'll probably need some patience to see one, though if you startle a feeding vole on the bank you may notice the sharp 'plop' as it drops into the safety of the water.

In autumn, the waders make their return journey and some species stop off here in large numbers. Migrating birds of prey may also show up – Hobbies hunt the Swallows and martins that gather here in autumn, and if you're very lucky you may see an Osprey fishing the lakes. Other uncommon visitors have included Spoonbill and Great White Egret.

The winter Golden Plover flock at Old Moor is quite breath-taking in the air, though the well-camouflaged birds virtually disappear when they settle.

How to get here

Grid ref./postcode SE422022/S63 7

By road From the M1, leave at Junction 36 and take the A61 towards Barnsley. At the small roundabout, continue straight ahead on the A6195 towards Doncaster for approximately 4 miles. After passing the Morrisons supermarket, follow the brown RSPB Old Moor signs. From the A1: leave at Junction 37 (for Doncaster), follow the A635 towards Barnsley, then follow the brown RSPB Old Moor signs.

By public transport The nearest rail stations are Wombwell and Swinton, both 3 miles away, with regular connections to Doncaster. A number of buses run from Wombwell and Swinton stations and stop near the entrance to the reserve on Manvers Way. Buses also run to the reserve from Barnsley, Doncaster and Meadowhall. Please check with bus operator TravelLine on 01709 515151 for further information.

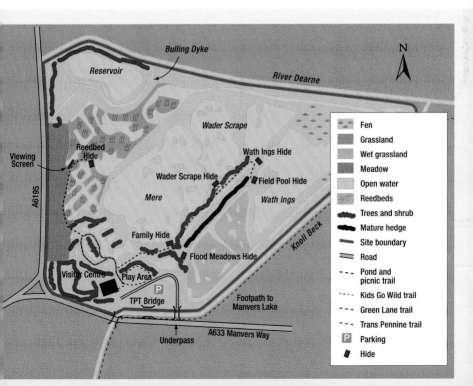

NORTHERN ENGLAND

FAIRBURN INGS SSSI, LNR

Tucked in the outskirts of Leeds, close to the A1, this excellent reserve has a great range of wildlife in beautiful surroundings. Fairburn Ings lies alongside the winding River Aire and is based around a series of pools originally formed from mining subsidence – in the 30 years the RSPB has managed the site, they have worked to maintain the water levels of the lakes and the wetness of the surrounding grassland for maximum attractiveness to wildlife. Artificial islands in the lakes attract breeding birds, the old spoil heaps are now clothed with trees, and the grassland is rich with wild flowers. Fairburn has plenty of facilities for visitors, and as it lies on a key cross-country bird migration path, it attracts more than its share of rare birds.

● Access, facilities, contact details and accessibility

Fairburn Ings is a family-friendly reserve with full facilities. You can hire binoculars from the visitor centre, and book guided walks. Refreshments are available from the shop. Children can enjoy free pond-dipping from a permanent platform – there's also a free 'Discovery Trail'. The events programme includes regular optics demonstration days, talks, walks and fun family days.

- **Telephone** 01977 628 191; **email** fairburnings@rspb.org.uk; **web** www.rspb.org.uk/fairburnings
- **Opening hours** The main car park and Lin Dyke car park are open at all times. The visitor centre is open Monday to Sunday 9am–5pm, except on Christmas Day and Boxing Day.
- **Entry fees** Free to RSPB members. For non-members there is a £2 charge for parking.
- **Accessibility** The visitor centre and the boardwalk are wheelchair-accessible, and there is also an accessible toilet.
- **Dogs** Allowed anywhere, but they must be kept on a lead

WILDLIFE BY SEASON

SPRING

Kingfishers are particularly noticeable at this time. Summer visitors such as Reed and Sedge Warblers, Little Ringed Plovers and Garganeys arrive, and birdsong is at its peak.

SUMMER

Look for ducklings on the lake, and enjoy the bustling tern and gull colonies on the islands. Dragonflies and damselflies hawk over the water, while butterflies patrol the flowery grassland areas.

AUTUMN

Migration time, and a variety of waders will call in at Fairburn on their journeys south. Look out for Ruffs and Green Sandpipers. Winter visitors – wildfowl, waders and wintering thrushes – will start to arrive.

WINTER

Redwings and Fieldfares are stripping the last berries from the bushes, while on the lakes wildfowl such as Goldeneyes, Goosanders and Smews gather to feed and display to one another – the males' plumage is at its resplendent best in winter. Visiting Peregrine Falcons may harry the flocks of Lapwings and Golden Plovers.

What to look for

Fairburn is a partly artificial but very valuable area of wildlife habitat. Formed by the collapse of coal-mining pits, the lakes here are vulnerable both to drying out and to flooding, depending on weather conditions. The RSPB's management involves careful control of water levels and the water table in the land surrounding the lakes, to maintain the lakes' attractiveness to wildlife and to develop areas of wet grassland for breeding and wintering birds.

good for waders and wildfowl, especially when water levels are lower. The trail passes the reserve's bird-feeding station, which attracts a variety of small birds, especially in winter – perhaps the most interesting are the Tree Sparrows, which differ from the familiar House Sparrow in their chestnut crowns and neat black cheek spots. Other visitors to look out for include Siskins and Lesser Redpolls in the Alders, and, sometimes, Bramblings.

You'll find a picnic area

The Tree Sparrow is country cousin to the familiar House Sparrow – look for its chestnut-brown cap and black cheek-spot.

There are three parking areas at Fairburn, each of which gives you access to trails and/or viewpoints across the various lakes. From the main parking area, you'll reach the visitor centre, and from here the short loop of the 'Discovery Trail' heads west (a boardwalk here ensures you keep your feet dry and it's navigable with a pushchair and by wheelchair). You can follow it to the Pickup hide, positioned to overlook a shallow lake. The lake is

close to the visitor centre and the pond-dipping platform is opposite. The reedy areas are good for Reed and Sedge Warblers in summer and numerous dragonflies will be hunting over the open water – an impressive 18 species have been seen here.

Another trail – the 'Riverbank trail' – goes east around adjacent marshy and lightly wooded patches, following the course of the River Aire and finally arriving at Fairburn village.

Grey Partridges have declined sharply in the wake of industrialised farming. At Fairburn, weedy fields provide them with the seeds they need.

You can walk the trail in reverse if you opt to park in the village. The trail first passes areas of spoil heaps (in spring and summer look for warblers in the scrubbier areas, and Skylarks and Meadow Pipits in the more open areas) and then two sizeable lakes, overlooked by three hides. In summer Common Terns and Black-headed Gulls nest on purpose-built islands placed in the lakes by the RSPB, while in winter you may see water birds like Smew, Goldeneye or Goosander alongside large flocks of commoner species like Tufted Ducks and Pochards. There is also a swan-feeding platform here – leave the unhealthy sliced white at home and buy bags of grain at the

visitor centre to throw to the Mute Swans and other wildfowl. Kingfishers are common and often easy to see here – listen for their piercing whistle as they skim by, low over the water.

Heading west along the road from the visitor centre, you'll come to a further car park after a mile or so. From here, the Lin Dike trail (which is wheelchair-accessible) leads past a collection of small lakes to the Lin Dike hide, overlooking a narrow lake called Spoonbill Flash. This part of the reserve is best for waders, which congregate in spring on their way to their northern breeding grounds, and again in autumn, when they're on their way back south. Controlling water levels is an inexact science and sometimes heavy rain can mean the water is too high to leave the exposed muddy shores that the waders need to feed, so bear this in mind when planning your visit. In winter, the pastureland around the lakes attracts Wigeons and Bewick's and Whooper Swans.

As you explore the reserve, look out for Water Voles swimming across the ditches – you may also hear them jumping into the water with a loud 'plop' when they notice you coming. More elusive is the tiny Harvest Mouse, which weaves its neat little nest in stands of long grass. The RSPB manages grassland here to provide a

WHEN TO VISIT

Although the reserve's wildlife changes dramatically through the seasons, Fairburn is well worth a visit at any time of year. The car park and trails are open at all times, so you can make a dawn start if you wish, or stay on until dusk – birds are often more active early and late in the day. For insects, warm and still spring, summer and autumn days are best. Pond dipping will be most enjoyable in summer.

mosaic of habitat types, catering to the needs of a wide variety of wildlife. Cattle are used to graze the wet grassland to keep the grass an optimum length for breeding Redshanks and Lapwings, while occasional mowing of the dry grassland encourages weedy plants to thrive and provide food in the form of seeds for many farmland species, especially finches and partridges.

Fairburn is truly a reserve for all people, with its top-notch visitor facilities, children's activities, wild corners, potential for attracting rare birds and trails that link up with public footpaths for those who want a longer and invigorating walk with excellent wildlife-watching along the way.

How to get here

Grid ref./postcode SE 451277/WF10 2
By road Leave the A1 at Junction 42 for the A63, and follow signs for Fairburn village on the A1246. Once in the village turn right at Wagon and Horses public house. At the T-junction turn right, and the reserve is 1.5 miles on the left.
By public transport The closest train station is Castleford, five miles away. The 950 Metro Daytripper service runs through August from Leeds and Castleford three times a day and stops at the main entrance.

The drake Gadwall isn't the showiest of ducks but has a quiet charm. Both sexes have the distinctive white wing patch.

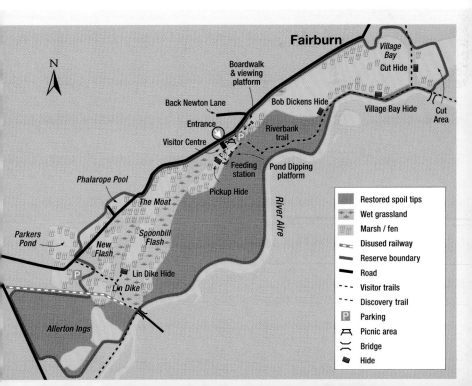

Legend:
- Restored spoil tips
- Wet grassland
- Marsh / fen
- Disused railway
- Reserve boundary
- Road
- - - Visitor trails
- - - Discovery trail
- **P** Parking
- Picnic area
- Bridge
- Hide

NORTHERN ENGLAND

GELTSDALE SSSI, SPA, SAC, AONB, NATURA 2000

Here in the north Pennines, you'll find stunning landscapes of steep and rolling hills, scattered woodlands and rushing streams. Geltsdale reserve is home to a wide variety of upland breeding birds and other wildlife, including many scarce species, and offers a great walking experience for those who enjoy an energetic ramble over hill and dale.

●Access, facilities, contact details and accessibility

There are four way-marked trails, the shortest of which will take an hour or more to complete. There is also an information point.

● **Telephone** 0191 233 4300; **email** northernengland@rspb.org.uk; **web** www.rspb.org.uk/geltsdale

● **Opening hours** Trails are open at all times, and the information point between 9am–5pm

● **Entry fees** Free, but donations to help continue the work here are welcome

● **Accessibility** Wheelchair access can be pre-arranged to the reserve information point at Stagsike cottages – call 01697 746717. The Tarn viewpoint will soon be accessible.

● **Dogs** Welcome but please keep them on a lead, as the reserve is a working farm

What to look for

There are four way-marked trails leading from the car park at Howgill. The Stagsike Trail will take at least an hour to walk and the other trails a little longer. Stagsike Cottages are approximately a 40-minute walk from the parking area and provide an information point and toilets.

The breeding waders of Geltsdale are a highly visible and audible component of the scene in spring. Listen for the gorgeous liquid bubbling song of the Curlew – you shouldn't have to wait long before you hear the first one. Lapwings and Redshanks are nesting here too – a carefully

WILDLIFE BY SEASON

SPRING
Breeding waders are calling and displaying, and small birds are singing in the woodland.

SUMMER
Flowers and butterflies are abundant. Cuckoos call through early summer, Whinchats are common around the moorland edge and birds of prey are busy hunting.

AUTUMN
Winter thrushes arrive and wildfowl come to the tarn.

WINTER
The best time to see Black Grouse. Wildfowl on the tarn may include Smews. Look out for Buzzards and Hen Harriers.

planned grazing rota keeps the grass conditions ideal for these ground-nesting birds.

Black Grouse and Hen Harriers nest here too – both species are rare and declining in England, so their conservation at Geltsdale is a matter of extreme importance. The grouse are elusive all year round, but winter is perhaps the best time to see them. You might see Hen Harriers – and also Barn and Short-eared Owls – in summer, as they have to hunt increasingly to keep their chicks supplied with voles and other small prey.

The hillsides become flushed with flowers in summer, which attract butterflies. Two local specialities fly in late spring to early summer – the Green Hairstreak and the small Pearl-bordered Fritillary. Another special insect of the reserve is the striking Golden-ringed Dragonfly. The reserve also has many species of mammals – Red Squirrels hang on, Otter sightings are increasing and there have even been reports of Pine Martens.

Through autumn, winter thrushes migrate overhead,

WHEN TO VISIT
The beautiful scenery is well worth exploring year-round. Wildlife interest is also present throughout the year, although winter is probably the quietest season.

and family parties of Whooper Swans visit the tarn, the youngsters greyish replicas of their parents. By winter a good range of wildfowl will be on Tindale Tarn, perhaps including a Smew or two.

How to get here
Grid ref./postcode NY 588584/ CA8 2
By road From the A69 near Brampton, take the A689 to Hallbankgate and Alston. At Hallbankgate, take the minor road that runs in front of the Belted Will pub; follow this minor road to the reserve car park at Clesketts.
By public transport Brampton Junction, on the Carlisle to Newcastle line, is the nearest station, around 2 miles from the reserve.

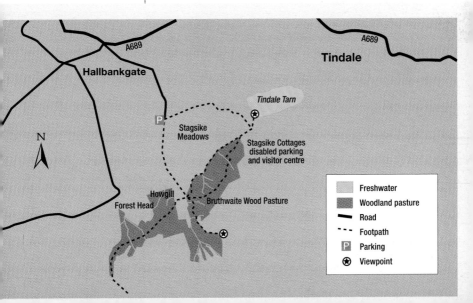

NORTHERN ENGLAND

HAWESWATER

Only in the Lake District is the English landscape rugged and remote enough to attract Golden Eagles – since 1969 Haweswater has been home to the country's only breeding pair. Just a single male is here at present, performing his annual spring displays over the rolling hills and wooded valleys to attract a new mate.

● Access, facilities, contact details and accessibility

The viewpoint has RSPB staff on hand and telescopes set up to help you see the Haweswater Golden Eagle. **P**

● **Telephone** 01931 713 376; **email** haweswater@rspb.org.uk; **web** www.rspb.org.uk/haweswater
● **Opening hours** The reserve is always open; the viewpoint is open at all times but is only manned between April and August from 11am–4pm on weekends and bank holidays.
● **Entry fees** Free, but donations are welcome
● **Accessibility** The trails are unmade and rugged, so not suitable for the mobility-impaired
● **Dogs** Allowed anywhere, but must be kept on leads as this is a sheep-farming area

What to look for

This is a wonderful reserve for peaceful walks in a wild landscape. Many visitors come in the hope of seeing the lonely male Golden Eagle, and the best time is spring, when he performs aerial displays in the hope that a female will pass by and see him. Pick a fine day from mid-morning and follow the trail from the car park up to the viewpoint. If you visit at a time when the viewpoint is manned (see above for times), the RSPB staff will be able to update you on the eagle's activities that day.

Spring is a good time to see other wildlife on the reserve. The woodlands attract Pied Flycatchers and Redstarts, both summer visitors.

WILDLIFE BY SEASON

SPRING

The Golden Eagle displays on fine days. Wheatears, Ring Ouzels, Redstarts and Pied Flycatchers arrive, Goosanders breed on the reservoir.

SUMMER

Look out for Red Deer and Red Squirrels. Breeding birds are caring for well-grown chicks.

AUTUMN

Red Deer are rutting. The eagle may still be seen on the wing. Many of the breeding birds prepare to depart.

WINTER

The eagle is at his most elusive but you may still be lucky. Thousands of gulls roost on the reservoir.

Redstarts have a pleasant, rather Chaffinch-like song, while Pied Flycatchers produce a more repetitive ditty, but the males of both species are attractively patterned and well worth searching out. Keep your eyes open for Red Squirrels in the woods too.

On the streams, look for Dippers. These portly, Wren-shaped but Starling-sized, birds forage for aquatic prey items in the streams, immersing themselves completely in the clear water and walking along the stream-bed.

Out on the open slopes, you'll probably see Skylarks and Wheatears. With luck you could also see a Ring Ouzel – look for a Blackbird-like bird with a striking white (or off-white in the females) crescent-shaped mark across the chest.

By summer, the Goosanders that nest on Haweswater reservoir have broods of ducklings in tow – enchanting brown-and-cream fluffballs that follow their mother across the water in a neat line and sometimes clamber onto her back for a free ride.

WHEN TO VISIT

To see the male Golden Eagle displaying, visit in spring. The reserve is stunning year-round but winter can be quiet for wildlife.

Winter is a quiet time, but watching the gull roost assemble on the reservoir at dusk is an exciting seasonal highlight.

How to get here

Grid ref./postcode NY 469108/ CA11 0

By road For the eagle viewpoint, aim for the small village of Bampton, 10 miles south of Penrith. From Bampton, head south towards Haweswater reservoir. Drive down the unclassified road alongside the Haweswater reservoir, the road ends at a car park. From here you will need to walk.

By public transport The nearest railway station is Penrith, 14 miles away. There is an occasional bus service to the Haweswater car park – phone Traveline for information on 0871 200 2233.

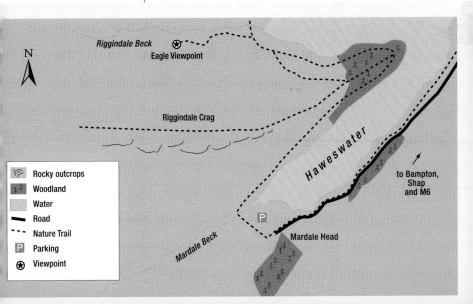

NORTHERN ENGLAND

Red-breasted Merganser

HODBARROW

SSSI, SPA, SAC, RAMSAR, NATURA 2000

Tucked into the Duddon Estuary just north of Morecambe Bay, this reserve is centred around a large lagoon that holds a lively breeding colony of Little, Sandwich and Common Terns. The RSPB hide gives you exceptionally close views of the birds, enabling you to look in on their family life from just a few feet away.

●Access, facilities, contact details and accessibility

The hide here offers excellent close views of nesting terns. The surrounding area is good for walking.

● **Telephone** 01697 351 330; **email** campfield.marsh@rspb.org.uk; **web** www.rspb.org.uk/hodbarrow

● **Opening hours** Open at all times

● **Entry fees** Free, but donations are welcome

● **Accessibility** The main trail is suitable for pushchairs and wheelchairs, but other pathways are not

● **Dogs** Allowed anywhere

P

What to look for

The sea wall has a rough track that leads to the RSPB hide. This is where you'll want to head in spring to see the nesting terns. The birds nest on an artificial shingle island in front of the hide, which is carefully maintained and kept free of excessive vegetation to encourage the birds. The Little Tern is especially prone to disturbance

and predation, so the conservation work at Hodbarrow is closely focused on supporting this species. Though small, Little Terns are loud and feisty birds. They are less elegant on the wing than their relatives, their jerky flight style reminiscent of a clockwork toy.

Besides the terns, the island also has breeding

WILDLIFE BY SEASON

SPRING

See breeding Little, Sandwich and Common Terns. Several warbler species sing in the scrub.

SUMMER

Orchids flower in the grassland. Look out for Dark Green Fritillary and Grayling butterflies on sunny days.

AUTUMN

Migrating waders feed in front of the hide, while large numbers of moulting Red-breasted Mergansers visit the lagoon.

WINTER

Large flocks of Redshanks, Knots, Black-tailed Godwits and Lapwings roost on the island in front of the hide, and wildfowl visit the lagoon.

Ringed Plovers, Lapwings, Redshanks and Oystercatchers, while out on the lagoon you'll see water birds like Great Crested Grebes.

An impressive show of Bee Orchids is to be found on the scrubland bare ground in June, and there are also Dark Red Helleborines. Butterflies, including Graylings and Dark Green Fritillaries, are on the wing, and warblers such as Lesser Whitethroats will be singing. The RSPB has created a number of small ponds throughout the reserve as breeding sites for the rare Natterjack Toad.

During autumn, the lagoon island provides a high-tide refuge for migrating waders, such as Greenshanks and Black-tailed Godwits. Out on the water, nearly 200 Red-breasted Mergansers gather here in autumn into winter, undergoing their main annual moult. These 'saw-billed' ducks are adept fish-hunters and you can watch them dive for prey, swimming underwater for long intervals.

In winter, the lagoon attracts other wildfowl, and wintering waders continue to shelter on

WHEN TO VISIT

To see the nesting terns, visit in spring or summer. The reserve is interesting at other times of year too.

the island when high tides cover up the estuarine mud beyond the lagoon.

How to get here

Grid ref./postcode SD 174790/ LA18 4
By road From Millom town square, continue east beyond the pedestrian crossing, taking the second right (Mainsgate Road signposted for Hodbarrow RSPB). Continue for about half a mile, turning left by the lagoon for the reserve car park.
By public transport Millom, 1.5 miles away, is the nearest rail station. Turn left out of the station. From Millom town square continue east beyond the pedestrian crossing, taking the second right (Mainsgate Road signposted for Hodbarrow RSPB). Continue for about half a mile.

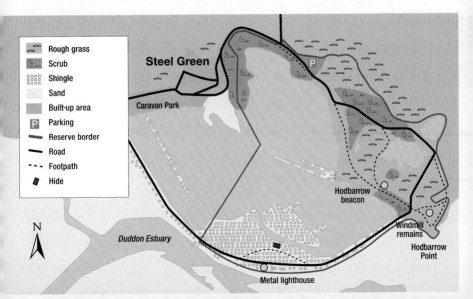

Rough grass	
Scrub	
Shingle	
Sand	
Built-up area	
P	Parking
Reserve border	
Road	
Footpath	
Hide	

Steel Green

Caravan Park

Hodbarrow beacon

Windmill remains

Hodbarrow Point

Duddon Estuary

Metal lighthouse

N

LEIGHTON MOSS

SSSI, SPA, SAC, AONB, NATURA 2000

Incongrously nestled amongst rolling farmland, this remnant of the once extensive Lancashire meres and mosses standes out from miles away – a reedy oasis among farmland, it is home to a range of wildlife more closely associated with altogether flatter, wetter and more southerly terrain. Here you can hear Bitterns booming, watch Marsh Harriers displaying and even see Otters at close quarters if you're lucky, all on easy-walking trails. Close by is RSPB Morecambe Bay, with hides giving views across pools and saltmarsh.

● Access, facilities, contact details and accessibility

Leighton Moss is a well-appointed reserve designed to welcome visitors of all ages. You can buy refreshments and hire binoculars from the shop. There are regular events held for all ages, and a lively education programme. The reserve has seven hides and three nature trails.

- **Telephone** 01524 701 601; **email** leighton.moss@rspb.org.uk; **web** www.rspb.org.uk/leightonmoss
- **Opening hours** The reserve and visitor centre are open daily all year round (except 25 December). The reserve is open from 9am to dusk and the visitor centre from 9.30am–5pm (4.30pm November–January inclusive).
- **Entry fees** There is free entry to the visitor centre and tearoom. Admission to hides and nature trails: £4.50 adults, £3 concessions, £1 children, £9 family. Free to RSPB members and those who come by public transport or by bike.
- **Accessibility** Four of the hides and some of the trails are wheelchair-accessible, and a wheelchair is available for hire from the visitor centre
- **Dogs** Allowed in the car park and on the Causeway but not elsewhere

WILDLIFE BY SEASON

SPRING

Bitterns boom at dawn and dusk. Marsh Harriers are displaying over the reeds, and later in spring Pearl-bordered and Small Pearl-bordered Fritillary butterflies can be seen in the wooded parts of the reserve.

SUMMER

Marsh Harriers pass food to one another for the chicks. Young water birds are out and about – if you are very lucky you could see Water Rail chicks. Marshland flowers bloom, and many butterflies and dragonflies are on the wing.

AUTUMN

Bearded Tits roam in family groups, sometimes picking up grit from the paths. Waders on return migration stop off at the reserve. Large flocks of Starlings swirl over the reedbeds in the evenings.

WINTER

Wildfowl numbers increase, and cold weather may mean increased sightings of Bitterns and Water Rails at the reeds' edges. Wigeons and Greylag Geese gather in the fields, and Peregrine Falcons and Merlins hunt over the reserve.

What to look for

From the car park, a choice of trails takes you around and between the reserve's stretches of open water. The seven strategically placed hides provide views across various inlets, lakes and stretches of reedbed. The northern corner of the reserve has an area of wet woodland that is good for warblers and butterflies.

Leighton Moss is almost synonymous with Bitterns – the famously shy brown herons are here all year but to hear the extraordinary 'booming'

ship display in spring, and also the food pass in which the male passes an item of prey to the female in mid-air, the female flipping upside-down to catch the gift.

Visit the woody areas from late April on sunny days to see two of the reserve's special butterflies – the Pearl-bordered and Small Pearl-bordered Fritillaries. These two species are bafflingly similar and are best told apart by subtle differences in the patterns on their underwings. They will bask

The star of Leighton Moss is the Bittern. You may see one flying over the reeds, looking a little like a heavy-set owl with its broad, mottled wings.

of the males you'll need to visit in spring. Listen for a deep, airy foghorn-like sound – but remember it carries a tremendous distance so hearing the call is unfortunately not necessarily going to help you see the bird itself. Your best chance of seeing one is to hold a patient vigil in one of the hides – keep scanning the reeds and one may wander into the open.

Marsh Harriers nest here too, and you may see their spectacular 'sky-dancing' court-

for long spells in the mornings to warm up enough for flight, looking like beautiful tawny flowers as they rest, wings spread, on the foliage. Both species lay their eggs on violets, which can also be seen flowering in spring.

Warblers like Blackcaps, Willow Warblers and Sedge and Reed Warblers arrive in spring to breed. Waders arrive too but most stay only briefly, continuing their northwards migration once they've refueled.

Seeing Otters in England is rarely easy, but you have a fair chance at this reserve, especially early or late in the day, if you're willing to wait patiently in the hides.

You could see Black-tailed Godwits, Ruffs and others on the Eric Morecambe pools in spring – while Avocets stay here to nest.

Through summer, the breeding birds are rearing their chicks. This is also a good time for mammals – Red Deer graze on the Tim Jackson and Griesdale meres in the evenings, and there are sporadic sightings of one or more Otters, which recolonised in 2007, from the hides. You could also see hunting Barn Owls on summer evenings. In the woods, another fritillary is on the wing from late June – the very uncommon

High Brown Fritillary, a bigger and more dramatic butterfly than the spring fritillaries.

In autumn, the Bearded Tits that have nested in the reeds through summer become suddenly more visible, moving about in family groups and visiting the grit trays provided for them. Though mostly insectivorous in summer, they switch to eating reed seeds in autumn, and like many seed-eaters they also eat a little grit to help their systems grind up the hard seeds. The young birds are yellower than their parents, with bold dark stripes along their backs and long tails to help them balance while clambering through the reeds.

Migrant waders are more numerous in autumn than in spring. This is also the time that the reedbed Starling roost starts to form, providing one of the most awe-inspiring spectacles nature has to offer. Up to 100,000 birds may eventually gather when the roost is

WHEN TO VISIT

There is always interesting wildlife to enjoy at Leighton Moss. To hear Bitterns booming, you'll need to visit early in the day in early spring.

at its peak, the massed birds performing stunning mass manoeuvres in the darkening sky before dropping down into the reeds for the night.

Winter brings wildfowl to Leighton Moss, with flocks of Teals, Wigeons, Gadwalls and Shovelers joining those that have bred here. Hard weather will concentrate them in unfrozen areas of water – a partial freeze also increases your chances of seeing Bitterns and Water Rails, as both must abandon their secretive ways to search out the best foraging grounds. The feeding stations provide a welcome source of sustenance for the resident songbirds of the reserve, their numbers boosted in winter by visiting flocks of Siskins, which also feed in the Alder trees. Flocks of Black-tailed Godwits and Lapwings may take refuge on the reserve at this time (a few godwits stay on all year), and birds of prey that breed in the local uplands – Peregrine Falcons, Merlins and Hen Harriers – head for lower ground and easier hunting opportunities.

Reedbed management mainly takes place in winter. It is essential work, with reed cutting, raking and burning to stop the reedbed from drying out and eventually turning to woodland, which would be no good for the rare and special wildlife that depends on the Leighton Moss reedbed to live.

How to get here

Grid ref./postcode SD 478750/LA5 0

By road The reserve is 4 miles north of Carn-forth. Take Junction 35 off the M6 (signposted Carnforth), then follow the A6 north (signposted to Milnthorpe). Brown tourist signs direct you to the reserve off the A6 and take you through the villages of Yealand Redmayne and Yealand Storrs. Alternatively, to come from Carnforth, follow signs to Silverdale, passing through the village of Millhead. Shortly after entering Warton, turn left and follow the road until you come to a T-junction beyond the level crossing, where you turn right, then right again just before the Silverdale railway station.

By public transport Silverdale station is on the Manchester Airport/Preston to Barrow line and is only 150 metres from the reserve. Turn left out of the station entrance, then left again and then right. The nearest bus stop is immediately opposite the reserve entrance. The Silverdale shuttle bus meets the trains and provides a shuttle service between Silverdale Railway Station and Silverdale Village.

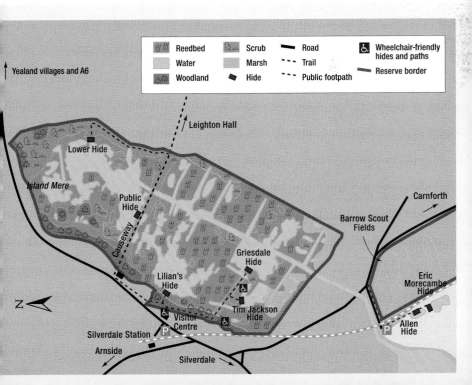

NORTHERN ENGLAND

MARSHSIDE SSSI, SPA, NATURA 2000

Just at the mouth of the Ribble Estuary, Marshside is a wonderful coastal reserve within easy reach of western Lancashire. The RSPB leases this site from Sefton MBC. The coastal grassland and pools provide breeding sites for wading birds, and rich feeding grounds in autumn and winter. 'Mad March' hares race across the fields in springtime, while summer brings butterflies.

● Access, facilities, contact details and accessibility

There are two hides, a viewing platform and three viewing screens. With the nature trails plus existing footpaths you can do a round walk of 4.3 miles. Guided walks can be arranged.

- **Telephone** 01704 226 190; **web**: www.rspb.org.uk/marshside
- **Opening hours** Sandgrounders hide is open daily 8.30am–5pm (dusk in winter). Nels hide is open daily but times vary.
- **Entry fees** Free, but donations are welcome
- **Accessibility** The trail to Sandgrounders Hide from car park (200m) is wheelchair-accessible, as is the trail from Nel's Hide to the car park (550m)
- **Dogs** Some access is permitted – please contact the reserve for details

What to look for

From the car park, trails go in a loop around the outside of the reserve, along the sea wall. You can reach the first hide very quickly, but if time and mobility permits, the circular walk that picks up the Sefton Coastal Footpath is well worth taking.

If you come in spring, you'll be treated to the sight and sound of around 80 pairs of Lapwings establishing and defending their territories. These colourful waders are agile in flight, rolling, climbing and tumbling, and calling all the while up to 40 pairs of Avocets nest on islands in the ponds, right in front of Sandgrounders Hide.

WILDLIFE BY SEASON

SPRING
Lapwings and hares express the joys of spring with tumbling aerial displays and boxing bouts respectively. Migrating waders visit the muddy edges of the pools.

SUMMER
Redshanks and Avocets are nesting, and the grassland is full of flowers and butterflies.

AUTUMN
Pink-footed Geese start to arrive to roost on the mudflats. Look out for Migrant Hawker dragonflies on sunny days.

WINTER
Water birds gather in huge flocks on the marsh. Look out for raptors.

Brown Hares lose their habitual shyness in spring and pursue one another across the fields, occasionally standing up on their hind feet to 'box' when a female tires of a male's attention and tries to fend him off.

Common Blues, Wall Browns and other colourful butterflies start to appear on warm days in April, and the grassland is rich with flowers and insects throughout the summer. The RSPB uses grazing, cutting and controlled drainage to keep the grass suitable for the nesting waders. A reintroduction programme for Natterjack Toads is underway here.

The mudflats provide a roosting place through autumn and winter for Pink-footed Geese – you can see the noisy skeins on the move late or early in the day. In total some 40,000 wildfowl are here over winter, an astounding spectacle. Lapwings and Golden Plovers form large foraging flocks, often spooked by passing Peregrines.

How to get here

Grid ref./postcode SD 353205/PR9 9

WHEN TO VISIT
Visit early or late on autumn and winter days to see the Pink-footed Geese leaving or returning to their roosts. Otherwise, the reserve is interesting year-round, and time of day is not critical.

By road From Southport, follow the coast road north (1.5 miles from Southport Pier) to the small car park by the old sand works.

By public transport Southport (Chapel Street Station) is the nearest rail station. From here follow London Street until it joins Lord Street and then go straight across Lord Street and on down Nevill Street to the Promenade. From here turn right to follow Marine Lake to its northern end; turn left onto Fairway and then right on to Marine Drive. The reserve begins at Hesketh Road after 0.6 miles; take the first turning on right. Total distance is 1.8 miles. You can also take bus 42 or 44 from Lord Street to Marshside Road – from here walk to the sea wall.

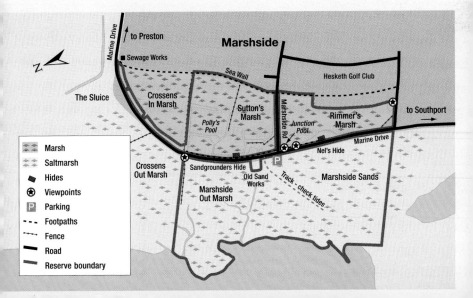

Legend:
- Marsh
- Saltmarsh
- Hides
- Viewpoints
- Parking
- Footpaths
- Fence
- Road
- Reserve boundary

NORTHERN ENGLAND

SALTHOLME SSSI, SPA

Here in the Tees Valley, the RSPB joined with the Teeside Environmental Trust and many other local funders and supporters to establish a brand new nature reserve and discovery park. Pools, scrapes, reedbeds and grasslands have all been created. A wonderful award-winning centre with café and shop completes the picture.

● Access, facilities, contact details and accessibility

There is a well-stocked shop, a café serving meals and drinks and an adventure playground for younger visitors. There is a full programme of events and you can arrange a guided walk or a group visit.

- **Telephone** 01642 546625; **email** saltholme@rspb.org.uk; **web** www.rspb.org.uk/saltholme
- **Opening hours** Open daily Oct–March 10am–4pm, April–Sept 10am–5pm, closed Christmas Day
- **Entry fees** Entry Fees free for RSPB members. £3 per car for non-members (free to all staying less than one hour)
- **Accessibility** The trails, shop and café are accessible
- **Dogs** Please contact the reserve for advice

What to look for

A massive amount of time, planning and hard physical labour has gone into making Saltholme the reserve it is today, and its potential for wildlife is only just coming into full flower. As development and study continues and the site matures, it will only become richer and more important.

The wet grassland has nesting waders – Redshanks, Lapwings and Snipes can all be seen and heard in spring. Winter grazing helps prepare a perfect nursery for wader chicks, which need shallow pools and ditches to search for the tiny flies and other insects they eat.

WILDLIFE BY SEASON

SPRING

Watch Lapwings, Brown Hares, Great Crested Grebes, Common Terns and many other species getting amorous and territorial.

SUMMER

Yellow Wagtails flycatch in the fields and butterflies, dragonflies, orchids and other wild flowers bloom.

AUTUMN

Migrant waders are arriving by late summer, their numbers growing into autumn. Winter wildfowl arrive later on.

WINTER

Thousands of birds feed and roost on the wet grassland and around the pools. Peregrines and other raptors hunt overhead.

The pools attract nesting Gadwalls, Mallards, Pochards, Tufted Ducks and Shelducks, while Great Crested Grebes cruise across the water with their humbug-striped babies riding on their backs, peering out from between the adults' folded wings. Swallows and Sand and House Martins hoover up the swarms of flies dancing above the surface. On the fields, Yellow Wagtails are also avidly snapping up the fly bounty.

Migrant ducks, waders and other birds start to arrive in autumn. The reserve has also attracted rarities in the form of Great White Egret, Glaucous-winged Gull, Long-toed Stint, Semipalmated Sandpiper and Lesser Yellowlegs, among others.

Large flocks of Lapwings and Golden Plovers overwinter on the fields, and winter wildfowl includes Wigeons and Teals. Water Rails venture out in into the open on cold days. The sudden arrival of a Peregrine Falcon causes mass panic. Lucky visitors could witness the falcon swooping into a whirling flock and smacking an unlucky victim out of the sky

WHEN TO VISIT

Saltholme is a great place to visit at any time of year, with each season offering its own particular combination of species and wildlife activities. Time of day is not important.

– a shocking sight perhaps but proof positive that the ecology of Salthome is thriving and set to go from strength to strength.

How to get here

Grid ref./postcode NZ 506231/ TS2 1

By road Saltholme is six minutes from the A19; turn east off the A19 north of Stockton along the A689. After half a mile, take the A1185; in 4 miles join the A178 at a mini-roundabout and take the third exit. The reserve entrance is 250m on the right-hand side.

By public transport The nearest bus stop is outside the entrance to Saltholme, on the Seaton Carew Road. Bus 1 stops here and is run by Stagecoach in Hartlepool. During peak hours it runs every half hour every day.

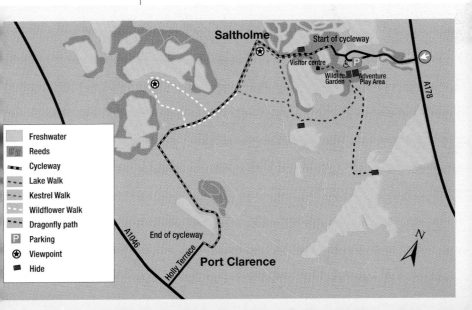

Map legend:
- Freshwater
- Reeds
- Cycleway
- Lake Walk
- Kestrel Walk
- Wildflower Walk
- Dragonfly path
- P Parking
- Viewpoint
- Hide

NORTHERN ENGLAND

ST BEES HEAD SSSI

These towering cliffs south of Whitehaven host a bustling colony of seabirds through spring and summer. Take a bracing walk along the cliff-top paths and enjoy great views of the seabirds, as well as scrubland songbirds like Stonechats, Linnets and Whitethroats. This is a good vantage point to look for migrating seabirds in autumn.

● Access, facilities, contact details and accessibility

The cliff-top path runs for 2.8 miles, and there are three strategically placed viewing platforms along its length.

- **Telephone** 01697 351330; **email** stbees.head@rspb.org.uk; **web** www.rspb.org.uk/stbeeshead
- **Opening hours** Open at all times
- **Entry fees** Free, but donations to help continue the work here are welcome
- **Accessibility** The cliff-top paths are steep and uneven, so not suitable for the mobility-impaired
- **Dogs** Only allowed on public footpaths and bridleways

What to look for

The cliffs at St Bees Head are spectacular for a walk at any time of year, but in spring and summer the wonderful views are just part of the story, as the cliffs become home to thousands of seabirds. This is one of the most southerly places to see the UK's rarest breeding auk species, the attractive Black Guillemot.

Fulmars and Herring Gulls are the first seabirds on site. At first glance they can be difficult to tell apart, but Fulmars are not closely related to gulls and if you see one close up you'll notice it has distinctive tubular nostrils, and big black eyes that seem to frown under heavy eyebrows.

WILDLIFE BY SEASON

SPRING
The first Fulmars and Herring Gulls take up their territories in early spring, with the other birds arriving later.

SUMMER
Activity is in full swing, with auks, Kittiwakes, Fulmars and Cormorants all busy rearing their chicks.

AUTUMN
The seabirds depart by early autumn, but windy days may bring migrating shearwaters and skuas close inshore.

WINTER
The seascapes can be especially dramatic. The cliffs are quiet but you could see Peregrine Falcons and Ravens.

The commonest auk here is the Guillemot, but Razorbills are present too. The Black Guillemot is smaller than both and is black all over apart from a big white oval on the wing. Look out for Black Guillemots in Fleswick Bay, between the North and South Heads, if you visit early in the day in spring. They can be hard to pick out on the cliffs but are easier to spot when they're on the sea. South Head has a large colony of Cormorants, and you may see dolphins or Harbour Porpoises.

Kittiwakes contribute much of the St Bees soundtrack with their deafening and raucous calls. More pleasant altogether are the songs of Linnets, Whitethroats and other small birds that nest in the gorse bushes that line the cliff-top paths.

Most of the seabirds leave at the end of summer, and the cliffs are quiet, but Black Guillemots usually remain close to their breeding sites in winter. Two other birds that you could see at any time of year are Peregrine Falcons and Ravens. These two species liven up many a quiet cliff-top walk – especially when they meet and antagonise each other with dramatic chases and tumbles through the air. You could imagine that they are actually playing together, practising their respective flight skills while waiting for spring to come again.

How to get here
Grid ref./postcode NX 959118/ CA27 0
By road From St Bees village, take Beach Road, parking in the shore-front car park at the end. Access to the reserve is via the path over the wooden footbridge at the north end of the promenade.
By public transport St Bees station is three-quarters of a mile away. Follow the directions as above.

WHEN TO VISIT
The seabird colony is active from mid-spring through to late summer. Time of day is not important.

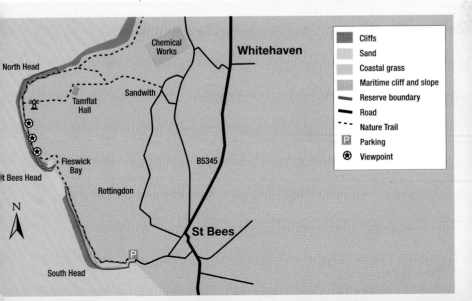

	Cliffs
	Sand
	Coastal grass
	Maritime cliff and slope
—	Reserve boundary
—	Road
- - -	Nature Trail
P	Parking
✱	Viewpoint

BELFAST HARBOUR RESERVE

ASSI, SPA, RAMSAR, NATURA 2000

Belfast Lough is a wide sea lough, formed where the River Lagan joins the sea. The RSPB reserve here is deep in the inner lough, close to the city of Belfast with its famous harbour, offering close-up views of wildlife and easily accessible facilities for those living in the city or visiting the area. The reserve famously offers incredible close-up views of waders, particularly Black-tailed Godwits. In the summer there is also a busy colony of Arctic and Common Terns, which nest on islands in the lagoons. The mudflats and lagoons attract wading birds in spring and autumn, while the reserve's areas of wet grassland support even more wildlife. Staff at the observation room can tell you what's about and help you get the most from your visit.

● Access, facilities, contact details and accessibility

The observation room is a comfortable place to enjoy close-up views of shorebirds and terns. There are also two hides on the reserve. You can arrange group visits, and educational events are held.

● **Telephone** 02890 491 547; **email** belfast.lough@rspb.org.uk; **web** www.rspb.org.uk/belfastlough

● **Opening hours** Viewpoints open at all times; observation room open Tuesday to Saturday (9am–5pm), Sundays (1–5pm). Closed Mondays and Sunday mornings and 25 December and 1 January.

● **Entry fees** None, but donations to help continue the work here are appreciated

● **Accessibility** There is easy access for wheelchair users to the observation room and one outdoor viewpoint, 150m from the observation room, with excellent views over the lagoons. The other viewpoint is inaccessible to wheelchair users.

● **Dogs** Only allowed on public footpaths and bridleways

WILDLIFE BY SEASON

SPRING

Common and Arctic Terns are back at the colony in April and pairing up. Roseate Terns may visit. Swallows, martins and, by late spring, Swifts are hunting over the water. Migrating waders visit the reserve on their northbound journeys.

SUMMER

The terns are busy feeding their chicks, while Mallards, Coots and Moorhens are escorting their fluffy offspring across the water. Wetland insects like damselflies flit over the lagoon. By late summer waders are already arriving on return migration.

AUTUMN

Migrating flocks of Black-tailed Godwits, Oystercatchers, Redshanks, Dunlins and Curlews gather in autumn. There's a chance of a wandering North American wader or two showing up. Winter wildfowl and birds of prey start to arrive.

WINTER

Numbers of winter wildfowl build up, with Teals and Wigeons the most numerous but many other species, including Scaups, also possible. A few Brent Geese overwinter too.

What to look for

This reserve offers a great opportunity to watch nesting and wintering water birds, on the Harbour Lagoon. Part of the challenge the RSPB face here is making sure the lagoon is just as appealing to these two categories of birdlife, with their different requirements.

Nesting birds need safety from predators. For terns, which nest on the ground, an island will always be the best choice as it is safe from most predatory mammals. The RSPB has gradually increased the size of the islands in Harbour Lagoon

RSPB hopes they will one day stay and breed – nestboxes on the ground are provided to offer them even safer nesting places.

Various common water birds, like Mallards, Moorhens and Coots, also nest on the lagoon. The nearby areas of wet grassland provide breeding grounds for Redshanks, Snipes and Lapwings, and the drier areas have Skylarks and other songbirds.

Outside the breeding season, the lough mudflats attract feeding waders, especially in spring and autumn, when large

The black head, white collar and neat white moustache livens up the male Reed Bunting's plumage, making him one of the more handsome reedbed birds.

so that they will be able to hold more pairs of terns, while electric fencing helps keep out determined predators that might otherwise swim to the islands. Two species of terns nest here, the Common and the Arctic. They are very similar at first glance, but you'll rarely find a better opportunity to compare the two side by side than from the observation hide here. The rare Roseate Tern does not breed here but individual birds show up now and then, and the

numbers stop off on migration. They include Curlews, Dunlins, Oystercatchers, Lapwings, and Icelandic Black-tailed Godwits, with smaller numbers of Curlew Sandpipers, Spotted Redshanks and Little Stints. A handful of rarities are found most years, the majority of them in autumn. Many of the rarity reports involve species that hail from the other side of the Atlantic, such as Pectoral Sandpiper, Long-billed Dowitcher and Buff-breasted Sandpiper.

With a very good view, it's easy to see the shortish, all-red bill of the Arctic Tern – the Common Tern's is longer and has a distinct black tip.

The combination of inexperienced young birds making their first ever migration with prevailing winds blowing across from North America means that on any given autumn day there may well be at least one lost American wader staying on the reserve.

Many of the waders have moved on by late autumn, but wildfowl numbers are just starting to build up. The commonest two species are the Wigeon and the Teal – like all ducks they look their best in winter and early spring as the males are in full breeding plumage. If you see a duck that has a Teal-like pattern but with a white line running down its body instead of along, you could have found an American Green-winged Teal – ducks from North America are just as

TAKE YOUR TERN

In some parts of the UK, the easy way to tell Common Terns from Arctic Terns is to look at a map. If you're in southern England, it's probably a Common Tern. If you're in northern Scotland it's probably an Arctic Tern. If you're inland, it's probably a Common Tern as Arctics stick mainly to the coast. But that leaves a big area of overlap and, wherever you are, unless you get a good look it's hard to be sure. Many birdwatchers' notebooks will refer to 'commic terns' – the nickname for a tern that could have been a Common, but could also have been an Arctic. However, at Belfast Lough in spring, with both species on show right in front of you, you can take the time to learn the differences between the two, which are summarised below.

Bill – longer, more orangey and with a dark tip in Common Terns; shorter and more crimson in Arctics.

Legs – shorter in Arctics, which also means they 'waddle' more than the longer-legged Commons.

Tail – longer in Arctics, reaching beyond the tips of the wings when the bird is at rest.

Underparts – cleaner white in Commons; often slightly greyish in Arctics.

Wing translucence – in Arctics the long wing feathers are all translucent; in commons just a narrow panel is.

Wing edges – the underside of the trailing edge of the wing-tip has a neat, narrow dark edge in Arctics, but Commons have a wider and blurrier dark edge.

Voice – the Arctic has a harsher voice than the common. To be fair though, both species make a fairly awful racket.

susceptible to losing their way as waders. North America's version of the Wigeon – the American Wigeon – is also occasionally seen here. Other, commoner ducks you may see on the lagoon include Shelducks, Shovelers and Scaups. A small flock of Brent Geese also winters here. The observation hide provides a comfortable place for cold-weather bird-watching, with telescopes available to help you identify the tricky distant birds.

How to get here

Grid ref./postcode NW 488307/BT4
By road The reserve is located within Belfast Harbour Estate. Two main entrances lead into the harbour estate; both are signposted along the A2 (Belfast to Holywood dual carriageway).

A tiny wader, hardly bigger than a sparrow, the Little Stint visits the Lough in autumn. Juveniles are particularly smartly marked.

WHEN TO VISIT

With breeding terns in summer, flocks of wildfowl in winter and migrant waders in between, this is a reserve for all seasons, and the time of day you visit is not important.

From the Dee Street entrance the reserve car park is a further 2 miles; from the Tillysburn entrance it is 1 mile.
By public transport Translink's Metro bus stops close to the reserve (service 26A and 27).

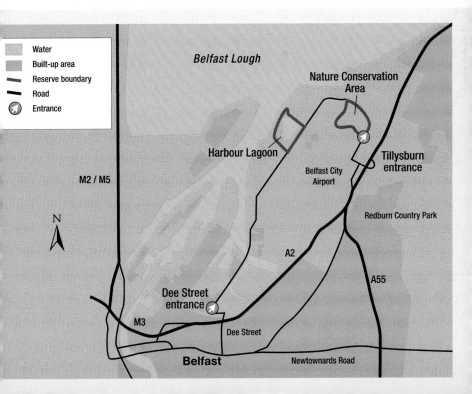

Legend:
- Water
- Built-up area
- Reserve boundary
- Road
- Entrance

Belfast Lough

Nature Conservation Area

Harbour Lagoon

Tillysburn entrance

Belfast City Airport

M2 / M5

Redburn Country Park

N

A2

A55

Dee Street entrance

M3

Dee Street

Belfast

Newtownards Road

NORTHERN IRELAND

LOUGH FOYLE

ASSI, SPA, RAMSAR, NATURA 2000

Lough Foyle, a sea lough on the north coast of Northern Ireland, is an important refuge for thousands of migrating waders and wintering wildfowl. The RSPB protects and manages an area on the south-eastern shore of the lough to provide optimal habitat for the birds. You can view them from several good places on the road.

● Access, facilities, contact details and accessibility

This is a reserve mainly for the independent birdwatcher with a car, with no facilities or trails but the chance to see great numbers of birds in a stunning remote location.

- **Telephone** 02890 491547; **web** www.rspb.org.uk/loughfoyle
- **Opening hours** Open at all times
- **Entry fees** Free, though donations are welcome
- **Accessibility** The best viewpoints are from minor roads through the area
- **Dogs** Allowed on public footpaths and bridleways

What to look for

This reserve is best visited in autumn, for wading birds, or winter, for flocks of swans, geese and ducks. If you time your visit to coincide with high tide, you will have closer views as the mud is covered and the birds are pushed inshore.

Some of the waders that arrive here in autumn stay on for the whole winter, while others move on further south after a few weeks. The short-stayers include Whimbrels, Spotted Redshanks, Curlew Sandpipers and Little Stints, while the wintering flocks are mainly composed of Curlews, Oystercatchers,

WILDLIFE BY SEASON

SPRING
Generally quiet, although a few winter birds may not yet have moved on. You may see skuas and terns at sea.

SUMMER
Waders including Curlew Sandpiper, Little Stint and Spotted Redshank start to come through by late summer.

AUTUMN
The numbers of waders using the mudflats build up, and winter wildfowl starts to arrive.

WINTER
A variety of wildfowl and waders winter on the mudflats and this is also a good time of year to see birds of prey. Check the tideline for Snow Buntings.

Redshanks and Golden and Grey Plovers. This is a great place to compare and contrast waders' feeding behaviours and general appearance. If you're unsure whether you're looking at a Whimbrel or a Curlew, look at the bill first. Curlews' bills are often immensely long, with mature females the longest-billed of all, and the bill has a smooth downward curve. Whimbrel bills are shorter, and the curve is more abrupt, looking almost like a kink. Golden and Grey Plovers can be confusing in winter too – as well as being greyer, Grey Plovers are stockier, heavier-billed, and most helpfully of all, show a neat black armpit-patch when they fly. Sanderlings can be found on the sandier shore at Magilligan Point.

The wildfowl parade is led by flocks of wild swans, both Whooper and Bewick's. The beds of eelgrass that are exposed at low tide attract large flocks of Wigeons and Brent Geese. White-fronted Geese, Pintails, Teals and other wildfowl may also be seen. Out on the sea, there are often Slavonian Grebes, while flocks of Snow

WHEN TO VISIT
This reserve is best in autumn and especially winter. Visit as the tide is rising for closer views of birds on the mudflats.

Buntings with occasional Lapland Buntings pick their way along the tideline.

Always be alert to the chance of seeing a bird of prey in winter – Peregrine Falcons and Merlins are the likeliest suspects. The Peregrines hunt ducks and waders, while Merlins prey mainly on small songbirds which they catch after a lightning-speed chase.

How to get here
Grid ref. NV 714858
By road You can view the lough from Longfield Point, Faughanvale and Ballykelly, all reached by minor roads off the A2 Limavady–Londonderry road.
By public transport Difficult. The nearest station is Londonderry, 8 miles away, and the nearest bus stop is at Ballykelly, some 6 miles away in the other direction.

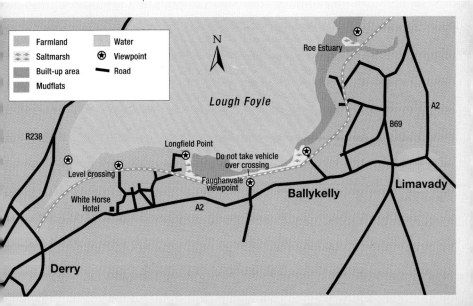

LOWER LOUGH ERNE   ASSI, NNR

The RSPB takes care of some 40 islands in the huge freshwater Lower Lough Erne, managing them for their breeding birds and other wildlife. You can see the islands while enjoying a walk through Castlecaldwell Wood on the shore, or if you are on a boating trip on the lough you can circumnavigate the islands and even land on two of them at certain times of the year.

● Access, facilities, contact details and accessibility

A good place for a quiet and interesting walk, this reserve also offers guided walks and boat trips by arrangement.
- **Telephone** 02866 341 456; **email** lower.lougherne@rspb.org.uk;
  web www.rspb.org.uk/lowerlougherne
- **Opening hours** The Castlecaldwell footpaths are open daily from dawn until dusk
- **Entry fees** Free, but donations are welcome
- **Accessibility** Assistance would be required for wheelchair users to use the trails
- **Dogs** Only allowed on public footpaths and bridleways

What to look for

Wildlife interest here is found in the woodlands on the shore, on the islands and on the waters of the lough itself. Most visitors will be here to explore the woodlands, via the two nature trails, from which there are views across the lough. You'll see birdlife all year round in the woods, but spring is best.

Castlecaldwell Wood is alive with birdsong in the spring, with migrants like Blackcaps joining the resident species. Once a conifer plantation, it is now a more diverse mixed woodland and attracts a range of birds. Listen for the distinctive 'spinning coin' song of the Wood Warbler – this beautiful little yellow-and-green bird is an

WILDLIFE BY SEASON

SPRING
Migrant warblers arrive. Sandwich Terns return to their breeding colony, and grebes and ducks display on the lough.

SUMMER
The birds are rearing their chicks. A good time of year to see mammals, including Red Squirrels and Otters.

AUTUMN
The woodland assumes its array of autumn colours. Migrant birds are preparing to depart.

WINTER
Wildfowl numbers increase on the lough – Goldeneyes and the occasional Whooper Swan may be seen. Redpolls join the woodland birds.

occasional breeder here. The wood is also very good for mammals. The species you're probably most likely to see is the Red Squirrel, chasing through the treetops. However, there are also Badgers and Pine Martens here – visit early or late in the day to improve your chances of seeing them. Both of these predators are nocturnal, but the shorter nights in summer mean this season is best for seeing them.

On the lough islands, several species of birds nest, including Redshanks and Lapwings. The most remarkable breeding bird is the Sandwich Tern, a large and handsome tern that does not make a habit of breeding at inland sites like this. In fact, Lough Erne holds the only inland colonies of the species in the UK. Sandwich Terns are robust, short-tailed terns, long-billed and shaggy-crested. With luck you'll have close views of them as they hover over the water and drop down to snatch up a small fish from the surface. Common Terns breed here too, but the two species are not difficult to tell apart if you get a reasonable view.

WHEN TO VISIT
The reserve is interesting and worth a visit at any time of year, but spring into early summer is perhaps the most exciting time. Time of day is not important.

The lough has a few species of breeding wildfowl, including Red-breasted Mergansers. Through autumn into winter the numbers and variety of wildfowl increases, with diving ducks like Goldeneyes and Pochards, and dabblers like Wigeons arriving. Whooper Swans put in appearances on occasion, as do White-fronted Geese. Otters use the lough and you could see one at any time of year.

How to get here
Grid ref. NV 126271
By road In north Fermanagh on A47 Kesh to Belleek Road, the reserve is signposted to the south around 6 miles east of Belleek.
By public transport There is no convenient public transport access to this reserve.

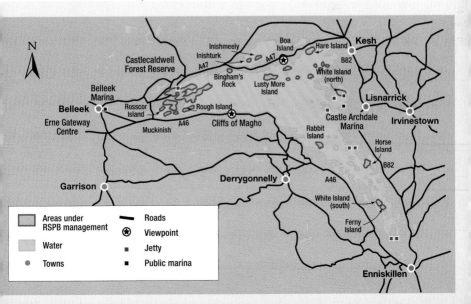

NORTHERN IRELAND

PORTMORE LOUGH

ASSI, SPA, LNR, RAMSAR, NATURA 2000

Portmore Lough's undisturbed shoreline is attractive to waders and other wetland birds. The RSPB manages an area of wet meadowland, reedbed and marsh on the south-eastern shore, and runs many exciting events to help you get to know the wildlife.

● Access, facilities, contact details and accessibility

There is a 0.6-mile nature trail leading to a hide. Educational events are regularly held here and you can arrange guided walks, group visits and binocular hire.

● **Telephone** 02890 491547; **web** www.rspb.org.uk/portmorelough

● **Opening hours** The reserve is open at all times. When the car park is locked please park outside the gates.

● **Entry fees** Free, but donations are welcome

● **Accessibility** A 500m all-weather path suitable for wheelchairs extends from the car park to a grassed picnic area. The main trail hide and meadows are not suitable for wheelchairs.

● **Dogs** Allowed anywhere but must be kept under close control at all times

What to look for

For wetland and meadowland wildfowl, this reserve offers a great wildlife-watching experience whatever time of year you visit. In springtime, you'll hear an array of birds, large and small, singing or calling to establish their territories. Listen for the tumbling notes of Skylarks and the comical whoops of Lapwings as you walk through the meadows, and the songs of Sedge Warblers and Reed Buntings from the reedbed and tangled vegetation around the ditches. The RSPB has put up nestboxes to encourage the reserve's Tree Sparrows, while on the lough itself, Common Terns nest on the rafts provided for them and Great Crested Grebes

WILDLIFE BY SEASON

SPRING
Skylarks sing over the fields and reedbed birds from the ditches. Early insects are on the wing, spring flowers bloom and ducks and grebes display to each other on the lough.

SUMMER
All the birds are rearing chicks, and insects abound.

AUTUMN
Swallows and martins flock before beginning their southbound migrations. Duck and wader numbers start to build up.

WINTER
The flooded meadows attract huge flocks of Lapwings and Golden Plovers, while Pochards, Tufted Ducks and other wildfowl assemble on the lough.

display from February.

The meadows have a rich community of flowering plants, which in turn support a diversity of insects. Look for Orange-tip butterflies from early spring, the males displaying neat orange wingtips and the duller females busy visiting Cuckoo Flowers on which to lay their eggs. Throughout spring and summer, large numbers of dragonflies and damselflies hunt over the reserve. Winter grazing with Polish Konik ponies (the only ones in Ireland) helps maintain the richness of the meadows for the summer.

Once the business of rearing chicks is out of the way, summer migrant terns and songbirds depart, but wildfowl numbers start to increase, peaking in winter. The lough attracts many Tufted Ducks and Pochards, both diving ducks that favour fairly shallow water. Colder weather may bring other, scarcer diving ducks such as Goldeneyes or Scaups. The meadows often flood, and become feeding grounds for flocks of Lapwings and Golden Plovers. As dusk falls, large and noisy flocks of Greylag Geese and Whooper Swans flight onto the lough to roost for the night.

WHEN TO VISIT
This reserve is well worth a visit at any time of year, and time of day is not important.

How to get here
Grid ref. J 104687
By road Leave the M1 at Junction 9, Moira roundabout, and head up the A26 towards the International Airport and Antrim. After the Glenavy Road Service Station on the right, take the second road on the left, signposted Aghalee. At Aghalee Village turn left at the T-junction then right into the Ballycairn Road which is signposted Portmore Lough Reserve. After 3 miles turn right at the T-junction opposite the Gawleys Gate inn. After a series of bends RSPB Portmore Lough is signposted to the right, up Georges Island Road.
By public transport There is no easy public transport access.

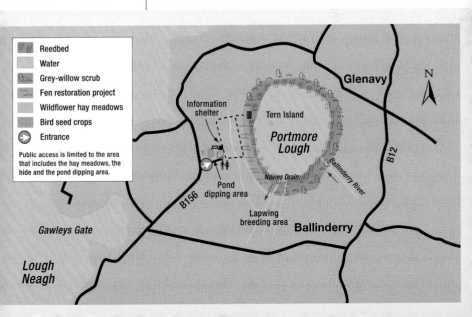

Reedbed
Water
Grey-willow scrub
Fen restoration project
Wildflower hay meadows
Bird seed crops
Entrance

Public access is limited to the area that includes the hay meadows, the hide and the pond dipping area.

Information shelter

Tern Island

Portmore Lough

Navies Drain

Ballinderry River

B12

Glenavy

N

B156

Pond dipping area

Lapwing breeding area

Ballinderry

Gawleys Gate

Lough Neagh

NORTHERN IRELAND

RATHLIN ISLAND SEABIRD CENTRE

ASSI, SPA, SAC, AONB, NATURA 2000

From the moment the ferry pulls out of Ballycastle harbour, the excitement of a trip to Rathlin Island begins. Seabirds fly or furiously paddle out of the way of the boat – auks, Gannets and Fulmars all pass at close quarters, and seals and Eider Ducks bob about in Rathlin harbour. Once you reach the reserve itself, go to the viewing platforms to enjoy astonishing views right into the heart of the bustling seabird colony. Rathlin Island offers an awesome, almost overwhelming experience – a ring-side view into one of the most high-octane wildlife spectacles available anywhere. As well as the reserve itself, the island offers a mini-world of wild beauty and fascinating history, so if time permits you could spend the night and explore the island from end to end at your leisure.

● Access, facilities, contact details and accessibility

The viewing platforms here are staffed by RSPB wardens and volunteers, who will help you and your family see and identify the various different seabirds. Telescopes are provided and staff will help children get used to using them.

- ● **Telephone** 02820 760062; **web** www.rspb.org.uk/rathlin
- ● **Opening hours** 11am–3pm daily from April to mid-September
- ● **Entry fees** Free, but donations to help continue the work here are welcome
- ● **Accessibility** Access is currently being improved for mobility-impaired visitors. For more information, please contact the warden's office.
- ● **Dogs** Access for dogs under control and on lead is permitted

WILDLIFE BY SEASON

SPRING

The cliff-nesting seabirds start to return from February, with Fulmars the first to arrive. Soon all the other species are *in situ* and nesting has begun. Wheatears and other songbirds visit the clifftop fields. Eiders court each other offshore.

What to look for

The boot-shaped Rathlin Island, with a lighthouse at each corner, lies 6 miles north of County Antrim, and just 15.5 miles south of the Mull of Kintyre in Scotland. It is about 4 miles long from end to end, and marks the most northerly point in Northern Ireland. It is inhabited, but only just, with almost 100 hardy residents staying put through the winter and a few hundred extras visiting just for summer.

The waters around the island are rich in marine life, and with

from the ferry crossing, as well as many of the seabirds that nest here. Walking or cycling the 4-mile trail from the harbour to the reserve is a great way to get to know the island itself. The trail is navigable by vehicle too, although the last stretch is very rough. Look out for Irish hares.

At the end of the trail at the western tip of the island, the Seabird Centre is set low down on the cliff to give you eye-level views of the birds nesting on the cliffs. From here, you can watch Guillemots, Razorbills,

Look out for Grey Seals and other sea mammals from the boat as you make the crossing to Rathlin.

SUMMER

Breeding activity is frenetic until the end of summer, when the cliff birds, adults and youngsters alike, depart and the cliffs are suddenly quiet. You could see Harbour Porpoises and dolphins offshore.

70m cliffs, the island offers an abundance of safe breeding habitat for seabirds. The RSPB manages some of the cliffs and cliff-top habitats for birds and other wildlife, and provides and maintains safe viewing places so visitors can enjoy great views of the island wildlife.

You could see dolphins, Harbour Porpoises and seals

Puffins, Kittiwakes, Fulmars and Shags going about their business – bickering over nest sites, incubating eggs, feeding chicks and flying to and from the sea on hunting expeditions. It is also interesting to see how the different species organise themselves, almost like geological strata, along and up and down the cliff-face. The

A big and sturdy auk, the Razorbill favours less crowded, more tucked-away ledges than its close cousin the Guillemot.

three auks for example, all black and white with frantic fast-flapping flight, have quite different preferred nest spots, with Puffins using burrows on the grassy tops, Razorbills choosing tucked-away nooks and crevices, and Guillemots packing as tightly as rush-hour commuters onto even the narrowest ledges.

Kittiwakes scream their name incessantly as they swirl around their nests, on ledges almost as narrow as those used by the guillemots. Fulmars like a little more personal space and choose awkward nubbins of rock – any other seabird venturing too close to a Fulmar's nest is liable to receive a nasty shock as the Fulmar vomits up a well-aimed crop-load of stinking, fishy oil to keep them away. Shags, which look like slimline Cormorants but have bright green eyes and a natty little curly crest, stand in groups on low rocks, holding their wings outspread to dry off after their fishing trips.

Not all the cliff-nesters are seabirds. Peregrine

Falcons enjoy the safe nesting spots and abundance of birds to hunt here – look out for a dark-backed, stocky, scythe-winged bird speeding along the cliff edge, its rump and tail often shining silvery when it catches the light.

In recent years, Choughs have returned to these cliffs to breed, following years of RSPB work to provide the right kinds of feeding conditions on the cliff-tops for them. Choughs are rather uncrowlike crows, with long, slender, downcurved red bills, and strikingly long-fingered wings that help them master the onshore breezes with effortless grace. They need open fields rich in invertebrate life in which to forage. The cliff-top fields are good for other birds too, such as Wheatears, Skylarks and Stonechats.

Besides the wildlife, there is much of interest to see on the island, including Bruce's Cave, which some say was the place where Robert the Bruce had his famously inspiring encounter with a spider (though similar claims are made for another three caves in Scotland!) The ruined castle on Rathlin also bears the name 'Bruce's Castle' – although historical details are few, it seems beyond doubt that the famous warrior did indeed visit and stay on Rathlin.

The waters around the islands have claimed many ships and boats over the centuries, and

WHEN TO VISIT

The reserve is open from late morning to mid-afternoon in spring and summer only, as the seabirds depart by the end of summer.

today Rathlin is popular with scuba divers, with a wealth of wrecks to explore. Divers whose interest lies in natural history will find much of interest here too – new species of anemone have been found, and a population of the rare Fan Mussel discovered. More than 130 species of sponges have been recorded – and 29 species new to science were discovered here in 2007. All in all, Rathlin offers an unforgettable experience for anyone with an interest in wildlife and an appreciation of remarkable wild places.

How to get here

Grid ref. NR 282092

By road You can reach the island by ferry from Ballycastle, County Antrim – it is possible to take your vehicle across or you can take a foot-passenger ferry and use the (private) minibus service or bicycle hire available on the island. You can make a day trip or stay overnight in one of the guesthouses in the harbour area, the hostel nearby or the camping barn close to the RSPB viewpoint – more details of available accommodation can be found by searching 'Rathlin Island' at www.discovernorthernireland.com/accomfinder. Visit www.rathlinballycastleferry.com for details of the ferry service.

The Juniper bush's attractive berries look at first glance like a collection of seaside pebbles.

By public transport The nearest railway station from Ballycastle is Ballymoney, some 15 miles away. Occasional buses run from Ballymoney to Ballycastle.

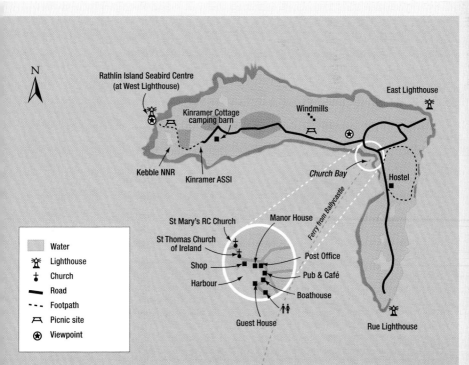

N

Rathlin Island Seabird Centre
(at West Lighthouse)

East Lighthouse

Kinramer Cottage
camping barn

Windmills

Kebble NNR

Kinramer ASSI

Church Bay

Hostel

St Mary's RC Church

Manor House

St Thomas Church
of Ireland

Post Office

Shop

Pub & Café

Harbour

Boathouse

Guest House

Rue Lighthouse

Ferry from Ballycastle

Water
Lighthouse
Church
Road
Footpath
Picnic site
Viewpoint

BARON'S HAUGH

A stone's throw from the town of Motherwell, this reserve is on the bank of the Clyde and includes woodland and scrub as well as the river itself. It is a good place to watch wildfowl, especially in winter, and to hear warblers and other songbirds in spring and summer. You can while away two hours or more taking a circular walk around the nature trails.

●Access, facilities, contact details and accessibility

The reserve has four hides, and a network of paths that can be joined up to make a circular walk.

- **Telephone** 0141 331 0993; **email** barons.haugh@rspb.org.uk; **web** www.rspb.org.uk/baronshaugh, www.dalzellandbaronshaugh.co.uk
- **Opening hours** Open at all times
- **Entry fees** Free, but donations are welcome
- **Accessibility** Some paths in the area are suitable for wheelchairs, but the circular trail is not
- **Dogs** Please ensure dogs are kept under proper control and away from the livestock, wetlands and pools

What to look for

Celandines flowering and Sand Martins returning are signs of spring at this riverside reserve. You can hear Sedge, Reed and Grasshopper Warblers all singing from mid-April. The Grasshopper Warbler is a very shy, mouse-like bird. Its song sounds like an angler's reel – easy enough to identify but the bird chooses very well hidden song perches and also has impressive ventriloquism skills.

The scrubby areas support Lesser White-throats and Bullfinches, while the woodland has the usual variety of birdlife. One interesting resident here is the Nuthatch, which was formerly a great rarity in Scotland but has been

WILDLIFE BY SEASON

SPRING
Songbirds and flowers are much in evidence in the woodland and scrub. Listen for singing Grasshopper Warblers. Ducks and swans are courting on the river.

SUMMER
Ducklings are out on the river, while dragonflies and butterflies are on the wing. Late butterflies and dragonflies are active on sunny days.

AUTUMN
Migrating waders visit the reserve, and winter wildfowl start to arrive.

WINTER
Wildfowl numbers peak, with Wigeons and Whooper Swans joining the resident species.

steadily pushing northwards. Nuthatches are agile birds, capable of scampering headfirst down a tree trunk. Their name comes from their trick of wedging a nut securely in a crack in the bark, then hammering it open with their serviceable, dagger-like bills.

The reserve has breeding Mute Swans, Mallards and other common water birds. Look out for the electric-blue flash of a passing Kingfisher, or the bow-wave formed by a swimming Otter. Colourful dragonflies and damselflies are out hunting and courting each other through summer, while butterflies patrol the scrubland and sunny woodland patches.

Many waders call in during the autumn, including Oyster-catchers and Redshanks. Wild-fowl start to arrive later on, with Whooper Swans and Wigeons among the more numerous. Gadwalls and Coots increase at this time too, the Gadwalls often 'stalking' the Coots as they dive for weed, then stealing a share of the bounty; scientists call this villainy 'commensal feeding'. In the winter woodlands, parties of small birds forage for food, flocking together to improve their chances of detecting a hunting Sparrowhawk before it's too late.

WHEN TO VISIT
At any time of year there is something interesting to see at this reserve. Early morning is best for songbirds.

How to get here
Grid ref./postcode NS 756553/ ML1 2
By road From Junction 6 of the M74, take the road to Motherwell. Bear right at the next traffic lights signposted to Wishaw. Turn right at the third mini roundabout, and follow the road to the junction, turn left then immediately right to enter the reserve.
By public transport Airbles Road is the nearest railway station. Turn right onto the main road, right at the second mini roundabout, then turn left and immediately right to enter the reserve.

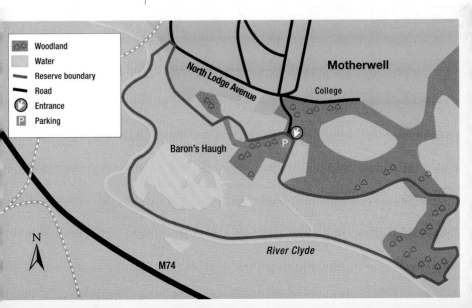

SOUTH AND WEST

Corncrake

COLL SSSI, SPA, SAC, NATURA 2000

If you have yet to visit a Hebridean island, you could do a lot worse than choosing Coll for your first. Famous among birdwatchers for its large and relatively easy-to-see Corncrake population, this beautiful island is rich with other wildlife too. The RSPB reserve covers 1,221 hectares of grassland, bog and dunes, managed to benefit Corncrakes and other wildlife.

● Access, facilities, contact details and accessibility

Three suggested walking routes lead from the two car parks. There is an information centre.
- **Telephone** 01879 2303 01; **web**: www.rspb.org.uk/coll
- **Opening hours** Open at all times. Please avoid walking through fields of hay and crops.
- **Entry fees** Free, although donations are welcome
- **Accessibility** Walking the paths may be difficult for some – contact the reserve for more details
- **Dogs** Only allowed on public footpaths and bridleways. Please keep them under proper control.

What to look for

If you're exploring the reserve in spring or summer, you'll probably hear Corncrakes easily. They give a very distinctive rasping, monotonous call, transcribed accurately in the species' scientific name as 'crex, crex'. Seeing one is more difficult, as they are shy and well-camouflaged – look out for a partridge-like sleek brown bird, with reddish wings and a grey head.

Corncrakes nest in the hayfields, while out on the machair (grass growing on limestone-rich soil derived from shell fragments) there are breeding waders. Red-throated Divers may visit the small pools in the boggy areas, while Great Northern Divers can be seen offshore in their splendid breeding plumage before they head north to Iceland to nest. The higher ground has

WILDLIFE BY SEASON

SPRING

Corncrakes are calling and breeding waders are displaying. Great Northern Divers are offshore. A few geese may still be around.

SUMMER

Many seabirds can be seen offshore, while Hen Harriers and Merlins are hunting over the machair.

AUTUMN

Barnacle and White-fronted Geese start to arrive for the winter. Migrating waders and thrushes pass through.

WINTER

Large numbers of geese have gathered. Seaducks and other seabirds may be seen offshore and farmland songbirds flock on the stubble fields.

Merlins and Hen Harriers, while the dunes support a number of nationally scarce insects. Look out for Otters around the coast.

In autumn, migrating waders visit the reserve, and winter birds start to arrive. Coll attracts large numbers of Barnacle and White-fronted Geese in winter, feeding and resting on the fields. Stubble fields hold a valuable supply of seeds through winter, which attracts flocks of farmland birds like Linnets, Twites, Skylarks and Rock Doves – the wild descendents of our familiar street pigeons. At sea, look for Long-tailed Ducks, divers and other seabirds.

How to get here

Grid ref./postcode NM 167563/ PA78 6

By road Coll is reached by ferry from Oban, landing at Arinagour on Coll. Contact Caledonian MacBrayne on 08705 650 000 for details. You can take your car across – the reserve is 6 miles west of Arinagour on the B8070. Emergency vehicles on the island do not use blue flashing lights – give way to any vehicle if it flashes its headlights as it comes up behind you.

By public transport There is no public transport on Coll. You can bring a bike across on the ferry, hire one on the island or get around on foot.

WHEN TO VISIT

Visit from late April through to late summer to hear and see Corncrakes. Otherwise, there are interesting birds and other wildlife here all year.

CRAKE IN THE GRASS

Many Corncrake chicks used to die when the crofters cut their hayfields in July – the birds were unable to escape the mower. By asking the farmers to cut one month later, when the young birds are more mobile, and by recommending that fields be cut from the inside outwards to give the birds an escape route, the RSPB has helped to massively increase the breeding success of Corncrakes on Coll and on other reserves.

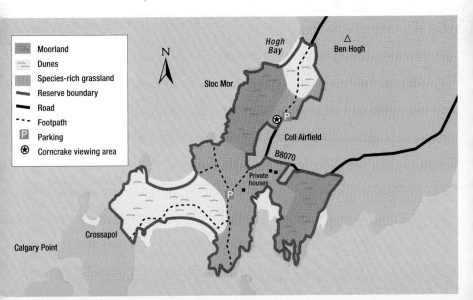

Moorland
Dunes
Species-rich grassland
Reserve boundary
Road
Footpath
P   Parking
✪   Corncrake viewing area

N

Hogh Bay
Ben Hogh
Sloc Mor
Coll Airfield
B8070
Private houses
Crossapol
Calgary Point

SOUTH AND WEST

INVERSNAID   SSSI, SAC, NP, NATURA 2000

On the shores of Loch Lomond, this reserve is an area of woodland that cloaks the hills before being replaced by moorland on the higher ground. It is a beautiful spot, offering excellent walking and an exciting range of wildlife to see, from Redstarts to wild swans, and magnificent Black Grouse to Golden Eagles. It lies on the long-distance West Highland Way path.

●Access, facilities, contact details and accessibility

The woodland nature trail here is a 0.6-mile loop off the West Highland Way.
- **Telephone** 0141 331 0993; **email** Inversnaid@rspb.org.uk; **web** www.rspb.org.uk/inversnaid
- **Opening hours** Open at all times
- **Entry fees** Free, though donations are welcome
- **Accessibility** Difficult for the mobility-impaired, as most paths are steep and rugged in places
- **Dogs** Allowed, but must be kept under control and away from livestock

What to look for

Inversnaid forms a part of the Great Trossachs Forest, which is in turn a part of the Scottish Forest Alliance, a partnership of the RSPB, the Forestry Commission Scotland, the Woodland Trust and BP. Inversnaid's woodland is comprised mainly of oak trees, around the bases of which grow many colourful spring flowers before the leaf canopy forms in May. The woods are home to a classic triptych of migratory songbirds – the Wood Warbler, Pied Flycatcher and Redstart. All three are attractive and worth searching out – the male Redstart especially attractive with his blue-grey back, bright red-orange belly, black throat, white eyebrows and constantly quivering red tail. His mate is a less exciting 'little brown job' but she too has the red and restless tail.

WILDLIFE BY SEASON

SPRING

Wood Warblers, Pied Flycatchers and Redstarts arrive. Golden Eagles fly over the hill and butterflies and flowers are out. Black Grouse lek throughout spring with activity peaking in April to May – visit around dawn to see them.

SUMMER

Woodland birds are feeding young, and butterfly numbers peak. A good time to see woodland mammals.

AUTUMN

Migrating wildfowl are moving down the loch. Winter thrushes arrive.

WINTER

Resident woodland birds are easiest to see while the trees are still leafless.

The woods are also home to many woodland mammals, such as the elusive Pine Marten, a large and beautiful member of the weasel family. The RSPB is increasing the area of broad-leaved woodland to encourage Black Grouse – up to six have lekked here in recent springs.

On the higher ground, you could see many interesting birds soaring over the moorland. Three of the biggest are the Buzzard, the Raven and the Golden Eagle. Buzzards are all broad wings and shortish, often fanned tail – they are also much commoner than Golden Eagles. You'll probably know an eagle when you see one – they are massive, long-winged birds of prey with a decent length of tail and an obviously projecting head. Ravens are crow-shaped, but larger with a wedge-shaped tail – you may also be able to make out a massively sturdy bill and 'full-throated' look – the deep, sonorous croaking call is another giveaway.

Inversnaid is quieter in autumn and winter, as many songbirds depart and the birds of prey become elusive. Still,

WHEN TO VISIT

This reserve is at its best in spring, with summer migrant songbirds, divers on the loch and a good show of woodland flowers. Your best chance of seeing a Golden Eagle is several hours after sunrise.

autumn can be exciting with wildfowl moving down the loch, while winter is a good time to see resident woodland birds.

How to get here

Grid ref./postcode NN 337090/ PA26 8
By road From Aberfoyle, follow the B829 sign posted to Inversnaid. After 12 miles on single track, turn left at a T-junction. Garrison Farm is on the right before the Inversnaid bunkhouse. For the other section of the reserve, continue down the hill to the Inversnaid Hotel and car park and then walk the West Highland Way to the north.
By public transport Stirling is the nearest station, 35 miles away. No buses serve this remote area.

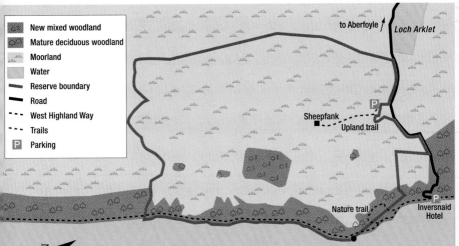

- New mixed woodland
- Mature deciduous woodland
- Moorland
- Water
- Reserve boundary
- Road
- West Highland Way
- Trails
- P Parking

to Aberfoyle
Loch Arklet
Sheepfank
P
Upland trail
Nature trail
Inversnaid Hotel
P
Rob Roy's cave

N

SOUTH AND WEST

Red Squirrel

KEN-DEE MARSHES

SSSI, SPA, RAMSAR, NATURA 2000

The reserve at Ken-Dee Marshes lies around the shore of Loch Ken, the largest lowland river and floodplain system in south Scotland. The reserve also includes areas of woodland, overlooking the beautiful wide river with its many islands. A great variety of wildlife is found at this tranquil and remote reserve, as you'll discover from a stroll around the pushchair-friendly nature trail.

● Access, facilities, contact details and accessibility

There are two hides and a goose viewing point, as well as a 3-mile nature trail.

- **Telephone** 01556 670464; **web** www.rspb.org.uk/kendeemarshes
- **Opening hours** Open at all times
- **Entry fees** Free, but donations to help continue the work here are welcome
- **Accessibility** The nature trail is wheelchair-accessible, and there is wheelchair access via a boardwalk to one hide
- **Dogs** Welcome, but must be kept under control

What to look for

If you're visiting or lucky enough to live in this picturesque part of Scotland, you'll find this reserve a lovely place to visit at any time of year. The woodlands are probably at their best in spring, with a fine show of Bluebells, Bugle, Enchanter's Nightshade and other attractive spring flowers. Early butterflies visit the flowers and songbirds hunt the insects, sing and build their nests. Pied Flycatchers and Redstarts are among the summer visitors, while Great Spotted Woodpeckers and Willow Tits are here all year.

The wet meadowland holds breeding Lapwings, Curlews and Oystercatchers. Water Rails and the rare Spotted Crake also breed

WILDLIFE BY SEASON

SPRING
Redstarts and Pied Flycatchers arrive in the woods. A variety of woodland plants flower.

SUMMER
Woodland songbirds are nesting, as are Oystercatchers, Lapwings and Curlews in the fields. Butterflies and dragonflies are at their most numerous.

AUTUMN
A good time to see Red Kites as the young birds disperse. Winter thrushes arrive.

WINTER
Greenland White-fronted Geese and Greylag Geese flock in the fields. Red Squirrels are easiest to see at this time of year.

here – both are shy and hard to see but the former gives itself away with a loud pig-like squealing, while the latter makes a remarkable whip-cracking sound, most commonly at dusk. The RSPB are planting new areas of reeds here to encourage these and other reedbed and wetland birds – reeds are also good for Harvest Mice which, along with Otters, are among the mammals you could see here.

Summertime is good for insects, with Ringlet butterflies over the grasslands and Purple Hairstreaks swirling around the oak canopy. If you use the hides at this time, be careful not to disturb the pipistrelle bats that roost in them during the daytime.

Autumn is a good time to see Red Kites – about 100 birds were reintroduced in Galloway at the start of the 21st century and numbers have soared. These distinctive raptors with their long wings, deeply forked tails, bold black, white and red pattern and marvellously effortless flight are a joy to watch. Autumn is also perhaps the best season to see Red Squirrels,

WHEN TO VISIT
To see the geese you'll need to visit in winter, but the reserve has plenty of wildlife on view in the other seasons. Woodlands in spring tend to be more lively early in the day.

exploiting the annual bounty of acorns in the oak woods.

White-fronted Geese from Greenland overwinter on the wet meadows. You can see them from the goose viewpoint, along with Greylag Geese. The loch edges also attract Teals and other wildfowl in winter, while woodland birds which remain here are easier to see at this time of year.

How to get here
Grid ref./postcode NX 699684/ DG7 2
By road There is a car park on the minor road 3.5 miles north from Glenlochar on the A762.
By public transport Dumfries railway station is 30 miles away. Buses call at Glenlochar, 3.5 miles south of the reserve.

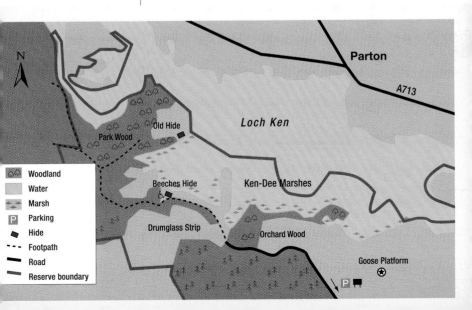

Legend:
- Woodland
- Water
- Marsh
- P Parking
- Hide
- Footpath
- Road
- Reserve boundary

Parton
A713
Loch Ken
Old Hide
Park Wood
Beeches Hide
Ken-Dee Marshes
Drumglass Strip
Orchard Wood
Goose Platform
N

SOUTH AND WEST

LOCH GRUINART

SSSI, SPA, SAC, RAMSAR, NATURA 2000

Islay, the fifth largest Scottish island, is a horseshoe-shaped, hilly land mass with a unique atmosphere and a superb range of wildlife. Loch Gruinart is one of two RSPB reserves on the island, and is famous for the large flocks of Barnacle and White-fronted Geese that winter on the wet grassland. The reserve also includes a wide range of habitats from saltmarsh to blanket bog.

● Access, facilities, contact details and accessibility

The wheelchair-accessible hide and viewing platform offer comfortable viewpoints, while the visitor centre staff can help you to find the wildlife. Regular guided walks are held – please contact the reserve for details.

- **Telephone** 01496 850 505; **email** loch.gruinart@rspb.org.uk; **web** www.rspb.org.uk/lochgruinart
- **Opening hours** The reserve is open at all times. The visitor centre is open daily from 10am–5pm.
- **Entry fees** Free, but donations to help continue the work here are welcome
- **Accessibility** Special needs visitors may drive to the hide, which is wheelchair-friendly. Most other trails are not easily accessible. The visitor centre and toilets are wheelchair-accessible.
- **Dogs** Allowed on the woodland trail provided they are kept under proper control, but not permitted in the hide.

What to look for

A 2¼-hour ferry trip from the Scottish mainland brings you to this wonderful island, home to thousands of Barnacle Geese, Golden Eagles, Otters, Hen Harriers, Marsh Fritillary butterflies and a host of other exciting wildlife. The RSPB's

Loch Gruinart reserve is managed for a range of breeding and wintering species.

From the car park close to the hide, a track takes you through some sheltered woodland, from which there are views over the sea loch,

WILDLIFE BY SEASON

SPRING
Wading birds display over the fields, and Corncrakes are calling from mid-May.

SUMMER
A good time to see Otters and seals, also hunting birds of prey such as Hen Harriers and Short-eared Owls.

AUTUMN
Barnacle and White-fronted Geese start to arrive. Migrating waders visit the estuary. Young Choughs and birds of prey disperse.

WINTER
Wintering waders and other wildfowl join the geese. A good time to see Choughs and birds of prey.

and on to the viewing platform.

From meadows to moorlands, this is a haven for breeding waders including Dunlins, Curlews, Snipes, Redshanks and Lapwings. Hen Harriers and Short-eared Owls nest on the moors.

The meadows are rich with insect life in the summer. From May look out for Marsh Fritillary butterflies – very beautiful with their intricate wing patterns in orange, black and cream. Choughs probe for beetles, ants and other invertebrates in the fields with their long, curved red bills, and Corncrakes call from the long grass.

In autumn and winter, look out for birds of prey, including Hen Harrier, Merlin, Peregrine, Buzzard, Kestrel and Sparrowhawk. You could even see a Golden Eagle – an unforgettable experience. These huge birds are especially distinctive in juvenile plumage, with their white wing-patches and tail-bands. Rarities occasionally found on the reserve in winter have included the superb Gyr Falcon.

WHEN TO VISIT
The reserve is exciting year-round – visit in winter to see the geese.

How to get here
Grid ref. NR 275672
By road To reach Islay, you can fly from Glasgow or take the ferry from mainland Kennacraig to Port Askaig or Port Ellen. The reserve is signed from the A847 Bridgend to Bruichladdich road, and 3 miles from the turn-off.
By public transport Once on Islay, the nearest bus stop is at the junction on the A847 Bridgend to Bruichladdich road, a 3-mile walk from the reserve.

WHY BARNACLE?
Back in the 12th century, naturalists were mystified by Barnacle Geese, because their nesting grounds could not be found. We know now that they breed further north and east, but back then the preferred explanation was that the birds hatched out of Goose Barnacles, elegant crustaceans which grow on driftwood. Hence the species' peculiar name.

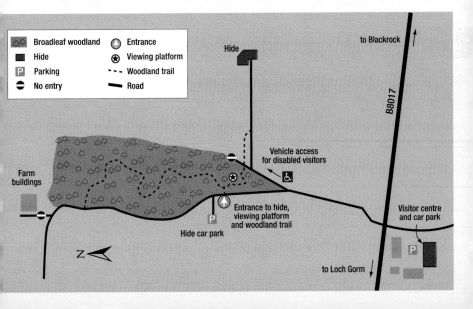

SOUTH AND WEST

LOCHWINNOCH SSSI

Today, western Scotland has very little in the way of wetlands, so it is good news for wildlife that one of the best remaining sites is under the care of the RSPB. The reserve includes two shallow lochs (Barr Loch and Aird Meadow Loch), together with their surrounding water meadows, marshes and woodlands – a real oasis for wetland and woodland wildlife. In spring and summer warblers sing, flowers bloom and water birds court one another before guiding their new chicks out onto the water, while autumn and winter brings flocks of ducks and Whooper Swans from their northerly breeding grounds. With easy-walking nature trails, hides, daily activities for children and families and many other visitor facilities, this is one for the whole family.

● Access, facilities, contact details and accessibility

Lochwinnoch is a popular reserve with good facilities for all visitors. There are two hides and two nature trails (one a quarter of a mile and one just under a mile). The shop sells refreshments, optics, books, garden wildlife supplies and gifts. With a picnic area, pushchair-friendly paths and binocular hire available this is a great place for a family day out, and you can book group visits and guided walks.

● **Telephone** 01505 842 663; **email** lochwinnoch@rspb.org.uk; **web** www.rspb.org.uk/lochwinnoch

● **Opening hours** The reserve is open at all times. The visitor centre is open daily from 10am–5pm, but is closed from 25–26 December and 1–2 January.

● **Entry fees** Free entry to visitor centre, viewing area and shop. Nature trails access is free for RSPB members and those who used green transport, otherwise £2 adults, £4 families and 50p for children/ concessions.

● **Accessibility** The trails, hides and visitor centre are all wheelchair-accessible

● **Dogs** Allowed on all footpaths; must be kept under close control

WILDLIFE BY SEASON

SPRING

Great Crested Grebes are courting on the lochs, while newly arrived warblers sing from the reedbeds. Species to listen for include Reed, Sedge and Grasshopper Warblers. Look out for frogs and toads spawning in the smaller ponds.

SUMMER

The wildfowl will be out on the lochs with their chicks, stripy baby grebes riding on their parents' backs. Many flowers are blooming, including rarities like Greater and Lesser Butterfly Orchids.

AUTUMN

Swallows, martins and wagtails roost in the reedbeds, forming large and noisy flocks in the evenings. Fungi flourish in the woodlands, and winter ducks and swans start to arrive.

WINTER

Whooper Swans and many species of ducks, including Smews, Goosanders and Goldeneyes, spend winter on the reserve, with small birds roaming the woodland in feeding parties. This is a good time to see birds of prey such as Hen Harriers.

What to look for

This reserve, within striking distance of Glasgow, is a great place to observe wetland wildlife and enjoy a well thought-out visitor infrastructure. From the visitor centre, the two trails lead in opposite directions, the shorter Dubbs Water trail heading to a viewing area between the two lochs, and the longer Aird Meadow trail passing the two hides on its way to the far end of Aird Meadow Loch. Both trails give you views over reedbeds, open water and, in the case of the offering bill-loads of waterweed to each other, and fanning and shaking their impressive head-dresses with elegantly choreographed grace. Other water birds are courting too, and by the end of spring the first cygnets and ducklings will have appeared. Frogs and toads also get together in the springtime, filling the ponds with clouds and strings of frogspawn and toadspawn respectively.

The reedbeds are home in spring and summer to Reed Buntings and Sedge Warblers,

Perhaps the most endearing of all our ducks, Goldeneyes have distinctive patterning and perpetually surprised expressions.

Aird Meadow trail, takes you through meadowland, scrub and woodland.

One of the highlights of early spring takes place out on the open water. If you notice a couple of Great Crested Grebes showing an interest in each other, wait and watch and you could witness the famous courtship display. This impressive performance between the two birds involves a sequence of eye-catching moves including synchronised diving, with Grasshopper Warblers in the drier areas. The woodland patches and scrub have a different selection of warblers, including Blackcaps and Whitethroats. The meadows come to life through summer with a show of flowers and plenty of butterflies. Dragonflies roam across the reserve, hunting for insect prey, while the daintier damselflies tend to stay closer to water. Dusk and dawn are the best times to see Otters.

Young Swallows and martins

The smallest bird you're likely to see swimming in the water, the Little Grebe looks beautiful in breeding plumage with its rich dark colours.

join their parents to feed over the lochs into autumn, hunting constantly to build up their fat deposits before they begin their long journey to Africa. The flocks roost in the relative safety of the reedbeds, along with chattering parties of wagtails. Flocking is very much the theme of the season, with the resident woodland birds banding together while the migrants prepare to depart. The feeding station starts to get busier at this time of year, with visitors like Redpolls and Siskins joining the growing flocks of Chaffinches, Greenfinches and other common birds.

The lochs attract large numbers of ducks in winter. Handsome Goosanders and perky Goldeneyes join the Tufted Ducks, with dabbling ducks represented by Wigeons and Teals.

Whooper Swans visit in variable numbers, as do Greylag Geese. The dainty Smew, our smallest saw-billed duck, is a regular visitor in winter – the males are particularly attractive with their almost pure white plumage relieved by elegant black accents on the head, breast and wings.

Birds of prey are more in evidence during the winter too. Hen Harriers visit most days, either ring-tailed females or ghostly grey males rafting across the reeds and water. The busy feeding station draws the occasional Sparrowhawk, looking to grab an easy meal from the flocks of tits, finches and other small birds.

How to get here

Grid ref./postcode NS 358580/PA12 4
By road The reserve is located 18 miles south-west of Glasgow, beside the A760 Largs Road, which is off the A737 Irvine Road (easily reached from the M8 at Junction 28A). Car parking facilities are available.
By public transport Lochwinnoch railway station is situated 400m south-east of the visitor centre. The nearest bus stops are on the A737

WHEN TO VISIT

Lochwinnoch is exciting for wildlife throughout the year. Autumn evenings can be exciting for seeing roosts of small birds – otherwise, time of day is not important.

FEATHER IN THE CAP?

One of the special birds of Lochwinnoch, the Great Crested Grebe, has a special place in the history of the RSPB. The luxuriantly soft body plumage that helps waterproof and insulate these supreme divers was once highly sought after as a fur substitute, and those splendid head plumes became a popular decoration for ladies' hats. The demand led to the near extinction of the species in the UK, and many other species were badly affected, but this devastation was what brought about the creation of the organisation that was to become the RSPB. A group of women established a pressure group – the Fur and Feather League – aimed at curtailing the killing of wild birds for their plumage, but the group quickly expanded its interest to further the conservation of all birds and their habitats. Fifteen years later the society received its royal charter and was renamed the Royal Society for the Protection of Birds.

Confused by reedbed warblers? The Sedge Warbler is quite distinctive if you get a good view, with its prominent creamy eyebrows and streaky back – Reed Warblers are much plainer.

at Roadhead roundabout (half a mile south-east of the reserve entrance) and on the A760 at Newton of Barr (just under a mile north-west of the entrance).

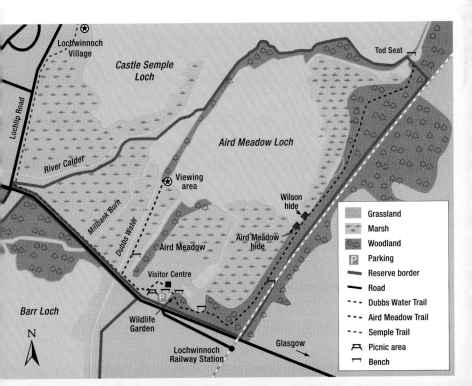

MERSEHEAD

SSSI, SPA, pSAC, NSA, RAMSAR, NATURA 2000

The Solway Firth, a dividing line between north-west England and south-west Scotland, is of immense importance to wildlife, especially for wildfowl. The entire population of Barnacle Geese that breed in Svarlbard spends winter on the Solway, and Mersehead provides ideal feeding and resting grounds for them. The reserve also has breeding and migrating waders, mammals including Otters, large flocks of buntings, Skylarks and finches in winter, and a fine show of coastal wild flowers in summer. There is a visitor centre, two nature trails and two hides.

● Access, facilities, contact details and accessibility

There is a viewing room in the visitor centre, and two hides out on the reserve. There are two nature trails – the out-and-back Wetland trail is about 1.2 miles long, the circular Coastal trail about 2.4 miles. The visitor centre has a refreshments stand selling drinks and snacks, and you can hire binoculars and book guided walks here. Fun and educational events are held from time to time.

- **Telephone** 01387 780 579; **email** mersehead@rspb.org.uk; **web** www.rspb.org.uk/mersehead
- **Opening hours** Visitor centre 10am–5pm, hides and trails open dawn to dusk
- **Entry fees** Suggested donation of £1
- **Accessibility** The Wetland trail is wheelchair-accessible, but the circular Coastal trail is not as it includes grass tracks, saltmarsh and beach with soft sand. There are two benches along the trail. Visitors with restricted mobility can take vehicles to within 300m of the hide to designated parking spaces. Both the Bruaich and Meida Hides are wheelchair-accessible with purpose-built viewing areas and two single seats each.
- **Dogs** Must be kept under control at all times

WILDLIFE BY SEASON

SPRING
Waders and warblers are proclaiming their territories with display and song respectively. Some of the winter geese will hang on into early spring.

SUMMER
A great time for insects, flowers, mammals and seabirds. Butterflies and dragonflies explore the fields and ditches, while shoreline flowers are in colourful bloom. You could see Roe Deer, Otters and Badgers, especially at the end and start of the day, while shearwaters and Gannets may pass close inshore.

AUTUMN
The Barnacle Geese start to return from mid-September, soon followed by other wildfowl. Migrating waders visit the wetlands.

WINTER
Thousands of geese, ducks and swans feed on the fields and wetlands. Masses of small farmland birds flock on the stubble fields and set-aside, and birds of prey such as Hen Harriers, Merlins and Short-eared Owls visit the reserve. There may be large numbers of Scoters, divers and grebes on the sea.

What to look for

This reserve is mainly grassland, both wet and dry, with some lagoons and ditches and a length of shoreline. It's well worth planning your day to walk both of the nature trails, as they take you through quite different parts of the reserve.

If you visit in early spring, you may see some lingering Barnacle or Pink-footed Geese out on the fields. In the far northern regions where these birds breed, the summer is short and intense and their time on the breeding grounds is

ideal habitat for nesting waders. It also suits Skylarks – dozens of singing males serenade you as you walk the trails. Another less conventional songster can be heard at dusk – dozens of Natterjack Toads breed in the pools by the shore. These rare amphibians have been reintroduced here and are prospering under careful management.

Wet scrubby areas have one or two breeding pairs of Grasshopper Warblers, giving their fishing-reel songs throughout

Barnacle Geese are beautifully marked and charming little geese – with 10,000 of them here in winter you'll have great opportunities to enjoy their social interactions.

brief. However, by mid-spring virtually all will have gone, leaving the fields to the nesting waders. Snipes, Lapwings, Redshanks and Curlews all breed here – there are about 100 pairs altogether with Lapwings and Snipes the commonest, up from just one or two of each species back in 1993 when the RSPB first acquired land here. A management routine of the wet grassland and merse (saltmarsh) involving winter grazing and water-level control has created

the day but favouring only a lucky few visitors with an actual sighting. Reed Buntings are much more extrovert, the handsome males singing from prominent vantage points, showing themselves off as if to make up for the rather unexciting simple song. Yellowhammers and Linnets are among the true farmland birds that prosper under the wildlife-friendly field management systems used here. Spotted Flycatchers breed in the wooded patches.

The most elegant duck at Mersehead has to be the Pintail. Its scientific name, *Anas acuta*, could accurately be translated as 'pointy duck'.

Come summer, and the reserve is looking splendid with coastal flowers in bloom and many insects on the wing – an impressive 240 species of butterflies and moths have been seen here. Birds can be elusive in summer, with the waders no longer loudly displaying but furtively attending their chicks in the long grass or moving off on to the estuary, but this is a good time to see Barn Owls, and the lagoons have a few breeding ducks including Shelducks, Wigeons, Teals and Shovelers.

Summer is also good for mammals. Brown Hares live out on the grassland, while you may see Otters along the coast. Harbour Porpoises come close inshore at times, while bats hunt over the fields and lagoons – tiny pipistrelles and much larger Noctules.

Barnacle Geese are the harbingers of winter, arriving from mid-September and building up to nearly 10,000 birds. They are joined by a few hundred Pink-footed Geese and a dozen or more Whooper Swans. The grassland that provided breeding grounds for waders through spring and summer is now a refuge for the geese and swans, while the saltmarsh and lagoons provide feeding grounds for more wildfowl, including large numbers of Pintails. Migrating waders arrive – Knots, Curlews and especially Oystercatchers are numerous, but you could also see Golden, Grey and Ringed Plovers, Sanderlings and both species of godwits. Some of these birds will stay on for winter.

The RSPB manages some fields traditionally, harvesting a crop of wheat or barley and leaving the stubble for farmland birds to feed on through the winter. Other set-aside fields offer a rich crop of weed seeds, so sparrows, finches and buntings are well provided for through the winter months. You can see massive flocks of these small birds descending on the fields on winter days – among the commoner Linnets, Twites, Reed Buntings and House Sparrows there may be a few Yellowhammers, Bullfinches and perhaps even a Corn Bunting – this species has become extremely rare in Scotland.

Naturally, such gatherings of birds attract predators. The usual suspects are involved here – birds that breed inland on the uplands of the Galloway hills and further afield. Come winter,

WHEN TO VISIT

Mersehead is alive with wildlife throughout the year. Perhaps the biggest highlight is the arrival of the Barnacle Geese, which begins in late September. Dawn or dusk visits in summer are best for mammals. Generally, however, time of day is not important.

many upland birds leave the hills for the coast, and the predators follow suit – look out for Hen Harriers, Short-eared Owls, Merlins and Peregrine Falcons. The sudden arrival of one of these will send a flock of waders or songbirds into a panic – somehow the predator sometimes manages to single out an unlucky victim among the confusion of fleeing wings.

It's worth taking the coastal trail and spending some time sea-watching in winter. Rafts of Common Scoters gather offshore – the males sleek and black, the females dusky brown with pale cheeks. Other seaducks you could see include Scaups, while there are often many Great Crested Grebes and a few divers.

Perfectly adapted for a life on the ocean wave, the Common Scoter forms large flocks or 'rafts' at sea, especially in winter. Males are glossy black, and females are grey-brown with striking creamy cheeks.

How to get here

Grid ref./postcode NX 928566/DG2 8
By road From Dumfries, take the A710 Solway Coast road, passing through the villages of New Abbey, Kirkbean, Prestonmill and Mainsriddle. The reserve is signposted just before the village of Caulkerbush, on the left. A single-track road with passing places runs for a mile down to the car park, adjacent to the visitor centre. From Castle Douglas, take the A745, then the A711 to Dalbeattie before joining the A710 Solway Coast road, passing through the villages of Colvend, Sandyhills and Caulkerbush. The reserve is signposted just after Caulkerbush bridge, on the right. **By public transport** Dumfries is the nearest railway station, about 16 miles away. From here you can take a bus to the village of Caulkerbush, from where the reserve is signed (about a mile's walk).

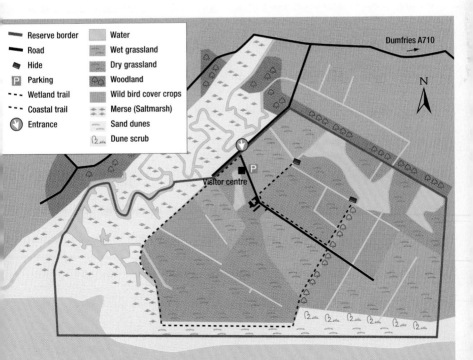

Reserve border	Water
Road	Wet grassland
Hide	Dry grassland
P Parking	Woodland
- - - Wetland trail	Wild bird cover crops
- - - Coastal trail	Merse (Saltmarsh)
Entrance	Sand dunes
	Dune scrub

Dumfries A710

N

P

Visitor centre

SOUTH AND WEST

MULL OF GALLOWAY SSSI, pSAC

At the tip of a tiny south-eastern projection from the hammerhead-shaped peninsula at the south-western corner of Scotland is this spectacular seabird reserve. Visit in spring and summer to see the colonies of Guillemots, Black Guillemots, Razorbills, Fulmars, Kittiwakes and Shags, and take in the sensory overload of one of our greatest wildlife spectacles. You could see whales or porpoises in summer, and in autumn migrating seabirds go by offshore while landbirds may stop off on their migratory journeys. The Mull of Galloway is the jewel in the crown of this lovely and unspoilt part of Scotland, offering an unforgettable experience for anyone with an interest in wildlife and wild places.

● Access, facilities, contact details and accessibility

There is a circular trail around the reserve, and a viewing platform giving good views of the cliffside. The visitor centre can provide information and has live CCTV footage from the colony, and you can arrange a guided walk. Refreshments are available from the nearby Gallie Craig café.

- **Telephone** 01776 840539 (Easter to October) or 01671 404975 (November to March); **web** www.rspb.org.uk/mullofgalloway
- **Opening hours** The reserve is open at all times; visitor facilities are open from Easter to end of October
- **Entry fees** Free, but donations to help us continue our work here are welcome
- **Accessibility** Disabled access is possible at the visitor centre (where there is disabled parking) and café, but the trail and viewing platform are not suitable for wheelchair users
- **Dogs** Allowed, but keep them under close control at all times

WILDLIFE BY SEASON

SPRING

The nesting seabirds arrive and begin to establish their territories. Fulmars are back on site as early as February, with the other species arriving later on. Migrant songbirds may be seen around the trail.

SUMMER

The seabird colony is full of activity with adults coming to and fro bringing fishy meals for their growing chicks. Cliff-top flowers bloom around the trail. You could see Otters along the shore, or Minke Whales or porpoises further out to sea.

AUTUMN

Seabirds move on, and large numbers of migrating songbirds may pass overhead. At sea, migrating shearwaters and skuas may be seen, along with the locally nesting seabird species.

WINTER

The reserve is very quiet, although the cliff-nesting Peregrine Falcons are present throughout the winter. You may still see Black Guillemots offshore in their pale grey and white winter plumage – they don't wander as far as the other auks outside the breeding season.

What to look for

This isolated peninsula-on-a-peninsula is a real UK landmark, with wonderful seascape views from the tops of the 80m cliffs. The trail is a short circular walk, with an offshoot leading down steep steps to a viewing platform, from which you can enjoy great views of the seabirds massed on the cliffs and going past offshore.

As with many seabird colonies, the commonest species are Guillemots and Kittiwakes, a long way to prevent accidents.

The other auks here are less noticeable than the Guillemots, because they prefer more tucked away nesting sites, under overhangs or between boulders. You stand a good chance of seeing Puffins and Black Guillemots if you scan the sea for them. Shags, Fulmars and Herring Gulls also nest on the cliffs.

Gannets don't nest on the Mull itself, but they do breed

The Black Guillemot is the only auk with a black belly. Its scarlet bill and gape (the inside of its mouth) add a touch of colour to its monochrome plumage.

as these two are able to use tiny ledges that the other species eschew. You'll see hundreds of both from the viewing platform. Kittiwakes gather bill-fulls of seaweed in early spring to construct their simple nests. Guillemots don't bother with nests at all and lay their eggs straight onto the bare rock. Inevitably, a few Guillemot eggs end up in the sea, the price paid for using such marginal nesting places, although the egg's unique tapered shape goes on Scar Rocks, a small rocky outcrop that lies 10 miles offshore and is also managed by the RSPB. Some 2,500 pairs of these large, graceful birds nest on the rocks – representing 1.1 per cent of the UK's entire Gannet population. The birds can be seen easily from the Mull of Galloway, hanging in the air currents as they prepare to plunge-dive into the water after a fish. Scar Rocks also has small numbers of other seabirds, although the Gannets have

Grabbing a bite: Otters hunt for fish and shellfish in the seas around the Mull, and you may spot them from the clifftop.

virtually taken over the island following 30 years of strong population growth.

The cliff-top grassland and heathland on the Mull of Galloway is a rich and important habitat in its own right. By early summer many of the local specialised plants are in flower, including Spring Squill, Sea Thrift, Sea Campion, Sheep's-bit and Wild Carrot. These attract butterflies, with Wall Brown and Grayling among the more interesting species. The Wall Brown is a particularly stunning butterfly with rich red-gold wings marked with a bold and intricate pattern in black. The reserve also attracts migrant butterflies and moths, including the handsome Clouded Yellow butterfly, and the Silver-Y moth which is often active in the daytime and can be incredibly numerous at times. You'll recognise the Silver-Y by the delicately inscribed white 'Y' mark on

its forewings – its scientific name *Autographa gamma* shows that the mark looked to earlier European civilisations like the ancient Greek character for the letter gamma. In years when their numbers increase enough to trigger an 'invasion', most recently 2009, Painted Lady butterflies can arrive here en masse as at other coastal sites. The salmon-pink, black and white butterflies are large, very attractive and, unsurprisingly, powerful flyers.

Through summer, Otters, Grey Seals and Harbour Porpoises are regularly seen in the sea. Grey Seals' heads are easily mistaken for small rocks – if you notice a particularly round rock that seems to keep moving, take a closer look! A few very lucky observers could see a Minke Whale offshore, spouting or flicking a fin into the air. Small birds using the heathy areas to breed during summer include Stonechats and one or two pairs of Twites. The Linnet, a close relative of the Twite, also breeds here, listen out for its beautiful song. Male Linnets are very pretty with their rosy-pink chests and scarlet foreheads.

By autumn, the breeding seabirds and their young have all moved on, although on days when the wind is favourable you could see many seabirds, including shearwaters and

WHEN TO VISIT

Visit in spring or summer to see the seabirds. The reserve offers stunning views throughout the year, but wildlife interest is limited outside of the breeding season.

skuas, migrating past the Mull. This is also a good place to see landbird migration, with large flocks of finches and thrushes flying over, challenging the identification and counting skills of birdwatchers.

A pair or two of Peregrine Falcons nest on the cliffs, and you could see them at any time of year, but in winter they may be the only birds you see. Peregrine Falcons travel far and wide for prey, so the sudden disappearance of all the other cliff birds does not spell disaster for them. You may hear the birds' loud screeching calls, especially towards the end of winter when courtship behaviour becomes more frequent.

By late winter, Fulmars are back around the cliffs, sorting out their nesting sites for the new breeding season. The other species soon follow, and the whole process begins all over again.

With its beautiful, subtle colours and lovely song, the Linnet is one of the most attractive songbirds you're likely to encounter at this reserve.

How to get here

Grid ref./postcode NX 156305/ DG9 0
By road The reserve is 5 miles south of Drummore. Follow the brown tourist signs from Drummore.
By public transport Stranraer, 27 miles from the reserve, is the nearest railway station. From here you can take a bus to Drummore, 5 miles from the reserve, but there are no formal walking paths to the reserve from Drummore so you will need to cycle or take a taxi from Drummore.

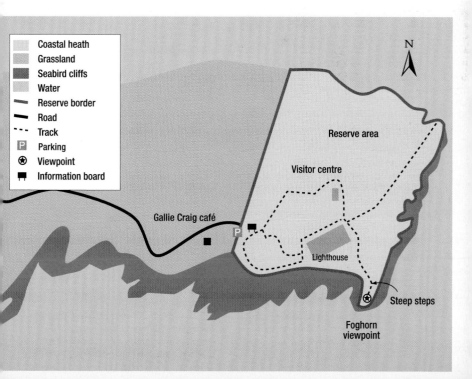

- Coastal heath
- Grassland
- Seabird cliffs
- Water
- Reserve border
- Road
- Track
- P Parking
- Viewpoint
- Information board

N

Reserve area

Visitor centre

Gallie Craig café

P

Lighthouse

Steep steps

Foghorn viewpoint

THE OA SSSI, SPA

One of the RSPB's two reserves on the lovely island of Islay, The Oa is situated on the rugged southern tip of the island. Here Golden Eagles fly over the moorlands, Choughs play in the cliffside air currents and Red-throated Divers nest on the lochans. This reserve offers a dramatic contrast to Loch Gruinart to the north – if you come to Islay, be sure to visit both.

● Access, facilities, contact details and accessibility

There is a picnic area, and two marked trails (1.25 miles and 2 miles).
- **Telephone** 01496 300118; **email** the.oa@rspb.org.uk; **web** www.rspb.org.uk/theoa
- **Opening hours** Open at all times
- **Entry fees** Free, though donations are welcome
- **Accessibility** Unfortunately the trails are not wheelchair-accessible
- **Dogs** Please keep dogs under close control and stay clear of cattle, especially those with young calves

What to look for

The Oa comprises wild, hilly moorland, blanket bog and grassy cliff-tops with views towards Jura and Northern Ireland. The two nature trails offer real leg-stretching walks and give you the chance of seeing exciting wildlife throughout the year.

The bird most visitors will want to see above all others is the Golden Eagle, and The Oa regularly offers excellent sightings against a striking moorland and clifftop backdrop. On the wing, the Golden Eagle's silhouette is huge, yet beautifully balanced and proportioned – once seen never forgotten. Another less dramatic bird of the uplands is the Twite

WILDLIFE BY SEASON

SPRING
Breeding birds, including Choughs and Golden Eagles, are courting and gathering nesting material.

SUMMER
Twites and Skylarks are breeding on the moorland, insects are on the wing.

AUTUMN
Farmland birds begin to form large flocks. Young Choughs and Golden Eagles disperse from their breeding grounds.

WINTER
Finches and buntings feed on stubble fields. Raptors like Peregrine Falcons move down from the uplands.

– a small brown finch (the males have pink rumps but are otherwise much like the females). It is the northern counterpart of the Linnet and at first glance is much plainer than its cousin, but take time to look closely when you find some, and you'll appreciate their warm cinnamon-washed plumage and rather cute, small-billed faces.

Also busy nest-building are Choughs, which nest in cliff hollows or sea caves. Peregrine Falcons may be seen on the reserve too – you might hear them screaming to each other in courtship or in dispute over mates, or see them stoop on their prey. The small lochans may have Red-throated Divers, while on the grassland, a few Lapwings and Redshanks breed. Hopefully the reserve will also attract breeding Corncrakes in due course. Marsh Fritillary butterflies breed here too, the caterpillars spinning communal feeding webs on their food plant, Devil's Bit Scabious, which you may see from summer but especially in early spring.

WHEN TO VISIT
The Oa has exciting wildlife to see throughout the year, and time of day is not important (though note that Golden Eagles are not early risers!)

In winter, farmland birds from a wide area come to The Oa for the stubble fields and set-aside that the RSPB provides. Another winter speciality is the White-fronted Goose – hundreds winter on the grassland.

How to get here
Grid ref./postcode NR 282423/ PA42 7
By road The reserve is approximately 6 miles south-west of Port Ellen, Isle of Islay. You can reach Islay by flying from Glasgow, or take the ferry from mainland Kennacraig to Port Askaig or Port Ellen.
By public transport The nearest bus stop is in Port Ellen – from here you'll need to cycle or take a taxi.

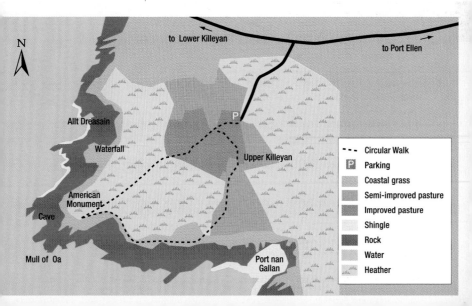

Map key:
- - - - Circular Walk
- P Parking
- Coastal grass
- Semi-improved pasture
- Improved pasture
- Shingle
- Rock
- Water
- Heather

Map labels: to Lower Killeyan, to Port Ellen, N, Allt Dreasain, Waterfall, Upper Killeyan, American Monument, Cave, Mull of Oa, Port nan Gallan

WOOD OF CREE SSSI, SAC, NATURA 2000

In a landscape of rolling moorland and hill farms, the Wood of Cree is one of Scotland's few ancient deciduous woodlands – the largest in southern Scotland and home to wildlife that's otherwise hard to find in this part of Scotland. The RSPB also owns an area of meadowland and floodplain on the banks of the River Cree.

● Access, facilities, contact details and accessibility

The woodland trail is 1.25 miles, to which you can add on a 1.25-mile loop through scrubland.

- **Telephone** 01671 404975; **web** www.rspb.org.uk/woodofcree
- **Opening hours** Open at all times
- **Entry fees** Free for everyone, but please make a donation to the RSPB if you can
- **Accessibility** The trails around this reserve are unimproved, and in some areas are steep, rutted or muddy so unsuitable for wheelchairs
- **Dogs** Allowed but please keep them under close control at all times

What to look for

In spring, when the Bluebells are out and the birds are singing, the Wood of Cree is at its very best. Take the marked trails through the woodland, keeping your ears open for the special birds of the oakwood – Redstart, Pied Flycatcher and Wood Warbler all breed here and your best chance of seeing them is to listen for singing males. There are other woodland birds here too, including Tawny Owls (look out for smaller birds behaving in an agitated manner – they may be harassing a sleeping owl). Another local speciality is the Willow Tit, which has a distinctive nasal 'buzzing' call. The trails take you to progressively higher ground and eventually

WILDLIFE BY SEASON

SPRING

Redstarts, Pied Flycatchers and Wood Warblers arrive and begin to sing. Bluebells and other woodland flowers are in bloom.

SUMMER

Birds are rearing their chicks. Many insects are on the wing. Best time to see mammals.

AUTUMN

Wintering wildfowl begin to arrive on the marshes. As the acorns start to fall, this is a good time to see Red Squirrels.

WINTER

Parties of small birds such as tits and finches are moving around the leafless trees, joined by noisy but colourful Jays.

out onto the moors – here you might see (and hear) Tree Pipits. Red Squirrels, Roe Deer and a variety of bats, including the rare Leisler's Bat, live in the woodlands; look out for Red Deer in the more open areas.

The RSPB's work here is focused on expanding the area of oak woodland, while maintaining its diversity of plant and animal life. They also work to control bracken encroachment on the moorland, and to maintain the attractiveness of the riverside meadows to breeding waders with grazing and hay-cutting.

The River Cree is home to Otters, Dippers and Grey Wagtails, with Oystercatchers and Snipe breeding in the wet meadows. In winter, wildfowl like Whooper Swans and diving ducks come to the river and meadows. In the evenings, Barn Owls patrol the fields in search of mice and voles. Close to the car park you'll find the Otter viewing platform, which gives you views over the river. If you can spare some extra time, it's worth waiting here for views of

the river wildlife, though you will need a dose of luck to see an Otter.

How to get here

Grid ref./postcode NX 381708/ DG8 6

By road Travel north along the minor road from Newton Stewart through Old Minnigaff. Turning left past Monigaff church, continue along the minor C50 for a further 3 miles to the car park.

By public transport Rather difficult. The nearest rail stations are in Dumfries, nearly 50 miles away, and the sporadically served Barrhill and Stranraer (14 and 29 miles away respectively). Newton Stewart, 4 miles (6.4 km) away, has the nearest bus stop.

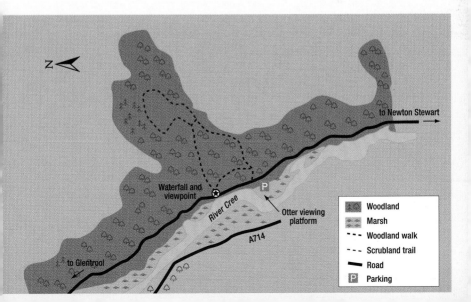

🌳	Woodland
	Marsh
- - -	Woodland walk
- - -	Scrubland trail
▬	Road
P	Parking

to Newton Stewart

Waterfall and viewpoint

River Cree

Otter viewing platform

A714

to Glentrool

EAST SCOTLAND

BIRSAY MOORS   SSSI, SPA, NATURA 2000

The splendour of an Orkney moorland appeals to the adventurer in all of us, and in spring and summer that adventure gains an extra edge as Great and Arctic Skuas wheel overhead, Golden Plovers and Curlews call from the heather and Hen Harriers patrol low over the ground. You can enjoy close-up views of stunning Red-throated Divers with their chicks, and with luck see several species of birds of prey at this exciting reserve.

● Access, facilities, contact details and accessibility

The Stromness RSPB office has Wildlife Explorer backpacks for hire. The reserve has two trails and a hide.
- **Telephone** 01856 850 176; **email** orkney@rspb.org.uk; **web** www.rspb.org.uk/birsaymoors
- **Opening hours** Open at all times
- **Entry fees** None, though donations are welcome
- **Accessibility** The hide on Burgar Hill is accessible to wheelchair users. Much of the reserve's best bird life can be easily viewed from the B9057.
- **Dogs** Please keep them under close control at all times and stay on tracks. Please be aware of livestock.

What to look for

Like some other Orkney RSPB reserves Birsay Moors has nesting Great and Arctic Skuas - both of these formidable seabirds are vulnerable to disturbance and will attack visitors who stray too close to their nests, so they are best admired from a distance. Nevertheless, it's a wise precaution to wear a hat.

The noisy honking of Greylag Geese, many of them soon to move on to breeding grounds elsewhere, adds a different note to

WILDLIFE BY SEASON

SPRING

Curlews, Skylarks and Meadow Pipits are singing. Skuas and Red-throated Divers return to the moors.

SUMMER

Great and Arctic Skuas are nesting and vigorously seeing off intruders. Hen Harriers and Merlins hunt prey for their chicks. Red-throated Diver chicks can be viewed from the Burgar Hill hide.

AUTUMN

Young raptors disperse – many species can be seen. Hen Harriers roost communally at Durkadale.

WINTER

Winter thrushes and finches may visit. Red Grouse begin their courtship displays in late winter

Birsay's springtime soundtrack of Skylark and Curlew song. Both of these species are birds of open countryside which have suffered large population declines in many parts of the UK mainland. They thrive here and both are rightly famed songsters. Birds of prey like Hen Harriers and Short-eared Owls breed here too – their rodent prey is numerous thanks to sympathetic modern peat cutting which helps maintain a diversity of habitats.

Another special nesting bird of the moors is the Red-throated Diver. If you have only seen this species in its pale grey winter plumage, you're in for a treat – the spring birds are resplendent with their bold neck stripes and deep red throats. The hide at Burgar Hill looks out onto a lochan where the divers nest – visit in summer to see them with chicks.

Autumn and winter are quieter times. Small songbirds like Meadow Pipits, Twites, Linnets and Skylarks remain, attracting the attention of birds of prey like Hen Harriers and

WHEN TO VISIT

This reserve is at its best in spring and summer, when skuas and Red-throated Divers nest on the moors. Winter can be good for birds of prey.

Merlins. In winter, there is a large roost of Hen Harriers at Durkadale – ask at the Stromness office for advice about seeing them.

How to get here

Grid ref./postcode HY 340240/ KW17 2
By road The main section of the reserve is west of Evie and the A966. Durkadale is west of the Birsay Moors and extends to the southern shore of the Loch of Hundland. The B9057 (Hillside Road) between Evie and Dounby cuts right through the reserve.
By public transport Buses stop at Evie, 2 miles to the east of the reserve, and also in Dounby, 3 miles to the west of the reserve.

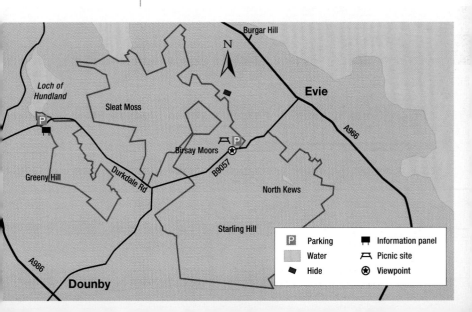

BRODGAR

Lying on a thin strip of land between the Lochs of Harray and Stenness, Brodgar reserve is a haven of wet grassland, surrounding the ancient stone circle Ring of Brodgar – a spectacular Neolithic monument with an atmosphere to rival Stonehenge. The path through the reserve provides easy walking and great views of the reserve's many breeding and wintering birds.

● Access, facilities, contact details and accessibility

This small but lively reserve is ideal for family walks. The car park is shared with the Ring of Brodgar World Heritage Site.

- **Telephone** 01856 850176; **email**: orkney@rspb.org.uk; **web**: www.rspb.org.uk/brodgar
- **Opening hours** Open at all times
- **Entry fees** None, though donations are welcome
- **Accessibility** The main path is a wheelchair- and pushchair-accessible, non-metalled track – however please take extra care in wet weather
- **Dogs** Allowed but must be kept under close control at all times. Please be aware of livestock.

What to look for

This compact reserve is as interesting to those keen on archaeology as it is to wildlife enthusiasts, with birds everywhere and a host of standing stones and cairns to see as well as the Ring of Brodgar itself. The RSPB and Historic Scotland have both managed the land here, to preserve its historical integrity and to protect

and encourage the breeding birds.

An impressive seven species of waders breed here, and eight species of ducks. Spring is the time to see and hear their courtship displays. Birds of prey nest locally – Hen Harriers and Short-eared Owls hunting Orkney Voles, Merlins chasing Skylarks and other small songbirds. The

WILDLIFE BY SEASON

SPRING
The air is filled with the sounds of Skylarks and waders. Ducks are courting on the lochs, and you could see hunting birds of prey.

SUMMER
Ducks and waders are breeding, with fifteen species present altogether. Great Yellow Bumblebees visit the flowers.

AUTUMN
Migrating waders visit the loch shore. You could see a rarity at this time of year.

WINTER
Farmland finches and waders visit the stubble fields. Wildfowl flock on the lochs.

RSPB is replacing pasture with flowery grassland to encourage insects and Corncrakes.

Migrating and wintering waders and wildfowl start to arrive through autumn. This is the likeliest time of year for rare birds to be found, perhaps a vagrant wader on the shoreline or lost North American duck on the loch. Loch of Harray attracts thousands of ducks by mid-winter, mainly Wigeons and Teals. Loch of Stenness is tidal and therefore more appealing to seaducks like Long-tailed Ducks. The fields in between the lochs attract noisy flocks of Whooper Swans and Greylag Geese, and Skylarks, Reed Buntings and Twites visit the stubble fields.

How to get here
Grid ref./postcode HY 294135/ KW17 2
By road From Stromness or Kirkwall, take the A965 toward Finstown and turn onto the B9055 (signposted for Ring of Brodgar). There is parking available 1.2 miles along this road on the right.
By public transport Take bus 91, which runs between Kirkwall and Stromness. Ask the driver to drop you at the Ring of Brodgar stop. Walk along the A965 to the signposted turn for Ring of Brodgar (B9055).

WHEN TO VISIT
The reserve is well worth a visit at any time of year, and time of day is not important.

BUZZ OF EXCITEMENT
The impressively furry Great Yellow Bumblebee lives in several Northern Isles RSPB reserves, including Brodgar. Conserving this very rare species is an RSPB priority, and researchers are studying the ecological needs of the bee to help improve the habitat here – for example, the bee has an exceptionally long tongue and so specialises in flowers with long corollas, like Red Clover. Ensuring suitable flowers are present on the reserves is key to keeping the bees' numbers healthy.

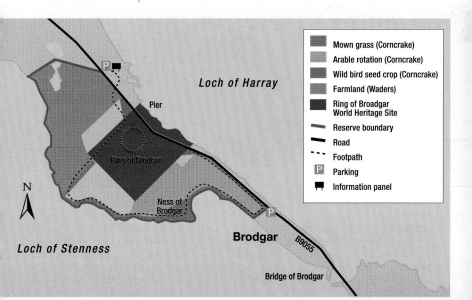

Mown grass (Corncrake)
Arable rotation (Corncrake)
Wild bird seed crop (Corncrake)
Farmland (Waders)
Ring of Broadgar World Heritage Site
Reserve boundary
Road
Footpath
P Parking
Information panel

Loch of Harray
Pier
Ring of Brodgar
Ness of Brodgar
Loch of Stenness
N
Brodgar   B9055
Bridge of Brodgar

Merlin

EAST SCOTLAND

COTTASCARTH & RENDALL MOSS

SSSI, SPA

A landscape primarily of rugged moorland, Cottascarth and Rendall Moss comes to life in spring when upland birds are breeding. Birds of prey nest on the moors too – spend a little time here and you could meet some of the UK's most exciting species.

● Access, facilities, contact details and accessibility

Park in the farmyard (limited space) to access the trail to the hide (1km). Otherwise, good views can be had from the roadside.

- **Telephone** 01856 850 176; **email** orkney@rspb.org.uk; **web** www.rspb.org.uk/cottascarth
- **Opening hours** Open at all times
- **Entry fees** Free, but donations to help continue the work here are welcome
- **Accessibility** The hide is not accessible to wheelchair users. However, much of the reserve's best birdlife can be easily viewed from a car.
- **Dogs** This is a working farm and as such it is preferred that dogs are not brought to the reserve

What to look for

Whether you choose to walk the moors or birdwatch from the minor roads in the comfort of your car, you should enjoy views of a select group of interesting bird species in this remote and dramatic landscape.

One of the stars of this reserve is the Curlew,

which breeds here at a density unmatched almost anywhere else in Europe. It is famous for its voice, giving a wild rolling, bubbling song in spring that captures the spirit of the moorland. The Curlew's immensely long curved bill (longer in the female), used to locate estuarine

WILDLIFE BY SEASON

SPRING
Upland birds on the reserve, including Curlews, Snipes, Meadow Pipits and Skylarks, are all singing and displaying.

SUMMER
Birds of prey are easiest to see at this time – Merlins, Hen Harriers and Short-eared Owls are all busy hunting to feed their chicks.

AUTUMN
Adult and young birds start to disperse from the breeding grounds.

WINTER
Very quiet on the reserve, as upland birds move away to lower ground when the weather turns colder.

worms deep in the shoreline mud in winter, is just as effective at probing the soft, peaty soil of the moorland breeding grounds or picking insects and even berries from the surface.

Skylarks and Meadow Pipits are both streaky brown above and streaky off-white below, they are easily confused until you get used to the Skylark's stockier build. Both species sing in flight, the Skylark climbing and climbing until it is lost to view, when the sweet jingling song seems to come from the sky itself. The Meadow Pipit flies up just a short distance, singing shrilly with zest if not particular musical skill, then drops slowly to earth on fanned wings.

The hunters of the uplands are well represented here, and you can see them all in spring and especially summer, hunting prey for their chicks. Short-eared Owls are agile, long-winged fliers, dipping and twisting over the moors as they search for voles. Hen Harriers search more methodically, cruising low on wings held in a shallow 'V' shape. This species is polygamous, each

male often providing for two or more nesting females. The other moorland predator is the Merlin, a compact little falcon with a breathtaking turn of speed. It also practices aerial deception, adopting an innocuous thrush-like flight to get closer to its unsuspecting prey before launching the lightning-speed final attack.

How to get here
Grid ref./postcode HY 369195/ KW17 2
By road The reserve is 3.1 miles north of Finstown off the A966. Take the minor road west at Norseman Village to Settisgarth and then north for 0.6 mile to Lower Cottascarth Farm.
By public transport Buses stop at Norseman Village, 2 miles to the east of the reserve, on the Kirkwall to Tingwall route.

WHEN TO VISIT
The reserve is very much at its best in spring and summer, and there is little to see in winter. Time of day is not crucial.

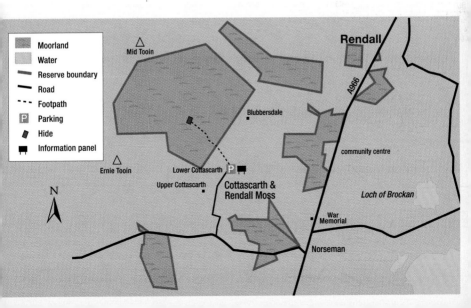

Red-necked Phalarope

FETLAR   SSSI, SPA, SAC, NATURA 2000

A small island marking the north-easterly corner of the Shetland group, Fetlar is a wildlife paradise and the best place in the UK to see some very rare and interesting nesting birds – most notably the charming Red-necked Phalarope. The island is wonderful at any time, but visit between late May and July to see the phalaropes and many other species.

● Access, facilities, contact details and accessibility

A hide overlooks the Mires of Funzie. Footpaths on the island allow you to explore a wide area.

- **Telephone** 01957 733 246; **email** fetlar@rspb.org.uk; **web** www.rspb.org.uk/fetlar
- **Opening hours** The hide is open from April to October at all times of day
- **Entry fees** Free
- **Accessibility** The track to the hide is not suitable for wheelchair users
- **Dogs** Allowed on all footpaths, but please keep them on a short lead due to the presence of ground-nesting birds

P

What to look for

The island of Fetlar has a rocky shoreline, and inland there are farmed crofts and rolling moorland with many lochans. The Loch of Funzie is frequently used by phalaropes and is a great place to watch them as they feed along the shoreline. The RSPB protects and manages the nearby Mires of Funzie, which is a phalarope breeding site and is overlooked by a hide.

Red-necked Phalaropes are tiny wading birds that actually spend most of their time swimming, spinning on the surface to disturb tiny invertebrates, which are then snapped up. The females are more colourful, and they display and compete for males. This role-reversal continues through the breeding season, as the females migrate after egg-laying, leaving the

WILDLIFE BY SEASON

SPRING
Migrating birds visit the island. Breeding birds start to arrive.

SUMMER
The time to see Red-necked Phalaropes, Red-throated Divers, Great Skuas and many other exciting nesting birds.

AUTUMN
Breeding birds depart. Passage migrants from Northern Europe may visit the reserve at any time.

WINTER
Winter wildfowl including Goldeneyes and Whooper Swans may be present. You could see Great Northern Divers around the coast.

males to rear the family.

Red-throated Divers nest on the lochans across the island, while the moorland provides a breeding ground for skuas – both Great and Arctic – and Whimbrels, Golden Plovers and other wader species as well as upland songbirds including Twites. Please treat Fetlar's special birdlife with great respect, especially in the breeding season, as several species are extremely vulnerable to disturbance.

If you head for the coast, look out for auks nesting on the low rocky cliffs – they include good numbers of Puffins. Otters forage amidst the kelp close to shore.

The island is quieter outside the breeding season. Migrants could show up in autumn – historically a number of very rare species have been found here. The island once held the UK's only nesting pair of Snowy Owls, though sadly they stopped breeding here in the 1980s. Great Northern Divers can be seen offshore in winter.

How to get here

Grid ref./postcode HU 655900/ ZE2 9

WHEN TO VISIT
Summer is the best time to visit to see Fetlar's breeding birds. Other times are quieter but there is always wildlife to see, and time of day is not important.

By road To get to Fetlar from mainland Shetland requires two ferry crossings, the first from Toft mainland to Ulsta, Yell, and from there it is a 25-minute drive north to Gutcher, Yell, for the ferry to Hamarsness, Fetlar. For ferry times and bookings, call 01957 722 259. From the ferry terminal at Hamarsness, drive 6 miles east. Park at the small car park to the west of the Loch of Funzie. Walk east about 100m and follow signs to the hide, about 300m from the road. Note that no fuel is sold on Fetlar.

By public transport You can take a bus on Yell from Ulsta to Gutcher to make the ferry connection to Fetlar. There is no public transport on Fetlar itself – a bicycle would be a good alternative.

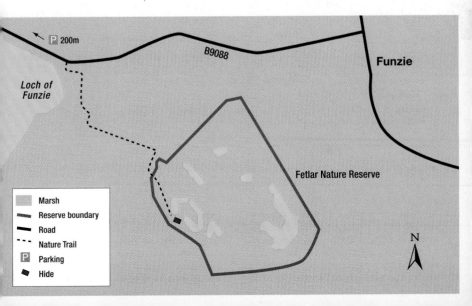

EAST SCOTLAND

FOWLSHEUGH SSSI, SPA, NATURA 2000

Down the coast from Aberdeen, the 65m cliffs of Fowlsheugh teem with nesting seabirds
through spring and summer. The RSPB's nature trail provides viewpoints into the colony, which
is one of the easiest to view on the Scottish mainland. This is a great place to experience the
magic of a busy seabird colony, and enjoy a bracing cliff-top walk.

●Access, facilities, contact details and accessibility

There is a 0.75-mile out-and-back trail from the reserve entrance, which includes several viewing points.
You can arrange guided walks here.

P

- **Telephone** 01346 532 017; **email** strathbeg@rspb.org.uk; **web** www.rspb.org.uk/fowlsheugh
- **Opening hours** Open at all times
- **Entry fees** Free, but donations to help continue the work here are welcome
- **Accessibility** Two sets of steps at the beginning of the reserve make Fowlsheugh inaccessible for wheelchair
  users and less accessible for other disabled visitors
- **Dogs** The RSPB requests that you do not bring your dog onto this reserve (registered guide dogs excepted)

What to look for

From the reserve entrance, follow the cliff-top
path (which includes some steep steps) along
to the viewpoints. The main viewpoint is into
a deep rock fissure called Henry's Scorth,
from which many seabirds can be seen, but do
continue to the path's end, as you are most likely
to see Puffins from the furthest point.

The most numerous species here are, as is
often the case, Guillemots and Kittiwakes, while
other species present in smaller numbers include
Razorbills, Fulmars, Herring Gulls, Shags and
Puffins, while you may see Gannets and skuas

WILDLIFE BY SEASON

SPRING

The seabirds start to return to the cliffs, and by late spring breeding activity is well underway.

SUMMER

With about 130,000 birds on the cliffs, Fowlsheugh is a riot of noise and action. This is the best time to see whales and dolphins.

AUTUMN

The seabirds have left the cliffs by early autumn. Many seabirds move past offshore. Migrant land birds may visit.

WINTER

The quietest time, although Fulmars return to the cliffs in February. A good time to see Grey Seals offshore.

going past at sea, and Eiders on the water.

Summer is the best time to see sea mammals, although their appearance is by no means as predictable as the seabirds'. Both Grey and Common Seals are often seen, while Common and Bottlenose Dolphins are the likeliest of the cetacean species. With good views it's easy to tell them apart, as Bottlenoses are plain grey, while the smaller Common Dolphins are dark grey above with a wide and clear-cut stripe of cream down their sides. Minke Whales and White-beaked Dolphins are seen occasionally.

By the end of summer, all of the seabirds must leave – the young gulls and Fulmars lifting off the cliff edge into their first flights, while the young auks are not yet able to fly so must plummet seawards, attended by their anxious fathers. They stay together for the coming weeks as the youngster learns to fish.

Although the cliffs are now quiet, seabirds pass by throughout the autumn, sometimes in large numbers and at close quarters if onshore

WHEN TO VISIT

Come in late spring or summer to experience the seabird colony in full swing – but before mid-July if you are hoping to see Puffins. Time of day is not important.

winds push them inshore – they include terns, skuas and divers as well as the cliff-nesting auks.

How to get here

Grid ref./postcode NO 879808/ DD10 0

By road The reserve is 3 miles south of Stonehaven. On the A92 heading south from Stonehaven, take the turning on the left signed for Crawton. The reserve car park is just before the end of this road, with limited parking.

By public transport Stonehaven is the nearest station. From here follow the directions above. There is a request bus stop at the start of the road to Crawton on the Stonehaven to Johnshaven route – just over a mile's walk to the reserve.

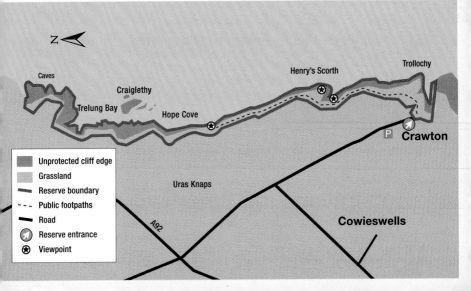

EAST SCOTLAND

HOBBISTER   SSSI, SPA, NATURA 2000

Here at Hobbister, the wild beauty of the landscape is matched by the variety of wildlife you could encounter as you walk the moorland and coastal trails through the land that runs alongside the coast, and is in marked contrast to the grim naval encounters played out here in the strategically important Scapa Flow, in both the First and Second World Wars.

● Access, facilities, contact details and accessibility

The reserve has nature trails to points that overlook Scapa Flow and Waukmill Bay.

- **Telephone** 01856 850176; **email** orkney@rspb.org.uk; **web** www.rspb.org.uk/hobbister
- **Opening hours** Open at all times
- **Entry fees** None, but donations to help continue the work here are welcomed
- **Accessibility** There are council-maintained stepped paths down to Waulkmill and a clifftop walk on mown paths – not accessible for wheelchairs
- **Dogs** Welcome, but please keep them under close control at all times. Please be aware of livestock.

P

What to look for

This is a reserve that rewards time spent in exploration, especially in spring and summer when the birds of the moorlands are present. You can enjoy long walks here, although come prepared (even in summer) with sturdy walking boots as the ground may become wet and muddy.

Curlews, Twites, Skylarks and Meadow Pipits are the voices of the moorland. The coastal path is probably best for Twites. Birds of prey are often in evidence too, with Short-eared Owls, Merlins and Hen Harriers the classic trio of this part of the world. You could be lucky enough to witness a stunning aerial chase when a Merlin

WILDLIFE BY SEASON

SPRING
Upland birds are singing and nesting. Red-throated Divers display on the lochs, Fulmars and Black Guillemots nest on the rocky coast.

SUMMER
Birds of prey hunt over the moorlands. Twites and other upland songbirds are busy feeding their chicks. Red-thoated Divers nest on the lochans.

AUTUMN
Wintering water birds are gathering in Scapa Flow and Waukmill Bay.

WINTER
Waterbird numbers in Scapa Flow and Waukmill Bay peak, with many Slavonian Grebes, Long-tailed Ducks and divers.

targets a Meadow Pipit or a defiantly singing male Skylark.

Fulmars breed on the low cliffs, while Black Guillemots nest among the boulders. Great Northern Divers call from Scapa Flow on still spring evenings, while Red-throated Divers in splendid breeding plumage dive for fish through summer. As summer turns into autumn, waders visit the shoreline in Waukmill Bay, and more birds arrive in the Flow, including Shags and Slavonian Grebes. By winter, Great Northern and Black-throated Divers have joined the Red-throateds, giving you the opportunity to compare all three species in their confusing winter plumages.

How to get here

Grid ref./postcode HY 395069/ KW17 2
By road For flights and ferry information to Orkney, contact VisitOrkney at www.visitorkney. com or at 6 Broadstreet, Kirkwall KW15 1NX, or call 01856 872856. The reserve is 3.1 miles west of Kirkwall off the A964. The main access

points are from the car park at grid ref HY 395069 or from Waulkmill Bay at HY 382068.
By public transport Buses run along the A964 five times per day. Contact the Orkney Tourist Board on 01856 872856.

SCAPA SECRETS
Scapa Flow is an extraordinary rich marine environment, attracting numerous scuba-divers to enjoy the undersea world as well as hordes of hunting birds. All this is a far cry from the Scapa Flow of wartime, when it was an important naval base. In the First World War, 74 interred German ships were scuttled in the Flow – eight of them were never salvaged. In World War II, the German U-Boat U-47 attacked and sank the *HMS Royal Oak* in the Flow. Many scuba divers come to see the wrecks, as well as the sealife that has colonised them.

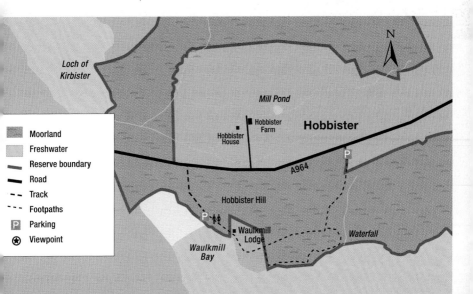

HOY SSSI, SPA, NCR, SCA, NSA, NATURA 2000

Hoy is the most south-westerly of the Orkney islands. The RSPB manages a large swathe of moorland and cliff-top in the north of the island. Wrap up well and enjoy a walk along the rugged paths – you'll see the famous Old Man of Hoy, a 150m-high sea stack, and a variety of sea and moorland wildlife.

● Access, facilities, contact details and accessibility

There are two footpaths through the reserve, plus a more challenging cliff-top track (for which you'll need a compass). Guided walks on the reserve can be arranged.

P

- **Telephone** 01856 850 176; **email** orkney@rspb.org.uk; **web** www.rspb.org.uk/hoy
- **Opening hours** Open at all times
- **Entry fees** None, but donations are welcome
- **Accessibility** The trails are quite rough and hilly, so not suitable for the mobility-impaired
- **Dogs** Some access is permitted for dogs – please contact the reserve for details. Please be aware of livestock.

What to look for

With towering cliffs packed with seabirds to one side and rolling heather moorland on the other, this wild and wonderful reserve is an exciting wildlife-watching destination and offers the kind of bracing walks that really make you feel you've earned your dinner and evening bath.

Seabirds abound in spring and summer, with

Guillemots, Razorbills, Puffins, Kittiwakes, Shags and Fulmars all nesting on the high cliffs. There are colonies of Manx Shearwaters and Common and Arctic Terns nearby and you may see these birds going past at sea. The pigeons that nest on the cliffs are as close as any you'll see to pure wild Rock Doves, the species

WILDLIFE BY SEASON

SPRING

Seabirds are beginning to nest, while Hen Harriers are breeding on the moorland and Emperor Moths are emerging.

SUMMER

There is a fine show of flowers, including seven species of orchids, along the Post Road footpath, and this is the best time to see whales and dolphins.

AUTUMN

Migrating birds fly overhead, sometimes in huge numbers, and rarities are found in most years.

WINTER

Divers and seaducks may be offshore. Mountain Hares are in their stunning white winter coats.

from which all our street and domestic pigeons are descended. Ravens and Rock Pipits nest here too, while inland on the moors there are Great Skuas on the higher tops and Arctic Skuas further down, as well as Golden Plovers, Red Grouse and Mountain Hares. The hares are smoky-grey at this time of year, with bold black ear-tips.

The moorland is alive with Emperor Moths for a few weeks in late spring to early summer. These fat, fluffy moths with their bold eye-shaped wing markings fly by day and so are easy to see – the males homing in on females the moment the latter emerge from their cocoons, drawn in by the females' powerful pheromones.

Many breeding birds vacate the area completely in autumn, but you could see masses of migrating geese, finches, thrushes and other birds at this time, as well as countless seabirds going by offshore. By winter, only a few hardy residents remain, including the Red Grouse and the Mountain Hares – the latter moulting into a snowy-white pelage to provide winter camouflage but retaining the black ear-tips. At sea, Long-tailed Ducks and Great Northern Divers loiter close to the shore until spring returns.

WHEN TO VISIT

Winter is the quietest time. A wealth of interesting wildlife is present in spring and summer, autumn is unpredictable but sometimes excellent for migrants, and time of day is not important.

How to get here

Grid ref./postcode HY 222034/ KW16 3

By road From Stromness, take the passenger ferry *MV Graemsay* to Lyness on Hoy. From Lyness ferry turn right (signposted 'Hoy') onto the B9047 and take the first left (signposted for Dwarfie Stone) toward Rackwick. Park at Dwarfie Stone or Rackwick beach.

By public transport Follow the same directions as above (about 1.5 miles total distance).

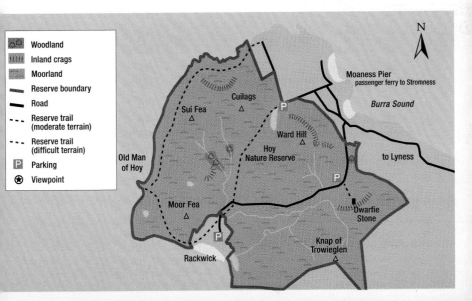

Legend:
- Woodland
- Inland crags
- Moorland
- Reserve boundary
- Road
- Reserve trail (moderate terrain)
- Reserve trail (difficult terrain)
- P Parking
- ★ Viewpoint

N

Cuilags

Sui Fea △

Moaness Pier
passenger ferry to Stromness

Burra Sound

Ward Hill △

Hoy Nature Reserve

Old Man of Hoy

to Lyness

Moor Fea △

Dwarfie Stone

Rackwick

Knap of Trowieglen △

EAST SCOTLAND

LOCH OF KINNORDY

SSSI, SPA, RAMSAR, NATURA 2000

This shallow loch with its marshy surroundings is important for wildfowl and waders through-out the year. It is also a popular hunting spot for local Ospreys, and you can enjoy great views of these fantastic raptors swooping low to swipe fish from the water. The feeding station attracts a variety of woodland birds and also Red Squirrels.

● Access, facilities, contact details and accessibility

There are three hides along the 300m overlooking the loch, and a feeding station. You can arrange guided walks and group visits.

- **Telephone** 01738 630 783; **web** www.rspb.org.uk/lochofkinnordy
- **Opening hours** Open daily from dawn to dusk, but is closed occasionally on Saturdays in autumn (please contact the reserve to check).
- **Entry fees** Free, but donations to contribute to the work here are welcome
- **Accessibility** The reserve trail is suitable for wheelchairs, although the path to Kirriemuir may not be
- **Dogs** Allowed on all footpaths, but must be under strict control at all times

What to look for

The picturesque Loch of Kinnordy sits in a natural basin, among farmed fields with small wooded copses. Part of the basin is marshland, while the rest is open water. If you visit in spring, you'll see wading birds like Lapwings, Curlews

and Snipes displaying over the marsh, while Black-tailed Godwits visit on their way to Iceland.

Ospreys return from Africa in March – they nest nearby and visit the loch throughout spring and summer to fish. Watching them hunting is

WILDLIFE BY SEASON

SPRING

Ospreys fish the loch from mid-March. Waders display over the marsh, and warblers return to nest.

SUMMER

Wildfowl on the loch have chicks, and flowers and insects are most abundant at this time.

AUTUMN

Waders come to the loch shore to feed, and wintering swans and geese start to return.

WINTER

The loch is busy with Whooper Swans, Goldeneyes, Goosanders and Wigeons. Many birds – and Red Squirrels – visit the feeding station.

one of the highlights of a visit to this reserve – sometimes there are heart-in-mouth moments when the Osprey seems to have trouble taking off from the surface with its catch, but a few strokes of those powerful wings against the water soon gets it airborne again.

Several species of wildfowl nest discreetly in the marshland, and in summer they venture out onto the open water with their chicks to feed – they include Shovelers, Gadwalls and Mute Swans. An impressive show of wetland flowers, along with butterflies and damselflies in profusion, is some compensation for this. This is a particularly good time to look for Otters.

Autumn brings more wildfowl, including Whooper Swans and Pink-footed and Greylag Geese, and passage waders too, especially when water levels are low and a more muddy foreshore is exposed. The feeding station starts to become busier at this time, with Red Squirrels joining the flocks of tits and finches at the peanut feeder. You could see Roe Deer at any time of year but they tend to

WHEN TO VISIT

Ospreys are present in spring and summer and into early autumn. Otherwise, there is much to see here throughout the year, and time of day is not important.

come out into the open more in winter, as do the usually skulking Water Rails. Diving ducks like Goldeneyes and Goosanders also visit in winter.

How to get here

Grid ref./postcode NO 361539/ DD8 5

By road The reserve is located 1 mile west of Kirriemuir on the B951 to Glenisla road. Follow the tourist signs to The Glens, Alyth and Blairgowrie until you reach the Glenisla road. The reserve is on the right.

By public transport The nearest railway station is Dundee, 19 miles away. From here, buses call at Kirriemuir town centre. From here the reserve can be reached on foot either along the B951 or along the footpath from the top of Kirriemuir Den.

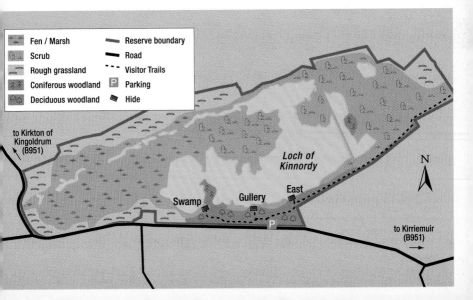

Map legend:
- Fen / Marsh
- Scrub
- Rough grassland
- Coniferous woodland
- Deciduous woodland
- Reserve boundary
- Road
- Visitor Trails
- Parking
- Hide

to Kirkton of Kingoldrum (B951)

Loch of Kinnordy

Swamp
Gullery
East

N

to Kirriemuir (B951)

EAST SCOTLAND

Whooper Swans

LOCH OF SPIGGIE SSSI, SPA, NSA

The Lochs of Spiggie and Brow make up this reserve, which is one of Shetland's most important lochs for water birds. You can view the birds very easily from the roadside, so any mobility difficulties won't stop you enjoying the spectacle of thousands of Whooper Swans, ducks and other wildfowl on the lochs, especially in winter.

● Access, facilities, contact details and accessibility

With great views from the roadside, it's easy for everyone to enjoy the wildlife of this reserve. There is an RSPB information hut at the north end of the loch.

P

- **Telephone** 01950 460 800; **web** www.rspb.org.uk/lochofspiggie
- **Opening hours** The loch can be viewed from the road all year-round
- **Entry fees** Free, though donations are welcome
- **Accessibility** The loch is best viewed from the roadside
- **Dogs** There are no dog-walking areas on the reserve

What to look for

This fine loch is a magnet for water birds throughout the year. Once a sea loch, it was cut off from the sea by the natural formation of a sand bar, and now offers a sheltered refuge to a host of species. Visit in spring to see the breeding waders – Oystercatchers, Redshanks, Lapwings, Snipes and Curlews – displaying and calling around the north-west marsh. Through

summer, the Great and Arctic Skuas, Kittiwakes and Arctic Terns that nest locally come to the loch to bathe, rubbing shoulders with the Teals, Shovelers and Mallards that nest here. The Loch of Spiggie is very popular with anglers. You may even catch a glimpse of a Sea Trout leaping out the water to catch insects.

In late autumn, 100 or more Whooper Swans

WILDLIFE BY SEASON

SPRING
Nesting waders are noisily displaying overhead. Ducks display on the loch before they depart for their breeding grounds.

SUMMER
Many locally breeding birds come to the loch to bathe, while Tufted Ducks, Teals and Mallards nest here.

AUTUMN
A wide variety of wild birds begins to arrive on the loch, including Whooper Swans.

WINTER
Goldeneyes, Teals, Wigeons, Long-tailed Ducks, Greylag Geese and Whooper Swans are present in large numbers.

join the wildfowl that has already arrived. Some continue their journeys south after a short stay but others spend their winters here. These wild swans have a bugling call so you can hear them coming from a long way off – just as vocal are the Greylag Geese that also winter here.

By mid-winter, the reserve becomes busy with wildfowl. The geese and swans are joined by a wide variety of ducks, including Tufted Ducks, Pochards, Goldeneyes and Wigeons, and the Teals are joined by a fresh influx from northern Europe and Iceland. Rarities are sometimes found – this is a good hunting ground for vagrant ducks from North America, such as American Wigeon and Lesser Scaup. In late winter, this is a great place to watch drake Goldeneyes and Long-tailed Ducks in their smart breeding plumage, displaying to the females.

As well as the open water of the reserve, the RSPB owns a small piece of land to the northern tip of Loch of Spiggie. This, the north-west marsh,

is managed for the benefit of breeding waders, including Lapwings and Redshanks. The management is also geared to attract new species. One of those on the target list is the extremely rare and very beautiful Red-necked Phalarope – management plans are geared towards attracting them to breed.

How to get here
Grid ref./postcode HU 374165/ ZE2 9
By road You can fly to Sumburgh from Edinburgh, Aberdeen, Inverness and Orkney. The reserve is about 2.5 miles north of Sumburgh Airport; turn off the B9122 near Scousburgh.
By public transport From Lerwick, take the bus to Sumburgh Airport. To reach the loch, alight at Robin's Brae and walk westwards for 2.5 miles.

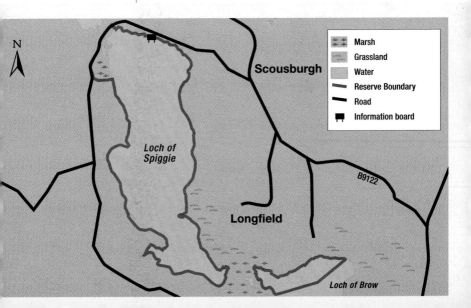

EAST SCOTLAND

LOCH OF STRATHBEG

SPA, NATURA 2000

The mesmerising spectacle of countless wild geese flighting off their roost in winter, the enchanting sight of terns feeding their fluffy offspring right before your eyes in summer, and exciting migration action through spring and autumn... the remarkable Loch of Strathbeg is truly a reserve for all seasons. The RSPB works hard to maintain the appeal of this fragile habitat for wildlife, and you can enjoy it all year round from the trails and hides – for a full day's walking you can also explore the beach and wider area.

● Access, facilities, contact details and accessibility

The visitor centre provides hot drinks, and Wildlife Explorer backpacks for children. Reserve staff are on hand to help with any identification queries and to direct you to any interesting sightings. The reserve runs regular wildlife-watching events, and guided walks can be arranged.

- **Telephone** 01346 532017; **email** strathbeg@rspb.org.uk; **web** www.rspb.org.uk/lochofstrathbeg
- **Opening hours** The visitor centre is open daily from 8am–6pm, while the Tower Pool and Loch hides are open dawn to dusk.
- **Entry fees** Free, but donations to help continue the work here are welcome
- **Accessibility** All infrastructure on the reserve, including access routes, is currently being upgraded to ensure that it is suitable for users of all abilities. All hides and paths will be adapted to accommodate wheelchairs. For more information, please contact the reserve. Neither of the two picnic tables are wheelchair-adapted at present.
- **Dogs** You may bring your dog but please keep it under close control at all times to prevent disturbance to wildlife.

WILDLIFE BY SEASON

SPRING

The last of the winter wildfowl depart in early spring. Breeding waders display around the fields and other waders stop off on migration. Tree Sparrows are using nestboxes around the visitor centre.

SUMMER

Terns are feeding their chicks on the visitor centre pools. Dark Green Fritillary butterflies fly over masses of dog violets on the dunes.

AUTUMN

The winter wildfowl starts to return, and waders including Ruffs, Greenshanks and Black-tailed Godwits stop off on their migration south. Sea-watching is most rewarding at this time of year, with terns, auks, skuas and shearwaters among the seabirds passing by offshore.

WINTER

Wildfowl numbers are at their peak, and the visitor centre pools are full of ducks in their most colourful plumage. Flocks of Lapwings, Curlews and Golden Plovers feed on the fields. A dawn visit will reward you with wonderful views of masses of Pink-footed Geese leaving the loch. Otters are easiest to see in frozen conditions.

What to look for

This 'dune loch', the largest of its kind in the UK, was formed naturally in 1720, when a huge storm shifted the sand dunes, cutting off the bay and transforming it into a loch. Since then, the sheltered shallow waters have attracted masses of water birds to feed, breed and rest here.

An autumn or winter sunrise at Strathbeg offers an unforgettable experience, as the great flocks of Pink-footed Geese that roost on the loch and dunes wake up and head close to their duller-billed offspring in close family groups.

A great variety of other wildfowl, including Wigeons, Teals, Goldeneyes, Barnacle Geese and Whooper Swans, come here in winter too. You can watch many of them at close quarters from the visitor centre, which overlooks a collection of pools. The trails lead to two hides overlooking the loch itself – from here you may see scarcer water birds like Scaups, Long-tailed Ducks and Slavonian Grebes. From November this

You'll recognise Pink-footed Geese by their shortish necks, dark heads, small bills and, at Strathbeg, by the fact that there are 80,000 of them.

off to nearby fields to feed. Up to 80,000 of them (a fifth of the world's population) may be here in mid-autumn, pouring overhead in endless noisy strings against the dawn sky. You can enjoy this amazing sight from the elevated Tower Pool hide, open from dawn until dusk and giving panoramic views across the loch and beyond. During the day the geese feed in the fields – watch long enough and you'll start to see order within the flocks, with adult pairs keeping

is one of the few places in Scotland where there is a chance of encountering a Bittern, especially from Fen Hide. Predators are more noticeable at this time too – look out for Peregrine Falcons sending the assembled flocks into a panic, or slowly patrolling Hen Harriers (replacing the Marsh Harriers that are here in summer).

The RSPB has re-routed the main stream that feeds into the loch, so that it now flows slowly through 23 hectares of reedbed.

The Dark Green Fritillary butterfly is on the wing from late June to early August. This one is feeding from a Common Spotted Orchid flower.

This helps to filter the water and maintain its quality, as well as providing new wildlife habitat, attractive to birds like Bitterns and Marsh Harriers. The RSPB has also improved the surrounding land to make it more attractive to farmland birds.

In spring, flocks of waders and wildfowl are on the move. By summer, the masses of wildfowl have departed but Common and Arctic Terns nest on the pools, and Tree Sparrows, Snipe, Redshanks and Lapwings breed on the farmland. You may be lucky and see an Otter from the visitor centre, and the reedbeds are full of singing warblers.

In autumn, a variety of waders calls at the loch on their migration south. Many are young birds hatched that year, unused to people and therefore often quite fearless, feeding right in front of the hides and giving excellent views. This is a great time to practise your wader identification – both species of godwits, Spotted Redshanks, Green and Wood Sandpipers, Little Stints, Curlew Sandpipers and Ruffs are all regular, and scarcer visitors from across the Atlantic show up from time to time.

Autumn is also a good time to turn to the sea, as seabirds are passing by in large numbers. Look out for terns, and also gannets and Manx Shearwaters – the former large and mostly white, the latter smaller and alternating black and white as they tip and tilt between the waves. Great and Arctic Skuas may also pass by, sometimes harrying the other seabirds as they go in dazzling aerial chases. These piratical birds often don't bother fishing for themselves but harrass other birds to drop or even regurgitate their lunch – a charming behaviour that the biologists term 'kleptoparasitism'.

WHEN TO VISIT

The Pink-footed Geese are on show from November til March, numbers peaking in mid to late autumn. Arrive just before sunrise to see them flighting off the loch. Otherwise, the loch is an exciting place to visit at any time of year, and time of day is not crucial.

How to get here

Grid ref./postcode NK 055577/AB43 8
By road From A90 in the village of Crimond, take the turn beside the church, following the brown tourist sign. At the T-junction at the end

IN THE PINK

If you're only used to the Greylag and Canada geese of city parks, the Pink-footed Goose will come as a pleasant surprise. Dainty, small-billed, gentle of expression and musical of voice, this goose is very different to its more ungainly cousins.

Although Pink-feet do not breed in the UK, a large proportion of the world's population winters here and having safe places to feed and rest here is just as important as having suitable safe breeding grounds up in Greenland, Iceland and Svarlbard. At the Loch of Strathbeg, the RSPB protects the loch and surrounding meadows, while local farmers grow extra crops for the geese, for which they are paid by Scottish Natural Heritage. Add in increased legal protection from shooting, and the result has been a big increase in the number of Pink-feet coming to Strathbeg and other sites in the UK. Many of the birds continue south to Norfolk as winter advances, so mid-autumn is the time to see the biggest numbers at Strathbeg.

Summer-plumaged Redshanks aren't as colourful as some waders but make up for it with their lively characters and loud voices.

of the road, turn left. After approximately 500m, turn right at the reserve entrance sign onto the entrance track and follow the track to the car park.

By public transport The nearest rail station is at Inverurie, 30 miles away – reaching the site by public transport is difficult if you are not based nearby. The nearest bus stop is in Crimond village. In the village, walk towards the church. Beside the church is a small road with a brown nature reserve sign. Follow signs to the visitor centre (roughly one mile from village).

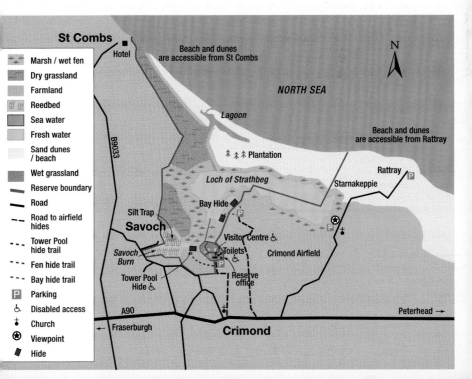

EAST SCOTLAND

MARWICK HEAD

SSSI, SPA, NCR, NATURA 2000

On the north-western corner of Mainland, Orkney, the towering sea cliffs host a busy seabird colony through spring and summer. This quiet and very out-of-the-way reserve is ideal for those who enjoy sharing a remote and dramatically wild location with only a noisy mass of seabirds. Even in winter it's worth a look for the breathtaking scenery alone.

● Access, facilities, contact details and accessibility

This remote reserve has no facilities, so suits the independent visitor.
- **Telephone** 01856 850 176; **web** www.rspb.org.uk/marwickhead
- **Opening hours** Open at all times
- **Entry fees** Free
- **Accessibility** Not suitable for the mobility-impaired
- **Dogs** Must be kept under close control at all times. Please be aware of livestock.

What to look for

The massive sandstone cliffs of Marwick Head hold an important mixed seabird colony. You can reach the cliff-top path from the bay or from the car park at Cumlaquoy. Good views are possible from this path but please take great care on the cliff edge.

If you are visiting in spring or summer, you'll enjoy the impressive sight, sound and smell of up to 32,000 Guillemots, 20,000 Kittiwakes, 2,000 Fulmars and 700 Razorbills, with a supporting cast of Puffins, Shags, Herring Gulls and Jackdaws. Rock Doves and Rock Pipits also nest here, while on the cliff-tops you could see Wheatears, and further inland there are breeding

WILDLIFE BY SEASON

SPRING

Seabirds return to the cliffs, with Fulmars arriving as early as late February.

SUMMER

Breeding activity is in full flow. August is a good time to see Great Yellow Bumblebees. By August most Puffins have disappeared out to sea.

AUTUMN

The seabirds leave the cliffs to the resident Jackdaws and Rock Doves. You could witness sizeable migrating flocks of various birds, over land and at sea.

WINTER

The reserve is very quiet, but westerly storms produce spectacular seascapes.

waders in the fields – Snipes, Oystercatchers, Redshanks, Curlews and Lapwings are all present and often very noticeable in spring, calling to one another and scolding any passing visitors. Snipes are the exception, but late in the day you may hear their bizarre 'drumming' display flight, when their vibrating tail feathers make an almost comical buzzing sound.

Up on the cliff-tops, Spring Squill and Thrift form a colourful carpet in summer, while down in the sea you could see Grey Seals bobbing about close inshore. Puffins are often easier to see when they're swimming on the surface, rather than in their tucked-away nesting spots.

You'll notice a prominent monument on the cliff-top. This sturdy stone tower is a memorial to Field Marshall Lord Kitchener, famous as the face of the wartime 'Your Country Needs You' posters, who was lost along with his ship *HMS Hampshire* in June 1916. En route to Russia, the ship hit a mine in rough sea, and was destroyed, with the loss of almost the whole crew.

WHEN TO VISIT

Visit in spring or summer to watch the action at the seabird colony.

How to get here

Grid ref./postcode HY 223248/ KW17 2

By road To reach Mainland, either fly from Edinburgh, Glasgow, Inverness or Aberdeen to Kirkwall, or take a ferry from Gils Bay or Scrabster to Stromness. From Kirkwall, follow the A960 for about 0.6 miles, then at the roundabout take the first exit onto the A965. Follow this road for 8 miles then turn right onto the A986, turning right again onto the B9056 after about 2 miles. Just after a crossroads take the minor road left, then first right, then left at a crossroads to take you to the Head. From Stromness, take the A967 heading north, then after about 4 miles turn left onto the B9056, and follow this road for about 6.5 miles, then directions are as above.

By public transport There is no public transport access to the reserve.

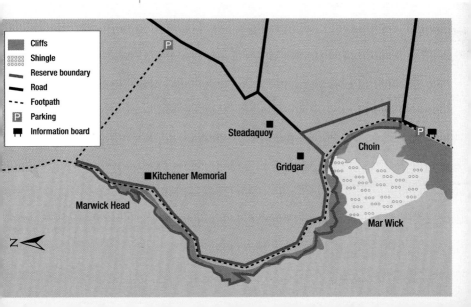

Map legend:
- Cliffs
- Shingle
- Reserve boundary
- Road
- Footpath
- P Parking
- Information board

Steadaquoy
Choin
Gridgar
Kitchener Memorial
Marwick Head
Mar Wick

EAST SCOTLAND

Pintails

MILL DAM IBA

This natural marsh, on the small central Orkney island of Shapinsay, represents a rare and important wildlife habitat in the islands. From the hide here you can see no fewer than nine species of ducks nesting, along with many other water and marshland birds, while winter brings large flocks of wildfowl including Whooper Swans.

● Access, facilities, contact details and accessibility

There is no public access to this reserve, but anyone may use the hide by the car park. You can borrow binoculars in the hide.

- **Telephone** 01856 850176; **email** orkney@rspb.org.uk; **web** www.rspb.org.uk/milldam
- **Opening hours** The hide is open at all times
- **Entry fees** None, though donations are welcome
- **Accessibility** The track from the car park to the hide is wheelchair-accessible
- **Dogs** Welcome but must be kept under control. Please be aware of livestock.

What to look for

The marshy habitats at Mill Dam are too fragile to allow visitor access, but a well-placed hide allows you to enjoy views of the wildlife without causing any damage or disturbance. In spring, you could see up to nine species of breeding ducks including the stunning Pintail, the male resplendent with his chocolate-brown, silver,

black and white plumage and long tail feathers.

Several species of waders breed here too, as do Little Grebes, Coots, Moorhens and a very lively and noisy colony of Black-headed Gulls. By summer the gulls are tending their endearing fluffy chicks, while you could see female Pintails, Shovelers and other ducks escorting their

WILDLIFE BY SEASON

SPRING

The marshes hold many breeding ducks and waders – see their courtship displays in spring.

SUMMER

Wetland birds have chicks, and the marsh is colourful with a variety of flowering plants including Northern Marsh Orchids.

AUTUMN

Whooper Swans arrive, along with the first of many wintering ducks and geese. Flocks of waders gather on the fields.

WINTER

The marsh, open water and fields are busy with ducks, geese, Whooper Swans and wading birds. Predators like Hen Harriers hunt over the reserve.

ducklings out onto the open water. The RSPB is clearing overgrown vegetation to increase the area of marshland available to the water birds, and also improving the drier areas in the hope of attracting breeding Corncrakes in the future. Marshland flowers including Bog Bean, Marsh Cinquefoil and Marsh Marigold lend a splash of seasonal colour to the reserve.

The ducks moult into their 'eclipse' plumage in late summer, and it can become a challenge identifying the species as the males lose their distinctive breeding colours. By the time the moult is ending, the first Whooper Swans of the winter have arrived, and a new influx of Teals, Wigeons and Mallards starts to arrive for the winter. Out on the fields, masses of Lapwings and Golden Plovers are joined by Redshanks and Oystercatchers.

Winter at Mill Dam is a busy time, with 100 Whooper Swans, thousands of Greylag Geese and large flocks of ducks and waders all feeding on the marsh. This is the best time to look for raptors, with Hen Harriers descending

WHEN TO VISIT

With a wide variety of both breeding and wintering birds, Mill Dam is worth a visit at any time of year, and time of day is not critical.

from the moors to winter in more agreeable hunting grounds like this, along with a few Merlins and Peregrines.

How to get here

Grid ref./postcode HY 483178/ KW17 2
By road Take a ferry to Stromness, Burwick or St Margaret's Hope on Mainland, then on to Kirkwall and from here take a ferry to Balfour on Shapinsay. The reserve is 1 mile north-east of Balfour village on Shapinsay, take the second left from the B9059 out of the village.
By public transport Take a ferry to Stromness, Burwick or St Margaret's Hope on Mainland, then a bus to Kirkwall and from here a ferry to Balfour on Shapinsay, then follow directions as above (1 mile's walk).

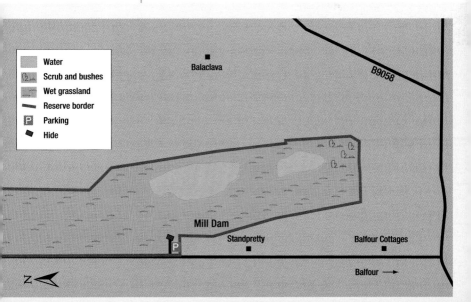

Water
Scrub and bushes
Wet grassland
Reserve border
P Parking
Hide

Balaclava

B9058

Mill Dam

Standpretty

Balfour Cottages

Balfour →

N

EAST SCOTLAND

MOUSA SSSI, SPA, SAC, NATURA 2000

Lying just off the south-eastern shore of Shetland Mainland is this small uninhabited island with its rich Iron Age history and wonderful wildlife. It is one of the best places in the world to see and hear Storm Petrels, but hosts many other seabirds and is famous for its seals.

Access, facilities, contact details and accessibility

There are way markers, information signs and a trail guide. The path to the broch is about half a mile long, while the circular path is 1.5 miles long. Guided walks and group visits can be arranged.

- **Telephone** 01950 460800; **web** www.rspb.org.uk/mousa
- **Opening hours** The ferry runs from 1 April until mid-September, weather permitting
- **Entry fees** Free, though donations are welcome
- **Accessibility** Disabled visitors should contact the ferry company to check suitability of crossing. The path around Mousa is uneven, and boggy in places.
- **Dogs** Permitted on the reserve providing they are under control. However dogs are not permitted on the ferry.

What to look for

From the ferry to Mousa you could see Harbour Porpoises and you will probably see Eiders and other seabirds before you land. Once on the island, you'll soon discover the Iron Age broch, which actually houses some of Mousa's 11,000 or so pairs of Storm Petrels within its walls. The petrels, being small and vulnerable seabirds, visit their chicks at night when the chance of being attacked by a passing skua or gull is reduced. You may hear the adults on their nests or, later on, chicks calling from within the burrows, but to see them you'll need to take one of the night crossings, which will give you an unforgettable hour on the island around midnight (of course the sky never completely darkens on summer nights this far north).

WILDLIFE BY SEASON

SPRING

Seabirds return and by late May breeding activity is underway. Black Guillemots nest among the boulders while skuas will be establishing their territories on the moorland. Storm Petrels arrive in late spring. Look out for seals in the East and West Pools.

SUMMER

Seabirds and many other birds, such as Ringed Plovers and Skylarks, are busy nesting and rearing chicks. Storm Petrel trips run from late May to mid-July. Seals haul out in large numbers to moult by the East Pool.

The island's other nesting birds include Arctic Terns, Black Guillemots, Eiders, Arctic and Great Skuas and assorted waders. The terns and skuas may give you a rather unfriendly reception, especially if they decide you are too close to their nests. Wear a hat to protect you from attacks. Common Seals give birth in June on the northern shores of the West Pool and move to the East Pool to moult in July and August. If you keep behind the walls, you will be rewarded with excellent views of these marvellous mammals.

How to get here

Grid ref./postcode HU 435248/ ZE2 9

Mousa is only accessible by boat. The ferry departs from Leebotten, Sandwick, on the east coast of the Mainland of Shetland, about halfway between Lerwick and Sumburgh Airport. Tom Jamieson (tel: 01950 431367) runs the ferry service to Mousa, offering trips during the day and unique night-time trips to see the Storm Petrels. The ferry crossing lasts about 15

WHEN TO VISIT

You can only visit between 1 April and mid-September. Take a night-time trip for an unforgettable encounter with the island's Storm Petrels.

minutes, and costs £12.50 for adults and £6 for children (5–16 years). There is a 10 per cent discount for RSPB members.

BROCH OF AGES

Mousa Broch is the best-preserved fortification of its kind in the British Isles, and lies on the south-western shore. The broch is a tall round stone tower, built around 100 BC, although no archaeological investigation has taken place. Many of the internal features have been lost, probably during Norse occupations. Its construction is of dry stones, which means that any disturbance could cause disastrous damage. This also means that there are numerous tunnels within the thick walls, perfect for Storm Petrels to nest inside, safe from the attentions of larger, fiercer seabirds.

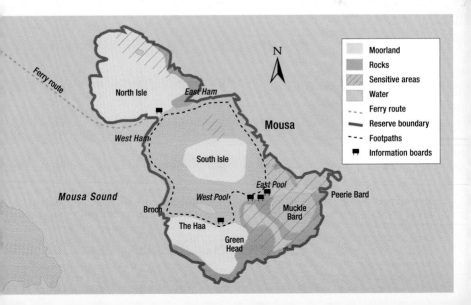

EAST SCOTLAND

NORTH HILL SSSI, SPA, NCR

Papa Westray is a small, narrow island in the north of the Orkney archipelago. The reserve at
North Hill comprises the moorland and cliff edge of the island's northern tip, and is home to
many rare breeding birds in spring and summer as well as the extremely rare and beautiful
Scottish Primrose. A great place for an invigorating walk for adults and older children.

● Access, facilities, contact details and accessibility

The main trail is about 3 miles long and there is a hide. Wildlife Explorer backpacks for children are
available from the warden at Rose Cottage.

- **Telephone** 01856 850176; **email** orkney@rspb.org.uk; **web** www.rspb.org.uk/northhill
- **Opening hours** Open at all times
- **Entry fees** Free
- **Accessibility** The trail is not suitable for wheelchair users
- **Dogs** Welcome but please keep them under close control. Please be aware of livestock.

What to look for

The cliffs and cliff-tops are marvellous from
mid-spring to late summer, with flowers
blooming in abundance and colonies of seabirds
nesting on the cliffs themselves.

The maritime heath on the cliff-tops has an
important vegetation community, including the
Scottish Primrose which flowers in late May and

again in July. Look out for its clusters of pink
flowers with yellow centres, borne on long stems
and resembling campions perhaps more than the
familiar primroses of southern woodlands and
gardens. To protect these and other flowers, stick
to the recommended routes. A seasonal grazing
regime helps the primrose to thrive and also

WILDLIFE BY SEASON

SPRING

Seabirds return to the cliffs. Flowers including Scottish Primrose are flowering by late spring.

SUMMER

Seabirds are feeding their chicks. Cliff-top flowers are at their best. The Scottish Primrose has a second flowering in July.

AUTUMN

Many migrant birds may pass overhead, and rarities are sometimes found. Look out for Orcas and other cetaceans on calm days.

WINTER

A quiet time, but look for Fulmars, Gannets and seals offshore. By late February the Fulmars have started settling down to nest on the cliffs.

provides ideal nesting habitat for skuas, terns and wading birds. Great and Arctic Skuas nest up on the heath.

By autumn, the cliffs fall silent, but this is the time for rare birds to arrive. Heavy weather tends to ground more land bird migrants, but if you do visit on a calm day you have a better chance of seeing cetaceans, including Orcas which travel in family groups and have distinctive tall, blade-like dorsal fins.

Papa Westray is a great wildlife-watching destination in winter, especially on the coast where you'll see Gannets, Fulmars, various waders, divers, seaducks and seals.

How to get here

Grid ref./postcode HY 495538/ KW17 2

By road Transport to Papa Westray is available by boat from Kirkwall, Orkney mainland (Orkney Ferries, tel: 01856 872 004), or by plane from Kirkwall (contact Loganair, tel: 01856 872 494). From the pier or airfield, travel northward along

WHEN TO VISIT

Spring and summer are the best times to visit, but time of day is not important.

the main road. From the shop/ hostel, travel up the road to the junction at Holland Farm, turning right onto the main road. Once on the main road, continue past Rose Cottage until the road bends sharply to the right at the reserve entrance. Limited parking is available here. **By public transport** There is no public transport on the island. See above for walking directions from the pier or airfield.

SOMETHING SPECIAL

Among the many migrating birds that arrive on our east coast each autumn are non-UK species from mainland Europe, like Bluethroat, Red-backed Shrike and Barred Warbler. Along with these fairly regular passage migrants, there is always the chance of something really exotic, from much further afield.

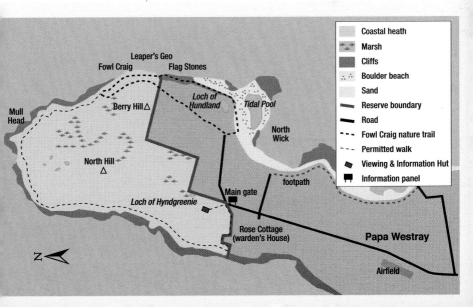

Legend:
- Coastal heath
- Marsh
- Cliffs
- Boulder beach
- Sand
- Reserve boundary
- Road
- Fowl Craig nature trail
- Permitted walk
- Viewing & Information Hut
- Information panel

Map labels: Leaper's Geo, Fowl Craig, Flag Stones, Berry Hill △, Loch of Hundland, Tidal Pool, Mull Head, North Wick, North Hill △, Loch of Hyndgreenie, Main gate, footpath, Rose Cottage (warden's House), Papa Westray, Airfield

N

EAST SCOTLAND

NOUP CLIFFS   SSSI, SPA, NCR, NATURA 2000

At the north-western tip of the island of Westray is Orkney's largest seabird colony. The sheer scale of the spectacle is breathtaking, but you'll need your wits about you to dodge the Arctic Terns that nest on the cliff-tops – they may 'bomb' you if you stray too close. The terrain can be hard going, so this is ideal for those who like a really invigorating walk.

●Access, facilities, contact details and accessibility

There is a 1.5-mile linear cliff-top trail, which joins up with the West Westray Walk for those who want a longer stroll.

- **Telephone** 01856 850176; **email** orkney@rspb.org.uk; **web** www.rspb.org.uk/noupcliffs
- **Opening hours** Open at all times
- **Entry fees** Free, but donations to help continue the work here are welcome
- **Accessibility** The trail is unsuitable for wheelchairs or pushchairs
- **Dogs** Welcome but please keep them under close control. Please be aware of livestock.

What to look for

The cliff-top leads to the lighthouse on Noup Head, giving you great views over the sea and, in places, of the cliff-face. The seabirds return to the cliffs through spring, with Fulmars leading the way as usual. By May there are up to 40,000 Guillemots packed onto the ledges (about a fifth of the Orkney population), each pair tending a

single egg. When the egg hatches, there follows two or three weeks of frantic feeding before it's time for the half-grown chick to take the big leap into the sea.

The cliffs also hold Kittiwakes, Razorbills, Black Guillemots and Puffins, while up on the tops there are up to 1,000 pairs of Arctic Terns

WILDLIFE BY SEASON

SPRING
Seabirds return to the cliffs to breed, and Arctic Terns are nesting by mid-May.

SUMMER
The flowers on the cliff-top are in full bloom, while below on the cliffs the auks and Kittiwakes are feeding chicks.

AUTUMN
Migration season, when the seabirds move on and large numbers of land birds may pass overhead, sometimes stopping on the island. Orcas move by offshore.

WINTER
A quiet time. Gannets and Fulmars may be seen offshore, likewise Grey and Common Seals.

nesting. Keep your distance from these noisy birds, for your own good as well as theirs. They will dive fiercely at visitors who they consider are too close to their nests, sometimes drawing blood with their sharp bills, and these attacks mean their eggs or chicks are left alone and vulnerable to becoming chilled. Wear a hat as a precaution, but don't stray too near.

The seabirds move on at the close of summer, the young, still flightless auks swimming east with their parents and the young Kittiwakes independent and flying free. Other birds are on the move too, and all kinds of birds could arrive at this time of year, including rarities blown off course from their migration routes. At sea, mammals are also migrating and the very lucky visitor could see a passing pod of Orcas or perhaps a Minke Whale. Seabirds are passing through too, though by winter there is little left to see either on land or at sea. You can still enjoy a bracing walk here – look out for Peregrine Falcons cruising alongside the cliffs, passing Gannets and Fulmars

WHEN TO VISIT
Spring and summer are the best times for a visit, to see the seabird colonies. Time of day is not important.

offshore, and seals surfing in the shallows.

How to get here
Grid ref./postcode HY 392499/ KW17 2

By road Transport to Westray is available by boat from Kirkwall (contact Orkney Ferries, tel: 01856 872 004) or by plane from Kirkwall (contact Loganair, tel: 01856 872 494). From Pierowall village, turn at the school, following the signs to Noup Cliffs. Turn left at the junction past Noltland Castle, following the road up the hill, eventually passing through Noup Farm. Follow the gravel road to the Noup Lighthouse where there is a car park at the reserve entrance.

By public transport See above for transport to Westray. Follow the minor roads as above to the reserve (about 4 miles).

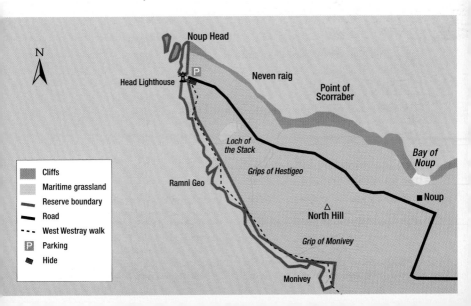

Noup Head · Head Lighthouse · Neven raig · Point of Scorraber · Loch of the Stack · Bay of Noup · Ramni Geo · Grips of Hestigeo · Noup · North Hill · Grip of Monivey · Monivey

Key:
- Cliffs
- Maritime grassland
- Reserve boundary
- Road
- West Westray walk
- P Parking
- Hide

N

EAST SCOTLAND

ONZIEBUST

One of the central Orkney islands, Egilsay is a small and relatively low-lying island with extensively managed farmland. Optimum Corncrake habitat has been created here. Corncrakes are still rare in Orkney and have not been present at Onziebust every year, but the habitat created is also perfect for other farmland birds including many Lapwings, Redshanks, Curlews and Skylarks.

● Access, facilities, contact details and accessibility

There is a 0.6-mile nature trail. You can arrange group visits.

● **Telephone** 01856 821395; **email** orkney@rspb.org.uk; **web** www.rspb.org.uk/onziebust

● **Opening hours** Open at all times

● **Entry fees** Free, but donations to help continue the work here are welcome

● **Accessibility** The nature trail is not suitable for wheelchairs or pushchairs

● **Dogs** Permitted, but please keep them under close control. Please be aware of livestock.

What to look for

This small island is home to a handful of farmers and smallholders and masses of wild birds and other wildlife. It is only about three miles from end to end, so although you can bring a car, you may well not need to.

The RSPB and the landowners have worked together to ensure that the timing and method of hay-cutting is Corncrake-friendly so that when birds do breed conditions are ideal for the rearing of chicks. Be patient if you want to see one – you may be lucky and spot one crossing a road, but they mostly skulk in the long grass, so look carefully for movement and check any areas of shorter grass. When calling, the males

WILDLIFE BY SEASON

SPRING
Waders and Arctic Terns are preparing to nest. Corncrakes are calling from May.

SUMMER
Flowers are everywhere, visited by Great Yellow Bumblebees. Nesting birds have chicks.

AUTUMN
More than 1,000 Greylag Geese arrive from Iceland, while many migrating birds pass through.

WINTER
Manse Loch attracts Wigeons, Teals and other wildfowl, while you'll see many divers and seaducks offshore. Farmland birds form feeding flocks.

stretch their necks out and point their bills upwards, making them more visible, so when you hear the call scan through the grass.

Other birds nesting in the meadows and pastures are much easier to see. Lapwings and Redshanks give themselves away with loud calls and, in the case of the former, an eyecatching tumbling aerial display. Snipes perform 'drumming' display flights and Oystercatchers standing in fields are noticeable from some distance with their pied plumage and long orange bills. Arctic Terns and Eiders nest on the beach.

The hayfields are flowery havens in summer, with Great Yellow Bumblebees visiting the clovers and vetches sown for them. Summer evenings are wonderful, with the fragrance of the meadows and the soundtrack of calling waders and Corncrakes.

All too soon the long summers are over, and autumn is announced by the arrival of more than 1,000 Greylag Geese, which winter on the island. Later on, other wildfowl comes to Manse Loch, including

WHEN TO VISIT
To see and hear Corncrakes, visit from late spring to late summer. Otherwise, the reserve is interesting throughout the year, and time of day is not important.

flocks of Teals and Wigeons, and a scattering of Goldeneyes. Around the coast you can see Great Northern Divers, Long-tailed Ducks and Eiders, males of the latter two beginning to call and display to the females by late winter.

How to get here

Grid ref./postcode HY 474289/ KW17 2

By road Take the roll-on/roll-off ferry to Egilsay from Tingwall on mainland Orkney. Call Orkney Ferries, tel: 01856 751 360. To reach the reserve from the pier, you won't need your car – walk up the road to the crossroads at the centre of the island. From there, follow the unsurfaced track that lies straight ahead, past the school.

By public transport See above.

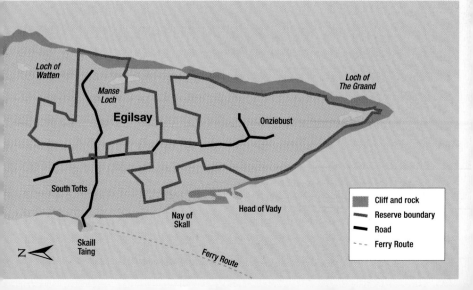

EAST SCOTLAND

Puffins

SUMBURGH HEAD

SSSI, SPA, NATURA 2000

At the southern tip of mainland Shetland, the land narrows to a point with high cliffs on all sides and far-reaching sea views. The beauty of the landscape is perennial, but it is in spring and summer that Sumburgh Head comes into its own, as masses of seabirds assemble on the cliffs for the breeding season. Boundary fences and walls let you view the action in safety.

● Access, facilities, contact details and accessibility

There are three viewing platforms around the reserve, and views from the path from the car park. This path is steep but negotiable with a pushchair.

- **Telephone** 01950 460800; **web** www.rspb.org.uk/sumburghhead
- **Opening hours** Open at all times
- **Entry fees** Free, but donations to help continue the work here are welcome
- **Accessibility** Disabled visitors may park by the lighthouse
- **Dogs** Permitted, but please keep them under close control

What to look for

The cliff-nesting birds are all back by mid-spring. You'll see countless Guillemots on the ledges – look out too for Razorbills, Kittiwakes, Shags, Fulmars and Puffins, each species finding its own ideal nesting site on the cliffs and on the stacks.

You can see an impressive panorama of seascape from here – if you have the time and inclination, it's worth looking for whales and dolphins from here, especially in summer. Harbour Porpoises, Risso's and White-beaked Dolphins, Minke and Humpback Whales and

WILDLIFE BY SEASON

SPRING

Seabirds start to arrive on the cliffs. Wheatears join the resident House Sparrows, Shetland Wrens and Starlings.

SUMMER

The cliffs are busy with seabird activity, and at sea you could see Orcas, White-beaked Dolphins, Harbour Porpoises and even Minke Whales.

Shetland Wren

Orcas have all been seen. Look out for spouts and for surfacing fins and flukes. Some individual Orcas, identifiable by their markings, have been returning here for years.

After the breeding season, Sumburgh Head offers exciting seawatching, with Little Auks sometimes passing in large numbers. These tiny auks breed in the Arctic, in huge colonies. Another seabird, the Sooty Shearwater, is also regularly seen from the headland in autumn, while flocks of Eiders gather offshore to moult.

Autumn brings many keen birdwatchers to Shetland in search of lost vagrant birds. The list of rarities found here includes such delights as Blyth's Reed Warbler, Thrush Nightingale and Black-throated Thrush. Migrant landbirds, whether common or scarce, should be left undisturbed to enable them to feed up in peace after their (sometimes epic) sea crossings. One landbird here through winter is the Twite, which flocks to eat up the canary seed provided for it by the RSPB.

WHEN TO VISIT

Late spring to summer is the best time to visit, and see the seabirds nesting on the cliffs.

How to get here

Grid ref./postcode HU 407079/ ZE3 9

By road Shetland can be reached by boat, from Aberdeen or from Thurso via Orkney (contact NorthLink Ferries, tel: 0845 600 0449), or by plane from Orkney, Edinburgh, Aberdeen, Inverness and Glasgow. The reserve is on the southernmost tip of Mainland Shetland. On the A970 about 0.3 miles east of the turn-off to Sumburgh Aiport, turn right (south-east) at Grutness and carry on for about 1.25 miles until you reach the main car park. From there it's a 0.3 mile walk to the lighthouse.

By public transport A bus runs between Lerwick and Sumburgh Airport. The reserve is located approximately 2 miles (3.5 km) from the airport.

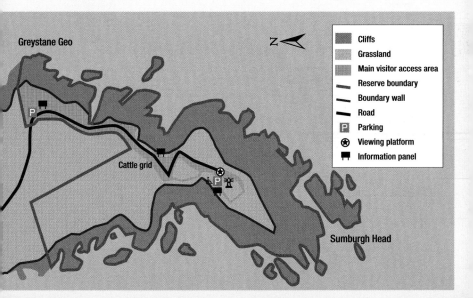

Greystane Geo

N

Cattle grid

Sumburgh Head

▨	Cliffs
▨	Grassland
▨	Main visitor access area
---	Reserve boundary
—	Boundary wall
━	Road
P	Parking
✪	Viewing platform
🛈	Information panel

EAST SCOTLAND

THE LOONS AND LOCH OF BANKS

SSSI, SAC, NATURA 2000

This area of marshland, flood-meadows and open water lies in a natural basin in the sandstone hills of north-western Mainland Orkney. Many species of wetland birds breed and winter here. The marsh is not open to the public, but is easily viewed from the perimeter road, the layby and the hide.

●Access, facilities, contact details and accessibility

There is one hide.

- **Telephone** 01856 850176; **web** www.rspb.org.uk/theloons
- **Opening hours** There is no access to the marsh, but good views can be obtained from the road and hide at all times
- **Entry fees** Free
- **Accessibility** Please contact the reserve for advice
- **Dogs** Not allowed on the reserve

What to look for

If you visit in early spring, you should see many ducks courting, the drakes showing off their fine spring plumage to the females with ritualised dipping, head-turning, flapping and bowing moves. Species that breed here include Red-breasted Mergansers, Pintails, Wigeons,

Teals and Shovelers. Look for the few breeding Dunlins, dramatically colourful if you're only used to them in their pale grey winter attire, and other waders including Oystercatchers. A handful of Black-tailed Godwits nest here too; careful grazing regimes to maintain optimum

WILDLIFE BY SEASON

SPRING
Eight species of ducks and several wader species are preparing to breed.

SUMMER
Nesting birds are busy tending their chicks. Activity at the Arctic Tern and Black-headed and Common Gull colonies peaks. Flowers blooming on the reserve include several species of orchids.

AUTUMN
Some breeding birds depart, while migrating waders and wildfowl visit.

WINTER
Overwintering species include White-fronted Geese. Ducks begin their courtship as winter ends.

conditions is helping their numbers to slowly increase.

By summer you can play 'spot the ducklings' as the female ducks cautiously bring their chicks out of nests hidden in the marsh. Although most of the duck species breeding here feed by dabbling rather than diving, the young ducklings dive frequently, especially when danger threatens from above. The many Black-headed and Common Gulls that nest here provide an early-warning system for when a potential predator is around – perhaps a passing Great Skua.

Summer flowers can be impressive. Look out for Grass of Parnassus, with its five-petalled white flowers, and carpets of Ragged Robin and the attractive Heath Spotted Orchid as well as two species of marsh orchids.

Otters visit the marsh now and then – the more patient you are the better your chances are of seeing one. The Orkney Vole, which as its name suggests lives only on these islands, is common here but not all that easy to see.

In autumn and winter, the fields will flood to a greater or lesser extent, and this attracts more wildfowl, with numbers of the breeding species increasing and new arrivals coming in, most notably a flock of White-fronted Geese.

Birds of prey are often attracted by the wintering wildfowl and waders. A good variety of species can be seen here, including Hen Harriers, Short-eared Owls and Kestrels hunting the grassland rodents, and Sparrowhawks, Peregrines and Merlins in pursuit of other birds. When spring returns, migrating Ospreys may be seen.

How to get here

Grid ref. HY 246241
By road The reserve is 3 miles north of Dounby on Orkney Mainland – take the A965 and then the A986 from Kirkwall.
By public transport No easy public transport access.

WHEN TO VISIT
The reserve is interesting year-round, but perhaps best in spring and summer. Time of day is not important.

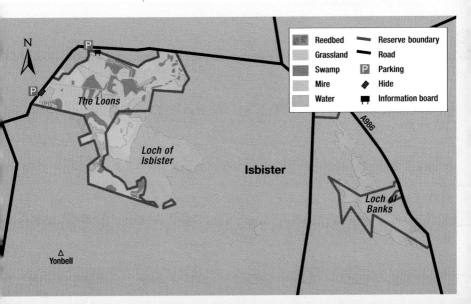

TROUP HEAD SSSI, SPA, NATURA 2000

Out on the North Sea coast, this cliff-side reserve holds mainland Scotland's only Gannet colony. It is a great place to watch these wonderfully graceful seabirds, and you'll see many other species of seabirds on the cliffs. You could also see the Moray Firth Bottlenose Dolphins, and perhaps other sea mammals.

● Access, facilities, contact details and accessibility

Guided walks and group bookings can be arranged.
- **Telephone** 01346 532017; **email** strathbeg@rspb.org.uk; **web** www.rspb.org.uk/trouphead
- **Opening hours** Open at all times
- **Entry fees** Free
- **Accessibility** Not suitable for the mobility-impaired
- **Dogs** Must be kept under close control due to the exposed cliff edges and nesting birds

What to look for

If you come to Troup Head any time from January, you'll see the Gannets, but it isn't until spring that the other seabirds arrive. However, the Gannets really do steal the show as they effortlessly hang in the updrafts, then dip down in measured steps before suddenly tipping over to plunge headlong into the waves to chase down a fish.

The other cliff-nesting birds here are Puffins, Guillemots, Razorbills, Kittiwakes, Herring Gulls and Fulmars, and it is fascinating to watch their very different flying strategies, from the stiff-winged flap-and-glide of the Fulmar and the loose, relaxed styles of the gulls to the frantic

WILDLIFE BY SEASON

SPRING
Gannets, Puffins and other seabirds return to the cliffs.

SUMMER
The colony is a hive of activity, while other locally nesting seabirds can be seen offshore.
A good time to look for sea mammals.

AUTUMN
Herring Gulls, Fulmars and Shags linger on the cliffs when the other birds have departed. Flocks of Redwings and Fieldfares from Scandinavia arrive.

WINTER
A quiet time, although you may see Peregrine Falcons. Gannets arrive back in January, Fulmars in February.

wing-beats of the auks, which seem to only become airborne by the narrowest margin. In summer, the cliff-tops flush pink with blooming Thrift and campions. Take the time to stare out to sea for a while, as you might just spot some of the Bottlenose Dolphins that live in the Moray Firth, and perhaps a Harbour Porpoise or Minke Whale. Closer inshore both Grey and Common Seals can be seen. Greys are bigger with a distinguished 'Roman-nose' profile, while Commons have a more dog-like face with a dip between snout and forehead. If you have good views, you may also notice that the Grey Seal's nostril slits are almost vertical and virtually parallel, while the Common's come close together at the bottom, forming a V-shape.

The cliff-nesters have left by autumn, and migrating flocks of winter thrushes make their first landfall here but soon move on to more productive feeding grounds. You can still see Gannets offshore through the winter, but this is a quiet time until the

Gannets return to their colony in January.

How to get here
Grid ref. NJ 822665
By road Troup Head is found between Pennan and Gardenstown on the B9031, east along the coast from Macduff. RSPB Troup Head nature reserve is signposted off the B9031. You will also see signs for Salix pottery and Northfield Farm at this turn-off. Follow the RSPB brown signs until you reach Northfield Farm. Continue through the farmyard and onto a rough track until you reach the Troup Head reserve car park. Park here and take the right-hand track through a gate (following RSPB brown signs) and follow the fence line until you reach the seabird colony.
By public transport Bus 273 calls nearby.

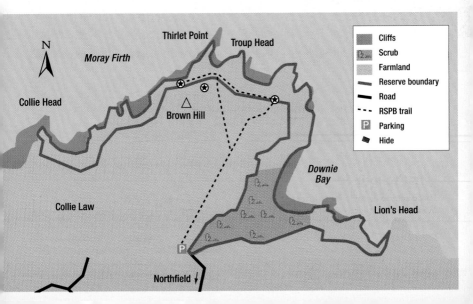

EAST SCOTLAND

TRUMLAND SSSI

Rousay lies off the north-eastern coast of Mainland Orkney, and is a rugged island with much moorland and a variety of interesting nesting birds, all of which you can see at the RSPB Trumland reserve. Two nature trails lead you through the best parts of the moorland – visit in spring or summer to see nesting raptors, waders and skuas.

● Access, facilities, contact details and accessibility

There are two nature trails (1 mile and 3.1 miles). You can book guided walks and group visits. There are toilets (including disabled access) at the Pier Head.

P

- **Telephone** 01856 821395; **email** orkney@rspb.org.uk; **web** www.rspb.org.uk/trumland
- **Opening hours** Open at all times
- **Entry fees** Free, but donations are welcome
- **Accessibility** The trails are not suitable for wheelchairs
- **Dogs** Must be kept under close control at all times. Be aware of livestock.

What to look for

Trumland is a fairly typical piece of Orkney moorland, managed by the RSPB to maintain a good mix of habitat types from blanket bog to wet heath. This helps maintain its appeal to special breeding birds such as Hen Harriers, Short-eared Owls, Merlins and Red-throated Divers.

The harriers display in spring, the males and females flying together in dramatic twists and turns, culminating in a food pass from male to female. Males also 'skydance' as they switchback freely high in the sky. Male Hen Harriers are often polygymous, provisioning two or more nesting females through the breeding season.

WILDLIFE BY SEASON

SPRING
Birds of prey such as Hen Harriers are courting. Golden Plovers are preparing to nest on the moor.

SUMMER
More birds arrive and begin to nest, including Arctic and Great Skuas on the moor and Red-throated Divers on the ochans. Moorland flowers create a carpet of colour.

Red-throated Diver

Females therefore value males who can demonstrate both good hunting abilities and efficient food-passing skills. Merlins nest here too, hunting Skylarks, Meadow Pipits and any other unfortunate small birds they find, while the moors' Short-eared Owls prey mainly on Orkney Voles.

Stay on the trails to avoid unwanted attention from the nesting skuas, which may dive at visitors. Both Arctic and Great Skuas nest here, and there are also Golden Plovers nesting out on the moor, looking very beautiful at this time of year with their spangled golden upperparts and black bellies. From the trail you can also see the pair of Red-throated Divers on Knitchen Loch, their sleek 'painted on' plumage looking marvellous at this time of year. The diver chicks are sweet, stubby-billed fluffballs, especially endearing when they hop aboard a parent's back for a lift across the water.

The main trail takes you to the highest point on Rousay, Blotchnie Field. Here is a good place to scan for birds of prey, but also to appreciate the wonderful far-reaching views – you can see the whole Orkney archipelago from here and on a clear day all the way to Fair Isle.

WHEN TO VISIT
The reserve is full of activity in spring and summer, but becomes very quiet from late autumn into winter.

How to get here
Grid ref./postcode HY 427275/ KW17 2
By road Take the roll-on/roll-off ferry to Rousay from Tingwall. Call Orkney Ferries, tel: 01856 751360. From the pier, follow the road uphill to the T-junction at Trumland Gate Lodge. Turn left and go past Trumland Wood until you reach the RSPB sign at Taversoe Tuick Cairn on your right.
By public transport See above for how to get to Rousay. A post bus is available from the pier – contact Royal Mail (tel: 0845 774 074) for further information

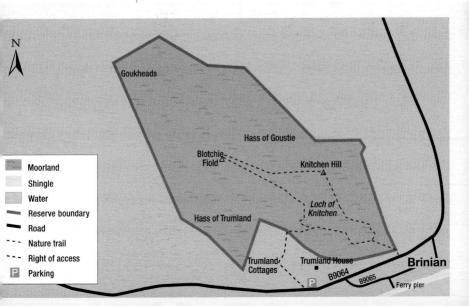

N

Legend:
- Moorland
- Shingle
- Water
- Reserve boundary
- Road
- Nature trail
- Right of access
- P Parking

Goukheads

Hass of Goustie

Blotchnie Field

Knitchen Hill

Loch of Knitchen

Hass of Trumland

Trumland Cottages

Trumland House

B9064

B9065

Brinian

Ferry pier

EAST SCOTLAND

VANE FARM NNR

On the southern shore of Loch Leven, this reserve takes in a varied slice of habitat, from loch shore with shallow lagoons and marshy patches, up through farmland, birch woodland and finally open moorland. Two nature trails give you great views over the lagoons and the loch beyond, out to Castle Island, where Mary Queen of Scots was held prisoner in 1567–1568. With mostly easy walking conditions, free binocular hire, CCTV cameras showing nesting birds on a big screen, regular family events and the chance to enjoy lunch while overlooking the reserve, this reserve offers a family-friendly and exciting wildlife experience throughout the year.

● Access, facilities, contact details and accessibility

With a coffee shop that doubles up as an observation room, Vane Farm offers comfortable and easy wildlife watching from the first moment you arrive. The shop sells a variety of wildlife-related goods. On the wetland trail there are three hides, the furthest 600m from the start of the trail, while the mile-long woodland trail is a little more rugged and remote. You can hire binoculars, arrange group visits and book guided walks.

- **Telephone** 01577 862355; **email** vane.farm@rspb.org.uk; **web** www.rspb.org.uk/vanefarm
- **Opening hours** Vane Farm Loch Leven visitor centre is open 10am–5pm daily, and the trails and hides are open 24 hours a day throughout the year (except Christmas Day, Boxing Day, New Year's Day and 2 January).
- **Entry fees** Adults £3, children 50p, concessions £2, family £6 and RSPB and Wildlife Explorer members are free.
- **Accessibility** The visitor centre is wheelchair-accessible, but the hides are not. The wetland trail is negotiable by wheelchair too but some help may be required.
- **Dogs** Permitted but please keep them under control

WILDLIFE BY SEASON

SPRING

Ospreys fish the loch from late March, their arrival overlapping with the departure of the last of the geese. Tree Pipits and other small birds sing in the birch woodland. Toads are spawning, wildfowl are nesting on the lagoons, and various waders are establishing territories on the marshland.

SUMMER

Mother ducks lead their broods out onto the loch. Damselflies swarm around the loch shore, while bats emerge at dusk to hunt moths and other flying insects. Long daylight hours make this a good time to see mammals on the reserve.

AUTUMN

The Pink-footed Geese and Whooper Swans start to arrive. Migrating waders stop off to feed at the loch shore, winter thrushes begin to arrive and late butterflies are still around on warm days.

WINTER

Some geese remain throughout winter but many continue their journeys south – numbers build up again in late winter as the southern winterers return. Dabbling and diving duck numbers build up, and the bird feeders are busy with tits and finches.

What to look for

From the visitor centre (which itself has an observation room with telescopes on the first floor) you have a choice of two trails – the wetland trail or the woodland trail. If you take your time on both trails you can easily spend the best part of a day here.

Loch Leven is internationally important for nesting ducks and many species use the lagoons at Vane Farm to nest and raise their broods. Ospreys may be seen fishing out over the loch toadlets leave the water.

Through early spring Pink-footed Geese are much in evidence, flying overhead in long noisy skeins or feeding on the flowery grassland, which provide winter and early spring food for a variety of small farmland birds as well as the geese. The observation room offers great views of them as they prepare to migrate north. Only a handful will remain by May, though it won't be long before they are back again with their young of

The smallest of Vane Farm's visiting wildfowl species, the Teal's a shy but pretty duck with a strangely fluty call. Important numbers winter at Vane Farm.

from late March. Their long-winged, casually langorous flight make them confusable with gulls at first glance, but when one heads purposefully low over the water there is no mistaking this superbly dynamic fish-snatcher in action.

The teaching pond by the visitor centre is a spawning ground for Common Toads, and you are most likely to see them here in early spring as the adults mate, or a few weeks later on when the masses of young

the year in tow, having raced through the short breeding season in the 'midnight-sun' summer of the far north, in Iceland or Spitsbergen.

Springtime up in the woods and the moorland beyond can be exciting too, with insectivorous birds such as warblers, Tree Pipits and Spotted Flycatchers. The woodland is rich in insects because grazing is managed to allow the growth of native broadleaved trees above a rich

Terror of the meadowlands, the beautiful Stoat is a ferocious and fearless predator, capable of felling a Rabbit four times its own size.

understory of woodland vegetation and upland heath. One of the rarer insects to be found is the Blaeberry Bumblebee, which feeds on blaeberry and heather when in flower on the hill. When these plants are not in flower the Blaeberry Bumblebee joins a wide range of other species in Vane Farm's bumblebee meadow – the world's first bumblebee sanctuary. A gentle stroll through the meadow will reveal the colourful and aromatic reason the bees visit as over 13 species of pollen- and nectar-rich flowers have been sown for them to feed on.

In summer damselflies are numerous around the loch shore, and you'll often see mating pairs flying in 'tandem', the male leading the way and gripping the female's head with special clasping appendages at the tip of his abdomen. When mating proper occurs, the pair form a 'wheel'

WHEN TO VISIT

The reserve offers a changing but always exciting wildlife-watching experience through all the seasons, with a rich variety of exciting breeding and wintering birds and other wildlife. Visit in spring or summer to see Ospreys fishing the loch, and in winter to see the wild geese. Time of day is not important.

as the female bends her abdomen forwards to make contact with the male. The Common Blue and Azure Damselflies can be difficult to tell apart – the Blue-tailed, Emerald and Large Red Damselflies are much more straightforward.

Waders migrating south will visit the lagoons any time from mid-summer. A good variety of passage waders can turn up at this time of year as they return from their high-Arctic breeding grounds. Many are in confusing transitional plumages at this time, but each species has its unique shape, proportions and way of moving, which will become as familiar as the mannerisms of an old friend after enough hours watching them.

The Pinkfeet return en masse from late September, along with a few Greylag Geese and variable numbers of Whooper Swans. Time taken to sift through the geese may be rewarded with the sight of some more unusual species that occasionally become attached to returning flocks of Pinkfeet, including Bean, White-fronted and Ross's Geese or even Bewick's Swans, while the resident wildfowl numbers are further boosted by arrivals of Shovelers, Goosanders, Gadwalls, Goldeneyes, a few Pintails and occasional Smews – Loch Leven is of vital importance to a whole variety of wildfowl. Cold weather may tempt a Water Rail out into view, while the loch sometimes attracts more coastal visitors, such as Slavonian Grebes or Red-throated Divers.

The feeding station comes into its own in the winter months. You could see Bullfinches alongside the more familiar garden birds. Roe Deer are easier to see in winter, when the tree cover is lighter. The cold weather also brings upland birds of prey down to lower ground in search of prey – Merlins cause much alarm among the small farmland birds, while Peregrine Falcons spook the ducks and waders on the marsh.

How to get here

Grid ref./postcode NT 160990/KY4 0
By road The reserve is well signposted 2 miles east of Junction 5 of the M90. Once on the slip road take a left turn and then a right turn onto the B9097 and drive for approximately 2 miles. The nature centre car park is on the south (right) side of the road.
By public transport Cowdenbeath (7 miles away) is the nearest rail station. There is no public transport from here; you would have to take a taxi. A limited bus service runs to the reserve from Kinross (4 miles) on Wednesdays and weekends. The first bus arrives at the

Confused about godwits? This Black-tailed Godwit shows off its best field marks – a white tail band and wingbars. The Bar-tailed has plain dark wings and tail.

reserve at 10.59 am. Contact Stagecoach Fife on 01383 511 911 for further details. Buses stop in Kinross and Ballingry but a taxi may be necessary from either of these.

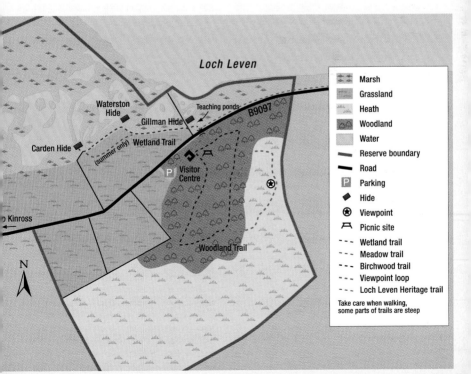

BALRANALD

SSSI, SPA, SAC, RAMSAR, NATURA 2000

A map of the Outer Hebridean island of North Uist reveals a mosaic of land and water, with the low-lying coastal grassland (or machair) surrounding a profusion of small lochs. Balranald has all this and more, with a sandy bay, dune system and rocky foreshore. It's well worth the long ferry ride to visit this superb and stunning reserve.

●Access, facilities, contact details and accessibility

This remote reserve has a small information centre, open through the summer, and a 3-mile circular nature trail. Guided walks take place on Tuesdays at 10am from May to August.

- **Telephone** 01463 715000; **email** nsro@rspb.org.uk; **web** www.rspb.org.uk/rbalranald
- **Opening hours** The reserve is open at all times; the visitor centre at Goular Cottage is open all the time
- **Entry fees** Free
- **Accessibility** The circular nature trail is unsuitable for wheelchairs
- **Dogs** Must be kept on leads

What to look for

Balranald is simply brimming with life all through the year. In spring, many migrating birds visit the reserve, stopping on the beach or machair to refuel. Look for Turnstones, Purple Sandpipers, Sanderlings and Dunlins on the shore, and look out to sea for passing skuas,

Manx Shearwaters and other seabirds heading north to their breeding colonies. The headland of Aird an Runair is a particularly good vantage point from which to seawatch.

Migrating Dotterels may stop off on the machair, briefly rubbing shoulders with the

WILDLIFE BY SEASON

SPRING
Migrating seabirds go by. Dotterels and Barnacle Geese visit the machair and nesting waders call over the grassland.

SUMMER
Corncrakes call from the fields. Flowers cover the grassland and machair and terns fish offshore.

AUTUMN
Flocks of Lapwings and Golden Plovers gather. Birds of prey become more numerous. A good time to see Otters.

WINTER
Wildfowl overwinter on the fields and marshes. Look out for eagles. Skylarks, Starlings, Twites and Snow Buntings forage on the shoreline.

many Redshanks, Oyster-catchers, Ringed Plovers, Lapwings and Dunlins that nest here. The real star of the machair is the Corncrake, doing well thanks to sympathetic management by the crofters who farm this land. Another farmland bird in need of RSPB help is the Corn Bunting, whose jangling-keys song is a classic Balranald sound.

The Outer Hebrides have a large Otter population and you can see them throughout the year here, though summer and autumn are perhaps the best times. They are as happy fishing in the freshwater lochs as they are in the sea, and if you keep quiet you could have great views.

The grassland attracts Greylag Geese and large flocks of Lapwings and Golden Plovers in winter, the latter themselves attracting the attention of Peregrine Falcons, while Merlins menace the flocks of Skylarks, Twites and Snow Buntings that feed along the shoreline. Further inland you might encounter a young Golden Eagle, born on the uplands and now off wandering

WHEN TO VISIT
This reserve is alive with wildlife throughout the year, each season offering a different experience. Time of day is not important.

the wider area in search of a territory of its own.

Flocks of wildfowl, especially Whooper Swans, Wigeons and Teals, spend winter on North Uist and you should see them gathered on the fields and marshes at Balranald. Some will linger into spring, as the migranting and nesting waders start to return.

How to get here
Grid ref./postcode NF 706707/ HS6 5

By road There is a ferry crossing from Oban to North Uist. The reserve is 3 miles north of Bayhead. Take the turn for Hougharry off the A865.

By public transport A Post bus service runs on the island. Contact Royal Mail on 08457 740740 for details.

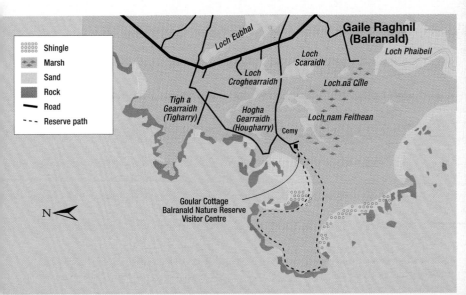

Legend:
- Shingle
- Marsh
- Sand
- Rock
- Road
- Reserve path

Map labels: Loch Eubhal, Gaile Raghnil (Balranald), Loch Phaibeil, Loch Scaraidh, Loch na Cille, Loch Croghearraidh, Tigh a Gearraidh (Tigharry), Hogha Gearraidh (Hougharry), Cemy, Loch nam Feithean, Goular Cottage Balranald Nature Reserve Visitor Centre, N

NORTH SCOTLAND

CORRIMONY

Caledonian pine forest and unspoilt moorland – Corrimony is a glimpse of a Highland world that has all but disappeared. There is a wealth of wildlife here, with Black Grouse the star of the show, and here you have the unmissable opportunity to watch the assembled males performing their spectacular courtship display.

● Access, facilities, contact details and accessibility

There is an 8.5-mile waymarked trail. Minibus 'safari' trips are run through the month of April to enable you to watch lekking Black Grouse without disturbing them.

P

- **Telephone** 01463 715 000; **email** nsro@rspb.org.uk; **web** www.rspb.org.uk/corrimony
- **Opening hours** Open at all times
- **Entry fees** Free, but donations are welcome
- **Accessibility** The waymarked trail is suitable for pushchairs and wheelchairs
- **Dogs** Must be kept on leads

What to look for

Corrimony is famous for its Black Grouse, and you could bump into one of these handsome birds at any time of year, but by far your best option is to book a place on one of the April Black Grouse safaris, and take a mini-bus ride to see the birds on their 'lekking' (communal courtship) ground at dawn, a wonderful experience. Lekking grouse are very vulnerable to disturbance, so viewing them in this way, with local advice about watching without disturbing them, is best for them too.

Another Corrimony star is the Crested Tit, which lives in the pine forests. Look out for these birds searching the lichen-encrusted

WILDLIFE BY SEASON

SPRING
Black Grouse are lekking – see them from the special safari trips. Ospreys fish the loch, and woodland birds are singing.

SUMMER
The hillsides have orchids and other flowers. A good time to see Red Grouse. Mammals, including Pine Martens, are active especially at dawn and dusk.

AUTUMN
It is rutting season for the Red Deer, while Whooper Swans and Pink-footed Geese are migrating through.

WINTER
Goldeneyes and Goosanders gather on the loch, parties of tits roam the woodland.

twigs for small invertebrates to eat. The RSPB is expanding and improving the woodland, thinning out the Scots Pines to make space for other Caledonian forest species like Juniper and Aspen, creating a more varied habitat for the Crested Tits and other forest wildlife. You may well see Red Squirrels here, and perhaps even a Pine Marten.

Red Grouse, Mountain Hares and Greenshanks are among the species living on the open moorland, along with herds of Red Deer.

A few wildfowl visit the loch in winter, mostly Goldeneyes and Goosanders. The woods can seem deserted, though feeding parties of tits and Goldcrests liven things up. These small birds glean a borderline living in winter, picking tiny invertebrates from the bark and lichens.

How to get here
Grid ref./postcode NH 383302/ IV63 6
By road The reserve is 22 miles south-west of Inverness, off the A831 between Cannich and Glen Urquhart. Park in the Corrimony Cairns car park.
By public transport Inverness station is about 25 miles away. There is a request bus stop 1.5 miles from the reserve on the Inverness to Cannich service.

WHEN TO VISIT
Safaris to see the lekking Black Grouse take place during April. Otherwise, the reserve is interesting throughout the year, and time of day is not critical.

GROUSE PARTY
The work 'lek' (Swedish for 'play') describes both the behaviour of the displaying Black Grouse and the place where it occurs. The lek is a grassy arena, and the lekking is the gathering of strutting, posturing, sparring male grouse, fanning their lyre-shaped tails and showing off their snowy-white underskirts, trying to impress the watching females. Only a few males will successfully mate, and they will have nothing further to do with the females until next year.

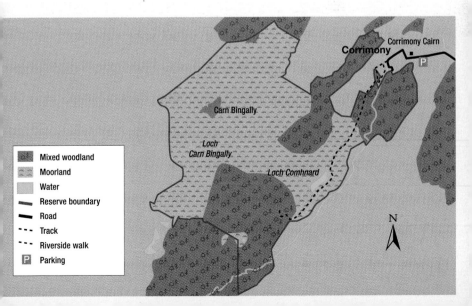

Legend
- Mixed woodland
- Moorland
- Water
- Reserve boundary
- Road
- - - Track
- - - Riverside walk
- P Parking

Corrimony Cairn
Corrimony
Carn Bingally
Loch Carn Bingally
Loch Comhnard

N

EAST SCOTLAND

CULBIN SANDS

SSSI, SPA, SAC, RAMSAR, NATURA 2000

Culbin Sands is a massive dune system on the southern side of the Moray Firth, backed by a large conifer plantation (managed by FCS). Here you can enjoy long walks and enjoy a rich variety of wildlife both on the beach and offshore, especially in winter when the sea can teem with rafts of seaducks. You could even see the famous Bottlenose Dolphins of the Moray Firth.

● Access, facilities, contact details and accessibility

This is a good reserve for a long or short walk and perhaps also a picnic.
- **Telephone** 01463 715 000; **email** nsro@rspb.org.uk;
  web www.rspb.org.uk/culbinsands and www.culbin.org.uk.
- **Opening hours** Open at all times
- **Entry fees** Free, but donations to help continue the work here are welcome
- **Accessibility** There is an all-abilities path from the East Beach car park to Ministers Pool (about 870m)
- **Dogs** Welcome but please keep them under close control, especially during the breeding season

What to look for

This reserve is part of a larger area of interest – when you visit, it's well worth exploring the adjacent forest (which has Crested Tits) as well as walking the dunes. In springtime, you'll see terns passing on their way to breeding colonies further north. Sandwich and Arctic Terns are the most numerous – the former sturdy and heavy-headed, the latter long-tailed and elegant.

Locally nesting Eider ducks rest on the shingle through summer, while the dune flowers attract butterflies. In late spring look for Small Blues, our smallest species and not actually blue

WILDLIFE BY SEASON

SPRING

Terns, including Sandwich, are passing on their way to their breeding grounds. You could see dolphins or Otters in the sea.

SUMMER

Eiders rest on the shingle bar. Butterflies flying in summer. Migrating waders start to arrive.

AUTUMN

Migrants may pass by. Large numbers of Bar-tailed Godwits, Oystercatchers and Knots flock at high tide. A small flock of Brent Geese visits.

WINTER

Numerous waders and seaducks may be seen, including scoters, Long-tailed Ducks, Eiders and Sanderlings.

but smoky dark brown with spotted fawn underwings. They lay their eggs on Kidney Vetch, which has a distinctive rounded hairy head.

More than 100 Bottlenose Dolphins live in the Moray Firth, and Culbin is a good place to see them – summer is probably the best time to look. You could also see Otters along the shore or swimming in the shallows.

Autumn brings migrating waders to the beaches, with large flocks of Knots, Oystercatchers and Bar-tailed Godwits pushed close to view by incoming tides. Seaduck numbers build up into winter – look out for Red-breasted Mergansers with their comical spiky head-feathers, chunky, ponderous Eiders, and rafts of scoters and Long-tailed Ducks. Common and Velvet Scoters both occur here, the Velvets catching the eye when they stretch and flap to show white wing-bars. Long-tailed Ducks are compact and extremely pretty, especially males in full winter plumage. You should also see several species of wintering waders.

WHEN TO VISIT

The greatest variety and numbers of birds are present during the winter, but Crested Tits may be seen in the forest all year.

How to get here

Grid ref./postcode NH 900576/ IV12 4

By road To access the west end of the reserve, the all-abilities trail and Minister's Pool, use the Highland Council's East Beach car park. After passing through Nairn on the A96 from Inverness, go over the river, take the first left towards the caravan park on Maggot Road. At the road end, turn right, through the caravan park to the car park.

To access the Hill 99 viewpoint, the adjacent forest and trails, use the Forestry Commission Scotland car park at Wellhill. Take the A96 from Nairn, turn left at Brodie, turn right at the T-junction. Turn left towards Kintessack, car park at end of road.

By public transport Nairn, 1.5 miles away, is the nearest station.

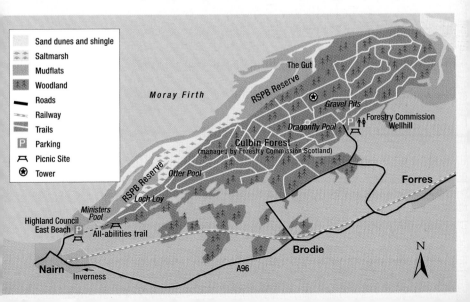

FAIRY GLEN

A stream rushes down this narrow, steep-sided glen, and broad-leaved woodland climbs the slopes on both sides. You'll see various woodland and riverside wildlife as you take the steep walk up alongside the stream, before you finally reach the waterfalls at the end of the trail. This beautiful reserve is worth a visit at any time of year.

● Access, facilities, contact details and accessibility

There is a 1-mile path up to the waterfalls.
- **Telephone** 01463 715000; **email** nsro@rspb.org.uk; **web** www.rspb.org.uk/fairyglen
- **Opening hours** Open at all times
- **Entry fees** None, though donations are welcome
- **Accessibility** The path up Fairy Glen is uneven and slippery and has several sets of steps
- **Dogs** Welcome provided they are under close control

What to look for

From the car park just outside Rosemarkie, the trail leads uphill, following the stream that has carved out this picturesque glen. In spring, before the trees come into leaf, the woodland floor is covered with Bluebells, Wood Anemones, Lesser Celandines and Primroses, and leafless twigs make it easier to see birds moving through the trees. Willow Warblers join the resident tits and finches in mid-spring, adding their distinctive sweet descending song to the soundscape, in sharp contrast to the harsh cacophony of caws from the Rooks in their nearby treetop colony.

The stream rushes at speed along its rocky

WILDLIFE BY SEASON

SPRING
Woodland flowers carpet the glen, and small birds are singing. The nearby rookery is busy with breeding activity.

SUMMER
The scent of Meadowsweet fills the air, and birds are foraging for food for their chicks.

AUTUMN
Young birds are out and about, and the woodland is resplendent in its autumn colours with the Norway Maples especially dramatic.

WINTER
Woodland birds form feeding parties that roam through the woodland. Roe Deer are easiest to see at this time.

course – an ideal habitat for Dippers. You're most likely to see just a plump, dark shape whirring away at your approach, but walk carefully and check ahead often and you may spot one resting on a mid-stream rock. These birds nest in rocky streamside hollows and are wholly at home underwater, gripping stones to keep their place as they catch aquatic invertebrates, and then allowing the rushing water to bear them along on the surface. Grey Wagtails are here too, showing their bright yellow rumps and undertails as they strut and flit from stone to stone, ceaselessly bobbing their long tails.

Summer flowers are fewer because the tree canopy takes much of the light, but Water Avens and Meadowsweet flower by the stream, the latter sweetly scenting the glen.

The leaves change colour in autumn, providing weeks of stunning and slowly changing colours before they fall. Once again the birds become easier to see, as do the Roe Deer that feed at the woodland's edge.

WHEN TO VISIT
Spring is probably the best time, to see the woodland flowers at their best, but the other seasons have their own attractions too. Visit early to hear the dawn chorus in spring.

Check overhead and you'll more than likely see a Buzzard soaring above on wide, long-fingered wings.

How to get here
Grid ref./postcode NH 732580/ IV10 8
By road From the Inverness direction, proceed through Rosemarkie village, passing the Plough Inn on your right and round the sharp left bend. After about 150m, you will see the car park on the right.
By public transport Inverness is the nearest rail station. Regular buses from Inverness and Cromarty (Stagecoach service no. 26) stop in the Highland Council-owned Fairy Glen reserve car park.

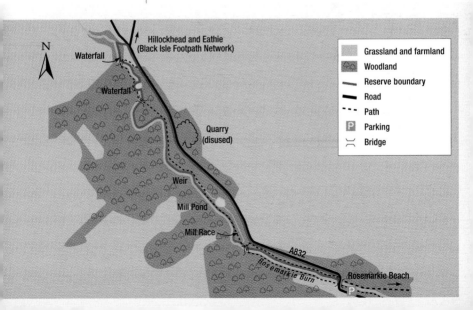

Map legend:
- Grassland and farmland
- Woodland
- Reserve boundary
- Road
- Path
- P Parking
- Bridge

Map labels: N; Waterfall; Hillockhead and Eathie (Black Isle Footpath Network); Waterfall; Quarry (disused); Weir; Mill Pond; Mill Race; A832; Rosemarkie Burn; Rosemarkie Beach; P

FORSINARD FLOWS

SSSI, SPA, SAC, NNR, RAMSAR, NATURA 2000

The Flow Country of northern Scotland is a wild landscape of windswept tussocky wet grassland, studded with stunningly clear dark lochans. Peat-cutting, drainage and forestry has destroyed vast swathes of this unique habitat; at Forsinard, the RSPB has turned back the tide.

● Access, facilities, contact details and accessibility

There are two trails – the mile-long Dubh Lochan trail and the 4-mile Forsinain Trail.

- **Telephone** 01641 571225; **email** forsinard@rspb.org.uk; **web** www.rspb.org.uk/forsinard
- **Opening hours** The reserve is open at all times; the newly upgraded visitor centre is open Easter to end of October daily 9am–5.30pm
- **Entry fees** Free. Guided walks are £2 for RSPB members, £5 for non-members and free for under-16s
- **Accessibility** The roadside offers good views. The first part of the Forsinain Trail is all-abilities.
- **Dogs** Bringing dogs is discouraged – if you do bring one it must be kept under close control at all times.

What to look for

From the visitor centre at Forsinard rail station, the Dubh Lochan trail heads out over the blanket bog, leading you first across an area cut for peat and then to an untouched expanse with numerous lochans. From the safety of the trail (it's narrow but passing places are provided!) you'll be able to see for miles across the bog

– look out for the special birds of the flows in spring and summer. They include Greenshanks, Dunlins and Golden Plovers, all in their smart breeding plumage and displaying over the bog.

The lochans hold no fish, but they teem with insect life and also attract frogs and newts. Out on the uncut bog you'll see unusual plants, like

WILDLIFE BY SEASON

SPRING

The breeding waders, Common Scoters, Red-throated Divers and birds of prey arrive on the bog.

SUMMER

Check the river for breeding Greenshanks and Teals. The bogland plants start to flower. Dragonflies are active around the lochans.

AUTUMN

Red Deer are rutting. Migrating geese and other birds pass overhead. The vivid colours of the sphagnum moss are at their best.

WINTER

Buzzards, Ravens, Red Grouse and the occasional Golden Eagle can be seen. Mountain Hares gain their white winter coats.

the tiny, carnivorous Sundews with their pincushion-like heads of sticky, insect-snaring red hairs, and the dense piles of multicoloured sphagnum mosses. By blocking hill drains on the cut sections of the bog, the RSPB is restoring more acres of land to the pristine state of the uncut bog.

The Forsinain Trail is a circular route which runs through RSPB and Forestry Commission ground. It begins at the roadside on the River Halladale before ascending the farm road through fields used intensively by feeding Golden Plovers and Dunlins. Breeding Lapwings, Curlews and Snipes can also be seen. Further on, there is a section of flagstone path through bog pool habitat and forest-to-bog restoration sites which passes close to a loch where Red-throated Divers sometimes breed. Descending on the forest road, the final section follows an unsurfaced route through the grassy riverbanks of the River Halladale where feeding Greenshanks and Dippers may be seen.

WHEN TO VISIT

Forsinard has most to offer in late spring and summer, when its breeding birds, flowering plants and water animals of the lochans are on show.

How to get here

Grid ref./postcode NC 891425/ KW13 6

By road The reserve is accessed from the A897, 24 miles (38 km) from Helmsdale. From Melvich on the north coast, turn south 2 miles (3.2 km) east of Melvich onto the A897 for 14 miles (22.5 km).

By public transport Forsinard station is the nearest station; the line runs from Inverness to Wick/Thurso, stopping at Forsinard three times a day. The reserve visitor centre is located in the station building. A Highland Council subsidised taxi service goes between the rail station to Melvich, Bettyhill or Thurso to the north. For booking and details call 01641 541 297.

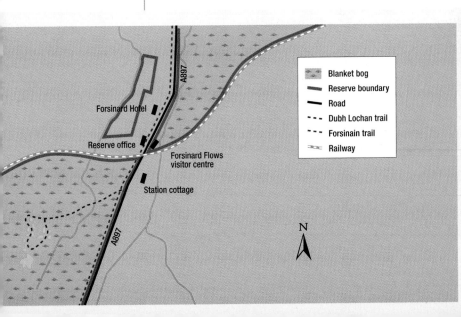

Legend:
- Blanket bog
- Reserve boundary
- Road
- Dubh Lochan trail
- Forsinain trail
- Railway

Forsinard Hotel

Reserve office

Forsinard Flows visitor centre

Station cottage

A897

N

GLENBORRODALE

SSSI, SAC, NATURA 2000

The Ardnamurchan peninsula is one of Britain's most remote, rugged and unspoilt places, home to such exciting wildlife as Scottish Wildcats, Pine Martens and Golden Eagles. The oak woodlands on the shore of Loch Sunart in the south-east of the peninsula are incredibly rich in species diversity. You can also explore moorland above the forest, and walk the loch shore.

● Access, facilities, contact details and accessibility

There is a shop and café in the Ardnamurchan Natural History Centre close to the reserve.

P

- **Telephone** 01463 715000; **email** nsro@rspb.org.uk; **web** www.rspb.org.uk/glenborrodale
- **Opening hours** Open at all times
- **Entry fees** Entry free, but donations are appreciated
- **Accessibility** The trails are unimproved and therefore not easily accessible for the mobility-impaired
- **Dogs** It is permitted to walk your dog on the public footpaths, however please keep it on a lead in the breeding season.

What to look for

The 2-mile trail starts close to the parking area, and heads up into the oakwoods. The RSPB protects this special woodland by ensuring that invasive plants are kept at bay and grazing is kept to a minimum to allow new saplings to grow, ensuring a woodland of mixed age. If you visit in spring, you'll enjoy the spectacle of a truly dazzling display of woodland flowers – Bluebells, Wood Anemones and primroses all grow in profusion. In the trees, Redstarts and Wood Warblers will be singing. Other woodland birds you may see in spring include Spotted

WILDLIFE BY SEASON

SPRING
Woodland birds are singing, migratory birds return to their breeding grounds. Woodland flowers carpet the forest floor before the trees come into leaf.

SUMMER
Butterflies and dragonflies are on the wing, reptiles are out and about on the moors.

AUTUMN
The woodland is at its most breathtaking as the leaves change colour before they fall.

WINTER
The best time to see eagles, Snipe and Woodcocks. Mammals may be easier to see as well.

Flycatchers – also, look out for Red Squirrels.

By June you may see the local butterfly specialities like the Scotch Argus and Pearl-bordered Fritillaries. Other special insects here include the Highland Darter and Northern Emerald dragonflies; Common Lizards and Slow-worms bask by the trail on sunny days. Birds of the moors include Whinchats, Wheatears, Ravens, Merlins and Golden Eagles.

The woodland has an exceptionally rich variety of mosses and lichens, which add their colours to the beauty of the turning leaves in autumn. The local Red Deer herds make their presence known at this time of year, roaring noisily during the rut.

The Ardnamurchan peninsula is a wonderful place for mammals, and many visitors will harbour hopes of seeing them. Your chances of finding a Scottish Wildcat are low, but Pine Martens are easier to see, some even visiting local gardens for a free handout of a jam sandwich. Perhaps the predatory mammal you're most likely to see is an Otter – they hunt in the loch

and often come to the shore. You could also see a seal bobbing about in the water. If you walk back to the parking area along the road, you'll pass close to the shore – look out for White-tailed Eagles overhead as well as Otters and seals, and Common Sandpipers and Oystercatchers feeding at the water's edge.

How to get here

Grid ref./postcode NM 595615/ PH36 4
By road Follow the B8007 from Strontian to Glenborrodale.
By public transport Fort William is the nearest station. Bus S48/500 calls at Glenborrodale twice a day, en route between Fort William and Kilchoan (contact Shiel Buses on 01967 431 272 or via www.shielbuses. co.uk for more information).

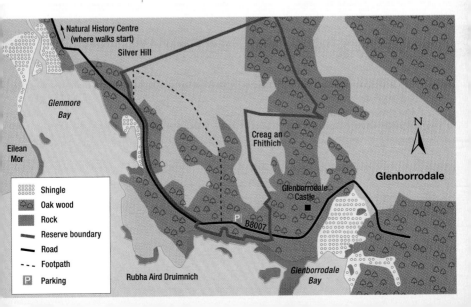

Legend:
- Shingle
- Oak wood
- Rock
- Reserve boundary
- Road
- Footpath
- P Parking

NORTH SCOTLAND

INSH MARSHES

SSSI, SAC, NNR, NP, RAMSAR, NATURA 2000

The Spey Valley is an area of rich lowland habitats running between some of the Highlands' most mountainous areas. A few miles south of the famous Loch Garten reserve, and in the shadow of the ruin that was Ruthven Barracks, Insh Marshes is an extremely important wetland reserve, alive with nesting waders in spring and swans and geese in winter.

●Access, facilities, contact details and accessibility

The reserve has one viewpoint, two hides and three woodland trails, ranging from 1.25 to 2.8 miles. An accessible reception hide will be completed by the end of 2009. Guided walks and group bookings can be arranged.

- **Telephone** 01540 661 518; **web** www.rspb.org.uk/inshmarshes
- **Opening hours** Open at all times
- **Entry fees** Free, but donations are welcome
- **Accessibility** The trails are not suitable for wheelchairs
- **Dogs** Allowed on all footpaths but please keep them under control

What to look for

Floodplain habitats are uncommon in the Highlands, making this wetland reserve an especially important wildlife haven. Some of the birds that nest here are extremely uncommon in a UK context.

Waders that nest here include Redshanks,

Lapwings and Snipes. A major rarity here is the Spotted Crake, whose distinctive whip-crack call can be heard at night in spring and summer although the bird itself usually remains stubbornly out of sight. Ducks including Wigeons and Teals nest on the marsh too, while the local Ospreys

WILDLIFE BY SEASON

SPRING

Waders are calling and displaying. Listen for Spotted Crakes calling. Goldeneyes are nesting in specially provided nestboxes and Ospreys fish the loch.

SUMMER

Nesting waders are still evident till June. The best time for flowers and insects.

AUTUMN

Greylag Geese and Whooper Swans start arriving for the winter. The Hen Harrier roost begins to form.

WINTER

Wigeons and Teals join the geese and swans. The number of birds in the harrier roost peaks.

---

fish the loch. In the drier and wooded areas, Woodcocks breed and you could also see Pied and Spotted Flycatchers, Redstarts, Grasshopper Warblers and, on the streams, Dippers and Pied Wagtails.

Insh Marshes has the fourth largest stand of Aspen trees in the UK, their leaves appearing to shiver in the wind. Rare species here include the Aspen Hoverfly and the Aspen Bracket Fungus. Tromie meadow is great for orchids in late spring to early summer, especially in the evenings when the Fragrant Orchids are at their best. Small White and Greater Butterfly Orchid also grow here.

There is a quiet interlude in midsummer when breeding birds become elusive. This is the time for flowers and insects – notable butterflies here include the Scotch Argus, while the truly spectacular (and inappropriately named) Kentish Glory moth is also on the reserve list, along with several dragonfly and damselfly species. A species of money spider new to Britain, the Hiawatha Spider, was discovered here in the late 1990s.

WHEN TO VISIT

Every season has something to offer at this reserve, and time of day is not important.

Otters use the loch and marsh, and Roe Deer often favour the woodland edges – they look wonderful in the evening sunlight with their bright russet summer coats.

Whooper Swans and Greylag Geese come to the marshes in autumn, soon followed by ducks including Wigeons and Teals. A number of Hen Harriers form a communal roost.

How to get here

Grid ref./postcode NN 775998/ PH21 1
By road From the A9, take the exit to Kingussie. Follow the B970 south from the village towards, and then beyond, Ruthven Barracks. The reserve entrance is 0.6 miles to the east of the barracks.
By public transport Kingussie station is a 0.9-mile walk away; buses stop there too.

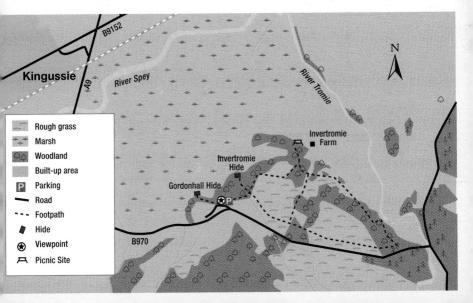

NORTH SCOTLAND

LOCH GARTEN & ABERNETHY

SPA, NATURA 2000

This flagship reserve was founded around the place that Ospreys chose to first nest in 1954 after a long absence from the UK. The RSPB reserve here offers much more than the chance to meet the famous Ospreys in person though – Loch Garten sits in the spectacular Abernethy Forest, one of Scotland's largest remaining fragments of native pinewood, and the area is home to Red Squirrels, Crested Tits, Scottish Crossbills, Capercaillies and a host of other wonderful wild creatures. It is also a place of intensely atmospheric beauty and magic all year round.

● Access, facilities, contact details and accessibility

The Osprey Centre offers telescope views of the Osprey nest as well as CCTV footage. You can also buy refreshments here. Staff are on hand to talk you through the action at the nest and provide other information. There are three forest trails you can walk, ranging in length from 1 mile to 2 miles – the Blue trail links up with the Speyside Way.

- **Telephone** 01479 831476 (April to August only, 10am–5pm); **email** abernethy@rspb.org.uk; **web** www.rspb.org.uk/lochgarten
- **Opening hours** The Osprey Centre is open daily from 10am–6pm from April to the end of August. Last entry to the centre is 5.30pm. The centre is also open daily for Caper-watch (to see Capercaillies) from 5.30am–8am through April and on to mid-May.
- **Entry fees** Adults £3, concessions £2, under 16s 50p. Family ticket £6 (up to two adults and two children). RSPB and Wildlife Explorer members – free. Caper-watch: adults – non-members £3, members £1, children free.
- **Accessibility** The Osprey Centre is fully accessible. The forest trails cannot be accessed by wheelchair.
- **Dogs** Not allowed in the Osprey Centre. Otherwise permitted but must be kept under close control.

WILDLIFE BY SEASON

SPRING

Ospreys are often back at the nest in late March and hopefully incubating eggs by mid-April. Capercaillies are easiest to see in April and May. Songbirds in the forest are singing to declare their territories.

SUMMER

From early June onwards the Ospreys should have young, which can be seen on the nest being fed by their parents. In July and August the chicks prepare to fledge, spending time jumping up and down on the nest as they learn to fly – an exciting time to visit. This is the best season to see mammals.

AUTUMN

Wildfowl come to Loch Garten to winter, including Whooper Swans, Greylag Geese, Goldeneyes and Goosanders. Young forest birds are dispersing. The Ospreys – adults and any youngsters fledged that year – are likely to have departed on migration by the end of August but may hang on into September.

WINTER

Although the Osprey Centre is closed, the bird and squirrel feeders are kept topped up – with patience you should see many species, including Crested Tits. A good time to see Roe Deer.

What to look for

If you visit in spring and your first port of call is the Osprey Centre, the staff will be able to talk you through the situation at the nest. Visitors and armchair Osprey fans alike have followed the twists and turns of the saga here for some years, as a succession of Osprey pairs have used the nest since the 1950s. With luck you'll see the male Osprey delivering a freshly caught trout to his mate – the female handles the incubation side of things mostly on her own are turkey-sized grouse, but despite their size they are very shy and very discreet in their habits. In spring, the males display communally to females on lekking grounds and are then a little easier to see, but very susceptible to disturbance. For this reason, it's best to avoid the forest trails in the early mornings at this time of year and attend the Centre instead – there has been an excellent rate of sightings since Caper-watch began in 1999.

Supper's ready: the Loch Garten Ospreys often bring Rainbow Trout back to the nest, caught at the nearby Rothiemurchus fish farm.

while the male must find enough fish for himself, her and, in due course, their chicks. If all goes well, there should be chicks in the nest by the end of May, with a corresponding increase in the frequency of fish-delivering visits from the proud father.

Much of the wildlife in the forest can be seen all through the year. Your best bet for seeing one of the most elusive species though, is an early-morning spring trip to the Osprey Centre for 'Caper-watch'. Capercaillies

There is a feeding station at the Osprey Centre which includes a large box feeder for squirrels. With no Grey Squirrels to worry about, the Red Squirrels steal the show at this feeding station – you shouldn't have to wait for too long before one or more comes spiralling down the tree trunk for a free lunch. The feeders are also visited by many Coal Tits (easily the commonest tit species here), Siskins, Chaffinches, Great Spotted Woodpeckers

A male Capercaillie in full courtship display is an imposing-looking (and sounding) creature. The daily Caper-watch at the Osprey centre in spring offers you a great chance of seeing it for yourself.

and, now and then, Crested Tits. There is a live webcam aimed at the feeders in autumn and winter, so you can keep tabs on the birds and squirrels at home before and after your visit. Other mammals present in the forest include Pine Martens and Scottish Wildcats, though regrettably your chance of seeing either is very small.

The two lochs (Loch Garten itself and the smaller Loch Mallachie) have relatively little birdlife in summer. Goldeneyes breed, and you may see a female surrounded by her swarm of cream-and-chocolate ducklings. Common Sandpipers nest around the shoreline.

The Ospreys depart in autumn for their leisurely southbound migration – before they do you could witness the chicks' first flights or see them trying out their fishing skills. The adults go first, leaving the youngsters to it, and soon they too have left. The loch now attracts wildfowl, with Whooper Swans arriving from the far north, joined by Greylag and Pink-footed Geese, Goosanders, Wigeons, Mallards and Teals. In the forest, look out for parties of crossbills feeding on pine cones – they may include the only bird species unique to Britain, the Scottish Crossbill. With Common and Parrot Crossbills here too, and identification very difficult and best done by analysing the calls, you may never be certain whether you've seen a 'Scotbill' or not, but crossbills of any kind are always worth a look.

How to get here

Grid ref./postcode NH 978183/PH25 3
By road In Strathspey, from the outskirts of Aviemore and Grantown-on-Spey, follow 'RSPB Ospreys' roadsigns.
By public transport The nearest mainline railway station is Aviemore (10 miles away). A steam railway runs from Aviemore to Boat of Garten (4 miles from the reserve) and Broomhill for Nethybridge (5.5 miles away) between April and October. For further information visit www.

WHEN TO VISIT

Spring and summer is the time to come and see the Ospreys at their nest. Caper-watch takes place from April to late May. Outside of this time, the reserve is still well worth a visit with much of the special wildlife present throughout the year. Caper-watch requires an early start (5.30–8am), otherwise time of day is not important.

CELEBRITY OSPREY

In the last decade, the long-standing Loch Garten female 'White EJ' has been wooed by two different suitors. In 2007 her regular mate 'Henry' returned late from Africa and EJ was already incubating a clutch of eggs fathered by Henry's love rival 'Orange VS'. Henry kicked the eggs from the nest but sadly it was too late for another breeding attempt. In 2008 Henry failed to return altogether and OVS stepped into the breach. Two chicks were reared, and for the first time thousands watched live action from the nest via a webcam. In another first, both chicks were fitted with GPS transmitters, so their migratory progress could be tracked when they departed for Africa in the autumn. At the time of writing in spring 2009, EJ has a brand new mate, Odin, who is taking great care of her as she incubates three new eggs while webcams and bloggers record every detail. From a single pioneering pair to stars of cyberspace – Loch Garten's Ospreys have certainly come a long way.

Only found in Scottish pinewoods in the UK, the Crested Tit is an enchanting little bird and easy to see at Abernethy.

strathspeyrailway.co.uk. The nearest bus stop is on the B970. Bus route 34 runs from Aviemore to Grantown-on-Spey (ask for Raebreck junction). From here a dedicated footpath leads to the Osprey Centre (1.6 miles away). A network of trails, stemming from the Speyside Way footpath, links the Osprey Centre with the villages of Boat of Garten and Nethybridge.

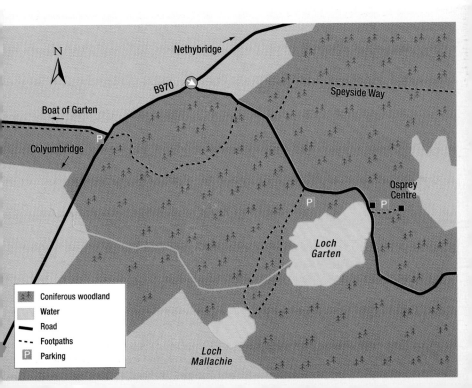

NORTH SCOTLAND

Sundew

LOCH NA MUILNE

On the peaty moorland close to the west coast of Lewis in the Outer Hebrides lies this shallow loch with its swampy fringes – a breeding ground for several species of ducks and waders, most notably the delightful Red-necked Phalarope. You can watch the loch's wildlife from a purpose-built viewing area.

● Access, facilities, contact details and accessibility

There is a viewpoint with an information panel. You can arrange guided walks on this reserve.

- **Telephone** 01851 703 296; **web** www.rspb.org.uk/lochnamuilne
- **Opening hours** Open at all times
- **Entry fees** Free, but donations to help continue the work here are welcome
- **Accessibility** The paths are rough and not suitable for the mobility-impaired
- **Dogs** Permitted, but please keep them under close control

P

What to look for

Loch na Muilne is a shining sheet of water within the gently rolling moorland of this part of Lewis, shallow enough to resemble temporary flood-waters but with marshy shores that reveal its enduring character. The wet moorland around is home to nesting waders, which you'll see from mid-spring. Redshanks, Dunlins,

Snipes and Lapwings are all here and thriving thanks to careful management of the habitat, which ensures that muddy areas and shallow pools are available for the small chicks to feed. The waders vigorously drive off crows and other potential predators, especially the Lapwings which energetically chase and dive-bomb intruders.

WILDLIFE BY SEASON

SPRING

Waders, including Dunlins, Lapwings and Snipes, display and select nesting sites. Golden Plovers flock here before dispersing out to the moorland to breed.

SUMMER

Red-necked Phalaropes are on the loch, along with Teals and Tufted Ducks. Sundews flower.

AUTUMN

Whooper Swans stop off on migration to refuel at the loch. Some of them will remain here throughout winter, while others continue to travel south.

WINTER

Very quiet, although you may see Snipes feeding at the loch shore.

The other breeding wader here is the Red-necked Phalarope, an extremely rare breeding bird in the UK (the only other place to see them nesting besides the Outer Hebrides is the Shetlands). Little bigger than a sparrow, this dainty and energetic little bird feeds mainly on tiny flies that swarm close to the water's surface, which it disturbs by rapidly spinning on the surface before snapping them up with its delicate bill. Another voracious fly-catcher is altogether more passive – the Sundew plant traps insects with sticky hairs on its leaves and secretes enzymes to digest them, a useful adaptation to survive in this nutrient-poor environment.

A few ducks are present on the loch in spring as well – Tufted Ducks and Teals – while Common Gulls nest on the fringes. Golden Plovers, looking extremely smart with their spangled gold and black upper-parts and black tummies, gather in the area before heading out to the higher moorland to breed.

Most of the birds leave the area in autumn, although Snipes are present year-round

WHEN TO VISIT

Visit between late spring and summer to see the phalaropes. Winter is the quietest time.

provided the loch shores remain unfrozen and accessible to their probing bills. Variable numbers of Whooper Swans visit in the autumn, feeding and resting at the loch before continuing their migration south.

How to get here

Grid ref./postcode NB 311494/ HS2 0

By road To reach Lewis, take the ferry from Ullapool to Stornoway. Take the A858 to Arnol and park near the Arnol blackhouse with due consideration for residents and other visitors. The nature reserve is accesssed by heading past the blackhouse and turning right. The reserve lies through a gate after a walk of some 800m.

By public transport Cross to Lewis as above. There are buses between Stornoway and Arnol, taking 1 hour 15 minutes.

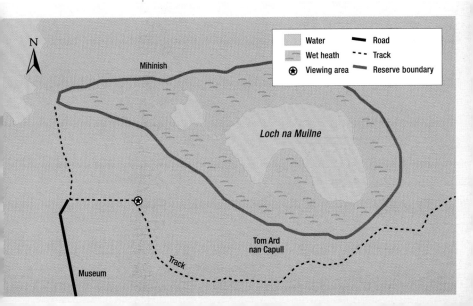

N

Water	Road
Wet heath	Track
Viewing area	Reserve boundary

Mihinish

Loch na Muilne

Tom Ard nan Capull

Track

Museum

LOCH RUTHVEN

SSSI, SPA, SAC, RAMSAR, NATURA 2000

The still beauty of this loch is disturbed only by some of the UK's most dazzling breeding birds. This is the place to see nesting Slavonian Grebes, resplendent in their breeding finery, and also Ospreys and divers – you should have good views from the hide.

●Access, facilities, contact details and accessibility

There is one hide at this quiet and peaceful reserve, at the end of a 500m trail.

- **Telephone** 01463 715 000; **email** nsro@rspb.org.uk; **web** www.rspb.org.uk/lochruthven
- **Opening hours** Open at all times
- **Entry fees** Free, but donations are welcome
- **Accessibility** The trail to the hide is not wheelchair-accessible
- **Dogs** Must be kept under close control. No dogs in the hide please.

What to look for

In the Highlands, many lochs lie in mountain valleys and are deep and dark with little shoreside vegetation. Loch Ruthven has rather gentler surroundings and is fringed with sedges, providing nesting places for the Slavonian Grebes that nest here. If you come in April, May or early June you should enjoy good views of the grebes looking their best.

The 'middle-sized' of the five grebe species that occur in Britain, Slavonian Grebes are gorgeous in their black and deep red breeding plumage, set off by an impressive pair of golden head tufts that are fanned out in the elegant courtship display. This one loch holds 50 per

WILDLIFE BY SEASON

SPRING

Slavonian Grebes arrive in March, becoming easier to see in April. Ospreys fish the loch, and Red-throated and occasional Black-throated Divers visit.

SUMMER

The grebes start to look more careworn as their chicks grow. Ospreys and divers continue to visit.

AUTUMN

The last grebes depart. There may be lingering Goldeneyes on the loch and Red-breasted Mergansers may visit.

WINTER

A quiet time – the loch is often iced over. A few songbirds remain in the woods.

cent of the UK's breeding population of the species, and conservation actions to help protect them include minimising disturbance and extending the area of sedgy nesting habitat.

If you spend long enough watching the grebes, you're almost sure to see a visiting Osprey too. The good fishing means that these graceful birds of prey, which nest locally, often stop by to grab a trout for their chicks. The few pairs of Black-headed and Common Gulls that nest here may rise up to try to chase away the Osprey.

The fish in the loch also draw in divers through the summer, mainly Red-throated but also the odd Black-throated, both species smart in their breeding plumage. In the birch woodlands, Redpolls and Siskins breed, and Sedge Warblers and Reed Buntings nest in the sedge fringes, the warblers singing a constant stream of squeaks, chirps, churrs and rattles.

Winter is a quiet time, although Pochards and Goldeneyes may visit the loch if it remains unfrozen.

WHEN TO VISIT

Visit in late spring or summer to see Slavonian Grebes and Ospreys.

How to get here

Grid ref./postcode NH 638280/IV2 6
By road Loch Ruthven lies 16 miles south-west of Inverness. Turn west off the A9 on the B851 towards Fort Augustus then after 8 miles turn right at Croachy onto the unclassified road (reserve is signposted).
By public transport Inverness is the nearest station but is about 18 miles away. An infrequent service runs through Croachy – the bus stop is approximately one mile from the reserve.

Slavonian Grebe

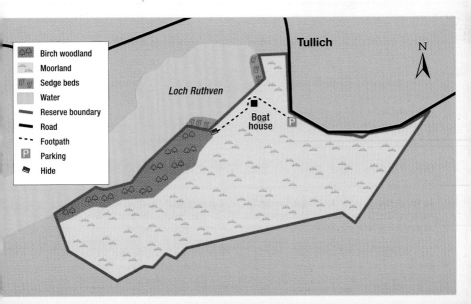

Birch woodland	
Moorland	
Sedge beds	
Water	
—	Reserve boundary
—	Road
- - -	Footpath
P	Parking
◣	Hide

Tullich

Loch Ruthven

Boat house

P

N

NIGG BAY   SSSI, SPA, RAMSAR, NATURA 2000

This estuarine basin on the Cromarty Firth provides a rich and sheltered feeding ground for thousands of waders and wildfowl through the winter. High tide shrinks the available mudflats and pushes the birds closer to view. A well-placed hide gives you a good vantage point to watch them as they feed.

● Access, facilities, contact details and accessibility

The reserve has one hide, giving views over the mudflats and wet grassland.
- **Telephone** 01463 715000; **email** nsro@rspb.org.uk; **web** www.rspb.org.uk/niggbay
- **Opening hours** Open at all times
- **Entry fees** Free
- **Accessibility** The hide is suitable for wheelchairs
- **Dogs** Must be kept under close control. No dogs in the hide please.

What to look for

For the spectacle of thousands of waders swirling over an expanse of mudflats and saltmarsh, come to Nigg Bay any time from early autumn to late spring. The hide, a short walk from the car park on wheelchair-friendly surfaces, is well screened off from the mudflats, allowing you to observe the birds without causing disturbance. If you have a telescope, you'll find it helpful here to see the more distant waders. On the opposite side of the Firth, Udale Bay, is also an RSPB reserve so it's worth visiting both in the same trip.

The main species present are Knots, Bar-tailed Godwits, Dunlins, Oystercatchers, Curlews and Redshanks.

Another habitat management scheme underway at this reserve involves the creation of some wet

WILDLIFE BY SEASON

SPRING

The last winter waders depart through April. A small number of wintering ducks remain into early spring, the males in their full colourful breeding plumage.

SUMMER

Some birds still use the saltmarsh and mudflats. Ospreys fish in the bay.

AUTUMN

Waders start to arrive at the end of summer, with good numbers present from October.

WINTER

Masses of waders feed on the mudflats, with Wigeons and Whooper Swans on the eelgrass beds. A few diving ducks winter on the sea here.

pasture behind the mudflats, which is encouraging waders to breed here as well as visit in winter. It is early days still, and the reserve is generally rather quiet in the summer but year-round wildlife interest is increasing. Meanwhile, the bay attracts a few diving ducks (mainly Goldeneyes) in winter, while Greylag and Pink-footed Geese and Pintails visit the inner bay.

By allowing the sea to breach the bay's coastal defences, the RSPB has created from unproductive fields more valuable intertidal habitat for the waders and for other birds, including the masses of Wigeons and Mute and Whooper Swans that come to feed on the eelgrass beds.

The work took place in 2003,

WHEN TO VISIT

The best time to visit is between September and March – arrive as the tide is rising (up to three hours before high tide) for the best views.

and the newly created areas of habitat already attract 11 species of waders and 10 of wildfowl.

How to get here

Grid ref./postcode NH 807730/ IV19 1
By road The reserve is 1 mile north of Nigg village on the B9175.
By public transport The nearest station is Fearn, 4.5 miles away. Local buses call at Nigg Village.

Bar-tailed Godwit

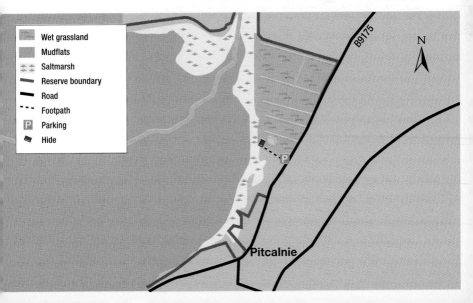

Wet grassland
Mudflats
Saltmarsh
Reserve boundary
Road
Footpath
P Parking
Hide

B9175

N

Pitcalnie

NORTH SCOTLAND

UDALE BAY

SSSI, SPA, RAMSAR, NATURA 2000

On the south side of the Cromarty Firth, opposite the Nigg Bay reserve, this reserve attracts many waders and wildfowl in autumn and winter. A hide overlooks the mudflats, giving good views of the assembled birds especially close to high tide.

● Access, facilities, contact details and accessibility

This reserve has a well-appointed hide, reached via a short path.
- **Telephone** 01463 715000; **email** nsro@rspb.org.uk; **web** www.rspb.org.uk/udalebay
- **Opening hours** Open at all times
- **Entry fees** None, but donations to help continue the work here are welcomed
- **Accessibility** The hide is wheelchair-accessible
- **Dogs** Must be kept under close control. No dogs in the hide, please.

What to look for

This reserve has a very similar mix of species to Nigg Bay. Pink-footed Geese pass through in spring – you may see them feeding on the grassland or flying overhead in wavering strings and 'V's. There are usually a few waders, gulls and Shelducks on the mudflats through summer, and Ospreys sometimes come to fish at high tide, but it isn't until autumn that the real numbers start to arrive. Wigeons form an impressive spectacle with up to 10,000 feeding on the eelgrass beds, though some of these birds will carry on travelling south after a short stay. Teals and Mallards arrive in smaller numbers, while Greylag Geese visit in variable numbers.

WILDLIFE BY SEASON

SPRING

Winter birds move on, while thousands of Pink-footed Geese visit on their northbound migration.

SUMMER

A few gulls, Shelducks and waders use the bay through summer. The first returning migrant waders will be arriving towards the end of summer.

AUTUMN

Winter visitors and passage migrants arrive, including some 10,000 Wigeons.

WINTER

The bay is busy with waders and ducks, with Peregrine Falcons occasionally panicking the flocks.

The predominant wader species are the same as in Nigg Bay. The rising tide pushes the birds closer to the hide, and you'll be able to compare and contrast the feeding styles of the various species, from the ceaseless scampering and picking of the Dunlins to the more leisurely searches of the Bar-tailed Godwits.

If time permits, it is worth checking the main channel of the firth (viewable from the B9163 to Cromarty) for diving ducks which prefer the deeper water here. Species that may be present include Long-tailed Duck, and sometimes there are Slavonian Grebes and Red-throated Divers here too. The grebes and divers retain their dull winter plumage till spring, but the male ducks look superb throughout winter. Male Long-tailed Ducks are unusual in having different winter and spring plumages, the former mainly white and the latter with much more black. There is also an internationally important flock of wintering Scaups here, which you can view from the car park on the B9163 to Cromarty, just east of the reserve boundary.

WHEN TO VISIT

Every season apart from mid-summer is interesting here, but the largest number of birds is present in autumn. Visit two hours or so before high tide for closer views.

How to get here

Grid ref./postcode NH 712651/ IV7 8

By road Travelling north along the A9 from Inverness, turn right onto the B9169 signed to Culbokie. Continue for approximately 9.5 miles. Take the next left (B9163) to Cromarty. After approx 0.6 miles, park in the lay-by on your left.

By public transport Dingwall, 15 miles away, is the nearest station. Buses call at Jemimaville, approximately 0.6 miles away. From Jemimaville, walk west along the footpath for about 0.6 miles. The reserve lay-by car park is on your right. For the latest travel information phone Stagecoach on 01862 892 683 or visit www.stagecoachbus.com

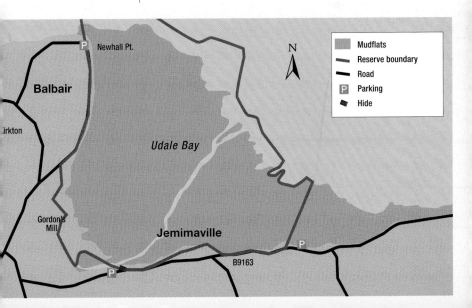

	Mudflats
	Reserve boundary
	Road
P	Parking
	Hide

WALES

CARNGAFALLT SSSI, SPA, SAC

Carngafallt is a summit of heather moorland, with woodland and hay meadow on its lower slopes, in the central uplands of Wales. A very beautiful and enchanting place, it holds a good variety of woodland and moorland wildlife, including native Welsh Red Kites, and is a great place for a rewarding walk in the hills – sturdy footwear is a must!

Access, facilities, contact details and accessibility

This is a remote site without facilities, though public footpaths and bridleways offer good access to the reserve.

- **Telephone** 01654 700 222; **email** carngafallt@rspb.org.uk; **web** www.rspb.org.uk/carngafallt
- **Opening hours** Open at all times
- **Entry fees** Free, but donations are welcome
- **Accessibility** The paths are steep in places and so not suitable for wheelchairs or pushchairs
- **Dogs** Allowed on public footpaths and bridleways, but must be under control

What to look for

While many of the interesting moorland birds are present year-round, you'll need to visit in spring to catch up with the greatest variety of woodland species. Those three key species of upland broadleaved woodland, the Pied Flycatcher, Redstart and Wood Warbler, all return here from Africa and can be seen and heard from mid-spring. The RSPB manages the wood for the benefit of for these birds, grazing the wood lightly with sheep and preserving the open sunny glades that help boost the woodlands' insect population. A dawn visit should reward you with an impressive chorus of birdsong, and woodland flowers add more interest.

WILDLIFE BY SEASON

SPRING

A wonderful chorus of birdsong includes contributions from newly arrived Pied Flycatchers, Wood Warblers and Redstarts.

SUMMER

The heather moorland flowers in July. Dragonflies and butterflies are on the wing.

AUTUMN

Winter thrushes and other birds feed on the berry and seed crop. The lichens and mosses look at their best in autumn. Young Red Kites are dispersing from their parents' territories.

WINTER

The quietest season, though you can still see Ravens, Red Kites and Buzzards overhead.

The heather flowers in summer, flushing the moorland purple and drawing in all manner of nectar-loving insects, along with the dragonflies which hunt them. Purple Hairstreak butterflies flit through the oak canopy from late June into August, Dor Beetles roll away neat balls of sheep dung, Tree Pipits and Whinchats nest at the woodland edges, and Red Kites and Buzzards soar overhead.

By the time the heather flowers fade away, the moorland and woodland mosses and lichens are starting to look their best, lending texture and colour to every surface and enhancing the impression of a magical, untouched natural world. The Rowan trees' red berries catch the attention of newly arrived Redwings and Fieldfares, which descend in ravenous hordes to strip off this colourful booty, sometimes joined by a Ring Ouzel or two.

The flycatchers, warblers and Redstarts head south for winter, leaving the woodlands quiet although the resident species are still here, just keeping a lower profile. Ravens, Buzzards and

WHEN TO VISIT

The reserve is best in spring and summer, though the scenery is of course marvellous in every season. Visit early in the day in spring to hear the dawn chorus.

Red Kites are still easy to see, however, and wintry weather reveals a new side of Carnafallt's atmospheric beauty.

How to get here

Grid ref./postcode SN 936652/ LD6 5

By road The main access point is at Elan village – there is an RSPB information sign at the eastern end of the village where the village road enters woodland at a cattle grid. Elan village is just off the B4518 approximately 3 miles south-west of the town of Rhayader, which straddles the A470 and A44, in central Wales.

By public transport Llandrindod Wells (13 miles away) is the nearest station. From here you can take a bus to Rhayader – the reserve is then a 3-mile walk away.

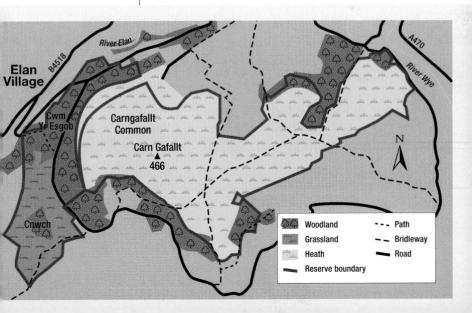

Legend:
- Woodland
- Grassland
- Heath
- Reserve boundary
- Path
- Bridleway
- Road

WALES

CONWY SSSI

On the east side of the Conwy estuary, a collection of lagoons forms the heart of this excellent reserve, which boasts great visitor facilities. Two nature trails form a circular walk that takes you right round the lagoons and alongside the estuary proper, providing opportunities for some great wildlife-watching. You'll also enjoy the far-reaching views inland to Snowdonia, with the splendid Conwy Castle with its numerous round towers poised on a hill-top on the other side of the estuary. As well as attracting a wide range of wildlife, this man-made reserve has been designed to offer something for all visitors, whether you fancy a gentle stroll or fun activities for the family.

Access, facilities, contact details and accessibility

The two trails form a 2-mile walk, and there are three hides and three viewing screens along the way. Back at base, there is a well-stocked shop and a tearoom serving drinks and snacks, as well as a visitor centre with information on hand about the reserve and the wildlife you can see. You can borrow binoculars, and guided walks and group visits can be arranged.

- **Telephone** 01492 584 091; **email** conwy@rspb.org.uk; **web** www.rspb.org.uk/conwy
- **Opening hours** The shop and visitor centre is open every day (except Christmas Day) from 9.30am–5pm. The coffee shop is open from 10am–4.30pm (4pm from November to March).
- **Entry fees** Adults £2.50, concessions £1.50, children £1, family £5. No charge for RSPB members.
- **Accessibility** The trails are firm and generally level though a little rough in places. Wheelchair access is recommended only for the first 0.6 miles – a loop that features two hides and a children's trail before returning to the visitor centre, but powered chairs can manage the whole 2-mile trail loop, as can pushchairs.
- **Dogs** Only registered assistance dogs allowed

WILDLIFE BY SEASON

SPRING

Lapwings tumble in the sky while Skylarks climb higher and higher, both species performing their own version of territorial song. Migrating land and water birds visit the reserve, with Sand Martins and Little Ringed Plovers first to arrive.

SUMMER

Reed and Sedge Warblers sing from the reedbeds. Butterflies are on the wing, many species of dragonflies and damselflies hunt over the reserve and ducks and waders have chicks on the lagoons.

AUTUMN

Whimbrels and other waders visit the lagoons on their southbound migrations. Winter wildfowl start to arrive, including Gadwalls, Shelducks, Shovelers, Teals and occasional rarities.

WINTER

Many Starlings gather to roost, sometimes attracting hungry Sparrowhawks and other birds of prey. The feeding station is busy with finches, buntings and other small birds. The best time of year to see Water Rails.

What to look for

In spring, late wintering waders are likely to still be around along with passage migrants – look out for Greenshanks and Black-tailed Godwits. High tide on the estuary may push more waders onto the lagoons.

The trails join up to make a loop, with hides and viewpoints on both the estuary side and the inland side. Islands in the lagoons are managed for breeding Lapwings – spring is the time to watch their exuberant rolling display flight,

out on the estuary. Little Egrets breed among the Grey Herons in Benarth Woods across the estuary and can often be seen hunting for food on the reserve.

Summer is the best time to look for insects on the reserve, and the RSPB arranges various bug-hunting events for children to show them the diversity of mini-beasts that live in the varied habitats of Conwy. Keep your eyes peeled and you could see some of the 11 species of dragonflies and damselflies and

On the wing from April, Common Blues may have three generations a year, so you could see them into early autumn.

conducted with a constant sound-track of weird whoops and yodels. Scrubby areas attract Chiffchaffs, Lesser Whitethroats and other warblers by mid-spring, while the reedbeds are soon resounding to a chorus of Reed and Sedge Warbler song. Out over the lagoons, Sand Martins fly-catch to replenish their fat reserves after migrating from Africa – soon there are Swallows and House Martins here too, and waders feeding on the lagoon shores as well as

22 species of butterflies on the reserve. Summer is also a good time for mammals. Stoats and Weasels are both seen regularly, and can be hard to tell apart if you only have a fleeting view of an elongated brown furry creature darting across the path ahead of you. If you do see one of these animals, keep still and wait – their natural curiosity could tempt them to reappear and give you a searching look. Occasionally, it might even approach you if you are very

A biggish, leggy and rather pale wader, the Greenshank is often to be seen striding confidently out into quite deep water, every now and then plunging its head under to grab aquatic prey.

still, and very lucky. Whether you get a good look or just a glimpse, try to see the tail tip, which is black in Stoats and brown in Weasels. Size is also a good clue, though variable – Stoats are bigger and more substantial-looking while Weasels often give the impression of stretched-out mice. Their big cousin the Otter occurs here too but is even more difficult to see.

In autumn, there can be large influxes of wading birds on migration, with Whimbrels, Dunlins, both species of godwits, Curlew Sandpipers and Redshanks flocking on the estuary, and smaller numbers crossing over to the lagoons. This is the time of year for rarities, and its west-coast location makes Conwy particularly good for vagrant waders from North America. The likeliest of these is the Pectoral Sandpiper, a solidly built bird rather like a

pumped-up Dunlin. In 2006 a Stilt Sandpiper was found on the reserve, while rare waders from the opposite direction have included Terek Sandpiper and Broad-billed Sandpiper.

Duck numbers also increase in autumn, with flocks of Teals and Wigeons gathering, along with Shovelers and Gadwall, with Goldeneyes out in the deeper water. Snipe numbers increase – check each Snipe you see carefully as there may also be one or two Jack Snipes here. They are smaller, shorter-billed and stripier than their more common cousins.

An early autumn roost of Starlings uses the reedbeds, swirling in mind-boggling formation overhead before they dive in. Birds of prey including Sparrowhawks, Kestrels and Peregrine Falcons may arrive at this time, trying their luck at seizing a Starling for an evening meal. The Water Rails that skulk in the reeds throughout the year are most likely to be seen creeping out into the open in winter, when the cold and a scarcity of prey forces them to forage more widely. Unusual birds to have appeared in recent winters include Firecrest and Bittern. The birdfeeders are busy at this time of year, with Reed Buntings, Siskins and Redpolls joining the more familiar garden species. Winter is a great time to try out your bird photography skills as you can often

WHEN TO VISIT

The reserve is well worth a visit at any time of year, with much to see in every season. Winter is the time to come if you particularly want to see the impressive reedbed Starling roost.

have very good views from the hides, and the birds on the feeders tend to be approachable.

How to get here

Grid ref./postcode SH 797773/LL31 9

By road From the A55, take Junction 18 (signposted Conwy and Deganwy) and follow the brown RSPB signs. The reserve is on the south side of the roundabout. From Conwy, Deganwy and Llandudno, take the A546/A547 to the Weekly News roundabout, drive south past Tesco and the cinema complex (Ffordd 6G) and cross the roundabout over the A55. The entrance to the reserve is on the south side.

By public transport The nearest train station is Llandudno Junction, a 10 minute walk away. Turn left out of the station and take the first left down Ferndale Road. Follow the footpath to the right and turn left over the road bridge. The road goes past Tesco and a cinema complex to the large A55 roundabout. The reserve is on the south side of the roundabout and is signposted. Bus 27 stops at Tesco, and many other buses from various destinations stop nearby. A footpath and cycleway from Conwy and Deganwy runs along the estuary, providing access to the reserve for pedestrians and cyclists.

It's related to Coots and Moorhens but is much shyer. Keep your eyes on the reedy, weedy shoreline if you want to spot a Water Rail.

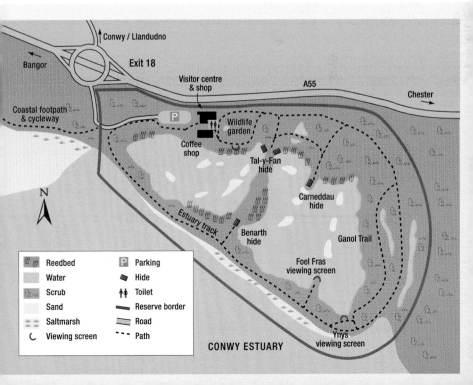

Conwy / Llandudno

Bangor

Exit 18

Visitor centre & shop

A55

Chester

Coastal footpath & cycleway

P

Wildlife garden

Coffee shop

Tal-y-Fan hide

Carneddau hide

N

Estuary track

Benarth hide

Ganol Trail

Foel Fras viewing screen

Ynys viewing screen

Reedbed
Water
Scrub
Sand
Saltmarsh
Viewing screen

P **Parking**
Hide
Toilet
Reserve border
Road
Path

CONWY ESTUARY

CWM CLYDACH

With oak and ash trees on the slopes on either side of the rushing Lower Clydach river, Cwm Clydach is a classic Welsh woodland reserve with many birds, butterflies and mammals. It's a great place for a walk at any time of year, though birdlife is probably most visible and varied in spring. With links to public footpaths, a long walk is possible.

●Access, facilities, contact details and accessibility

This reserve has two nature trails leading from the car park, which link up with a wider network of public footpaths.

- **Telephone** 01654 700222; **email** cwm.clydach@rspb.org.uk; **web** www.rspb.org.uk/cwmclydach
- **Opening hours** Open at all times
- **Entry fees** None, though donations are appreciated
- **Accessibility** The trails can be managed by wheelchair users with able-bodied assistants
- **Dogs** Allowed on all footpaths

What to look for

These woodlands provide a rich habitat for a variety of birds, and if you come in spring before the leaves are out, you should see many of them. Some of the more notable include Great Spotted Woodpecker, Nuthatch, Treecreeper and Tawny Owl, all of which are easiest to see in late winter and early spring. By mid-spring, the migrants are arriving, including Willow Warbler, Blackcap, Garden Warbler and Spotted Flycatcher. If you notice a group of small birds calling agitatedly, look where they're looking and you could find a roosting Tawny Owl.

WILDLIFE BY SEASON

SPRING

Migrating birds arrive in the woods, and all the birds are singing and preparing to nest. Wood Sorrel carpets the woodland floor.

SUMMER

Watch Dippers and Grey Wagtails feeding their newly fledged chicks along the river, and look for Silver-washed Fritillary butterflies in sunny clearings.

AUTUMN

Flocks of Siskins and Redpolls feed in riverside alder trees. The autumn colours are glorious.

WINTER

With the leaf canopy gone, it's easier to see Buzzards and Red Kites overhead. Woodland birds forage in flocks.

Once the birds have established territories and are rearing chicks, they become more difficult to see, especially as the canopy has grown in, but Dippers and Grey Wagtails remain fairly visible on the river, while butterflies visit flowers in the more open, sunny areas. The most eyecatching of them is the Silver-washed Fritillary, a large tawny-orange creature with impressive curved forewings and a lovely diffuse green and silver underwing pattern. Purple Hairstreak butterflies swirl around the oak canopy in July. If you are here early or late enough you could see Badgers ending or beginning their night-time feeding forays.

After the riotous colours of autumn and the departure of the summer visitors, the reserve seems much quieter. You could disturb a Woodcock as you walk, and the riverside Alder trees attract flocks of Siskins and Redpolls, two attractive and agile little finches with streaky underparts. Tits, Treecreepers and Nuthatches may join forces with feeding flocks of other tit species – safety in numbers with more pairs of eyes watching for Sparrowhawks. With no leaves obscuring the view, it's easier to see Buzzards and Red Kites overhead at this time of year. Both of these large birds of prey are expert soarers, but the Red Kite's deeply forked tail gives it away.

WHEN TO VISIT

Spring is probably the best time to visit, but there is much to see here throughout the year. Birdsong is best in the early mornings in spring.

How to get here

Grid ref./postcode SN 684026/ SA6 5

By road The reserve car park is situated in the village of Craig Cefn Parc, close to the New Inn public house on the B4291.

By public transport The nearest rail station is Swansea, 6 miles away; an hourly bus service from Swansea to Craig Cefn Parc stops at the reserve entrance.

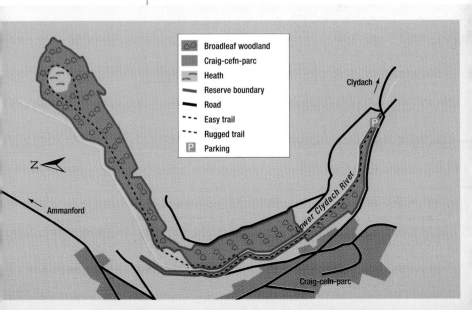

Legend:
- Broadleaf woodland
- Craig-cefn-parc
- Heath
- Reserve boundary
- Road
- Easy trail
- Rugged trail
- P Parking

Clydach

Ammanford

Lower Clydach River

Craig-cefn-parc

WALES

DEE ESTUARY – POINT OF AYR

SSSI, SPA, SAC, RAMSAR

A promontory at the western tip of the Dee Estuary, Point of Ayr is famous as a vantage point for watching migrating seabirds. It also overlooks estuarine mudflats where important numbers of waders and Brent Geese stop off to feed on their migration southwards – many of them overwinter too. Birdwatching here can be very exciting, especially in autumn.

● Access, facilities, contact details and accessibility

The sea wall path is 0.6 miles long and from here there are good views. You can book guided walks or group visits.
- **Telephone** 0151 336 7681; **web** www.rspb.org.uk/dee-pointofayr
- **Opening hours** Open at all times
- **Entry fees** None, but donations to help continue the work here are appreciated
- **Accessibility** It is possible for wheelchair users to access the 0.6-mile sea wall path, though access can be difficult. For more details, please contact the reserve office.
- **Dogs** Allowed on all footpaths

What to look for

Like many headlands, the Point of Ayr is a good place to observe bird migration in spring and autumn. In spring the main interest is provided by flocks of waders on the mudflats and terns going past offshore. Small landbirds like Wheatears, wagtails and assorted warblers may visit briefly in spring.

In summer, the action dies down for a while, though this is a good time to look for butterflies and other insects including scarce local moths like the Sandhill Rustic, and to watch terns, mainly Common and Sandwich but often also a handful of rarer species, fishing or loafing on the beach.

WILDLIFE BY SEASON

SPRING

Migrants passing at sea and overland, especially terns and small land birds.

SUMMER

Waders are migrating south by mid-summer. Terns roost on the shingle spit and beach.

AUTUMN

More passage migration is taking place, with north-westerly gales sometimes producing large numbers of seabirds, including Leach's Petrels.

WINTER

Peregrines hunt the wintering waders and wildfowl. Redwings and Fieldfares feed in the bushes behind the sea wall. Snow Buntings feed on the beach.

By late summer waders on their return migration are arriving on the mudflats, and numbers build up through the season to some 20,000 birds by winter. The main species involved are Oystercatchers, Knots, Dunlins and Redshanks, but others such as Greenshanks, Sanderlings, Curlews and godwits are scattered among them. The birds will be easiest to see around high tide. Brent Geese also arrive in autumn.

Seabird migration can be spectacular, with skuas, shearwaters, Gannets and Fulmars all passing close by when the wind is in the north-west. The most coveted seabird here is the tiny Leach's Petrel, and in good years there can be hundreds seen. If you are keen to see this species, keep an eye on weather reports and be ready to drop everything and head for the reserve if strong north-westerlies are forecast.

The wintering waders are joined by wildfowl, with many Mallards and Shelducks and smaller numbers of Wigeons and Pintails. On the sea you could see scoters, divers, grebes and auks, while Snow and Lapland Buntings, Twites and Shore Larks may be found by the sea wall. Birds of prey also visit in winter – Hen Harriers, Short-eared Owls, Merlins and Peregrine Falcons are all possible.

WHEN TO VISIT

Exciting all year round, but visit in early autumn for a chance of seeing Leach's Petrels, especially when onshore north-westerly winds are blowing.

How to get here

Grid ref./postcode SJ 124847/ CH8 9

By road The reserve is located at the end of Station Road, Talacre, which is reached off the coastal A548 road, 2 miles east of Prestatyn.

By public transport The nearest station is Prestatyn, 2 miles away. The nearest bus stop is on the A548 in Talacre; from here walk the length of Station Road and proceed to the end (approximately 1 mile's walk).

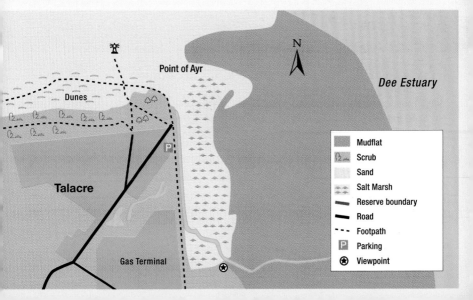

Point of Ayr

Dunes

Talacre

Gas Terminal

Dee Estuary

N

	Mudflat
	Scrub
	Sand
	Salt Marsh
	Reserve boundary
	Road
	Footpath
P	Parking
✪	Viewpoint

WALES

GRASSHOLM

SSSI, NNR, SPA, SAC, NP, IBA, NCR

This uninhabited 9-hectare island is home to an astounding 32,000 pairs of Gannets. Landings are not permitted to avoid disturbance, but the RSPB now offers guided boat trips that circumnavigate Grassholm before moving on to Ramsey Island, also an RSPB reserve (see page 312), where the boat lands.

● Access, facilities, contact details and accessibility

The RSPB-guided trips are run by Thousand Islands Expeditions. You must book in advance. Only light refreshments are available on Ramsey Island so you may wish to bring a packed lunch.

- **Telephone** 01437 721721 or 721686; **web** www.rspb.org.uk/grassholm and www.thousandislands.co.uk
- **Trip times** The boat leaves at 9.30am and leaves Ramsey Island at 4pm
- **Costs** Around £54 for adults, £42 for children, but check with the boat company. There is a small discount for RSPB members.
- **Accessibility** Contact the boat company for advice
- **Dogs** Only registered assistance dogs are permitted on Ramsey Island

What to look for

The gannetry on Grassholm is immense, covering a large part of the surface of the island, and you will enjoy stupendous views of the Gannets from the boat. Each pair maintains a tiny circle of territory immediately around its nest, so from a distance the island looks neatly polka-dotted with white. Things become less orderly as the chicks grow, becoming by the end of summer dark-brown replicas of their parents, but rather fatter thanks to lots of fish and very little exercise.

WILDLIFE BY SEASON

SPRING & SUMMER

Gannets and other seabirds can be viewed on the island and on the surrounding sea.

You also have a good chance of seeing Harbour Porpoises and Common Dolphins, with an outside chance of encountering a larger cetacean, perhaps a Minke Whale, Pilot Whale or even a pod of Orcas.

The adult Gannets fish by plunge-diving, and they may do this all around the boat, giving you amazing eye-level views as they slice into the water bill-first with wings drawn in and back to create a streamlined dagger shape that will propel them to deep water. When searching for fish, they can hang effortlessly on the updrafts, an amazing feat for such large and narrow-winged birds.

Grassholm was purchased by the RSPB in 1948, making it the oldest reserve in Wales. Back then there were just 8,000 Gannet pairs on the island, but given that they only first nested here in 1860, that too represents an impressive increase. Now the colony is at about 50 per cent

WHEN TO VISIT
The boat trips run from late May to mid-September.

capacity and is still growing. There is little space for other seabirds, either, although a few pairs of Guillemots, Razorbills and Kittiwakes manage to nest on the parts the Gannets can't reach. The birds are left to their own devices until October, when the warden (who also wardens Ramsey Island) visits with helpers, and they cut free any young Gannets they find that have become tangled in the fishing line that sometimes finds its way into the birds' seaweed nests.

While you're on the boat, look out for other wildlife (the RSPB guide will alert everyone to any interesting sightings). Harbour Porpoises, our smallest cetaceans, are regularly seen as are the attractively marked Common Dolphins, and larger cetaceans are seen now and then. You may also see Puffins swimming on the sea or flying past in tight, fast-flapping groups, and Manx Shearwaters, which breed on other Pembrokeshire islands, are also sometimes seen.

After circumnavigating Grassholm the boat moves on to Ramsey Island for the rest of the day – see page 312 for more on this reserve.

How to get here

Grid ref./postcode SM750249/ SA62 6

The nearest town to the departure point is St Davids. From the town centre (Cross Square) take a slight left onto Goat Street. Take a sharp right onto Pitt Street, then a left onto Feidr Treginnis and follow signs for St Justinians (1.5 miles/2.5 km), where the road ends. Parking is provided at St Justinians. Tickets are collected from the booking office in Cross Square, St David's.

Grassholm is a bustling metropolis of non-stop Gannet action – here you'll witness every detail of their daily lives.

WALES

GWENFFRWD-DINAS

SSSI, NNR, SPA, cSAC

This is a lovely woodland reserve set around a dramatic river valley. Many woodland birds will be singing from spring into early summer, with butterflies in sunny spots. The trail includes boardwalk sections to traverse steep gullys, and the river has its own interesting selection of wildlife.

● Access, facilities, contact details and accessibility

The nature trail is 2 miles long, but the terrain and wildlife interest means you should allow at least an hour and a half to walk it.

- **Telephone** 01654 700 222; **email** gwenffrwd.dinas@rspb.org.uk; **web** www.rspb.org.uk/gwenffrwd-dinas
- **Opening hours** Dinas nature trail is open from dawn to dusk
- **Entry fees** There is no fixed entrance fee. However, a suggested donation for non-members of a £1 parking fee is gratefully received to help maintain the reserve.
- **Accessibility** The trail has some rocky areas and so is not suitable for wheelchairs or pushchairs
- **Dogs** Allowed on public footpaths

What to look for

A typically scenic Welsh woodland reserve, Gwenffrwd-Dinas is a haven for birds and other wildlife, and a joy to anyone who appreciates a dramatic and beautiful landscape.

The river is home to Common Sandpipers in spring and summer, dapper long-bodied waders with the endearing habit of bobbing their back ends on the spot while contemplating their next move. There are also Dippers and Grey Wagtails, and sometimes also Goosanders,

WILDLIFE BY SEASON

SPRING

Migrant songbirds arrive in the woodlands, and Common Sandpipers by the river. Visit in mid-spring to see a good variety of songbirds before the leaf canopy grows in and hides them from view.

SUMMER

Butterflies and moths are on the wing. Dippers are feeding fledged chicks on the river.

AUTUMN

Autumn colours are wonderful, and many fungi species appear.

WINTER

Woodland birds form active flocks, and birds of prey and Ravens are more readily seen overhead.

which nest by upland rivers like this.

The trees are full of birdlife, thanks to a rich ecology that supports large numbers of invertebrates. The annual bounty of caterpillars, flies and other little creatures feeds the chicks of the tits, finches and other songbirds – Redstarts, Pied Flycatchers and Wood Warblers are all here too. The RSPB puts up hundreds of nestboxes here to make up for a shortage of natural tree holes. Pied Flycatchers use the majority of the nest boxes, assorted tit species the remainder.

The summertime is great for insect-watchers. More than 300 species of moths have been recorded here, including some scarce species. Butterflies on the reserve list include Purple Hairstreak and Silver-washed Fritillary.

This part of Wales has long been the stronghold for the UK's native Red Kites and the only place to see them before reintroduction schemes brought them back to England and Scotland. They are still here,

WHEN TO VISIT

Spring and summer are the best times to visit, with early mornings particularly good.

and are easy to see soaring high overhead throughout the year, along with Buzzards and Ravens. If you are having trouble identifying a silhouetted large soaring bird, look at its tail, which will be round-ended if it's a Buzzard, deeply forked for a Red Kite, and wedge-shaped if your mystery bird is a Raven. Winter, generally rather quiet otherwise, is a good time to look for all three, when the open canopy affords a clearer view of the sky.

How to get here

Grid ref./postcode SN 788471/ SA20 0
By road The reserve is 10 miles north of Llandovery on the minor road to Llyn Brianne.
By public transport The nearest station is Llandovery, but from here you'll need to cycle or take a taxi.

Llandovery

Llyn Brianne

P

P

Grassland
Oak wood
Wet alder wood
Crag and rock outcrop
Reserve border
Road
Nature trail
Rugged nature trail
P   Parking

River Tywi

N

WALES

LAKE VYRNWY

SSSI, NNR, SPA, SAC, NATURA 2000

Encircled by woodland with distant mountains beyond, the picturesque Lake Vyrnwy forms the centrepiece to this flagship reserve. Beyond the woodland there is high heathland and damp pasture, completing a diverse array of habitats with a great variety of wildlife. Here you can enjoy a long circular walk or just visit the first hide – however long you spend you're sure to want to return for more. Events held here include walks, art and craft workshops, pond-dipping, bat-watching and much more – this really is a 'hands-on' reserve where everyone can learn about wildlife and enjoy the great outdoors.

● Access, facilities, contact details and accessibility

There are five nature trails on the reserve, ranging from 1–2 miles to a circular walk of 5.5 miles, and three hides. There is a well-stocked shop that sells organic lamb and beef reared on the reserve, as well as the usual wildlife-related goods. Events for all the family are held here, and you can book group visits and guided walks.

● **Telephone** 01691 870278; **email** vyrnwy@rspb.org.uk; **web** www.rspb.org.uk/lakevyrnwy
● **Opening hours** 1 April to 31 October daily, 10.30am–5.30 pm. 1 November to 24 December daily, 10.30am–4.30pm. 1 January to 31 March, 10.30am–dusk.
● **Entry fees** Free
● **Accessibility** The shop and the trail to Coed y Capel hide are accessible for wheelchair users, as is the hide itself. Wheelchair users can also access the Sculpture Trail.
● **Dogs** Allowed, though please keep them under control

WILDLIFE BY SEASON

SPRING

Summer migrants like Redstarts arrive in the woods, joining resident songbirds, while out on the lake Great Crested Grebes perform their courtship dances from the end of February into mid-spring. Common Sandpipers and Goosanders also nest around the edges of the lake.

SUMMER

Golden-ringed Dragonflies and other insects are on the wing, and small birds and their fledglings visit the feeding station.
Falling water levels in the lake may reveal the remains of the flooded village of Llanwddyn.

AUTUMN

Mallards and Teals arrive on the lake, along with a few wading birds and also Little Grebes.
The fungi and autumn colours can be impressive. As the migrant birds feed up prior to departure, winter visitors like Redwings and Fieldfares begin to arrive.

WINTER

There is a small roost of Goosanders on the lake, and Bramblings, Siskins, Redwings and Fieldfares may join the commoner birds using the feeding station and taking natural food in the woodlands.

What to look for

This long, narrow lake was created by damming the River Vyrnwy to create a reservoir of clean water for the city of Liverpool back in 1881. The project was a success, notwithstanding the loss of the village of Llanwddyn. The people of Llanwddyn were given homes in a newly constructed village 2 miles away that bears the same name, but you can still see the remains of the original Llanwddyn when the lake water level drops very low. Sixty-eight miles of aqueduct still carry water from the lake to Liverpool.

There is one hide close to the

Goosanders and Great Crested Grebes through spring and summer. Watch out for courting grebes in early spring. The lake margins provide a suitable home for Common Sandpipers, which return in early spring and are often seen skimming low over the water, giving a volley of shrill, agitated calls.

The oak woodlands have the typical bird species of such upland Welsh woods, with Pied Flycatchers, Wood Warblers and Redstarts the stars. Tawny Owls, Nuthatches and Great Spotted Woodpeckers are here too. The RSPB is expanding the

Insects beware: the handsome Redstart is a skilled hunter of flies and creepy-crawlies alike.

visitor centre at the southern end of the lake, ideal for visitors with mobility difficulties or time constraints. There are two others at the northern end, reachable via the trails although they have their own parking areas too. A convenient minor road runs around the whole perimeter of the lake.

The lake is not overly hospitable to nesting birds but some species that do breed here are partly drawn by the sizeable fish stocks – you could see

area of broadleaved woodland, and managing it for wildlife by leaving plenty of dead wood for insect larvae to feed on and supplying nestboxes for Pied Flycatchers and other hole-nesting birds.

The coniferous woodland is less productive, but does have nesting Siskins, Goldcrests, Coal Tits and perhaps Goshawks. The best time to look for Goshawks is early spring, when the birds are displaying. They are big, broad, long-tailed and

Winter brings more wildfowl to the lake, including Goosanders. The males look their best from winter into early spring.

powerful predators, but beware confusion with large female Sparrowhawks. The key identification marks for a Goshawk seen in flight are a pronounced curve to the trailing edge of the half of the wing nearest the body (the secondaries), a well-protruding head (an odd but useful analogy – Sparrowhawks look like capital Ts, while Goshawks are more cross-shaped), a round-ended tail (Sparrowhawks' tails are squared off) and prominent fluffy white undertail feathers.

The heathy parts of the reserve are grazed by sheep at strategic times to keep down encroaching scrub and maintain a habitat that supports Red Grouse, Ring Ouzels and Curlews.

By mid-summer, young birds join their parents at the feeding station, and dragonflies patrol the lake, including the large and handsome Golden-ringed Dragonfly. You could see Buzzards and Ravens soaring overhead, perhaps also a Peregrine Falcon. Summer is also the time to look out for exposed parts of the ruined village of Llanwddyn, especially after long spells of dry weather.

When autumn arrives, a few extra ducks come to the lake, principally Teals and Mallards, with some Pochards and Tufted Ducks arriving

BIRD-RACING

It just so happens that the minor road that circumnavigates the lake is about 13 miles long – a more perfect setting for a half-marathon race is hard to imagine. If you enjoy wildlife and running, the Lake Vyrnwy Half-marathon is one of several places to combine the two. As it is run on the road, you won't see as much wildlife as you would on the trails, but there's no reason not to come up a day before the race and spend a few hours gently stretching your legs on the trails. You can enter the race online (visit the events section at www.runnersworld.co.uk) – it is held in autumn but fills up quickly. This is also an ideal opportunity to raise some sponsorship money for the RSPB. The Isle of Coll is another place where you can combine an RSPB reserve trip with a race – the Coll Half-marathon is held in August and there are also shorter races and children's events.

later on. A small winter roost of Goosanders also begins to form. By winter proper, there may be flocks of Bramblings, Redwings and Fieldfares visiting the reserve, perhaps at the increasingly busy feeding station. High over the hills, Ravens tumble and soar in their courtship display from mid-winter, ready to start the new breeding season.

WHEN TO VISIT

This reserve has interesting wildlife to see all year round, with the lake, forest and even the sky playing host to different species from season to season. The changing moods of the scenery also make every visit to Lake Vyrnwy a unique experience.

How to get here

Grid ref./postcode SJ 016192/SY10 0
By road From Llanfyllin, take the B4393 to

With its size and striking black-and-yellow colour scheme, the Golden-ringed Dragonfly is hard to miss.

Llanwddyn. Continue along the B4393 to Llanwddyn by taking a right turn. At the dam, turn left, then left at the end of the dam. The RSPB visitor centre is on the right.

By public transport The nearest railway station is Welshpool, more than 20 miles away. Buses stop at the end of the dam, although there is only an infrequent service to this rural location. Walk in the opposite direction to the lake, with the visitor centre on the right.

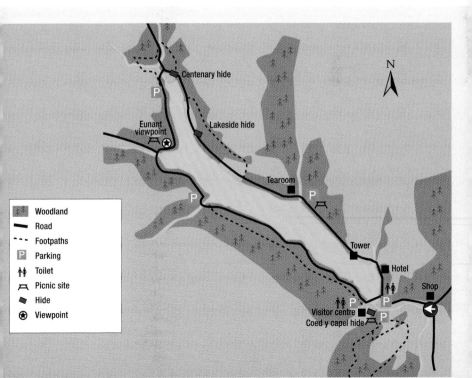

WALES

MAWDDACH WOODLANDS

SSSI, SAC

This reserve actually consists of two separate sites, with very distinct characters. Coed Garth Gell is a mixed broadleaved woodland on the steep slopes above the Afon Mawddach River, full of birdsong in spring, while Arthog Bog, on the other side of the river, is a raised bog with a variety of interesting plants, a good range of breeding birds and a wealth of butterflies and other insects. The views from parts of the reserve have often been described as the 'best in Wales' – quite a claim for such a generally picturesque country, but visit and decide for yourself while walking the trails and enjoying the wildlife of this lovely and unspoilt area.

● Access, facilities, contact details and accessibility

The two sites that comprise this reserve each have a nature trail – the one at Coed Garth Gell is circular, hilly and will take about two hours to walk. The nature trail at the nearby reserve of Arthog bog is shorter.

- **Telephone** 01654 700 222; **email** ynys-hir@rspb.org.uk; **web** www.rspb.org.uk/mawddachwoodlands
- **Opening hours** The reserve is open at all times
- **Entry fees** Free, but donations to help continue the work here are welcome
- **Accessibility** The 750m Arthog Bog trail is short and flat, though somewhat uneven. There are steep stairs in the visitor centre.
- **Dogs** Only allowed on public footpaths and bridleways, and they must be kept on a lead

WILDLIFE BY SEASON

SPRING

Resident woodland birds like tits, woodpeckers and Tawny Owls are joined by migrant visitors including Redstarts, Pied Flycatchers and Wood Warblers.

SUMMER

Still evenings are the time to listen for Nightjars, which begin their churring songs as the sky starts to darken after dusk. The greatest variety of butterflies and other insects can be seen in July – look for Purple Hairstreak butterflies around the oak canopy, and other species visiting flowers in sunny clearings.

AUTUMN

Summer visitors are feeding up prior to beginning their southwards migration. Wintering birds start to arrive. The birch leaves turn brilliant yellow before they fall, while the oaks are more richly coloured. Fungi sprout on dead wood and on the woodland floor.

WINTER

Winter finches and thrushes visit the woodlands. Over the hills you will still see Ravens and Buzzards, the former beginning their courtship displays in mid-winter. Tits forage noisily in the woodlands.

What to look for

The woodlands of Coed Garth Gell are wonderful in spring. If you make an early start you will be rewarded with a superb chorus of birdsong, and the opportunity to see and hear the special birds of the upland wood. This kind of steep oak and birch wood, so typical of this part of Wales, is the place to see Pied Flycatchers, Wood Warblers and Redstarts, three of our most charming songbirds.

Picking out small birds moving in the treetops can be challenging, especially when the leaves start to grow.

wood, males frequently singing and searching for prey at the same time. They glean insects from leaves and branches, but are also pretty mean fly-catchers themselves. Male Redstarts tend to sing from high perches, but they are not especially restless while doing so; with patience and trying different viewpoints you should eventually locate a singing male.

Another bird of the treetops is the Lesser Spotted Woodpecker, which is much smaller and considerably rarer than the more familiar Great Spotted

The Wood Warbler is the largest and most brightly coloured of our three breeding species of 'leaf warblers'.

Knowing something of your target bird's habits can help, though. Pied Flycatchers tend to have favourite perches from which they dart out to catch passing flies. If you glimpse one as it leaves its perch, wait and watch – it is likely to return to the same spot or somewhere nearby. With patience, you can enjoy great views of it doing what it does best, hovering and chasing through the dappled sunlight. Wood Warblers often forage at quite low levels in the

Woodpecker. Your best bet of seeing one is to visit in spring before the leaves come out. These little woodpeckers are as likely to be seen among the twigs as they are on tree trunks, and may excavate their nest holes in relatively small branches.

Arthog Bog in spring and summer is a good place for warblers, with Whitethroat and Sedge and Grasshopper Warblers all present and singing enthusiastically in the scrubby parts, and Redpolls nesting

That bright red backside means this woodpecker is a Great Spotted – Lesser Spotteds are all-white below (and much smaller).

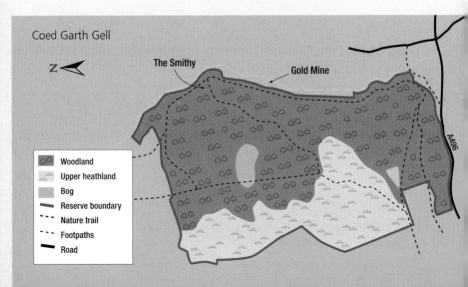

Coed Garth Gell

The Smithy

Gold Mine

Woodland
Upper heathland
Bog
Reserve boundary
Nature trail
Footpaths
Road

in the alders. Vegetation on this raised bog is interesting too – look out for Greater Spearwort, Wavy St John's Wort, Marsh Cinquefoil and Bog Myrtle. The last-named is a fairly unassuming plant, but is very fragrant.

Woodland mammals of the reserve may include Polecats, which were once very rare and confined to Wales, but are staging a gradual recovery. The ancestors of domestic ferrets, Polecats are related to Weasels but are larger, darker and have distinctive black markings, including a rogueish bandit-mask. Like most of our native predatory mammals, they are hard to see. The related Otter is also thriving in the Snowdonia National Park, and is seen in many rivers including the Afon Mawddach. Summer is probably the best time to see these and other mammals.

Summer is also butterfly season. The woodland has a good variety of species, including the Purple Hairstreak, although sadly Arthog Bog's population of Marsh Fritillaries seems to have died out. July is the best month for insects generally, although one local speciality, the Dark Green Fritillary, is on the wing from late June. From late May through to July, listen for Nightjars if you visit in the evening.

Autumn can be a quieter time but the wood looks particularly good at this time of year, with the changing leaf colours and fungi of all shapes and sizes adding further interest to what is already a magical place of luxuriant mosses, lichens and liverworts over every available surface. At this time, the summer migrant birds

are preparing to move on and they, as well as resident species, are feasting on abundant nuts, seeds and berries. Winter visitors from the north are soon here to join in the food-fest, with Redwings and Fieldfares seeking out berries and Siskins and Redpolls flocking in the alders on Arthog Bog. Overhead, Buzzards and Ravens soar, eyes down and scanning for something to eat. Other birds of prey here include Peregrine Falcons. On the river, Dippers continue, as they have done all year, to make a living finding small aquatic creatures on the river bed.

How to get here

Grid ref./postcode SH 695184/LL40 1
By road Take the A496 from Llanelltyd (near Dolgellau) to Barmouth. Between the villages of Taicynhaeaf and Bontddu there are several lay-bys and parking places where the reserve can be accessed via public footpaths.
By public transport Morfa Mawddach station is nearest – Arthog Bog is located half a mile from the station towards the A483. Coed Garth Gell is on the north side of the estuary on the A496 between Bontddu and Llanelltyd.

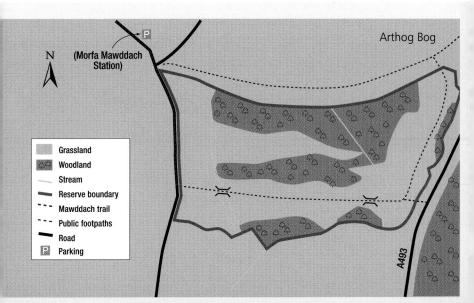

WALES

NEWPORT WETLANDS

NNR, SSSI, SPA, SAC

This popular reserve on the Usk estuary, itself on the north shore of the Severn estuary, is a stone's throw from Newport city but can feel far from civilisation. With saline lagoons and wet grassland as well as reedbeds, this reserve attracts an impressive array of bird species throughout the year, with a less obvious but no less fascinating supporting cast of insects, mammals, reptiles and wetland flowers.

● Access, facilities, contact details and accessibility   P

This reserve has a selection of nature trails of varying lengths, with viewing screens along the way. There is a shop, and group visits and guided walks can be arranged.

- **Telephone** 01633 636363 (or 0845 1306 229 for the Countryside Council for Wales); **web** www.rspb.org.uk/newportwetlands
- **Opening hours** Open every day (apart from Christmas Day), 9am–5pm (coffee shop open 10am–4pm)
- **Entry fees** Free
- **Accessibility** All of the trails are wheelchair-accessible
- **Dogs** There is some access for dogs – marked footpaths on perimeter of reserve. For more information, please contact the CCW (Countryside Council for Wales) enquiry line.

What to look for

This wetland was purposely created as a wildlife haven to compensate for the loss of mudflats at Cardiff Bay. Owned and managed by CCW, it already attracts an impressive tally of breeding birds, including Wales's first Avocet colony.

In the reedbeds, Reed and Sedge Warblers sing while Bearded Tits 'ping' – their strangely metallic tapping call-note often the first sign that

WILDLIFE BY SEASON

SPRING
Reed, Sedge and Cetti's Warblers are loudly sorting out their territorial boundaries. Bearded Tits call in the reedbeds.

SUMMER
A quieter time for birds, but great for insects and flowers. Often the best time to see mammals including the elusive Otter.

AUTUMN
Migrating waders arrive on the estuary, and winter wildfowl start to turn up.

WINTER
With up to 50,000 Starlings roosting in the reedbed, wintering waders and wildfowl and sometimes a Bittern, winter is a great time to visit.

they are nearby. In the scrub there are Cetti's Warblers, dozens of them, the males delivering an explosively loud song from well-chosen hiding places.

The estuary attracts waders on northbound spring migration and southbound autumn migration, with the greater numbers and variety in autumn. A few Aquatic Warblers lurk in the reedbeds each autumn.

Reed Buntings begin to search more widely for food in autumn, perhaps joining Goldfinches and other seed-eaters to raid the scrubland weeds of their seed crops.

Wildfowl soon join wintering waders, including Wigeons, Gadwalls, Pochards and Goldeneyes, with nationally important numbers of Shovelers. A Bittern has spent winter on the reserve in recent years, as has a Marsh Harrier. The resident Water Rails are easier to see at this time, and this is the time to see birds of prey like Hen Harriers, Short-eared Owls and Merlins.

The highlight of a late autumn or early winter visit is the reedbed Starling roost. The

WHEN TO VISIT
Visit in winter, towards dusk, to see the spectacular Starling roost. Otherwise, the reserve is full of interesting wildlife throughout the year.

impression left by the sight of 50,000 birds switchbacking across the dusk sky in high-speed formation, all calling to each other to create waves of sound in time with the swirling formations, is a lasting one.

How to get here

Grid ref./postcode ST 334834/ NP20 5

By road From junction 24 or 28, follow the A48 south of Newport looking out for the brown tourist signs that will lead you to the reserve and visitor centre car park.

By public transport Newport is the nearest rail station. From Newport Bus Station take service 63 to the reserve car park on West Nash Road. For times call Drake Travel on 01495 292 888 or Newport Bus Station on 01633 263 600.

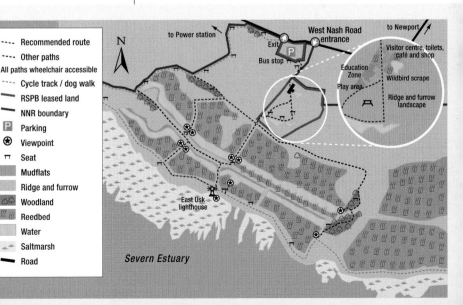

Legend:
- ---- Recommended route
- ---- Other paths
- All paths wheelchair accessible
- ---- Cycle track / dog walk
- ― RSPB leased land
- ― NNR boundary
- P Parking
- ⊕ Viewpoint
- ⊓ Seat
- Mudflats
- Ridge and furrow
- Woodland
- Reedbed
- Water
- Saltmarsh
- ― Road

N

to Power station
West Nash Road entrance
to Newport
Exit
P
Bus stop
Visitor centre, toilets, café and shop
Education Zone
Play area
Wildbird scrape
Ridge and furrow landscape

East Usk lighthouse

Severn Estuary

WALES

RAMSEY ISLAND

SSSI, SPA, SAC, NNR, NP, NATURA 2000

The rugged Ramsey Island, just a mile off the Pembrokeshire coast, belongs in its entirety to the RSPB and is a wildlife paradise, with the two wardens the only human residents. You can visit between April and October – the cliffs are busy with nesting seabirds until mid-summer, while the Grey Seals pup on the beach later on. If you've ever wondered what it's like to visit a truly wild island and share it with nature alone, Ramsey will satisfy your curiosity while leaving you eager to return for more.

● Access, facilities, contact details and accessibility

The trips are run by Thousand Islands Expeditions, and it's wise to book in advance. Only light refreshments are available on Ramsey Island so you may wish to bring a packed lunch. You can also book all-day trips that circumnavigate Grassholm Island in the morning before landing on Ramsey in the afternoons – see page 298 for more details.

- **Telephone** To book trips, call 01437 721 686; **web** www.rspb.org.uk/ramseyisland and www.thousandislands.co.uk
- **Trip times** Boats cross (weather permitting) from the Lifeboat Station at St Justinians at 10am and noon, returning at noon and 4pm
- **Costs** Various trip types are available, with prices starting at around £15 for adult non-members, £11 for adult RSPB members, £7.50 for child non-members and £5.50 for children that are members. There is a £2 landing fee for non-members, waived for RSPB members. Contact the boat company for more details.
- **Accessibility** Contact the boat company for advice
- **Dogs** You may bring your dog on the boat, but only registered assistance dogs may go on the island

WILDLIFE BY SEASON

SPRING
The cliffs start to become busy with seabird nesting activity – Choughs and Peregrine Falcons are also establishing nest sites on the cliffs. Land bird migrants arrive, including Wheatears, and Skylarks and Lapwings cavort above the fields. Cliff-top flowers are blooming.

SUMMER
The seabirds are rearing chicks, and the cliffs are alive with frenetic activity. The heather flowers in late summer.

AUTUMN
Seabirds vacate the cliffs, though the Choughs and Peregrine Falcons hang around through the whole year. Grey Seals give birth to their white-furred pups on the shore. Migrant birds pass through, and rarities are often found.

What to look for

All aboard for Ramsey island, one of Wales's real offshore gems. Whether you've booked a guided trip or will explore independently, you'll enjoy a unique experience on the island. With a maximum of 80 visitors here at any one time, the sense of isolation and of stepping into a corner of the world that truly belongs to nature is quite profound.

Ramsey is famously home to a population of Choughs, the rarest crow species in the UK and probably the least

The first seabirds to begin establishing their nest sites on Ramsey's cliffs are Fulmars, cruising stiff-winged along the cliff-face or cackling to each other from their nesting ledges. Other ledges soon become home to tightly packed ranks of Guillemots and Kittiwakes, the former resembling mini-penguins with their upright stance, sleek dark chocolate-and-white plumage and stubby wings, the latter are dainty, gentle-faced gulls with neat black wingtips, black feet and,

Fulmars greet their partners on the cliffs by loudly cackling to each other like throaty witches.

crow-like. Choughs are black, but this is relieved by striking red bills and feet, and they have unique silhouettes with round and very long-fingered wings, used to good effect to ride the cliff-side updrafts and perform impressive dives and climbs. They nest on the cliffs, bagging the best spots early in the year along with Peregrine Falcons, Kestrels, Jackdaws and Ravens.

A willingness to forage anywhere and everywhere serves Ramsey's Jackdaws in good stead.

interestingly, no hind toes. Razorbills are less social, often choosing tucked-away crannies – therefore there are fewer of them although perhaps they have a less stressful time. A few Manx Shearwaters nest here too, and Gannets often pass by offshore, some probably heading for Grassholm, another RSPB island reserve.

The most discreet of seabirds, the Storm Petrel, nests on other Pembrokeshire islands but only recently have there been signs

Guillemots are not the most agile fliers but somehow manage in their dense colonies without too many collisions.

of nesting on Ramsey – the island was rendered inhospitable to these little birds when rats were introduced to the island two centuries ago. An ambitious RSPB plan to eradicate the rats was completed in 2000, and since then there has been improved breeding success for the burrow- and ground-nesting birds. Even more excitingly, in 2008 five occupied Storm Petrel burrows were found. Because they only come ashore at night, you are only likely to see petrels going by at sea.

While the seabirds are getting themselves organised on the cliffs, land birds are also establishing territories. Skylarks and Lapwings

WHEN TO VISIT
Visit in spring and summer to see seabird breeding activity, and in autumn to see the Grey Seals pupping.

both advertise themselves with highly noticeable vocal and aerial displays, though the nests themselves are well hidden on the ground. A Skylark usually drops to the ground some metres from its nest, sneaking through the grass to the actual site to avoid giving away the location to any watching predators. Wheatears are everywhere on the tops, nesting among boulders and in stone walls.

In summertime the seabirds' lives become a constant cycle of heading out to sea, fishing and bringing the catch home to the chicks. Up on the cliffs, coastal flowers bloom, culminating in the flowering of the heather that carpets large parts of the island. This provides a splendid purple backdrop for the island's Red Deer as they approach peak condition in time for the autumn rut.

Although all the nesting seabirds have left their nests by the end of August, autumn can still be an exciting time to visit. You will still

RATTED OUT

Nesting halfway down a sheer cliffside is a good way to avoid losing your eggs or chicks to predatory mammals. This, however, still leaves the birds vulnerable to attack by predatory birds like large gulls. Larger seabirds can do a reasonable job of seeing off these marauders much of the time, but smaller species like Storm Petrels and Manx Shearwaters cannot, which is why they nest in burrows and pursue a nocturnal lifestyle. It's also why these species favour islands, because their adaptations to avoid predatory birds leave them vulnerable to attack from predatory mammals, and most small islands are historically more or less mammal-free. Unfortunately, humans have a habit of bringing rats with them when they land their ships on islands – not on purpose of course but that makes no difference. Rats have had a devastating impact on island shearwater and petrel colonies throughout the world, and eradicating them from such islands is the only effective solution. It has certainly worked on Ramsay, with 'Manxies' thriving and 'Stormies' returning within 10 years after the 200-year rat reign was put to an end.

see the Choughs and the falcons, and there is a good chance of a 'fall' of migrating land birds if the wind blows the right way. Extreme rarities from all points of the globe could show up too – Ramsey's tally includes Britain's first ever Indigo Bunting, which should have been in North America.

A different kind of autumn highlight is the pupping of the Grey Seals. Females haul out on the beaches to give birth to their pups while the burly adult males patrol the shallow waters – you can watch seal family life from various safe vantage points. Ramsey has more breeding Grey Seals than anywhere else in southern Britain and is a wonderful place to watch them.

How to get here

Grid ref./postcode SM 706237/SA62 6
The nearest town to the departure point is St Davids. From the town centre (Cross Square) take a slight left onto Goat Street. Take a sharp right onto Pitt Street, then a left onto Feidr Treginnis and follow signs for St Justinians (1.5 miles/2.5 km), where the road ends. Parking is provided at St Justinians. Pre-booked tickets are collected from the booking office in Cross Square, St. David's.

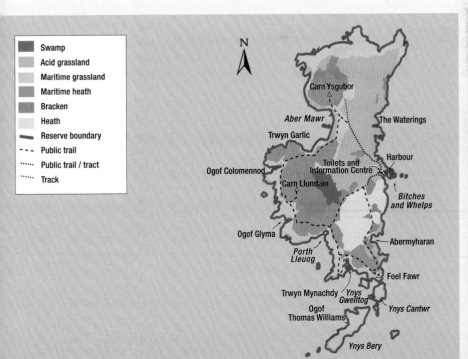

- ■ Swamp
- ░ Acid grassland
- ▒ Maritime grassland
- ▓ Maritime heath
- ▒ Bracken
- ░ Heath
- ▬▬ Reserve boundary
- - - - Public trail
- ······ Public trail / tract
- ······ Track

N

Carn Ysgubor
Aber Mawr   The Waterings
Trwyn Garlic
Harbour
Ogof Colomennod   Toilets and
                       Information Centre
              Carn Llundain
                                    Bitches
                                    and Whelps
Ogof Glyma
                              Abermyharan
    Porth
    Lleuog
                              Foel Fawr
Trwyn Mynachdy Ynys
              Gwelltog
       Ogof   Ynys Cantwr
Thomas Williams
                    Ynys Bery

WALES

SOUTH STACK

SSSI, SPA, SAC, AONB, NATURA 2000

On the west coast of Anglesey, from high on the cliff-tops you can see a white lighthouse standing on a rocky promontory off to the north, and in front of you the sea beats away at the bases of the towering cliffs. Here is South Stack, a stunning setting for a busy colony of seabirds and a rich cliff-top flora and fauna. Viewpoints within and in front of Ellins Tower, the RSPB centre, give you great views of the cliffside birds, while a network of footpaths enable you to explore the cliff-tops and see the special wildlife that inhabits the heathland.

● Access, facilities, contact details and accessibility

From the Ellins Tower visitor centre (open Easter to September) you can enjoy great views of the cliffside colonies – binoculars and telescopes are provided. There is also live CCTV. You can buy a meal or light refreshments at the nearby South Stack Kitchen café (not RSPB). There are no RSPB trails but there is a network of public footpaths around the cliff-top heathland.

- ● **Telephone** 01407 764973; **email** south.stack@rspb.org.uk; **web** www.rspb.org.uk/southstackcliffs
- ● **Opening hours** The reserve is open year round; Ellins Tower, the RSPB visitor centre, is open from Easter to September.
- ● **Entry fees** Free
- ● **Accessibility** Many paths are steep and rocky, and the visitor centre is accessed by steps with handrails. The most accessible path for people of impaired mobility runs from the RSPB car park into the heathland and onto a viewpoint in front of Ellins Tower. The track is well-surfaced and high quality (2m wide) with benches and leads from three marked disabled car-parking bays in the RSPB car park.
- ● **Dogs** Some access for dogs; please contact the reserve office for more information.

WILDLIFE BY SEASON

SPRING

Another breeding season gets underway on the cliffs, with seabirds establishing territories and nest-building. Stonechats, Linnets and Skylarks sing on the heath, which has patches of colourful Spring Squill.

SUMMER

Breeding activity peaks on the cliffs – the auk chicks leave the nests in mid-July and the other species are not far behind. Silver-studded Blue butterflies emerge on the heath from late June, while Adders and Common Lizards can be seen on warm days throughout spring and summer, often quietly basking in favourite sheltered spots.

AUTUMN

The heather blooms at the end of summer, and family parties of Choughs roam the cliff-tops, the youngsters noisily harassing their parents for food. Seabirds, Harbour Porpoises and dolphins go by offshore.

WINTER

The quietest time, though a good season to watch Choughs feeding on the RSPB-managed farmland. Ravens are first to kick off the new breeding season, beginning their courtship in midwinter.

What to look for

This wonderful reserve holds a large mixed colony of Guillemots, Razorbills, Puffins and Fulmars. Fulmars are first back, often arriving during February and most of the others are in place and busily preparing to nest by mid-April. From Ellins Tower you can watch them on CCTV through summer as they nest-build, lay and incubate eggs, feed their chicks and then head back to the open sea for the winter – the whole process is swift on or just below the surface (their long, curved bills are good for probing the soil), so regular grazing is required to keep the turf low and provide the dung that attracts the invertebrates that feed the Choughs!

Ravens also nest on the cliffs, mastering the updrafts just as the Choughs do, and involving themselves in frequent aerial tussles with the Peregrine Falcons that also nest here. It is always interesting to watch Peregrine Falcons and Ravens

Male Silver-studded Blues emerge from their chrysalids before the brown-winged females, and often bask together in large numbers.

and frantic and at its peak the activity is exhilarating.

Seabirds are just part of the story here. This is a great place to see Choughs, which although on the increase are still scarce birds, especially on the mainland. The RSPB manages a farm here at South Stack with Choughs in mind, providing suitable feeding conditions in the grassy fields throughout the year. Choughs require short vegetation in which to forage, finding their invertebrate prey interacting – both species are incredibly agile flyers, and often indulge in vigorous dogfights. Both species are hunters in their way, but Ravens are too large to be an easy prey option for Peregrine Falcons, and the falcons are far too quick and strong for Ravens to risk attacking. The two species seem to treat one another as annoyances at worst, playmates at best. Despite the skirmishes, they are far more tolerant of each other than either are of

Choughs do most of their feeding on the ground – their curved bills are ideal for probing soft earth for worms as well as snapping up speedier invertebrate prey.

other predatory species and often nest close together.

In spring and summer, enjoy a walk along the cliff-top and admire the impressive heath flower community, with stands of Spring Squill, Thrift, Heath Spotted Orchids and Gorse supplying the main colour scheme. There are rarities here too, including the pretty yellow Spotted Rock Rose, and a unique maritime variant of Fleawort. Butterflies roam the cliffs – Graylings in spring and again in late summer, and Silver-studded Blues in July. The latter appear just before the heather flowers and can be incredibly numerous. The shining-blue males are first out of their

WHEN TO VISIT

The seabird colony is active through spring and summer, and this is also the time to see the heath at its best. You can see Choughs here throughout the year.

chrysalises and are soon flying about in search of females, which they can detect by pheromones even before the females have emerged. Therefore, each female Silver-studded Blue is effectively being 'cheered on' by a crowd of eager males the moment she starts to break out of her chrysalis, and will find herself copulating with one of them before she has even taken her first flight.

Another heathland denizen is the Adder, arguably our handsomest snake with its bold zigzag pattern. Adders mate in early spring after a rarely seen, exquisite dancing display, but through the summer you could encounter them anywhere on the heath, usually basking in a secluded patch of bare ground. The presence of Adders is one good reason to keep to the footpaths – nesting land birds like Skylarks is another, and helping to prevent erosion is a third.

Seabirds are still very much part of the offshore scene in autumn, although the cliffs are now all but deserted. Look out for passing Manx

Shearwaters, long-winged birds that flash black then white as they tilt and turn on stiff wings, showing upperside and underside in turn and skimming the water with their wing-tips. On calm days, look out for Harbour Porpoises and dolphins.

Parent Choughs have their youngsters in tow through autumn, the babies begging to be fed for as long as they can get away with it. By winter, the groups have broken up, with the youngsters of the year teaming up with older sub-adults and roaming the fields and cliffs in these gatherings throughout winter. The farm is one of the best places to look for them. The cliffs and heaths are quiet at this time of year, but you'll still see Ravens and Peregrine Falcons holding their flying contests along the cliff edge. The Fulmars return in February and the whole cycle begins all over again.

How to get here

Grid ref./postcode SH 211818/LL65 1
By road Take South Stack Road out of Holyhead, following the brown tourist signs.
By public transport For access by bus, proceed to Summer Hill in Holyhead and catch the 22 bus which runs from April to October.

A more dapper and distinguished creature than the commoner auks, the Black Guillemot is one of South Stack's really special breeding birds.

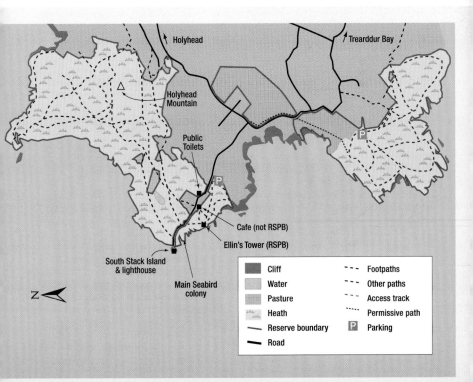

Holyhead

Trearddur Bay

Holyhead Mountain

Public Toilets

P

P

Cafe (not RSPB)

Ellin's Tower (RSPB)

South Stack Island & lighthouse

Main Seabird colony

Z

Cliff		Footpaths
Water		Other paths
Pasture		Access track
Heath		Permissive path
Reserve boundary	P	Parking
Road		

WALES

VALLEY WETLANDS SSSI, SAC

One of Anglesey's finest wetlands, this reserve is home to a good variety of birds and some interesting plants and insects, as well as Otters and Water Voles. Warblers sing through the summer and flocks of ducks visit in winter. The visitor route gives you views across the lakes and marshes.

● Access, facilities, contact details and accessibility

There is a public visitor route which goes around the reserve.
- **Telephone** 01248 421 100; **web** www.rspb.org.uk/valleywetlands
- **Opening hours** Open at all times
- **Entry fees** Free, but donations to help continue the work here are welcome
- **Accessibility** Not suitable for wheelchairs
- **Dogs** Allowed on footpaths

What to look for

This reserve consists of reedbeds and wet grassland around shallow lakes – perfect conditions for many species of birds. Springtime brings many Reed and Sedge Warblers to the reedbeds – look out for the latter species performing its sprightly song flight.

Where reeds grade into scrub, there are Cetti's Warblers, shy but pretty birds in their understated way with chestnut upperparts,

broad flicky tails and white throats.

Shovelers, Gadwalls, Pochards and Little Grebes all nest around the lake, and in summer there will be parties of ducklings being led by their mothers to the best feeding grounds, where they dabble and dive for food by themselves. Little Grebes fetch food for their chicks until the little ones are quite well-grown, the chicks making loud and piteous begging calls to make sure

WILDLIFE BY SEASON

SPRING

Sedge and Reed Warblers join the resident Cetti's Warblers. Several duck species nest, including Shovelers, Pochards and Gadwalls.

SUMMER

Wetland plants flower, and several species of dragonflies and damselflies are on the wing.

AUTUMN

Wildfowl numbers start to increase. This is the likeliest time of year to find a rarity, perhaps a vagrant American duck or wader.

WINTER

Wildfowl numbers peak, and unusual visitors could include Bittern. Freezing conditions force Water Rails into the open.

their parents aren't slacking off.

The smartly patterned Hairy Dragonfly is one of the earliest species to appear, often on the wing in May. Several other species occur here too, including Variable Damselfly. Flowering Rush is one of the many attractive wetland plants to look out for in summer, and listen for the songs of Grasshopper Warblers and Reed Buntings. Otters are present, but seldom seen.

Other ducks start to arrive through autumn, to spend winter enjoying the hospitable conditions of the lake. They include Wigeons and Golden-eyes, the former dabbling in the shallows, the latter diving in the deeper water. Every so often a rarity, perhaps a Green-winged Teal or a Ring-necked Duck from North America, is found, though an occasional wandering Scaup or Long-tailed Duck is far more likely. The coldest weather is the best time to look for Water Rails, while winter may also bring a Bittern. Freezing weather is best for Marsh Harriers and brings huge concentrations of ducks to remaining open water.

WHEN TO VISIT

There is interesting wildlife on the wetlands throughout the year, and time of day is not important.

How to get here

Grid ref./postcode SH313765/ LL65 3

By road Travelling west along the A55 dual carriageway from Bangor, come off at the junction between Bryngwran and Caergeiliog (signposted Bodedern and Caergeiliog) and turn left at the roundabout, following MOD signs for RAF Valley. Continue through a small village; the road will drop down a small hill and you will see a lake on the right-hand side. Carry on alongside the lake and reedbeds; the road will kink to the right and just as you are past the lake the entrance to the reserve car park is on the right-hand side next to a white gate with an RSPB logo.
By public transport The nearest railway station is Rhosneigr, 5 miles away. Bus services 4, 23 and 44 (Sundays only) run from Rhosneigr train station to Valley Wetlands (RAF Valley).

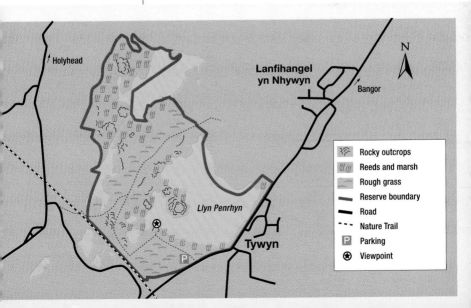

WALES

YNYS-HIR

SSSI, SPA, SAC, NNR, RAMSAR, NATURA 2000

On the south shore of the Dovey/Dyfi estuary, Ynys-hir has stretches of hilly oak woodland, complete with the rich flora and special birdlife of such habitats, while on lower ground there are damp pastures, saltmarsh and estuarine mudflats, attracting breeding waders in spring and a host of wintering water birds from autumn and into winter. With lengthy trails and seven hides that between them look over all of the reserve's many habitats, this is a great place for a day's wildlife-watching at any time of year. The RSPB shop sells refreshments in case you need to refuel.

● Access, facilities, contact details and accessibility

There are seven hides, two viewpoints and a feeding station outside the visitor centre. The two main circular routes are 1.5 miles and 3 miles. Wildlife-related goods are available from the shop, and you can also buy drinks and snacks. You can hire binoculars if required, and also book a guided walk with RSPB staff to gain more insight into the reserve and its wildlife. Group bookings are accepted.

● **Telephone** 01654 700 222; **email** ynys-hir@rspb.org.uk; **web** www.rspb.org.uk/ynys-hir

● **Opening hours** The reserve is open from 9am–9pm, or dusk if earlier. The visitor centre is open daily 9am–5pm from April to October and 10am–4pm from November to March (closed Mondays and Tuesdays).

● **Entry fees** Free for RSPB members. For non-members the cost is £3 for adults, £1 for children and concessions, and £6 for a family ticket.

● **Accessibility** Ynys-hir reserve is a rugged reserve unsuitable for wheelchairs. Access to the visitor centre and toilets is via steps or a steep slope.

● **Dogs** Not allowed, except registered assistance dogs

WILDLIFE BY SEASON

SPRING

The woodlands are full of birdsong and carpeted with spring flowers that attract early butterflies.

Special woodland birds here include Pied Flycatcher, Redstart and Wood Warbler, while the butterflies you may see in spring include Orange-tips and Brimstones. Migrant and breeding waders can be seen on the estuary and saltmarsh.

SUMMER

Waders on return migration arrive from mid-summer. Red Kites and Peregrine Falcons fly over the woodland. The best season for dragonflies and butterflies. The nesting waders in the meadows and ducks in the lagoons now have small chicks.

AUTUMN

Wildfowl arrive on the saltmarshes, including Wigeons, Teals, Shovelers. Goosanders and Greenland White-fronted and Barnacle Geese. This is also a good time of year to see waders and birds of prey.

WINTER

Wintering birds crowd onto the saltmarsh. Birds of prey around the reserve could include Merlins, Peregrine Falcons and Hen Harriers. The feeding station is at its busiest.

What to look for

Understandably popular, Ynys-hir is one of the key RSPB reserves in Wales, where visitors can enjoy a tremendous variety of wildlife and wonderful scenery throughout the year. The trails take you through woodland, past lagoons and down to the estuary.

In spring, the woodland is as full of life as any in the Welsh hills, with Wood Warblers searching for prey and singing their sweet 'spinning coin' song from the lower branches, Pied are preparing to nest. Lapwings, Redshanks, Mallards, Teals and Shovelers all breed here, the waders using the grassy fields and the ducks usually nesting by the water's edge. Reed and Sedge Warblers are here too, as are a few Grasshopper Warblers in the drier areas.

Later on in summer, migrating waders visit the estuary and the lagoons, some remaining through the whole winter. Dunlins form busy feeding flocks, scuttling on the mudflats among groups

Though not as distinctive as the male, her black-and-white wing pattern helps identify this female Pied Flycatcher.

Flycatchers making insect-catching forays through the shafts of sunlight, and Redstarts singing from the higher branches. Woodland flowers grow in profusion and Red Kites are regularly seen overhead, their distinctive fork-tailed silhouette representative of all that's wild and Welsh. A heronry uses the trees, and the woodland hide overlooks it – there are now Little Egrets nesting as well.

Out on the meadows and lagoons, waders and wildfowl of the larger, squatter Knots. Shape, size and character are far more useful clues to telling these species apart than plumage once their distinctive summer colours have been replaced with drab winter greys, but you could still see individuals wearing most of their summer feathers. The juveniles, which arrive soon after the adults, are also problematic to identify. The Knots stay only briefly, as do the Little Stints and Green Sandpipers that visit the pools.

The Small Red Damselfly is a dainty insect, often to be found resting on waterside vegetation.

Butterflies in the woods in summer include an impressive five species of fritillaries, and Graylings and Green Hairstreaks fly over the more open areas – the latter in spring only, the former with two generations a year, in spring and in late summer. Woodland mammals are very elusive but both Dormice and Polecats are present. Hares on the fields are, by contrast, not difficult to see.

Ringed Plovers and Turnstones are distinctive and easily recognised throughout the year, but the two godwit species can be difficult. In flight there is no question, because Black-tailed shows a broad white wingbar and Bar-tailed has plain brown wings, but with settled birds concentrate on leg and neck length (Black-tailed is longer), bill length and shape (Bar-tailed is usually longer, with a slight upward lift) and general pattern (Bar-tailed looks streakier in winter plumage, Black-tailed plainer). Also, Bar-tailed Godwits prefer the mudflats, while Black-taileds are more likely to be on the lagoons.

Late summer is a good time for birds of prey, with as many as eight species being seen in a day. Ospreys often visit in late summer, fishing on the river. Sometimes two or more will linger in the area for several days – for Ospreys migration down through the UK and southern Europe is a leisurely affair with stop-offs at many a good fishing ground, though they can certainly put on a turn of speed when crossing the fish-less Sahara a few weeks later.

As the weather cools and the days shorten, wildfowl begin to move onto the reserve. Wigeons are among the most numerous, the males announcing their arrival with their unmistakable 'wheeoo' whistle. As at home on land as in the water, they feed on the wet grassland, together with Teals. Geese also come to Ynys-hir – several hundred Barnacle Geese and a small flock of the Greenland subspecies of White-fronts which grows to around 60 birds by mid-winter.

WHEN TO VISIT

The wide variety of habitats at Ynys-hir means there is always a wealth of wildlife around, with the woodland at its best in spring and the estuary teeming with feeding birds through autumn into winter. Visit early in the day for spring birdsong, and shortly before high tide to see waders roosting on the fields in autumn, otherwise time of day is not crucial.

Big tides push waders off the beach and onto the fields, where you can see them from the Breakwater hide. By winter the flocks are mainly composed of Redshanks, Curlews and Lapwings, with a few godwits and the odd Spotted Redshank or Greenshank that has opted not to migrate any further. The bounty of birdlife attracts predators – Hen Harriers and Peregrine Falcons are seen daily, and Merlins hunt for the Meadow Pipits and other small songbirds that forage on the marsh. Marsh Harriers also visit on occasion, while Kestrels and Sparrowhawks are always present.

The woodland is quieter at this time of year, with some of the more interesting birds gone for the winter, but it is still worth a look for finches (including Siskin and Bullfinch) and flocks of tits which may be joined by Treecreepers or Nuthatches, and perhaps a Lesser Spotted Woodpecker.

With a lot of luck, you could see a Polecat in the oak woodlands – visit early or late in the day for the best chance.

How to get here

Grid ref./postcode SN 682961/SY20 8
By road The reserve is situated between Machynlleth and Aberystwyth. Turn off the A487 in the vilage of Eglwys-fach and proceed for 1 mile to the car park.

By public transport The nearest train station is Machynlleth. Proceed by bus or taxi to the reserve from there; there is a regular bus service between Machynlleth and Aberystwyth that stops in Eglwys-fach. If you are coming by bike, it is possible to get a train to Dyfi junction and cycle the 3 miles to the reserve.

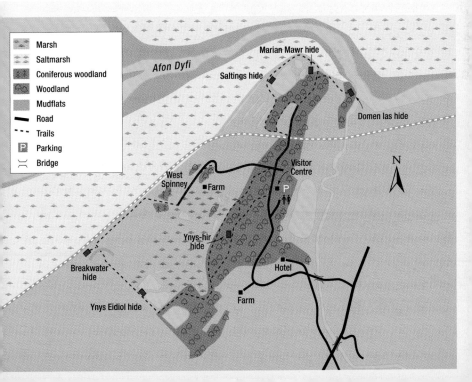

Marsh
Saltmarsh
Coniferous woodland
Woodland
Mudflats
Road
Trails
P Parking
Bridge

Afon Dyfi

Marian Mawr hide
Saltings hide
Domen las hide

West Spinney
Farm
Visitor Centre
P

Ynys-hir hide

Breakwater hide

Ynys Eidiol hide

Hotel

Farm

N

A DATE WITH NATURE

White-tailed Eagle

EAGLES

All birds of prey are impressive in their own ways, but for sheer jaw-dropping power and scale, you can't beat an eagle. The UK has two species, the Golden and the White-tailed, and both are seldom seen outside Scotland, particularly favouring the rugged islands of the west coast.

White-tailed Eagles became extinct in the UK in 1916, due to habitat loss and that old favourite, persecution. The RSPB began working with other conservation partners on a reintroduction scheme in the late 1970s, releasing young Norwegian-bred birds on the isle of Rhum. Eagles are slow to mature and choosy about mates and territories, but in 1983 breeding was finally confirmed. More young eagles were brought in over the next 15 years, to help the original birds along, and today there are White-tailed Eagles breeding on several of the Inner Hebrides and wandering more widely in western Scotland – more than 30 pairs altogether.

Soar points

Golden Eagles share some islands with the White-tails, but are also found across upland areas on mainland Scotland. They too have been much persecuted, often on the fallacious basis that they are voracious lamb-killers (in truth, they take only the occasional weak individual, though they will feed on lambs that have died of other causes). In some parts of their range, they are still subjected to persecution, with a shocking 85 cases of poisoning and shooting between 1980 and 2007.

The RSPB believes that stamping out ignorance about their way of life is as important as finding and bringing to justice those individuals who seek to harm them. Like White-tailed Eagles, Golden Eagles are slow to reproduce, and the loss of any one bird is seriously bad news for the whole population.

You can see eagles at several Scottish RSPB reserves, including the only English Golden Eagle at Haweswater, but your best bet is probably one of the 'Date with Nature' events that concentrate on these species.

WILDLIFE BY SEASON

Visiting an eagle
Date with Nature

One of the sites has CCTV footage from a White-tailed Eagle's nest and two give you the chance to see the adults at the nest from a watchpoint.

Golden Eagles are also present at two of the sites – take a guided walk with the RSPB experts to stand a good chance of seeing them.

SPRING

Courtship and nesting activity is taking place. Courting pairs may perform spectacular aerial displays above their breeding grounds. You may see birds renovating their nests and perhaps even laying eggs.

SUMMER

Chicks require constant care and food, so the parents are kept very busy. You can see all the action on the nest at the sites with CCTV.

AUTUMN

Young birds fledge and there are suddenly twice as many eagles on the wing. Youngsters of both species are easily told from their parents – young White-tails are dark-headed, while young Goldens have white wing-flashes and tail bands.

Golden Eagles tough it out in the mountains in weather conditions that send many other birds fleeing to the lowlands. Luckily, it's easy to see them in summer as well.

● Where to see them

Aros White-tailed Eagles, on Skye, is open from mid-March to the end of September, giving you camera views into a White-tailed Eagle's nest from the Aros Centre, just south of Portree on the A87. Staff will be able to advise you on seeing eagles (both species) elsewhere on the island.

Mull Eagle Watch has a hide giving views across to a White-tailed Eagle's nest. It is open August to early September, Fridays to Tuesdays. You can also see Golden Eagles on Mull. Signs will direct you from the A848 Tobermory to Salen road.

Go Wild on Arran and see both eagle species and much more besides, from mid-March to the end of July. Borrow RSPB binoculars and take a guided walk around the best spots. Local buses run to the event from the arrival of the Ardrossan ferry.

To find out more about Date with Nature events, visit www.rspb.org.uk/datewithnature.

OSPREYS

Few birds' recent histories in the UK have been so closely linked to the RSPB as the Osprey's. The nesting site at Loch Garten has attracted tremendous media attention over the years, initially as the first publicised place the species bred in the UK after a 42-year absence, and more recently when the nesting birds went through relationship dramas worthy of a soap opera. In 2008 the RSPB brought the magic of Ospreys to even more people by installing a live webcam aimed at the nest and satellite-tracking the 2008 chicks on their first migration.

This superb bird of prey is unique in the avian world in many respects. For a start, it has no close relatives and is the only species in its family. It isn't the only raptor to feed on fish, but it does so virtually exclusively while the other fish-catchers regularly take other prey. It is also unique-looking, with its long-winged, long-legged and rangy look, nearly white underparts, shaggy crest and staring yellow eyes set in a dark face-mask.

Gone fishing

Since the first birds nested in the Highlands, Ospreys have slowly but steadily recolonised Scotland and are now breeding in a few places in England and one site in Wales. They are also increasingly seen on migration at lakes, rivers and harbours up and down the UK, often staying for days at favourite fishing spots when travelling south in autumn. At this time of year, you could now see an Osprey almost anywhere, and every sighting is magical.

It is sad to reflect that in this day and age

there are still a few egg-collectors operating, determined to steal wild birds' eggs despite the stiff penalties involved and the undeniable fact that such activities are incredibly harmful. Therefore conservationists watch all known Osprey nests for intruders – but this also means in some cases that publicising the nest site is the safest thing to do, which allows the public at large to watch the action at the nest too.

Loch Garten is still the first place that springs to mind for many of us when Ospreys are

WILDLIFE BY SEASON

SPRING

Ospreys arrive back at their nests from March. Pairs are separated over winter, so on return there may be spectacular battles over mates and nest sites, with unmated challengers of both sexes trying their luck at usurping a nest site from its rightful owner.

SUMMER

The chicks hatch and the male must fish all day long to provide for them and his mate. From lake shores you can see the male fishing, and you can watch the trials and tribulations of family life at the nest via the CCTV camera.

AUTUMN

The adult Ospreys continue to feed the chicks for a few weeks after fledging, while the young birds must quickly learn the art of fishing before the parents head off on migration. The youngsters follow soon after.

mentioned. However, with more pairs now nesting in the UK now there are alternatives, and some of the best places to watch them are at Osprey-specific RSPB 'Date with nature' sites.

Visiting an Osprey Date with Nature

Besides the famous Loch Garten nest in the Abernethy Forest RSPB reserve (see page 276), the three Osprey sites at the time of writing are in Wales, Scotland and the Lake District. They give you the chance to spy on the nest via CCTV, as well as watch the adult birds fishing in 'real life'. Telescopes and binoculars are available, and you can find out more about the birds from the friendly and knowledgeable staff and volunteers.

A mother Osprey joins her two well-grown chicks at the nest. In just a few weeks these gawky babies will be beginning their first epic flight to Africa.

● Where to see them

Lake District Osprey Project runs from April to the end of August, and is situated in Dodd Wood. There is a free viewpoint and CCTV camera. Dodd Wood is about three miles north of Keswick on the A591.

Glaslyn Osprey Project is your chance to see what is so far the only pair of Ospreys nesting in Wales. There is a hide and also a nest-cam. It is open from late March to early September, and is on the B4410 at Pont Croesor.

The Aberfoyle live bird of prey viewing project is open from April to September, and offers you the chance to view not only nesting Ospreys but also Buzzards, Ravens and Peregrines on camera, and see them 'in the flesh' as well. The project is signposted from the outskirts of Aberfoyle.

To find out more about Date with Nature events, visit www.rspb.org.uk/datewithnature.

PEREGRINE FALCONS

The Peregrine Falcon is one of the most famous and iconic birds in the world – a beautifully engineered fighter jet of a falcon that dives on its prey at speeds unmatched by any other flying creature. We are very lucky to have a healthy population of Peregrines across the UK. However, it wasn't always so, and even today we can't afford to take the current good fortunes of the Peregrine for granted.

Like all predators, Peregrines inspire awe from many of us, but also anger and resentment from those who believe their livelihoods or pastimes are threatened by them. Gamekeepers traditionally shot or poisoned anything with a hooked bill and talons that dared encroach on their land. This kept Peregrine numbers down in large parts of the countryside.

Mixed fortunes

The two world wars helped the Peregrine's fortunes, as gamekeepers (along with everyone else) were called up for service and many country estates went unkeepered. However, the 1950s brought a new and more devastating threat to the recovering population. The introduction of organochlorine pesticides like DDT, which build up through the food chain to kill or render infertile the top-level predators, crippled populations of Peregrine Falcons and other birds of prey. For several decades until the chemicals were outlawed, Peregrines were real rarities, reaching an all-time low of fewer than 400 pairs, most of them in remote northern Scotland.

No more DDT and the threat of severe punishment for those who illegally kill Peregrines or disturb them at their nests (thanks to the Wildlife and Countryside Act of 1981) has enabled the UK's population of this magnificent bird of prey to recover to more than 1,400 pairs today. However, some gamekeepers still do illegally kill birds of prey. Another potential danger comes from the UK's many pigeon-fanciers – some groups have lobbied government for the right to 'control' Peregrine numbers, as Peregrines sometimes kill free-flying domestic pigeons. A third threat is the illegal removal of Peregrine eggs or chicks from the nest by

WILDLIFE BY SEASON

SPRING

Eggs are usually laid in early April and take about a month to hatch. During incubation you may see the male bringing food for his mate or perhaps the pair swapping shifts. When the chicks hatch, the male will be busy providing food for the family.

SUMMER

Throughout summer the adults will be run ragged hunting for their chicks. As the chicks get older the parents will leave them on their own for longer and both parents will bring back prey for the growing family. You may see the chicks being fed and, towards July, them making their first flights.

AUTUMN

The young Peregrines remain around the nest site into early autumn, being brought food by their parents as they practise and develop their flying and hunting skills until they are ready to fend for themselves and find new territories of their own.

WINTER

The adult Peregrines will be around, although they may make long hunting trips so allow extra time to see them. You might see courtship and nest-building behaviour in late winter.

falconers wanting to keep a Peregrine but lacking the means or morals to buy a legal, captive-bred bird.

Only a resilient and adaptable species could cope with all these assaults upon its population, and one of the most striking adaptations the Peregrine has shown is its willingness to adopt an urban lifestyle. Tall buildings are not so unlike sea cliffs and upland crags, and with a healthy population of street pigeons to eat, Peregrines have found a real home from home high above our city streets – these urban birds are, ironically, much safer from human persecution than their country cousins.

The RSPB is working hard to protect all birds of prey from the few individuals who think they are above the law – by investigating crimes, keeping watch over vulnerable nests, and raising public awareness of the situation. One way they achieve this last goal is by making it easy for ordinary people to see and enjoy the magnificent sight of Peregrines living wild and free in town and country alike, at a number of watchpoints on long-established nest sites up and down the UK.

Visiting a Peregrine Date with Nature

The many RSPB 'Date with Nature' Peregrine watchpoints are staffed by volunteers armed with telescopes, who are there to show you the birds themselves and also to tell you anything you may want to know about Peregrines in general. If you happen to be visiting a city with a Peregrine watchpoint why not come along and take a look at some of the city's most dashing newcomers? The best time to visit is in spring or summer when there will hopefully be a nest on the go, but you may also see the adult birds outside the nesting season.

● Where to see them

Peregrines at Malham has a viewpoint onto a nest on the limestone cliff at Malham Cove in the Yorkshire Dales National Park.

Manchester Peregrines can be seen on the BBC Big Screen, from their nest in Manchester's Exchange Square.

Peregrines at Lincoln Cathedral are on view from the grounds of the city's magnificent cathedral.

Birmingham Peregrines can be seen from the city watchpoint.

Worcester Peregrines are birds of taste, nesting on the spire of the handsome St Andrew's Church.

Symonds Yat Peregrine viewing offers a wilder Peregrine experience at this spectacular viewpoint, 400 feet above the River Wye.

Peregrines on the Clock Tower in Cardiff is a capital experience for seeing Welsh Peregrines.

Chichester Cathedral Peregrines are another pair appreciating great architecture – the viewpoint is in the centre of this Sussex city.

London Peregrines at the Tate can be seen on the Tate Modern from the RSPB watchpoint on London's South Bank.

Cheddar's gorgeous wildlife includes Peregrines and other species, at the famous Cheddar Gorge in the south-west of England.

To find out more about Date with Nature events, visit www.rspb.org.uk/datewithnature.

RED KITES

Anyone driving along the M40 around Ashton Rowant will have noticed them – dozens of big, fork-tailed birds of prey, soaring and circling overhead. They are Red Kites, among our most distinctive and attractive raptors, and they are here thanks to the RSPB and other conservation groups.

Over the past two centuries, the UK has treated its native birds of prey appallingly. Persecution by gamekeepers, farmers and others, saw many species all but wiped out, among them the Red Kite, a particularly undeserving candidate for anyone's wrath as it eats mostly carrion. By the early 1900s, the only place you could see these beautiful birds was central Wales, where a tiny population hung on in the wilder hills. Careful protection saw the population slowly expand and recover, and by the end of the 1980s, the law had changed to outlaw persecution and more enlightened attitudes had developed with regard to birds of prey. The time was right to plan the Red Kite's return to England, Scotland and Northern Ireland.

Back from the brink

The Welsh population was still relatively small and vulnerable, so the RSPB and the then Nature Conservancy Council brought young kites over from Spain, releasing them in a suitable area of quiet woodland and farmland in the Chilterns. The birds settled into their new environment beautifully, and were soon breeding and spreading across the wider area. The Chilterns project supplied the young kites for the next phases of reintroduction – to the East Midlands, Yorkshire and north-east England,

near Gateshead. Schemes in Scotland and Northern Ireland soon followed.

Now you can see Red Kites in many parts of the UK, just as you could have done 200 years ago. However, not all of the introductions have gone as well as the first project, and sadly that is mainly due to continued persecution – a handful of landowners and managers still resent the birds' presence and illegally shoot, trap or poison them and find and destroy their nests, risking heavy fines and jail sentences.

WILDLIFE BY SEASON

SPRING

Courtship and nesting is taking place. You may see courting pairs flying together, performing high-speed manouvres, or birds carrying sticks to build (or renovate) their tree-top nests.

SUMMER

Chicks are growing in the nests, so the male is kept busy finding food for them and for the female as well. Most of the kites you see at this time are purposefully looking for prey or carrion.

AUTUMN

The youngsters fledge, boosting the number of birds you'll see on the wing. Many young birds will then roam away from the breeding grounds.

WINTER

The kites are particularly social at this time of year, often flying, feeding and roosting in large groups. Feeding stations are especially busy.

All of this ill-feeling is especially misplaced in the case of the Red Kite, which is a very innocuous predator. Although it does sometimes hunt small birds and mammals, its main diet consists of carrion. Like the vultures of the savannah, kites help to keep the countryside tidy by clearing up the remains of other unlucky animals, and afford us great opportunities to admire their graceful flight as they cruise and circle, searching for the next meal.

Ending the persecution of birds of prey is an RSPB priority, tackled in several ways. Reports of raptor crimes are investigated and perpetrators brought to justice. The RSPB also seeks to educate everyone about the essential and entirely natural role birds of prey play in our ecosystems. Perhaps most importantly, they aim to enable as many people as possible to experience the beauty and grace of the birds first-hand, to help us as a nation develop a powerful sense of affection, pride and protectiveness towards these jewels of our countryside.

Visiting a Red Kite Date with Nature

You can watch Red Kites at several locations with the RSPB – some are seasonal but others run throughout the year, and all are in beautiful rural locations where you stand a good chance of seeing other wildlife as well. RSPB staff and volunteers will be on hand to show you the birds with telescopes and binoculars if required and answer any questions you may have. Some of the sites have a feeding station where the kites are given a daily supply of meat – often attracting other local raptors and carrion eaters as well.

● Where to see them

Red Kites at Top Lodge offers you the chance to see kites and other wildlife between May and July on a guided walk (£2) from Fineshade Woods visitor centre, signposted from the A43, two miles south of Duddington.

Yorkshire Red Kites are on view at Harewood House, a fine stately home in Yorkshire at the junction of the A61/A659 on the Leeds/ Harrogate road. Open from May to mid-December.

Galloway Kite Trail is a circular walk, open all year, through prime kite country in south-west Scotland. If you visit the feeding station as well you can enjoy amazing views of the birds coming down to feed. Follow signs from New Galloway.

Argaty Red Kites is open all year round and has a hide and a feeding station. The farm is near Doune, between Stirling and Callander. When you reach Doune, turn north up King Street to Argaty.

Northern Ireland Red Kites, one of the newest reintroduction projects, has telescopes and binoculars on hand at the watchpoint between mid-August and October. Turn off the A25 in Castlewellan on to the Drumbuck Road, and follow the signs.

Red Kites in Ceredigion feeding station, set in original 'kite country', is open from January to March. There is also CCTV footage from a kite nest. It's 2 miles west of the village of Ponterwyd.

Henley on Thames Red Kites is new for 2010, with guided walks and a live camera link to a Red Kite nest.

To find out more about Date with Nature events, visit www.rspb. org.uk/datewithnature.

Watching Kittiwakes at Seaford Head

SEABIRDS

The UK may not have the same number and variety of land birds as some larger and less developed European countries, but we make up for it with our seabirds. With nearly 8,000 miles of coastline altogether, the UK is of international importance for nesting seabirds, and our cliffside colonies provide some seriously exhilarating wildlife-watching.

The main species involved are the four species of auks – Puffin, Razorbill, Guillemot and Black Guillemot – and Kittiwakes, Shags, Cormorants, Fulmars and Gannets. Although they all live in these colonies, they are otherwise a most diverse group of birds, each with its own particular way of surviving on the cliffs and at sea. In addition, Great and Arctic Skuas nest on Scottish moorlands near the sea, and Manx Shearwaters and Storm Petrels in burrows or crevices on remote islands – they and many other seabirds migrate past our headlands every spring and autumn. These are all true seabirds, mostly coming to land to breed but dependent on the sea for the rest of the year. In addition, there are gulls and terns – many nesting on islands around our coasts.

Sea change

It is hard to see the changes taking place in the ocean environment as the planet gets warmer and human demands on the resources increase. However, one place where we can see change afoot is at our seabird colonies. Breeding success for many species has been falling in recent years, especially along the North Sea coast. A shortage of fish stocks, from a combination of global warming and overfishing, is the likely root cause. Not every colony, and not every species, is affected but the situation is dire enough to give serious cause for concern.

Many seabirds are long-lived, so a poor breeding season will have knock-on effects for years – a run of poor breeding seasons could prove disastrous. Many British seabird species depend on sandeels – small silvery fish which are – or were – exceedingly abundant in our waters. The fishing trade accounts for large quantities of sandeels for use in fertiliser and animal

WILDLIFE BY SEASON

SPRING
Seabirds return to their breeding colonies, and after skirmishes over territories (a matter of half a square metre or less in some species) nesting activity begins.

SUMMER
Eggs hatch and the hungry chicks immediately put their parents to work collecting fish. Birds are coming and going constantly and fishing at sea – the sight, sound and smell is quite awesome.

AUTUMN
Young birds fledge from mid-summer, the auk chicks making a leap of faith straight into the sea before they can even fly. Migrating skuas, terns and shearwaters are on the move.

Manx Shearwater

feed, and global warming has changed their distribution. This in turn caused serious declines in seabird species like Arctic, Sandwich and Little Terns, and Kittiwakes.

The knock-on effects of damaging the marine ecosystem are difficult to predict. One unexpected consequence has been an increase in the rate of predation of Great Skuas upon Arctic Skuas. These two big, fearsome seabirds nest in close proximity to one another on Scottish islands, and both feed by stealing fish from other seabirds. As the availability of this food source has declined, Great Skuas have turned to their smaller relatives instead and have begun to kill significant numbers of Arctic Skua chicks.

Turning things around for the seabirds is a task for the whole planet, as their problems are linked to environmental change. Do your bit by implementing green changes in your lifestyle, and if you need extra persuasion to start the process, you could do a lot worse than spending some time watching seabirds in their environment.

Visiting a seabirds Date with Nature

Many RSPB reserves give you views into cliffside colonies, where you can watch the various species coming and going and, later in the year, feeding their growing chicks. For a different perspective, you could take one of the seabird-watching boat trips that are run between spring and autumn, and get even closer to the birds. An RSPB guide on board will point out, identify and tell you more about the birds and any sea mammals you might encounter. Other events go in search of migrating skuas and shearwaters, spectacular seabirds that rarely venture close inshore away from their breeding grounds, or let you view busy colonies that don't lie within RSPB reserves.

● Where to see them

Firth of Forth Seabird Cruises are three-hour cruises from Hawes Pier, South Queensferry, Edinburgh, in search of seabirds. They take place through late spring and summer.

Shearwater and Skua Cruises take place in late summer and early autumn, and go in search of – yes – skuas and shearwaters, departing from Bridlington Pier. Puffin cruises are run here too.

Puffin Island Wildlife Cruise is a catamaran trip to Puffin Island off Anglesey. You'll see Puffins and other seabirds, with a chance of sea mammals. Boats leave from Beaumaris.

Lowestoft Kittiwake Colony is on Lowestoft Docks and is the most easterly colony of these beautiful gulls. Telescopes and RSPB staff are at the viewpoint on Lowestoft pier.

Avocet Cruises are winter boat trips to see the Exe's Avocet flocks. Cruises depart from Exmouth or Starcross.

Poole Harbour Wildlife Cruises explore the birdlife that winters in the bay. Boats depart from Poole Quay.

Seaford Kittiwake Colony occupies a huge slab of chalk at Seaford Head, and is alive with Kittiwakes through the summer. Enjoy great views from the telescopes available at the viewpoint. Follow the signs from Seaford town centre.

To find out more about Date with Nature events, visit www.rspb.org.uk/datewithnature.

A DATE WITH NATURE

Grey Heron and Black-headed Gulls

THE BEST OF THE REST

As anyone who's been inspired to join the RSPB knows, encountering birds and other wildlife can be a magical and uplifting experience, and having an expert onhand at the same time is an added bonus. It can start or fuel a lifelong passion and bring a new dimension to our lives. This is the rationale behind 'A Date with Nature' events, in which the RSPB's goal is to make sure we hang on to the excitement of seeing nature at first hand.

Many of the best bird-watching spectacles are obvious and enduring by nature – birds of prey nesting at the same site year after year, waders regularly using an estuary, seabirds breeding on cliffsides or migrating along well-established routes – and these form a large part of the RSPB's 'Date with Nature' programme. Others, however, are transient, or rather more subtle, or perhaps both.

The RSPB responds rapidly when rare birds nest in the UK, ensuring that the nest site is protected from disturbance, accidental or deliberate. Sometimes it is possible to arrange visitor access and create an opportunity for people to witness the unusual event, as happened in 2007 when a Montagu's Harrier nest site was made viewable in Lincolnshire.

City spectaculars

Some of the RSPB's most popular 'Date with Nature' events don't involve rare or especially glamorous species at all, but do open people's eyes to just how much birdlife we share our country with, even in the centres of our cities. Others are based in well-known but often overwhelming 'wild places' and will help you find the most exciting wildlife around. Others give you new insights into familiar species.

For the latest news on 'Date with Nature' events, visit www.rspb.org.uk/datewithnature/sites/index.asp and use the interactive map to see what's going on in your area – the map includes one-off events as well as regular fixtures. The established ongoing events are listed opposite, but be aware that new events are added all the time.

● Where to see them – a selection of events

A Date with Nature in the New Forest takes place all summer long, and has a viewpoint and CCTV footage from a Hobby and a Goshawk nest – staff can also help you find and watch the Forest's other special birds. The viewpoint is at the Forestry Commission's New Forest Reptile Centre, 2 miles south-west of Lyndhurst off the A35.

Brighton's Starling Spectacular runs from December to February, watching the massive flocks of Starlings that swirl over the sea as the sun goes down before going to roost. The viewpoint is on Brighton's Palace Pier.

Bewl Water Cruises traverse the south-east's largest water body in search of grebes and other water birds in March and April. Bewl Water is 1 mile south of Lamberhurst village – look for the brown tourist signs on the A21.

Leeds Castle Swans gives you the chance to enjoy watching regal Mute Swans nesting and rearing their chicks in the wonderful surroundings of the beautiful Leeds Castle near Maidstone in Kent.

Herons at the Regent's Park introduces you to these stately birds in their treetop homes in this elegant Royal Park in central London.

Cosmeston Lakes plays host to many ducks and other water birds in winter. The viewpoint staff will be on hand to lend you binoculars and telescopes and help with any identification problems. The main entrance is 1.5 miles south of Penarth town centre on the B4267 Lavernock Road to Sull.

Wildbirds at Westonbirt shows you the many wintering species that share the famous Westonbirt Arboretum with its collection of exotic trees. The arboretum is about 3 miles south-east of Tetbury.

Wildlife Wonders in Wimbledon Park is a great way to get familiar with common parkland birds on a summer's day. Follow the RSPB signs to the viewpoint. This is one of several London park events.

A Whirlwind of Waders treats you to the spectacle of thousands of Dunlins, Wigeons and other waders and wildfowl on the shores of the Medway. It is held at Riverside Country Park in February.

See the Essex Coast Come Alive and enjoy the sight of great flocks of Brent Geese and many other estuary birds. The viewpoint is at Victoria Wharf, about 15 minutes' walk from Leigh station.

Handsome Herons at St Albans is your chance to watch the action in a busy heronry in spring, from Verulamium Park, right in the heart of St Albans. A similar event takes place in Hartsholme Park in Lincolnshire.

Rutting Red Deer is a special event on a magical reserve at a spectacular time of year. The deer viewpoint is about half a mile beyond the Minsmere turn-off.

Choughs at Llechwedd Slate Caverns is a great chance to watch these rare and charismatic crows in spring and summer. Llechwedd Slate Caverns are situated on the A470 between Blaenau Ffestiniog and Dolwyddelan.

Ghosts of the Forest – Black Grouse Watch takes you on a guided walk through Coed Llandegla Forest to watch lekking Black Grouse from a hide. The walks take place in spring, and start from the Oneplanet Adventure visitor centre, off the A525.

Carsington Water is home to a variety of water birds in spring and summer – see them through RSPB optics and on CCTV from the viewpoint – follow signs off the B5035, north-east of Ashbourne. A similar event takes place at Loch Leven, near Kinross in Scotland.

Down on the Farm shows you the wildlife that can prosper on sympathetically managed working farms. Sheldon Country Park is signposted from Ragley Drive; and Northycote Farm is signposted from Underhill Lane.

A Date with Nature Glasgow is based at the Kelvingrove Museum and runs year-round. There is a great variety of interactive displays in the museum itself, and guided walks in Kelvingrove Park.

The Famous Grouse Experience takes place on the well-known whisky distillery, near Crieff village off the A85 near Perth. Sample the whisky and see Red Grouse among other upland wildlife.

Viewing Orkney's Birds runs through summer and gives you a look via CCTV into a Hen Harrier's nest – the staff at the viewpoint can help you see other local specialities too. It's at Kirkwall visitor centre.

To find out more about Date with Nature events, visit www.rspb.org.uk/datewithnature.

LIST OF CONSERVATION DESIGNATIONS

An **Area of Outstanding Natural Beauty (AONB)** is an area of countryside considered to have significant landscape value in England, Wales or Northern Ireland. The primary purpose of the **AONB** designation is to conserve natural beauty, which includes wildlife, geographic features and cultural heritage as well as the more conventional concepts of landscape and scenery. **AONBs** have equivalent status to **National Parks** as far as conservation is concerned. In Scotland, National Scenic Areas are broadly equivalent to **AONBs**.

An **Important Bird Area (IBA)** is an area recognised as being a globally important habitat for the conservation of bird populations. Currently there are about 10,000 **IBAs** worldwide. The program was developed by BirdLife International.

Local Nature Reserves (LNR) are for both people and wildlife. They are places with wildlife or geological features that are of special interest locally. They offer people special opportunities to study or learn about nature or simply to enjoy it. **LNRs** are of local, but not necessarily national, importance. An **LNR** can also be an **SSSI** or may have other designations (although an **LNR** cannot also be an **NNR**).

National Parks (NPs) are beautiful, spectacular and often dramatic expanses of countryside. In the UK people live and work within **National Parks** and the farms, villages and towns within them are protected along with the landscape and wildlife.

National Nature Reserves (NNRs) contain examples of some of the most important natural and semi-natural terrestrial and coastal ecosystems in Britain. They are managed to conserve their habitats or to provide special opportunities for scientific study of the habitats communities and species represented within them. These reserves help protect an amazing range of wildlife and landscapes, including many rare species and habitats of international importance.

National Scenic Area (NSA) is a conservation designation used in Scotland, currently administered by Scottish Natural Heritage. **NSAs** are defined as having outstanding scenic interest or unsurpassed attractiveness.

Natura 2000 is the name of the European Union-wide network of nature conservation sites established under the EC Habitats and Birds Directives. This network comprises **Special Areas of Conservation (SACs)** and **Special Protection Areas (SPAs)**.

Ramsar sites are designated under the Convention on Wetlands of International Importance, agreed in Ramsar, Iran, in 1971. Originally intended to protect sites of importance as waterfowl habitat, the Convention has broadened its scope over the years to cover all aspects of wetland conservation and wise use, recognizing wetlands as ecosystems that are extremely important for biodiversity conservation in general and for the well-being of human communities.

A Nature Conservation Review was published by Derek Ratcliffe in 1977. It set out to identify the most important places for nature conservation in Britain. The sites listed in it are termed **NCR** sites.

Sites of Special Scientific Interest (SSSI) (England, Scotland and Wales) and Areas of Special Scientific Interest (ASSI) (Northern Ireland) are a suite of sites providing statutory protection for the best examples of the UK's flora, fauna, or geographical features. These sites are also used to underpin other national and international nature conservation designations.

Special Areas of Conservation (SACs) are designated under the EC Habitats Directive as areas that have been identified as best representing the range and variety within the European Union of 220 habitats and 1000 (non-bird) species listed on Annexes I and II to the Directive. They are chosen from Sites of Community Importance (SCIs) and designated **SAC** by an act ensuring the conservation measures of the natural habitat. **cSAC** stands for **candidate Special Area of Conservation** and **pSAC** stands for **possible Special Area of Conservation**. **SACs**, together with **SPAs**, form the **Natura 2000** network.

Special Protection Areas (SPAs) are classified by the UK Government under the EU Birds Directive as areas of the most important habitat for rare and migratory birds within the European Union. **SPAs**, together with **SACs**, form the **Natura 2000** network.

PHOTO CREDITS

A & C Black would like to thank the following for providing photographs and for permission to reproduce copyright material. While every effort has been made to trace and acknowledge all copyright holders, we would like to apologise for any errors or omissions, and invite readers to inform us so that corrections can be made in any future editions of the book. Where more than one photograph appear on a single page the credits are listed from top to bottom.

1 Ben Hall (rspb-images.com)
3 Andy Hay (rspb-images.com)
3 David Tipling
3 Gary Smith (Photolibrary Group)
3 David Tipling
3 David Tipling
4 Mike Powles (Photolibrary Group)
4 Tracey Rich (Photolibrary Group)
4 Rebecca Nason
4 David Tipling
4 Mark Hamblin (Photolibrary Group)
5 David Tipling
5 Laurie Campbell (rspb-images.com)
5 Richard Revels (rspb-images.com)
5 Chris Gomersall (rspb-images.com)
6 Ben Hall (rspb-images.com)
7 David Tipling
8 David Tipling
9 Nigel Blake (rspb-images.com)
10 David Tipling
11 Ben Hall (rspb-images.com)
11 Mark Hamblin (rspb-images.com)
12 David Tipling (rspb-images.com)
13 Andy Hay (rspb-images.com)
14 David Kjaer (rspb-images.com)
15 David Tipling
16 Emanuele Biggi (Photolibrary Group)
17 David Tipling
18 David Wootton (rspb-images.com)
20 Andy Hay (rspb-images.com)
22 Clifton Beard
24 David Kjaer (rspb-images.com)
26 David Kjaer (rspb-images.com)
28 Chris Gomersall (rspb-images.com)
30 Chris Gomersall (rspb-images.com)
32 John Farmar (rspb-images.com)
34 Chris Gomersall (rspb-images.com)
36 Andy Hay (rspb-images.com)
38 Andy Hay (rspb-images.com)
39 Rebecca Nason
40 David Tipling
41 Mike Lane (rspb-images.com)
42 Andy Lane (rspb-images.com)
44 Richard Revels (rspb-images.com)
46 Andy Hay (rspb-images.com)

48 David Tipling
50 Andy Hay (rspb-images.com)
52 Robert Horne (rspb-images.com)
53 Rebecca Nason
54 Marko König (Photolibrary Group)
55 David Tipling
56 David Kjaer (rspb-images.com)
58 Andy Hay (rspb-images.com)
60 Steve Knell (rspb-images.com)
62 EA. Janes (Photolibrary Group)
64 Andy Hay (rspb-images.com)
66 Richard Revels (rspb-images.com)
67 Danny Green (rspb-images.com)
68 David Norton (rspb-images.com)
69 David Tipling
70 Chris Knights (rspb-images.com)
71 Horst Jegen (Photolibrary Group)
72 Elenor Bentall (rspb-images.com)
73 Andy Hay (rspb-images.com)
74 Gary Smith (Photolibrary Group)
76 Chris Gomersall (rspb-images.com)
78 David Tipling
80 Andy Hay (rspb-images.com)
82 Andrew Westley (rspb-images.com)
83 Steve Round (rspb-images.com)
84 Ben Hall (rspb-images.com)
86 Carolyn Merret (rspb-images.com)
87 David Tipling
88 Rebecca Nason
89 Rebecca Nason
90 Chris Gomersall (rspb-images.com)
92 Andrew Parkinson (rspb-images.com)
94 Chris Gomersall (rspb-images.com)
96 Tim Green
98 David Wootton (rspb-images.com)
100 Andy Hay (rspb-images.com)
101 Ben Hall (rspb-images.com)
102 David Tipling
103 David Tipling
104 Steve Knell (rspb-images.com)
106 Andy Hay (rspb-images.com)
107 Andy Hay (rspb-images.com)
108 Tony Hamblin (rspb-images.com)
109 David Tipling
110 David Tipling (rspb-images.com)

111 David Tipling (rspb-images.com)
112 Richard Brooks (rspb-images.com)
113 David Tipling
114 Andy Hay (rspb-images.com)
116 Mike Read (rspb-images.com)
118 David Tipling (rspb-images.com)
120 Ernie James (rspb-images.com)
122 Andy Hay (rspb-images.com)
124 Andy Hay (rspb-images.com)
125 Andy Hay (rspb-images.com)
126 David Tipling
127 Andy Hay (rspb-images.com)
128 Richard Revels (rspb-images.com)
130 Andy Hay (rspb-images.com)
131 Mike Powles (Photolibrary Group)
132 Klaus Honal (Photolibrary Group)
133 David Tipling
134 David Tipling (rspb-images.com)
135 Rebecca Nason
136 Ernie James (rspb-images.com)
138 Steve Janes (rspb-images.com)
140 Ernie James (rspb-images.com)
141 Malcolm Hunt (rspb-images.com)
142 Tracey Rich (Photolibrary Group)
143 Danny Green (rspb-images.com)
144 Mark Hamblin (rspb-images.com)
145 David Tipling
146 Steve Austin (rspb-images.com)
147 David Tipling
148 Andy Hay (rspb-images.com)
150 David Wootton (rspb-images.com)
151 Chris Gomersall (rspb-images.com)
152 Andy Hay (rspb-images.com)
153 Rebecca Nason
154 Alastair Shay (Photolibrary Group)
155 David Tipling
156 Andy Hay (rspb-images.com)
157 David Tipling
158 Danny Green (rspb-images.com)
159 David Tipling
160 Andy Hay (rspb-images.com)
162 Andy Hay (rspb-images.com)
164 David Tipling
166 Ben Hall (rspb-images.com)
167 David Tipling
168 David Tipling
170 Steve Knell (rspb-images.com)
172 Ray Kennedy (rspb-images.com)
174 Malcolm Hunt (rspb-images.com)
176 Andy Hay (rspb-images.com)
177 Steve Knell (rspb-images.com)
178 Rebecca Nason
179 David Tipling
180 Andy Hay (rspb-images.com)
182 Andy Hay (rspb-images.com)

184 Andy Hay (rspb-images.com)
186 Andy Hay (rspb-images.com)
187 David Tipling
188 Rebecca Nason
189 Sue Kennedy (rspb-images.com)
190 Andy Hay (rspb-images.com)
192 David Tipling
194 Mike Read (rspb-images.com)
196 Mark Hamblin (rspb-images.com)
198 Andy Hay (rspb-images.com)
200 Andy Hay (rspb-images.com)
201 Peter Cairns (rspb-images.com)
202 David Kjaer (rspb-images.com)
203 David Tipling
204 Kaleel Zibe (rspb-images.com)
205 David Tipling
206 David Tipling
207 Mark Hamblin (rspb-images.com)
208 Andy Hay (rspb-images.com)
209 Rebecca Nason
210 Mark Sisson (rspb-images.com)
211 David Tipling
212 Andy Hay (rspb-images.com)
213 Andy Hay (rspb-images.com)
214 Andy Hay (rspb-images.com)
216 Andy Hay (rspb-images.com)
218 Juan Carlos Munoz (Photolibrary Group)
220 David Tipling
222 Niall Benvie (Photolibrary Group)
224 Andy Hay (rspb-images.com)
228 Andy Hay (rspb-images.com)
230 Niall Benvie (rspb-images.com)
232 David Kjaer (rspb-images.com)
234 Steve Austin (rspb-images.com)
235 David Tipling
236 Steve Knell (rspb-images.com)
237 Ernie Janes (rspb-images.com)
238 Andy Hay (rspb-images.com)
240 Mike Read (rspb-images.com)
242 Steve Knell (rspb-images.com)
244 Andy Hay (rspb-images.com)
246 Andy Hay (rspb-images.com)
248 Andy Hay (rspb-images.com)
250 David Tipling
251 Michael Krabs (Photolibrary Group)
252 Andy Hay (rspb-images.com)
254 Andy Hay (rspb-images.com)
256 Andy Hay (rspb-images.com)
257 David Tipling
258 Andy Hay (rspb-images.com)
259 David Tipling
260 Mark Hamblin (Photolibrary Group)
261 David Tipling
262 Chris Gomersall (rspb-images.com)
264 Andy Hay (rspb-images.com)

266 Steve Austin (rspb-images.com)
268 Malcolm Hunt (rspb-images.com)
270 Andy Hay (rspb-images.com)
272 Peter Cairns (rspb-images.com)
274 Mark Hamblin (rspb-images.com)
276 Mark Hamblin (rspb-images.com)
277 David Tipling
278 David Tipling
279 Rebecca Nason
280 Laurie Campbell (rspb-images.com)
282 Steve Austin (rspb-images.com)
283 Sven Zacek (Photolibrary Group)
284 Andy Hay (rspb-images.com)
285 David Tipling
286 Andy Hay (rspb-images.com)
288 David Wootton (rspb-images.com)
290 Ben Hall (rspb-images.com)
291 Richard Revels (rspb-images.com)
292 Carlos Sanchez (rspb-images.com)
293 Steve Round (rspb-images.com)
294 David Wootton (rspb-images.com)
296 Graham Eaton (rspb-images.com)
298 John Archer-Thompson (rspb-images.com)
299 Lisa Morgan
300 David Kjaer (rspb-images.com)
302 Ben Hall (rspb-images.com)
303 Ben Hall (rspb-images.com)
304 Steve Round (rspb-images.com)
305 Steve Knell (rspb-images.com)
306 Chris Gomersall (rspb-images.com)
307 Richard Brooks (rspb-images.com)
308 David Tipling
310 Wales News Service (rspb-images.com)
312 Ben Hall (rspb-images.com)
313 Rebecca Nason

313 Genevieve Leaper (rspb-images.com)
314 David Tipling
316 Ben Hall (rspb-images.com)
317 Bjorn Forsberg (Photolibrary Group)
318 Mike Richards (rspb-images.com)
319 Danny Green (rspb-images.com)
320 Ben Hall (rspb-images.com)
322 Mike Read (rspb-images.com)
323 David Tipling
324 Richard Revels (rspb-images.com)
325 Michael Krabs (Photolibrary Group)
326 David Tipling
327 David Tipling
328 Peter Cairns (rspb-images.com)
329 Mark Hamblin (rspb-images.com)
330 Peter Cairns (rspb-images.com)
332 Danny Green (rspb-images.com)
333 Rebecca Nason
334 Andy Hay (rspb-images.com)
335 Chris Gomersall (rspb-images.com)
336 Nigel Blake (rspb-images.com)

Cover photos
Front: Red Squirrel, Niall Benvie (Photolibrary Group); Swallowtail, Richard Revels (rspb-images.com); Smooth Snake, David Tipling; Capercaillie, David Tipling; Sundew, Laurie Campbell (rspb-images.com).
Back: Brown Hare, David Tipling; Common Seal, David Tipling; Bearded Tit, David Tipling; Little Grebe, David Tipling.
Inside front: West Sedgemoor, Andy Hay (rspb-images.com).
Inside back: Insh Marshes, Mark Hamblin (rspb-images.com).

ACKNOWLEDGEMENTS

I would like to thank Nigel Redman at A & C Black for commissioning me to write this book. Julie Bailey at A & C Black and designer Julie Dando at Fluke Art pulled everything together and overcame endless obstacles on the way – you could not ask for a better team of Julies. Peter Holden at the RSPB helped to get the project off the ground, liaised with the RSPB over numerous issues and checked the draft text. Brian Southern undertook the mammoth task of drawing up a brand new set of reserve maps for the book. Too many RSPB staff to mention have helped with information on innumerable details. I'd particularly like to thank all the RSPB Site Managers, who not only helped us to double-check everything was accurate and up to date for their own reserves, but who also work every day to ensure that these wonderful wild places continue to bring unforgettable wildlife experiences to so many people. Mike Unwin provided invaluable advice and an undisturbed workspace for me during deadline week. Finally, I'd like to thank Rob for being a wonderful companion on many expeditions to RSPB reserves in the name of research, and for months of hot chocolate, cups of tea, patience, humour and support.

Marianne Taylor, July 2009

INDEX

Only the first mention of terms in each reserve has been indexed.

E

F

T

Every effort has been made to ensure that at the time of going to press the information presented in this book is as up-to-date as possible. However, access and facilities at RSPB reserves are constantly being upgraded, and other details, such as telephone numbers, opening hours, travel information and third-party website URLs, are subject to change. The publishers cannot accept responsibility for any material on third-party websites and cannot guarantee such sites will be a suitable source of information.

Before a visit to any RSPB reserve, in addition to using this book we recommend readers also refer to the RSPB reserves' home page to confirm up-to-date contact details and access information. An alphabetical list of all the RSPB's reserves can be found at www.rspb.org.uk/reserves